# CULTURES OF PEACE

Syracuse Studies on Peace and Conflict Resolution

Harrict Hyman Alonso,
Charles Chatfield, and
Louis Kriesberg, Series Editors

# CULTURES OF PEACE
## The Hidden Side of History

Elise Boulding

With a Foreword by Federico Mayor

*Syracuse University Press*

Library of Congress Cataloging-in-Publication Data

Boulding, Elise.
Cultures of peace : the hidden side of history / Elise Boulding ; with a
    foreword by Federico Mayor.— 1st ed.
    p.    cm. — (Syracuse studies on peace and conflict resolution)
    Includes bibliographical references and index.
ISBN 0-8156-2831-5 (cloth ; alk. paper) — ISBN 0-8156-2832-3 (pbk.: alk. paper)
    1. Peace.  2. International relations and culture. I. Title. II. Series.

JZ5538.B68 2000
306.2—dc21

                                                            99-087443

*To the children of the twenty-first century*

Born in Norway in 1920, Elise Boulding began her career as a scholar in the late 1950s, while still raising five children, by translating Fred Polak's Council of Europe Award–winning *The Image of the Future* from Dutch to English and by working with Kenneth Boulding to help found the International Peace Research Association. By the late 1960s she was a professor of sociology, first at the University of Colorado, then as chair of the sociology department at Dartmouth. Boulding has been active in developing the fields of future studies, peace research, and women's studies. An activist as well as a scholar, she has been international chair of the Women's International League for Peace and Freedom and is a past secretary-general of the International Peace Research Association and editor of its newsletter. She has served on the board of the United Nations University, the international jury of the UNESCO Prize for Peace, and the Congressional commission that led to the establishment by Congress of the U.S. Institute of Peace. She has also conducted numerous workshops on "Imaging a World Without Weapons." Her books include *Children's Rights and the Wheel of Life*; *Building a Global Civic Culture*; *The Underside of History—A View of Women Through Time*; *One Small Plot of Heaven, Reflections of a Quaker Sociologist on Family Life*; and, with Kenneth Boulding, *The Future: Images and Processes*. *Cultures of Peace* is written for the world in which her sixteen grandchildren will be growing up.

# Contents

# *Illustrations*

Figures

Tables

# Foreword

## Federico Mayor, Director-General, UNESCO

ELISE BOULDING brings to this interesting and thought-provoking publication, *Cultures of Peace*, an integrated social science and activist perspective. She explores the importance of cultural diversity and cultural pluralism, recognized by UNESCO as important in promoting sustainable development and durable peace.

After the Cold War, the world witnessed an increase in conflicts whose causes—alleged or averred—were ethnic, cultural, or religious. But at the same time there has been a strengthening of dialogue and interaction between cultures and the shaping of cultural cohesion based on respect for diversity. UNESCO has demonstrated its capacity for intellectual leadership in this field through its activities in the fields of intercultural dialogue and the promotion of a culture of peace.

In *Cultures of Peace*, Dr. Boulding takes an interdisciplinary and interconnective approach to a culture of peace, examining the effect of war on families and communities and the links between family, community, and institutions of government. Part 1 assumes a historical perspective analyzing how past actions have contributed to the desire and call for a culture of peace. Part 2 presents the current world order with its peace cultures in action and gender roles in a postpatriarchal, partnership-based society. Part 3 explores the challenges of the twenty-first century in relation to future peace movements. These perspectives reflect UNESCO's view that peace, development, and equality are inextricably linked.

With the approach of the new millennium, this publication is as timely as it is relevant: encouraging readers to reflect on and to refine their visions and scenarios for the future and to commit themselves to eradicating that which is destructive to the survival of humanity and our environment. It points to the values and concepts of a culture of peace so much needed in the twenty-first century.

Only a thinker and person of true commitment like Elise Boulding could present—at the turn of the century and millennium, which will, I hope, be a turning point from a culture of violence to a culture of tolerance and peace—a text that embodies her experience and her vision in such a creative and engaging manner.

# Acknowledgments

THE GAP LEFT IN MY LIFE by Kenneth Boulding's death in 1993, after fifty-two years of marriage, can never be filled, but I want to thank my five children, Russell, Mark, Christie, Philip, and William, and their families for their love and moral support during the difficult years that followed his death. It is that support which made it possible for me to reengage in an earlier start on the topic of peace culture and write this book. My new "granny apartment" in the treetops at the back of daughter Christie's house in Wayland, Massachusetts, built by son-in-law Greg Graham, has been the best possible setting for this reengagement.

Another wonderful source of support has been the Boston Research Center for the Twenty-First Century; the entire staff has been like family to me. The center's director, Ginny Straus, played a very special role in the development of my thinking about cultures of peace by organizing seminars and programs on the subject, which led to many fruitful interchanges and new insights. I am grateful for the helpful critiques and suggestions from Randy Forsberg, Winston Langley, Saul Mendlowitz, Theta Crawford, and all who participated in the Boston Research Center seminars. I am also grateful to two colleagues at Brandeis University and their students — Gordon Fellman, who conducts an exciting course in peace studies, and Cynthia Cohen, director of the Brandeis Coexistence Program, who offered challenging ideas and put me in touch with students who checked out hard-to-find references. And it was very good to be able to consult from time to time with my old friend and colleague Louis Kriesberg at Syracuse University.

UNESCO itself played an important part in the preparation of this book. Many thanks to David Adams and Ingeborg Breines of the Culture of Peace Program for their helpful comments, and for the foreword so graciously written by Federico Mayor, Director-General of UNESCO.

It has been a pleasure to work with Syracuse University Press. I want to thank Mary Selden Evans for patiently initiating me into the in-house processes of the Press, and I am particularly grateful to Bettie McDavid Mason for her skill in untangling my sometimes overcomplicated sentences. And at a very basic level, I have been fortunate to have found so skilled and patient a typist as Carole Flynn, in nearby Sudbury, who typed her way through several versions of each chapter. Thank you, Carole!

And last but not least, thanks to all my friends and colleagues, near and far, who cheered me on when the task of completing this book seemed over-whelming!

# Abbreviations

ACCORD  African Center for the Constructive Resolution of Disputes
ACP  African-Caribbean-Pacific group
AFPRA  African Peace Research Association
AISES  American Indian Science and Engineering Society
APRA  Asian Peace Research Association
APRI  African Peace Research Institute
ASEAN  Association of Southeast Asian Nations
CDI  community-based development initiative
CND  Campaign for Nuclear Disarmament
CLAIP  Latin American Council on Peace Research
CORE  Congress of Racial Equality
CSCE  Conference for Security and Cooperation in Europe
DARPA  Defense Advanced Research Project Agency
ECOSOC  [UN] Economic and Social Council
END  European Nuclear Disarmament
GATT  General Agreement on Tariffs and Trade
GCC  Gulf Cooperation Council
GDP  gross domestic product
GPI  Genuine Progress Indicator
GROOTS  Grassroots Women Operating Together in Sisterhood
GRO  grassroots organization
HDI  Human Development Index
IALANA  International Association of Lawyers Against Nuclear Arms
ICDP  International Confederation for Disarmament and Peace

| | |
|---|---|
| IFOR | International Fellowship of Reconciliation |
| IGO | intergovernmental organization |
| IIUP | International Interparliamentary Union |
| ILCOP | International Liaison Committee of Organizations for Peace |
| INES | International Network of Engineers and Scientists for Global Responsibility |
| IPB | International Peace Bureau |
| IPPNW | International Physicians for the Prevention of Nuclear War |
| IPRA | International Peace Research Association |
| IPS | Inter Press Service |
| IWGIA | International Work Group for Indigenous Affairs |
| LETS | Local Economic Trading System |
| | Labor Exchange Trading System |
| | Local Employment Trading Systems |
| | Local Exchange Trading System |
| MASA | Men Against Sexual Assault |
| MAP | Men Against Patriarchy |
| | Men Against Pornography |
| MEG | Men for Gender Awareness |
| MIPE | Men's International Peace Exchange |
| MOVE | Men Overcoming Violence |
| NAFTA | North American Free Trade Agreement |
| NATO | North Atlantic Treaty Organization |
| NGO | nongovernmental organization |
| NIC | newly industrialized country |
| NOCM | National Organization for Changing Men |
| NOD | nonoffensive defense |
| NOMAS | National Organization for Men Against Sexism |
| NWICO | New World Information and Communication Order |
| OAS | Organization of American States |
| OAU | Organization of African Unity |
| OPEC | Organization of Petroleum Exporting Countries |

OSCE Organization for Security and Cooperation in Europe
PAPSL Participatory Assessment and Planning for Sustainable Development
SAHD Stay at Home Dads
SANE Committee for a Sane Nuclear Policy
SAP structural adjustment program
SARC South Asian Regional Cooperation
SIPRI Stockholm Peace Research Institute
SNCC Student Nonviolent Coordinating Committee
TNC transnational corporation
TOES The Other Economic Summit
UNCED UN Conference on Environment and Development
UNDP UN Development Program
UNEP UN Environment Program
UNESCO UN Educational, Scientific, and Cultural Organization
UNICEF UN International Children's Emergency Fund
UNIDIR UN Institute for Disarmament Research
UNIFEM UN International Fund for Women
UNRISD UN Research Institute for Social Development
UNU United Nations University
USIP U.S. Institute for Peace
WAND Women's Action for Nuclear Disarmament; later, Women's Action for New Directions
WCTU Women's Christian Temperance Union
WEDO Women's Environment and Development Organization
WFM World Federalist Movement
WILPF Women's International League for Peace and Freedom
WOMP World Order Models Project
WRI War Resisters International
YWCA Young Women's Christian Association
ZOP Zone of Peace

# CULTURES OF PEACE

# Peace Culture
## An Overview

P<small>UT IN THE SIMPLEST POSSIBLE TERMS</small>, a peace culture is a culture that promotes peaceable diversity. Such a culture includes lifeways, patterns of belief, values, behavior, and accompanying institutional arrangements that promote mutual caring and well-being as well as an equality that includes appreciation of difference, stewardship, and equitable sharing of the earth's resources among its members and with all living beings. It offers mutual security for humankind in all its diversity through a profound sense of species identity as well as kinship with the living earth. There is no need for violence. In other words, peaceableness is an action concept, involving a constant shaping and reshaping of understandings, situations, and behaviors in a constantly changing lifeworld, to sustain well-being for all.

This is a far cry from stereotyped notions of peace as a dull, unchanging end state. A static image of peace, as reflecting human inactivity, is dramatically opposed to the characterization of peace as process, of peacebuilding as adventure, exploration, and willingness to venture into the unknown. *Pacifism*, which literally refers to the *making* of peace (from *pace* and *facere*) is often mistakenly understood as passivism. One major attitudinal obstacle to the acceptance of peaceableness as a desirable social norm is the connotation of inactivity associated with it.

Society does not exist apart from the activities and environments that sustain, shape, and reshape it. The ceaseless culture-creating activity that characterizes the social body involves interaction at every level, from the intrapersonal (the inner life of the individual human being) to the interpersonal—in household, neighborhood, and community, on through successive levels of civic organization from city to the United Nations, and finally to interaction with the planetary lifeworlds of which we are a part. Because there is constant interpenetration of levels, the societal capacity for aggression or peacebuilding depends on patterns developed in every domain, from the individual and the interpersonal to the national, and interenvironmental, for dealing with the ever-present conflicts that arise from the great diversity of human and more-than-human wants and needs.

It is how we deal with difference that determines how peaceable society is. Nature never repeats herself. Therefore, no two human beings are alike. Difference is a basic fact of life. Among the needs every person is born with are two of special importance to our capacity for peaceableness. One is the need for bonding, for closeness to and acceptance by other human beings. The other basic need is the need for space, separateness from others, room to be one's own self, to be autonomous. A society with only bonding relationships would be a passive, dull, enclosed society. A society in which separateness predominated would be an aggressive society in which everyone would be concerned with their own space. When groups of humans hold the need for bonding and autonomy in balance—nurturing one another, engaging in many cooperative activities, but also giving each other space—then we find the conditions for peace culture. Another very important dimension of that peace culture is bonding with, feeling at home in, the living bioregion that the members of that culture inhabit. Groups characterized by power struggles, patterns of domination of the strong over the weak, of men over women, by frequent physical violence and constant competition, and seeing nature as something to be conquered can be thought of as warrior cultures. We will not find either peace cultures or warrior cultures in a "pure" form. Peaceable societies will have some conflictual behavior, and war-prone societies have some patterns of nurturant behavior in certain settings and under certain conditions.

There is a vast literature on the issue of whether humans are by nature cooperative and peaceful or by nature competitive and violent. Writings that treat human aggression as biologically inherent include Robert Ardrey's *African Genesis* (1962), Lyall Watson's *Dark Nature* (1965), Lawrence Keeley's *War Before Civilization* (1996), and Richard Wrangham and Dale Peterson's *Demonic Males* (1996). Recent writings on inherent peaceableness include Irennaus Eibl-Eibesfeldt's *Love and Hate* (1972), Stephen Kellert and Edward Wilson's *The Biophilia Hypothesis* (1993), and Frans de Waal's *Good Natured* (1996). A more cosmic approach to peaceableness that includes all living systems is found in *What Is Life?* by Lynn Margulis and Dorion Sagan (1995) and in *Earthdance: Living Systems in Evolution* by Elisabet Sahtouris (1995).

A third alternative to the essentialist arguments about human nature is a social learning approach. In this approach, humans are seen as having the potential for both aggressive and peaceable behavior and are socialized into the behavior patterns that have evolved in the course of dealing with conflict and danger in each society. The UN Educational, Scientific and Cultural Organization (UNESCO) was founded on the assumption that attention to the process of peace learning was necessary to avoid the development of fear and mistrust and to encourage understanding and cooperation among peoples. The Seville Statement on Violence, written by an international team of scientists to address the myth that violence is inherent in human nature (at a UNESCO Conference in Seville in 1986), is the classic statement of war as learned behavior, inspired by Margaret Mead's often quoted remark that war is a social invention. This gave rise to UNESCO's Culture of Peace Program, as well as to UNESCO's biosphere-geosphere program, which evolved out of the understanding that part of that peace learning was learning how to interact sensitively with the planet itself.

Gene Sharp's earlier pathbreaking work on *The Politics of Nonviolent Action*[1] has drawn attention to the superior effectiveness of nonviolent action as an instrument of struggle in conflict situations, particularly for the powerless (who, in attempting violence, would only invite extermination). Sharp and his colleagues at the Albert Einstein Institution have undertaken extensive documentation of the widespread use throughout history of nonviolent action by the oppressed.[2] While not always successful, nonviolent struggles have often achieved their goals—unlike violent struggles, in which at least one side loses. Gordon Fellman, in *Rambo and the Dalai Lama: The Compulsion to Win and Its Threat to Human Survival*,[3] points out that while a compulsion to win is often found, it is not inevitable and leads to poor survival strategies. He develops the concept of mutuality as an alternative strategy that is superior to adversarialism in solving human problems. According to that view, peaceable societies are those that have discovered the advantages of mutual aid and teach the skills of mutuality to their children. The fact that historians overwhelmingly focus on the history of violence and war accounts for the widespread ignorance about nonviolence as an effective survival strategy. The conditions under which the strategy evolves and is practiced, taught, and passed on are still not well understood and represent an urgent research agenda. The Earth Charter movement and the antecedent deep ecology movement are beginning to extend our understanding of mutuality and nonviolence to the human relationship with the natural world.[4]

This book can be thought of as a story of human potentials for peaceableness. Setting aside the debate over what humans are really like, I offer examples of social settings in which the human capacity for peaceable behavior in the face of conflict and difference emerges as the prevailing social pattern. As I read the evidence, cooperative and autonomy-seeking behavior evolved together and had survival value when kept in balance. Among humans, there is clearly a capability for both cooperative and violent behavior, and children are socialized from infancy into behavioral sequences that either tend to be cooperative or tend to be violent or—not infrequently—represent some combination of cooperation and violence. These are learned behaviors, based on genetic predispositions, but there is no specific genetic programming for either nurturant or aggressive behaviors. The actual patterns are the result of social learning.

In general, societies tend to be a blend of peaceable and warrior culture themes—the balance between the themes varying from society to society and from historical moment to historical moment. In our time, the tensions between the two themes have become a heavy social burden as a worldwide military forcing system linked to a destructive, planet-harming mode of industrialization and urbanization is distorting the human capability for creative and peaceful change. No sooner did the fears of nuclear holocaust fade with the end of the Cold War than the fear of genocidal ethnic warfare reducing once proudly independent countries to a series of dusty battlegrounds rose to take the place of earlier fears. Urban violence—now manifesting itself in gun battles in the cities and neighborhoods and even the schoolyards and playgrounds of the industrial West—has unleashed other terrors. If every society is a blend of the themes of violence and peaceableness, why is the peaceableness so hard to see?

It is there, but not well reported. The tendency of planners and policymakers to prepare for worst-case scenarios leaves societies unprepared for the opportunities involved in best-case scenarios. Nevertheless, the longing for peace has not gone away. The hiddenness, and the longing, create an urgency to understand what works to strengthen one of the two cultures and what works to weaken the other. We are not helpless. We have at our fingertips an incredible storehouse of wisdom and knowledge from the past and new knowledge, new wisdom, new science and technology from our discovery-minded present that, together, offer great resources for the rebuilding of peaceful lifeways for the planet as a whole. A richer and more diversified peace culture than any of us can now easily imagine, an interconnected global peace culture, is there to be built out of the languages and lifeways and knowledge and experience worlds of the "10,000 societies"[5] now spread across the 185 states of today's world. The possibilities for the transformation of our current war- and violence-prone international system into an interconnected localist world of adventurous but peaceful problem solvers, using technology to nurture the planet rather than to stress it, are what this book is about.

Because we live in a much more multicultural world than most Westerners realize, and because the failure to understand that variety is a continuing source of anger in the non-West, there will be a continuing emphasis in what follows on the diversity of the peace cultures that hold the promise of our future. "Ignorance of each other's ways and lives has been a common cause, through the history of mankind, of that suspicion and mistrust between the people of the world through which their differences have often broken into war" (from the UNESCO Constitution). A prescient 1972 report from a Bellagio Conference on "Reconstituting the Human Community" speaks of the need for "a transcendence of 'only a European point of view' in regard to the origins of science, democratic development, nationalism and the United Nations, as well as transcendence of the psychology of dominance, especially in regard to the power of science and technology."

It is a great tragedy that the UNESCO World Decade of Cultural Development, 1988–97, with its major projects of reporting on cultures and patterns of cultural development in the Two-Thirds World, has received so little attention in the West, and least of all in the United States. The globalizing effect on other cultures of Western culture is slowly beginning to decline, as Eleanora Masini predicts in *The Future of Asian Cultures*.[6]

Slowly, we are learning from many sources that monocultures are dangerous both for humans and for the natural environment. Cultural diversity is as important as biodiversity for the survival of the planet. Maruyamah, who has written a great deal about the importance of heterogeneity, entitles a chapter in a recent book "Diversity Enables Mutual Benefit: Sameness Causes War."[7] He describes how African elders teach children about diversity by means of metaphoric tales. For example, an old man says: "Look at your hand. All fingers are different; that is why a hand can do its work. If all fingers are the same, your hand cannot function." The philosophy in Malinke culture is that all individuals, both humans and animals, are different, and if you force them to be the same, the only way left to them to be different is to get on top of one another. This creates conflicts and war. For the Malinke, heterogeneity means interaction for mutual benefit (positive sum relations), while for many of the Europeans and North Americans, heterogeneity tends to mean competitive, adversarial diversity (negative sum relations). A paradigm shift in the West is clearly in order. UNESCO's Culture of Peace Program, which this book celebrates, will help bring about that paradigm shift.

Since both the culture of war and the culture of peace are deeply rooted in history, part 1 is devoted to a historical overview. Chapter 1 discusses the historian's preoccupation with the documentation of war, which is buttressed by the doctrine of holy war in the major religious traditions, and considers the minority record on holy peace. Chapter 2 considers the persistence of attempts to think, dream, and sometimes actually design social orders that will correct the evils of a violent and unjust present, with emphasis on utopian thinking in recent centuries. Chapter 3 gives glimpses of social movements protesting war and witnessing to peaceful alternatives over the centuries.

Part 2 moves to peace cultures in action. Chapter 4 gives a selective overview of peace behaviors in certain notably peaceful societies, as well as examining peace behavior in everyday life in families, schools, and communities. Chapter 5 is intended to dispel stereotypes about women as primarily guardians of peace in the home, having no place in the public arena or, at best, secondary and supportive roles outside the home. Chapter 6 looks beyond the social dynamics of "traditional" gender roles, considering how men's movements as well as women's movements are redefining those roles to do away with traditional dualities and to release both male and female peacemaking capabilities in an interactive way. Chapter 7 looks beyond the social dynamics of traditional age-based roles. Children are not ordinarily thought of as having a part in peace processes at all, but as creatures needing protection. That view, however, leads to a vast underestimation of children's understanding of the world they live in and what they have to contribute to its betterment.

Part 3 focuses directly on what peace researchers call structural violence, that is, institutionalized patterns of behavior and structures that generate violence. In chapter 8 ethnic violence is viewed as a problem in the governance structures of the modern state and ethnicity as a potential resource for problem solving rather than simply a source of violence.

The theme of structural violence is continued in chapter 9 with an examination of the effects of corporations and international monetary institutions on local environments and local development, particularly in the Two-Thirds

World. Ecologically oriented development in an alternative economy, based on grassroots movements on each continent, is also given a careful look.

Chapter 10, which looks at the ambiguities of modern communication systems, considers how multinational corporations shape a global consumer culture. Exploitative information highways have swamped authentic communication and the creative arts potentials of the new communication technologies, stultifying the social imagination and offering ersatz images of the future. Grassroots cultural responses to that onslaught and alternative images of the future of culture are considered.

Chapter 11 gives an overview of the effects on the contemporary world of the global military forcing system, in both its high-tech and low-tech aspects. It reports on efforts to dismantle that forcing system by regional groupings of states and by the UN, and on NGO efforts to end war, with specific attention to year 2000 initiatives.

The closing chapter offers an overview of the challenges and possibilities for the twenty-first century. Unavoidable consequences of the abuses of the planet and its peoples that have taken place in the twentieth century will have to be dealt with. The redevelopment and rebuilding of the environment and of social institutions that will be needed to enable societies to live peaceably together in the twenty-first century will not be easy. But we cannot achieve what we cannot imagine. The book closes with an image of a more just and peaceful twenty-first century, based on awareness of both the challenges and possibilities for future generations of humans to live in peace with each other and the biosphere.

*Part One*
*A Historical Overview*

# Introduction

We will begin our exploration of peace culture with a journey through history. First, we will see how the story of wars won and lost has come to dominate our history books and our sense of who we are as human beings. We will also see how the warrior god has dominated the stories of our faith communities, so that the other story, the story of human caring and compassion and reconciliation, is often difficult to hear.

Next, we will see how that other story is found in the history of the imaginings of what life could be like if humans did deal with all life's obstacles and human needs peacefully. We will also see that people have not only imagined such good and peaceful places, such utopias, they have actually tried to create them in miniature—with varying degrees of success. Why the making of utopias is so difficult—and so important—will be explored.

Finally, there is still another history, the history of peace movements. Peace movements, like utopian experiments, have arisen through the centuries in response to a rejection of violent and oppressive societies, but they are primarily concerned with the remaking of such societies, with showing different ways of managing human conflict when differences arise within and between states.

These other stories from the past will give us the context for looking in part 2 at how we do manage much of our lives peacefully in today's conflicted world and how movements for social change may strengthen that capacity for peaceableness in tomorrow's world.

*1*

# History at Sword's Point?
## The War-Nurtured Identity of Western Civilization

HISTORY is generally thought of as the story of the rise and fall of empires, a chronicle of reigns, wars, battles, and military and political revolutions; in short, the history of power—who tames whom, who controls whom. The story of the ingestion of weaker societies by stronger ones and of rivalries among the strong is the story of humankind, says macrohistorian William McNeill.[1] In his version of history, every empire eventually reaches a limit-boundary region beyond which it has no control. When that point is reached, its people can either sit down and write poetry, opting out of history, or fight and push on.

Arnold Toynbee notes a countervailing fashion of a more complex story-telling, one that involves interspersing records of military activity with accounts of art, religion, and technology.[2] However, he points out that very few historians attempt to record that complex interplay of human activities in the various domains of life—work and play, art and architecture, intellectual inquiry and spiritual search. Why? At least part of the answer lies in the records intentionally left for posterity, in the rulers' habits of erecting monuments that glorify achievements in battle. The great invention of writing, the developments from pictographs and hieroglyphics through cuneiform to actual alphabets, while developed by priestly classes for the keeping of economic and administrative records, is better known for its use to record the triumphs of priest-kings and their gods in this world and the next. Voices from the past—Mesopotamian, Egyptian, Greco-Roman, Hindu, Chinese, and Mayan civilizations and others—have each left ample monuments and records attesting to their conquests.

The very identity of Western civilization at the end of the twentieth century is intimately bound up with its Greco-Roman heritage: the destruction of Troy in 1193 B.C.E.; the Battle of Marathon, when the Greeks defeated the

Persians; the Battle of Thermopylae, when the Persians defeated the Spartans; the three decades of Peloponnesian Wars between Athens and Sparta; the century of Punic Wars, ending with the destruction of Carthage and the triumph of Rome in 146 B.C.E. In the West we think of this as *our* history. The great cultural achievements of Greco-Roman civilization ("our past") are seen as the fruits of military power. Simone Weil, in her haunting study *The Iliad: A Poem of Force*, shows how the sword, in the West, has derived much of its power from the culture of that famous work of Homer.[3] Less noticed are the ecological fruits of military power—the destruction of the once luxuriant forests of the Mediterranean for timber for battleships and war chariots, leaving the stripped and parched earth we see today on the northern and southern shores of that great sea. Moving on to the Common Era, *our* history records the rise and decline of the Holy Roman Empire and centuries of war in Europe, including two centuries of crusades to reclaim the Holy Land and the holding at bay of a spreading Islam that threatened the very heart of Europe as the Turks reached the gates of Vienna. This history is seen as holding the seeds of the greatness of the West. Even the Vikings, ruthless pirates of the far North who plundered Europe for over two centuries, are part of our glory. William, the Norman Conqueror, was victorious in 1066 at the Battle of Hastings. This victory is taken as a major milestone in British history.

That heritage received a different input from a fortunately sheltered community of European monks and scholars. This community maintained peaceful contact with their more advanced colleague-scholars who were generating Islamic science and technology in Andalusia during the very centuries when Christian and Muslim soldiers fought for control of the Mediterranean. That knowledge transmission from Islam to Christianity, however, set the stage for a new series of conquests—the conquest of nature, the conquest of the world's seas, and the colonizing of the world's continents by Europeans.

Seen through the eyes of the colonized, the 1400s began a five-century process of forcible imposition, based on superior military force, of European values and culture on the many cultures, lifeways, and civilizations of the Asia-Pacific, Africa, and the Americas. This imposition was accompanied by a process of systematically mining the resources and the labor power of the colonized. From the perspective of the colonizers, these centuries nurtured the unprecedented flowering of Western science, technology, and culture. They furthered what was considered an evolutionary process resulting in a new universal civilization with values, material culture, and lifeways surely destined to supersede all other cultures and civilizations. A necessary part of this civilizing process was the development of military and political technologies to destroy competing or resisting societies in the name of social progress.

One drawback to the tremendous success of advanced military technologies, however, is that they have made present-day wars increasingly gruesome. In response, some societies retreat to the reliving of ancient, more glorious wars. Histories of famous battles become best-sellers.[4] In the United States, groups of patriots annually reenact famous battles of the Revolutionary War and, in the South, of the Civil War.

However, changes have been taking place in the attitude to war as a central mechanism in human history, as a more sophisticated civil society and a culture of transnationalism have evolved in the nineteenth and twentieth centuries, both in the One-Third World of Euro–North America and the Two-Thirds World of other continents. Among historians, Toynbee has in this century been a widely noted member of an innovative group of scholars who have broadened the agendas of macrohistory. He writes: "I hate war, and at the same time I am fascinated by the study of it, and give a great deal of attention to it. At the same time, too, I am reluctant to admit that the use of force has had decisive effects on the course of human history."[5] Toynbee, in fact, goes to great lengths to maximize the effect of what he calls spiritual factors. This, however, hardly affects the centrality of war in public consciousness. Rather, it spiritualizes it. The missing element in social awareness of the nature of the human experience through history is an image of the dailiness of life — of the common round from dawn to dawn that sustains human existence. The fact that most human activity revolves around raising and feeding families, organizing the work of production, solving problems and meeting human needs, interspersed with times of feasting and celebration of human creativity in poetry, song, dance, and art, rarely shows through in history books.

Yet a closer inspection of social records, the bias toward reporting wars notwithstanding, reveals a much richer tapestry of human activities. Samuel Kramer was a pioneer recorder of the quality of everyday life in ancient times, using documents from early Sumer.[6] He gives vivid evidence of what went on in families, schools, and public life, and of debates over morality and the nature and purpose of human existence. At the macrohistorical level, the remarkable historical undertaking of Bernhard Grun's *Timetables of History* is a brave beginning for a fuller account of the range of human doings over time.[7] *Timetables* tabulates events year by year from 501 B.C.E.(and by half-centuries before that starting at 4000 B.C.E.). The column entries for the year-by-year record include (a) History, Politics; (b) Literature, Theater; (c) Religion, Philosophy, Learning; (d) Visual Arts; (e) Music; (f) Science, Technology, Growth; and (g) Daily Life. The (a) column, listing the battles and kingdoms won and lost, is the fullest, but other columns get fuller over time, recording peaceful human activities in the civil society.

The importance of war is, of course, not to be downplayed. In fact, it is the recurring distortions war inflicts on everyday life that help perpetuate the systemic reproduction of war, fighting in generation after generation. Current research on violence in contemporary societies suggests that high levels of aggression in the civil society are associated with recent participation of that society in war. The socialization for aggression involved in the preparation for and fighting of wars has subsequent effects on civilian behavior. In short, wars produce socialization for aggression as well as socialization for aggression producing war.[8] This free-floating aggression affects the language and behavioral responses in political life, in social movements (including peace movements!), in sports, in the visual and performing arts; and it affects the content and style of social reporting by the media. Characterized as a rise in the level of incivility and meanness in public life, it is being widely commented on in contemporary U.S. circles concerned with this development in their own society.

If we add to this postwar syndrome of learned behavioral violence the abundant imagery about war in the historical record, civilian society has to deal with a heavy burden of war-consciousness in "peacetime." The religious consciousness of the societies nurtured within each major civilization reflect their war-consciousness in various ways, which we will now explore.

## War- and Peace-Consciousness in Religious Traditions

One way in which this war-consciousness appears is indirectly—in visions of warriors enjoying interludes of peace between battles, in special tranquil spaces hinting of utopia. In India we find that the ancient tradition of sacred warfare (symbolized by the chariot wheel) is transformed in the time of the Buddhist Emperor Ashoka into a tradition of sacred peacemaking (symbolized by the truth wheel), thus setting the stage for brief historical periods when spaces for nonviolent peacemaking appeared, in between the longer and more frequent periods when sacred warfare predominated, led by warrior monks. From the Greeks we have pictures of Elysian fields, where heroes hung their swords and shields on trees and walked arm in arm, discoursing of philosophy and poetry. The Hebrew Bible gives us Zion, the holy mountain where the lion shall lie down with the lamb and none shall hurt nor destroy. The Koran gives us the sanctuary in the desert, from which no one shall be turned away. Even in Valhalla, the warriors who fought each other by day feasted and sang together at night in the great hall of Asgard, drinking mead from a cow that never ran dry.

A second and far more direct way in which this war-consciousness appears in these same religious traditions is in visions of holy war, of divinely legitimated violence. Either God enjoins battle on his people to destroy evildoers, as happened frequently enough in Judaism, Christianity, and Islam, or violence itself is elevated to the realm of the sacred, as a part of the created order, as in some Hindu and Buddhist teachings. This set of violence-justifying teachings has made it possible for religious communities to support the state that houses them in times of war (with exceptions in the case of dissenting minority faith groups).

Every religion then contains two cultures: the culture of violence and war and the culture of peaceableness.[9] The holy war culture calls for mobilization against evil and is easily politicized. The culture of the peaceable garden relies on a sense of the oneness of humankind, often taking the form of intentional communities based on peaceful and cooperative lifeways, sanctuaries for the nonviolent.

It is important to understand the power of the holy war teachings, since they are intertwined with deep spiritual yearnings for relationship with the divine and shape perceptions of right conduct for believers. Holy war teachings in Buddhism, a nontheistic religion, express the sacredness of violence against the enemy differently, but the sense of mystical oneness with all being of the Buddhist warrior in the act of overcoming evil is not dissimilar to the sense of holy obedience to God of the Christian warrior who also fights to overcome evil.

## The Holy War Culture

The holy war culture is a male warrior culture headed by a patriarchal warrior-god. It demands the subjection of women and other aliens to men, the proto-patriarchs, and to God (or the gods). We see it in the ancient Babylonian epics, in the *Iliad*, in the Bhagavad Gita, in the Hebrew scriptures used by Jews and Christians, and in the Koran. There are many who argue that, while battle-scene scriptures were taken literally at the time they entered the written record, literal meanings have been gradually replaced by metaphoric meanings. The true holy war, according to this view, is the holy war in the soul. Mohandas Gandhi, notably, reinterpreted the warfare depicted in the Gita as a parable of the spiritual struggle between light and darkness. Many Jews and Christians do the same with the "Old" Testament. Yet, the template of patriarchy as a social institution continues to mold generation after generation in each tradition, continuing the practice of warfare and the subjection of women. Here we will look at some features of the holy war culture in Judaic, Christian, and Muslim traditions in terms of the sociopolitical outcomes for the societies in question. Ideally, Buddhist and Hindu traditions should also be included. However, the complexity of the elements involved would require more space than can be given here, so the overview will be confined to the Abrahamic traditions. After reviewing the holy war cultures, we will do the same for the peace cultures, and then consider how those two cultural themes interact over time.

**Judaism.** Much of the history of Israel relates to the central theme of Jehovah's release of his people from bondage in Egypt and of his leading them to a Promised Land. Since this land happened to be occupied by seven Canaanite nations, the Hebrew scriptures provide instructions on clearing the land for settlement through destruction of the previous inhabitants. The many different instructions were brought together in the Code of Maimonides. Treatise Five, Laws Concerning Kings and Wars, gives specific commandments concerning the destruction of the seven Canaanite nations. No life is to be spared, and the seed of Amalek is to be blotted out. There are precise instructions about the conduct of wars, even to the building of latrines. Peace terms are to be offered before war is waged, but not negotiated. If the unilaterally proposed terms are not accepted, a war of extermination may be waged. (There are modifications in dealing with non-Canaanites.) The behavioral code of the warrior is spelled out repeatedly for the Israelites. They are to fight bravely and not turn back because Jehovah is at the head of their army. However, they are also to protect the future productivity of the land on which they are fighting and not lay it to waste. Generally, they are also to spare women and children.

The institutional outcome of this warrior period was the fall of Israel and the Diaspora, followed many centuries later by the ingathering of the modern state of Israel. The Diaspora produced a great flowering of scholarship within its scattered communities. The scholarship has borne fruit in a sophisticated

Zionism and the remarkable social invention of the kibbutz. The modern state of Israel is, in many respects, a model democratic polity. However, a political willingness to negotiate with surrounding Arab neighbors on the part of many of its citizens stands in contrast with Zionism as a national liberation movement calling for war against the Arabs. Continual border warfare and a highly trained military reinforces war-readiness.

The role model in the holy war culture of Israel is the warrior with sword ever at hand to defend city or kibbutz. Whereas in the early days of modern Israel women were both to fight and to till the fields side by side with men, the pressure of continuing hostilities and earlier traditions returned women to more traditional hearth-bound and social service roles and to a more traditional obedience to men. Women are not primary participants in the warrior system; they are chiefly reproducers of it (this in spite of a tradition of charismatic women leaders from Deborah to Golda Meir and a practice of educating the minds as well as the hands of women).

**Islam.** Like Israel, Islam has an early history of fighting tribal wars for the survival of its religious faith. Islamic warriors fought for Allah, under his prophet Mohammed. Therefore, the Koran, like the Book of Judges, lays down specific commandments about the conduct of war. Both codes, incidentally, prohibit the destruction of fruit trees and fields where crops have been planted. They also command the protection of women and children. Jihad, or holy war, is to be conducted in a literal sense in the defense of *dar al-Islam*, the Islamic world, from intrusion by non-Islamic races. There is, however, significant reference in the Koran to the figurative jihad, the inner battle against the forces that prevent humans from living according to Allah's commands. In an oft-repeated story about the Prophet returning from a battle, he says to his companions that they have returned from the lesser holy war to the greater holy war—the inner struggle against evil. Nevertheless, there is a strong sense in which the Prophet and his companions are to be thought of as an all-male warrior band. Like the Jews, they rapidly expanded their domain under the leadership of Allah. Unlike the Jews, they had some centuries of political success.

The outcome of the successive expansion and contraction of Islam was the development of some unique institutions of governance codified in the shariah. The millet system, allowing for limited self-governance of non-Muslims under Muslim rule, is an example. The expulsion of Muslims from Spain in the late 1400s, followed two centuries later by the defeat of the

Turks at the gates of Vienna, led to a prolonged period of isolationism for Islam, a period that has ended abruptly in this century with the twin developments of modernization and fundamentalism. Like Israel, Islam is struggling to use its more evolved system of governance in the face of a fundamentalist revival that has declared jihad not only on Christians and Jews but on nonfundamentalist Muslims as well.

The role model in the jihad culture is the warrior with sword ever at hand to defend hearth, village, or pastureland from marauders, but always ready for the inner war as well. The pilgrimage to Mecca and the five daily calls to prayer are also part of the warrior's life. The taking of the sacred Mosque at Mecca by an armed fundamentalist Moslem group several years ago suggests how thin the line is between inner and outer warfare. In countries where it is practiced, the veiling and seclusion of women gives them little role in public life and emphasizes their role as obedient reproducers of the warrior society. That power has been exerted by charismatic women from behind the veil goes without saying; however, as in the case of Israel, it has been power exerted to maintain the warrior society.

*Christianity.* Unlike Judaism and Islam, Christianity started out as a pacifist sect. Only when the persecuted minority attained a protected position within the Roman Empire did it begin to see war as a legitimate instrument to protect its lands against intrusion by heretics and infidels. The just war doctrine, developed from the days of Augustine of Hippo onward, contained provisions similar to those of the Code of Maimonides and the Koran, particularly for the protection of the innocent and for proportionality, which can be translated as "protect those fruit trees for the future"! Over time, the crusade developed as the Christian counterpart of the jihad. Protective war changed to expansionist war when Pope Urban II in 1095 urged Christian princes of Europe to liberate the Holy Land from the Muslims. Three hundred years of crusades against the infidels were followed by three hundred more years of war between and within Christian denominations, finally brought to a close by the Treaty of Westphalia. Male warrior bands, fighting under the banner of king, pope, Holy Roman Emperor, or as independent warrior orders like the Knights Templar, roamed Europe from 500 C.E. on. Not a few of them were funded and equipped from monastic houses. They fought not only under a warrior God, but under a warrior king Jesus, transformed from peace-bringer by the just war doctrine.

The institutional outcome of these centuries of warfare has been a gradual separation of church and state and a decline in overtly religious wars in the West. The church, however, supports the secular state. The nineteenth century, century of political revolutions, eschewed support of churches. In a twentieth-century reversal, states have welcomed the legitimation of war provided by the enthusiastic blessing of the churches within their respective borders. The state is now seen as upholding the moral order and must be defended. The attempts in this same century, beginning with the Hague conferences, to create agreements that would outlaw the use of force in settling international differences were undertaken without the formal participation of any church. The peace-maintaining machinery of the League of Nations and the United Nations was also formed without a specific role for churches. At the same time, the new role of the church as backstop for the nation-state has greatly multiplied the incidence of war in this century, since there are many more states than religions and, therefore, more potential enemies.

The role model in the Christian secular state is once again the warrior, most recently exemplified in the United States by Rambo. The cigarette-smoking, hard-drinking cowboy warrior in blue jeans is a particularly American version of the warrior model. He is tough and keeps his women under tight control, equal opportunity and affirmative action notwithstanding. While the women's peace movement is trying to create an alternative role model of woman as autonomous peacemaker, rejecting the warrior support option, many women nevertheless support the role of reproducing the warrior society.

At the same time, the development of the welfare state has involved a much higher standard of living and greater opportunity for citizen development, male and female, than existed before. Social technologies are racing with physical technologies for the honor of defending the social order, with the nuclear technological fix apparently winning the race at the moment. Fundamentalist Christian movements strengthen this tendency.

There is no question but that some politically more progressive systems of governance have evolved alongside the warrior culture in each of the traditions mentioned. It is also a fact that each of the three traditions is now experiencing fundamentalist revivals that are promoting a return to a more overt reliance on the holy war culture. These revivals are aided by the continuing presence of the warrior-hero role model and by the powerful emotions evoked by that model.

The holy war culture will not simply fade away. It is too deeply embedded in our consciousness. It has to be reworked. That reworking will involve reformulating the idea of struggle as conquest and destruction of the other; it will involve no longer seeing struggle as a zero-sum game with only winners and losers. When we consider, however, that for religious communities, people's deepest and most inward prayer life has been formed by battle language of one scripture or another, *even when they consciously try to reinterpret it,* there is a heavy loading toward violence in our mental life. The sheer repetition of words independently of the intentions of the hearer has its own effect, as the gradual acceptance of the Star Wars concept in a public initially hostile to it suggests. How, then, with the words calling the hearer to God's battle against the enemy?

But there are other words, calling for very different action. Every community of faith also has a peace culture, and these will be briefly reviewed here.

### The Peaceable Garden Culture

The peaceable garden culture is nonviolent. One of its most notable characteristics is that men and women move about in it with equal freedom. The elderly and the very young are also visible. Love of God and love of nature go hand in hand. The highest experience in this culture is the unitive experience—oneness with God, creation, and humankind. The culture comes in two versions: the mystical union version and the practical pacifist version. We will focus on the latter, but it should be remembered that a basic sense of oneness with creation underlies all religious peaceableness.

**Judaism.** Practical utopian-pacifist activism is well exemplified in that form of Zionism represented by Martin Buber.[10] He saw a Jewish national community in Palestine as an opportunity to create a model political community embodying the highest spiritual values of Judaism while practicing a nonviolent, reconciling relationship with Arab brothers and sisters as co-tillers of the same soil. He called for the following precepts of Leviticus: communal ownership of the land, regularly recurrent leveling of social distinctions, guarantee of the independence of each individual, mutual aid, and the Sabbath year of rest and enjoyment of the fruits of labor for all. The kibbutzim were to be the practical experiments in creating this model society, and men and women were to be equal partners in every respect.

**Islam.** Sufism is the best-known pacifist tradition in Islam, and while the special service of the Sufi is to be a silent witness to God, the Sufi play a special role within the polity, standing over against bureaucracy and formalism. The dervish orders perform a similar function. A social action version of the Muslim peaceable garden culture best known in the West is the Baha'i faith, which, while generally treated as a heresy in Islam, sees itself as having the same relationship to Islam that Christianity has to Judaism. The Baha'i make working for peace a high priority. They are associated with movements for gender and racial equality and social justice in all the countries where they are to be found. There is also a strong element of Sufi-type spirituality in their religious practice. Although Baha'i saints and martyrs provide strong role models for public witness on difficult social issues—for men and women equally—the practice of the Baha'i faith is severely constrained in many Muslim societies today.

*Christianity.* Mystical and contemplative traditions in Christianity, as in Islam, are themselves a source of peace witness, with monks and nuns considered role models for peace in the larger community and prayer interpreted as a form of social action. Turning to the Christian activist tradition, we find the Anabaptists and a strong social action wing of Catholicism. This social action wing, linked to concepts of serving the poor, has been particularly visible in recent decades in lay movements like the Catholic Worker, Catholic trade unions, and the base community movement. Both Protestant and Catholic social action traditions emerged in response to Joachim de Fiore's teachings about the postbureaucratic age of the Holy Spirit in the twelfth century. Men and women all over Europe translated and taught from the Bible in the vernacular, set up communities where goods were held in common, and generally worked to break the bonds of the feudal order. Many of the chiliastic sects went to excesses, but the Anabaptists kept to a disciplined, nonhierarchical, socially and spiritually open set of teachings. The participation of women as equal partners with men and an emphasis on nonviolence in the pursuit of social justice were notable characteristics of the Anabaptists. Their later descendants include Quakers, Mennonites, and Brethren, now known as the historic peace churches. These groups administered alternative service camps for conscientious objectors during World War II in the United States. Pacifist-activist saints and martyrs come from all denominations within Christianity, one of the best known among them in our time being the Baptist Martin Luther King, Jr.

The "peace face" of these different faith communities is hardly unknown. It does not, however, enter the popular culture in the same way that the "war face" does. Its contemplative, mystical component accentuates its invisibility.

The activist peace culture in each case is a small minority trying to apply spiritual understanding and egalitarian, nonviolent practices to the social problems and conflicts of community life. This minority shares a powerful emotional commitment to doing God's work as they understand it and a powerful sense of belonging to God's whole earthly family. It is the intensity of this larger belongingness that sets them apart in their respective faith communities.

### Societies Can Change

Although a strong commitment to peaceable ways may, in one sense, be thought of as representing minority, almost dissenting beliefs—the warrior theme being both spiritually and politically more accessible—belief in nonviolence nevertheless has great staying power and never completely disappears. In times of rapid social change, it is an especially important resource because of its emphasis on peaceful problem solving, cooperative human relations, and sharing. And cultures do change. UNESCO's *Peace Anthology,* through the proclamations of "peace kings" and "peace emperors" and quotations by wise public leaders from ancient times onwards, gives a vivid picture of dramatic shifts from the warrior stance to that of the peacemaker.[11] One well-known example can be found in the behavior of Emperor Ashoka of India, who, after great conquests of nearby peoples in the third century B.C.E., repented of his war making and issued the Rock Edicts, calling on all neighboring kingdoms as well as his own people to live in peace and joy with one another. He made his own empire safe for all travelers, with special protected resting places on every highway.

Another interesting example of culture change drawing on hidden resources is found in the history of an early European warrior society turned peaceful: the Vikings. The transformation of the Northmen, the "scourge of Europe," into the architects of the most peaceful region in Europe, Scandinavia, and the designers of strategies and institutions to replace war is an intriguing story.

The skills of negotiation developed in the pre-Viking institution of the *thing,* the gatherings of landholders to make decisions by consensus, were centuries later seen to be more useful in interaction with other peoples than the conqueror's approach. Similarly, negotiated trade turned out to be more productive than simple pillaging. Settlement replaced conquest in Britain. The Vikings left their warrior gods and adopted some of the gentler teachings of Christianity, meanwhile learning to listen to the soil as well as to the sea and increasingly becoming farmers. This new awareness also led to the eventual abandonment of the conquest of Russia. In much more recent times, the choice of a peaceful separation of Norway from Sweden in 1905, even though both sides had been armed for war, was a notable example of a new style of diplomatic initiatives that has been important in the evolution of the League of Nations and its successor, the United Nations, in this century.[12]

We will see in the next two chapters of part 1 that peace movements and images of alternative societies with alternative approaches to conflict are not new phenomena on the historical scene. They go back to antiquity. However, the latter part of the nineteenth century brought a new wave of awareness of the alternatives to war and violence. It is ironic that the greatest breakthroughs by scholars and diplomats in designing institutions for peaceful settlement of disputes came side by side with counterbreakthroughs in military technology.

The Hague Peace Conference that ushered in the twentieth century was intended to begin the construction of diplomatic structures and processes that would render war obsolete as means of settling disputes among states. In 1910, William James wrote his famous essay "The Moral Equivalent of War," proposing to replace the old morality of military honor with a new morality of civic honor and civic responsibility by instituting conscription for socially useful service instead of war.[13] The establishment of the League of Nations after the setback of World War I, and of the United Nations after the setback of World War II, each in turn demonstrated the seriousness of the social and political intentions of deeply thoughtful internationalists on several continents and the difficulties of realizing them. In 1926, Quincy Wright broke new leadership paths for American internationalist thought when he began the Study of War Project at the University of Chicago. The project's purpose was to initiate a multidimensional understanding of war and to pursue serious professional research on how war could be abolished. *The Study of War*, first published in 1942, was a major conceptual breakthrough in questioning the inevitability of war in human history.[14]

During the same period, Sorokin analyzed the dynamics of historical change in culture systems from the fifth century B.C.E. through the 1920s and the relationship between culture types (ideational/idealistic or sensate/materialistic) and the frequency of warfare over time.[15] From the macrohistorical perspective, was warfare dying out or increasing? The news was, *neither*. Sorokin found only random fluctuations over the centuries. Sometimes war was associated with cultural flowering, other times with cultural decline.

Sometimes it flourished during ideational/idealistic periods, sometimes during sensate/materialistic periods. There was only one clear trend: war was becoming more lethal over time. The very fact of random fluctuations gave hope to those who sought to create alternatives to war. Again the message was: war itself not inevitable!

During the 1930s, 1940s, and 1950s a small group of interdisciplinary-minded scholars and activists were working to lay the foundations of a new social science discipline that would focus on alternative methods of conflict resolution between states. Since the "war to end all wars" (World War I) had failed in its mission, they had to struggle against the continuing persistence of the idea that wars were inevitable and beyond human control.

### Historians Reconsider the Sword

By the early 1960s the international situation looked very bleak. A group of American historians, disturbed by the Cold War-fueled arms race and signals of rising levels of intra- and interstate violence, such as the assassination of President Kennedy and the early rumblings of the coming war in Indochina, became keenly aware of how little effort had been made in their field to study the causes and processes of peace. Accordingly, they formed the Council on Peace Research in History to encourage, support and coordinate peace research in history. These American historians at the same time also were active in the larger peace research movement within the social sciences that became the International Peace Research Association. By the early 1970s they were working closely with their European counterparts, who eventually formed the European Working Group on Peace Research in History and have, in the decades since, made remarkable contributions to the documentation of peace movements and peace processes in history. The members of these new networks of historians first drawn largely from North America and Europe, now include diplomatic historians, analysts of military policy, chroniclers of movements for peace and social justice, and teachers, students, peace activists, and concerned citizens from each world region.[16] Their task has been not only to change the image of human history as the record of war, by documenting the far more ubiquitous activities of everyday problem solving and conflict resolution at every level—from local communities to interstate relations—but also to demonstrate how often such behavior created effective alternatives to military action.

At the same time, UNESCO encouraged the establishment of bilateral committees of historians from European countries that had been at war to agree on textbook versions of the history of the relations between the countries that would not keep old animosities alive. UNESCO also commissioned several world history projects that emphasized the positive contributions of each civilization to humankind.[17]

While a number of scholars continue to hold to the conviction that war is both genetically programmed in the human species and essential to its survival fitness, a consensus is growing that war is, as Margaret Mead put it, "a social invention, not a biological necessity"[18]—and an increasingly dysfunctional invention at that. UNESCO's Culture of Peace Program provides many examples of peace processes as social inventions in conflict prevention. Macrohistorical studies of the effectiveness of military preparedness and of war fighting as an instrument of the state to achieve peace and security for its people show little relationship between military preparedness and security. Naroll and his coauthors' careful and methodologically brilliant analysis of deterrence in nine civilizations for periods ranging from four to twenty-five centuries shows that military preparedness does not deter enemies but may, rather, incite them.[19] Studies of the arms races that preceded World War I and World War II and continued through the Cold War dramatically emphasize that each increase in arms levels by one state will be matched by its opponent, thus ensuring that arms races increase the insecurity of each party and frequently end in war.[20] Recent analyses of the Cold War, considered by many strategists and international relations specialists to be a masterly example of the effectiveness of deterrence (because the United States "won" it solely by a superior level of military preparedness), are now suggesting different conclusions. New evidence indicates that the expensive deterrence policy may, in fact, have prolonged the Cold War by slowing down Soviet-initiated resolution processes that finally succeeded in spite of, and not because of, United States deterrence strategy.[21]

Warfare has traditionally put soldiers at risk—civilians rarely so. Today civilian casualties far outnumber military casualties. This pattern began to be true in World War I with the use of chemical and bacteriological warfare. During World War II the saturation bombing of European cities and the tragic nuclear bombing of Hiroshima and Nagasaki brought about a dramatic increase in civilian deaths. Today landmines primarily target civilians, perhaps children most of all, in the rural hinterlands of warfare areas—in Africa, Asia, Central America, and Europe as well. Such developments dangerously lower the social threshold for what is considered morally acceptable strategy in conflict situations.

The economic analyses of war that have come out of the peace research movement clarify the enormous cost of military preparedness to economic and social well-being.[22] While these costs are most damaging in the Two-Thirds World, they also drag down industrial economies, providing fewer jobs per dollar invested than civilian production and contributing to an increasing maldistribution of income. The environmental destruction involved—first in military preparedness on military reservations within the preparing state and then in the target states once weapons are unleashed—is enormous. And finally, World Health Organization reports on rising rates of mental illness around the world in current decades, the fruit of high levels of intrastate and interstate violence, remove from military supremacy the last vestiges of its credibility as symbol of a nation's true greatness.

In spite of the many delegitimating forces at work, the deeply held belief that war is a basic, inevitable, and divinely ordained process in human history will not easily be changed. In fact, change will come about only with a much wider recognition of the actual peace processes at work in every society and a wider awareness of the success stories of conflicts resolved and wars avoided. An important part of this change will be the increasing awareness of the peace cultures that have reproduced themselves side by side with the war cultures right inside the same society, over time, as in the examples given of the two cultures within each religious tradition.

Sometimes the peace culture has been a hidden culture, kept alive in the cracks of a violent society. At other times the peace culture has predominated, and violence has receded to a minimum. Given how destructive war has become in this century, we are lucky that we have living peace cultures to look to and to build on in this transition era for the human race. They can help us move away from global destruction and toward a world alive with a great diversity of peaceable lifeways. In the next chapter, we will look at one special type of peace culture that has managed to reproduce itself over and over in different ages on different continents—the culture of utopian visioning of a different and better future.

# 2

# *The Passion for Utopia*

Peace cultures thrive on and are nourished by visions of how things might be, in a world where sharing and caring are part of the accepted lifeways for everyone. The very ability to imagine something different and better than what currently exists is critical for the possibility of social change. The historian Fred Polak has documented how societies' images of the future have empowered their action in the present.[1] People can't work for what they can't imagine. Thoughts about the other and different, however, are also a specific response to existing reality. The utopian image is in a profound sense a critique of the present, although it often appears as an escape from that present—which is why the term "utopian" has developed negative connotations for many people. In this chapter we will consider utopianism as a source of positive social change, away from violence and injustice and toward a humane social order. However, we will also examine tensions and contradictions in utopian thinking, as well as the pitfalls that lie in the path of utopian experiments in social change. We will note particularly how difficult such efforts can be at the macrolevel, on the scale of the national state, but also note that small-scale utopian experiments, such as intentional communities, have their challenges, too.

This chapter is a substantial rewriting of an essay commissioned by the Committee for a Just World Peace for presentation at its Royaumont Conference, December 1985, with support from the North American program of the Peace and Global Transformation Project of the United Nations University. The original essay was published in *Alternatives* 11, no. 3 (July 1986), 345–66, under the title "Utopianism: Problems and Issues in Planning for a Peaceful Society."

## Historical Overview

The human capacity to visualize *The Other* as different and better than the
experienced present is found in archetypal form in all civilizational traditions
through legends of the Elysian Fields, the Isles of the Blessed, Zion, Valhalla,
paradise. These legendary settings predate civilizations. Anthropologists report that blessed isles are part of the dream-world of tribal peoples. They are
not confined to the West. Utopian elements are found in Taoism, Theravada
Buddhism, and medieval Islam, and in Chinese, Japanese, and Indian stories
about imaginary havens of delight.[2]

Under the pressure of social upheaval, the archetypal vision is transformed
into concrete imagery that answers specific social needs and dissatisfactions.
Thus, Plato's *Republic* was a response to the upheavals of the Peloponnesian
Wars. The hundreds of desert communes established by Christian men and
women in Egypt and Syria in the first few centuries of the common era were
a response to the corruption of urban life in Imperial Rome, an affirmation
of an alternative human potentiality that has continued as a viable monastic
tradition for two thousand years. The millenialist movements and utopian
communities that erupted by the hundreds in the Middle Ages were a series
of responses to plague, famine, and the gradual breakdown of the feudal
order.

It is ironic, then, that utopia ("no place," as Thomas More named his pat-
tern-setting *Utopia* in 1516) has come to be synonymous with a flight from reality.[3] All the great utopians have been masterful critics of their own time.
Utopias have many forms and functions, but one enduring function is to sati-
rize society as it exists; another is to describe a more desirable way of organizing human affairs. One key problem of utopia writing is that all utopias have
implicit political goals, but few utopists are able to devise political strategies
to achieve their utopia that do not destroy these very goals. Historically, the
theoreticians of utopia and the practitioners have not been the same people,
and when they have been, the results have sometimes been disastrous. Theoreticians, however, are in touch with the currents of the times in very special
ways. The evidence for this, as the Manuels point out, is that "virtually every
one of the major slogans that expressed the hopes of French and English
working-class movements of the first half of the nineteenth century was
plucked from the gardens of the printed works of utopian writers."[4]

Although utopianism is found in all cultural traditions, many of its modern
versions have a very western flavor. Since modern utopianism, beginning in

the eighteenth century, will be our focus here, we will pay particular attention to the difference in knowledge and experience worlds out of which Euro–North American utopianism arose, as contrasted with the rest of the world.

The particular set of upheavals that ushered in modernism originated in Europe, though they were deeply affected by earlier experiences of the crusaders in the Middle East. These upheavals, providing the ingredients for the great utopias of the past three centuries, included: (1) the voyages of discovery, which brought news of many different lifestyles and cultures and produced a rash of literary island utopias; (2) a rapid rate of scientific discovery and technological invention, which gave a new sense of control over the environment to human beings; (3) urbanization and industrialization, which introduced the concept of class interests for new social groupings, including industrial workers and the bourgeoisie, and (4) the rise of the modern nation state and military expansion of the industrial order through colonization. All four of these factors contributed to the sense of social progress and control over the future. The four major ideologies of socialism, Marxism, liberalism, and anarchism, which developed in different contexts within different social formations, all worked to realize their respective utopias.

However, the path of utopianism has not been smooth. *Utopia* became an increasingly bad word during the world revolutionary movements of the mid-nineteenth century. Marx himself was a relentless anti-utopianist. Even Toynbee saw utopian thinking as a symptom of a descending stage of the civilization cycle. It was not until Mannheim published *Ideology and Utopia*,[5] with its conceptual clarification of the function of utopian thinking as a response to pressing social problems, and its typology of kinds of utopian thinking from chiliastic to socialist-communist, that the concept was restored to respectability. Nevertheless, the Mannheimian discussion was a very western-oriented one.

The Two-Thirds World, meantime, was experiencing the upheavals of modernism very differently. For that world, the voyages of discovery led to conquest and colonization; science and technology came with no context, and was seen as magic; urbanization and industrialization meant the destruction of traditional patterns of landholding, agricultural production, and, in many areas, the traditional autonomy of women; it also meant the replacement of village self-sufficiency with landless urban poverty. National liberation movements alternated between feelings of empowerment—that they could shape the future—and feelings of helplessness and dependency in the

face of alien political and economic forces they could not control and technologies they could not understand. In short, utopianism has had very different contexts and dynamics in Euro–North America and the rest of the world.
The dominant Eurocentric concepts of utopia are not easily applied to the
Two-Thirds World, where many of the utopian experiments of the past century have taken place.

## Concepts and Issues

### The Passion for Order and the Longing for Nature

Two key aspects of utopian thought that are continually struggling with one
another are the passion for order and the longing for what is "natural." The
passion for order is the powerful drive to impose rational, efficient, just, and
peaceful behavioral protocols and structures on irrational, inefficient, untidy,
and impulsive human beings. Science and technology offer the tools for creating this rational and peaceful order. Boguslaw points out in his *New Utopians* that automation systems are designed to reduce as far as possible the
number of responses that humans can make (i.e., reduce human error) while
increasing as far as possible the number of responses the machine makes (the
machine being immune(!) to error).[6] Behavioral modification provides the
same effect with the use of psychological tools. Mendelsohn and Nowotny, in
a grim assessment of science and utopia, speak of the overloading of utopian
thoughts with a "surplus of order" in order to keep the incoherence of actual
societies at bay.[7]

Society as a perfectly functioning mechanism can become an attractive
idea. Planning becomes the central function of such a society. Everything becomes doable. Authoritarianism and military organization slip in easily.
Fourier's phalanx system is a good example of this type of utopia—a completely formalist design that provides for everything that can happen in the society.[8] And that is what Huxley's *Brave New World* and Orwell's *1984* were
written to denounce.

Clashing with the passion for order is the longing for the spontaneous untidy abundance of nature. This organic approach sees nature as evolving in its
own way, and humans need only happily go along with nature. A transformation is taking place, and a new consciousness is needed on the part of humans
to recognize the transformation and to work with it. The millennialist
Joachim de Fiore wrote in the thirteenth century about the transformation.[9]
He declared that the Age of the Holy Spirit had arrived to replace the age of

the bureaucratic institutional church. People needed only to follow the paths opened up by the spirit to enter into this new age. The Anabaptist tradition that grew from de Fiore's teachings is utopian in the best sense of the word. Anabaptists taught egalitarianism, both between classes and between men and women. Working for the ideals of social justice and peace in the postfeudal era, they empowered peasants and workers alike with the tools of literacy and the skills of craft and industry. But their openness to promptings of the spirit left them vulnerable to a charismatic leadership that violated their own intentions. Norman Cohn's *Pursuit of the Millennium* vividly documents the chiliastic uprisings of peasants and workers in the late Middle Ages in the name of the holy spirit—uprisings that sometimes turned into nightmares of cruelty and bloodshed as charismatic leaders carried themselves and their followers away in an excess of emotionalism.[10] The 1534 Anabaptist seizure of Münster under the leadership of John of Leyden, which ended in the death of most of its inhabitants, illustrates the tragic distortion of a noble vision. Twentieth-century charismatics have, on the whole, appeared to be more peaceable, though transformation of consciousness can still be accompanied by great violence, as in the Jonestown massacre a few years ago. Other examples of transformational violence include the Aum Cult's mass chemical poisoning of subway riders in Japan, evidently intended as the signal of a new order, and the bombing of a U.S. federal building in Oklahoma, evidently carried out by a very small group opposed to the power of the U.S. government.

The more peaceful orientation of attunement to nature and organically evolving processes has, however, been a primary and continuous tradition, both in religious and secular form, from the time of the Anabaptists. In religion we see this in the historic peace churches of the Quakers, Mennonites, and Brethren—the direct descendants of the Anabaptists. In the social sciences we find it in the theories of Herbert Spencer about society as an organism, evolving over time from savage tribalism through military order to the highly differentiated peaceable industrial society that Spencer saw as an evolutionary end product.[11]

Oddly enough, both the mechanistic and the organic models of utopia were based on deep convictions about continuing social progress. The mechanists saw progress as coming through the application of scientific principles to the designing of social structure. The organicists saw progress coming through an awareness of the nature of living systems, including human and social systems, working with that nature to achieve the good society. Both models were vulnerable to the distortions of authoritarianism and militarism. Spencer's theory of evolution toward a peaceable industrial society depended on a voluntaristic, nonbureaucratic relationship between industry and the state, which did not come about. The growth of government machinery (which he, in fact, feared as an inevitably pathological distortion of organic processes) has produced a world military order that is the antithesis of the industrial society he visualized. On the other hand, Toynbee's portrayal of a long-term historical trend toward an eventual universal state, with each major world empire a herald of that possible world state, is still taken seriously by various world order thinkers. His image of societies climbing from ledge to ledge up a cliff certainly suggests an organic model, albeit with mechanistic overtones.[12]

There is one special utopian tradition in the organic mode that stands as a critique of the vulnerability to authoritarianism: the feminist utopian tradition. The feminist tradition is based on careful attunement to the structures and processes of the natural order. This enables individual actors and social groups to work with the potentials in any organic entity without doing violence to those potentials. The shaping of the individual and the social order according to such principles is seen as a task demanding the utmost effort, both intellectual and intuitive. Charlotte Perkins Gilman's *Herland* exemplifies this approach to social evolution,[13] as do the novels of Ursula LeGuin. On the scientific side, the work of Barbara McClintock[14] and Lynn Margulis[15] demonstrates the kind of breakthroughs in understanding possible when this kind of disciplined attunement, drawing equally on mind and heart, is practiced in scientific research on living systems. Charlene Spretnak, a leading theorist and practitioner of ecofeminism, has added a new and powerful voice to organically based utopianism.[16]

Both the mechanistic and the organic models suffer from the deep ambivalence represented by the metaphor of the machine in the garden, a recurring motif in Western writing, particularly in North America. Part of the ambivalence stems from the double perception of America as the new Eden, the garden of the New World where life is to be shaped anew, as contrasted with America as the pioneer in the application of science and technology to the good life. Washington Irving's description of edenic Sleepy Hollow, a quiet pastoral place suddenly invaded by the thundering roar of a nearby passing train, is symbolic of the sense of invasion that machines bring with mobility, productivity, and progress. The doubts about the machine are clear already in the writings of Carlyle, who called attention to the dangers of reliance on mechanism for the development of the inner life.[17] Karl Marx's concept of alienation also reflects this ambivalence, though no one relied more heavily than he on the machine to further human progress. The suddenness of the entry of the machine into the garden heightens the trauma. Industrialization is sometimes thought of as a slow, gradual experience in the West, and sudden only for the Two-Thirds World. In fact, however, the machine, by its very nature, erupted with explosive and unexpected force, whether in the textile mills of Britain or New England, in the trackless prairies of the United States, or in the rural hinterlands of India and China.

In the United States, Emerson, Thoreau, Mark Twain, and Henry Adams all wrestled with the problem. At the very beginning of the Gilded Age in the 1870s, a group of American writer-activists attempted to develop populist political movements that would preserve the human scale and community values in the face of the machine's onslaught. Henry George, Henry Lloyd, and Edward Bellamy were three such writer-activists.[18] Their evangelical zeal petered out with the decline of populism, but the country-life movement, the community planning and garden city movements of the twentieth century, along with the more recent bioregionalism, continue to deal with the problem of the machine in the garden.

In Europe the same movements exist, although with less intensity. Europe, after all, has experienced urban population densities for a long time, and the factory predated industrialism. The romantic tradition from Rousseau to Ruskin, and the village utopia novels of nineteenth-century England by authors such as Morris and Hudson, kept the issue of how to deal with the machine alive. The back-to-the-land movement in Europe, however, took a different form than in the United States. "Back to the land" meant emigration, settling on other people's land on other continents. The same movement that brought emigrating Europeans closer to the land deprived many native peoples of their land through the process of colonization. Most of the migrations were personal, intended to better individual circumstances. Some, however, were purposeful in the utopian sense. Best known are those groups that migrated for reasons of religious persecution and established a series of religious utopian settlements in the Americas. Similarly, a smaller group of social utopianists, such as the Owenites, set up new communities in the United States. In each case these ventures were seen as contributing to the reconstruction of society by setting up working models, but their efforts were confined to the microlevel. They will be further discussed below in the section on microlevel utopias.

The important thing to bear in mind in considering the conflict between the passion for order, which relies heavily on science and technology to create that order, and the longing for the "natural," the organic connectedness with nature, is that the two impulses usually coexist in each camp. The failure of utopias, insofar as they can be said to have failed, lies to a considerable degree in their inability to resolve this particular set of dilemmas.

### The Role of Violence in Revolutionary Change

Because utopia is always *The Other*—something totally different from existing society, a radical restructuring of the existing order—the changes implied by utopia are, in effect, revolutionary whether based on a commitment to gradual evolutionary change or sudden restructuring. This is why revolutionary violence keeps appearing in many utopian efforts, even when there is a commitment to peaceableness, as with the medieval millennialists. If the goal is total restructuring of how humans live, whether on the micro- or macrolevel, then the destruction of existing arrangements, including the physical destruction of the human beings who maintain it, may come to be seen as a necessary wiping clean of the slate. In *The Magic Mountain*, Naphta sees the utopianism of Settembrini, "the man of progress, liberalism and middle-class revolution," as monstrous and declares that "the task of the proletariat is to strike terror into the world for the healing of the world, that man may finally achieve salvation and deliverance and win back freedom from law and from distinction of classes."[19] It was Napoleon who said there could be no revolution without terror, a theme reechoed in revolutionary change.

Violence has been particularly important in certain Two-Thirds World settings. Frantz Fanon, speaking of the process of liberation in Algeria, writes that "for the native, life can only spring up again out of the rotting corpse of the settler." And again: "violence is a cleansing force. It frees the native from his inferiority complex and from his despair and inaction; it makes him fearless and restores his self-respect."[20] In the West, the very size of the challenge posed by the abstract globalism of a revolutionary commitment to free all humans everywhere would seem to necessitate violence to prepare the ground for change. During the crisis, when the time is ripe, anything goes. There is time enough later for the gentler human virtues to reassert themselves. This argument operates as strongly for religious as for secular revolutionary change. A distillation of this reasoning is found in the *Reformatico Sigismundi* on the eve of the Reformation.[21] The argument goes: The final crisis is now;

this is a time for anger; our cause is just, so we must succeed; refuse to bow to present authorities, and listen to the prophetic revelation that gives us a mandate for action (cite favorite scriptural reference here). It is a call to holy war.

It is an oversimplification to say that the resort to violence has been the operative cause of utopian failures, since nonviolent utopias also fail. The same problems of human learning beset both types of utopia. It is true, however, that the visibility of revolutionary violence, and the pride and fear it engenders, deeply affects our assessment of radical change and, indeed, the assessment of utopias in general. With rising tides of violence in industrial countries (to say nothing of the Two-Thirds World), there is loss of faith today in the capacity for peaceful change. Cotta writes that "violence hides in the antinomies of our very ways of life, which are lawless and mass-dominated, intellectualized and emotive, artificial and natural, torn apart between the pressing urge (often brought about artificially) for productive activism and a spreading desire for amusement and happiness."[22] In short, generalized violence endangers the utopian commitment.

### The Centralization-Decentralization Debate

The centralization-decentralization debate mirrors the mechanistic-organicist debate. Shall the new order be centrally designed by those with competence and skill and imposed on people who could not in their present state of being achieve this way of life unaided, thus helping them in spite of themselves? Or shall the seeds of the new order be planted wherever the fertile soil of existing structures can be found at the local level, thus allowing the old to be gradually transformed into the new? Again, both positions are held within each camp, frequently even by the same person. Marx, who identified historical conditions necessary for the emergence of socialism, had nothing but contempt for the tinkering of his fellow socialists, which he saw as standing in the way of unfolding historical processes. It was the identification of these processes that rendered his socialism "scientific," in contrast to "utopian" (read "unscientific, unrealistic") socialism. Did this analysis lead Marx to study existing associational structures available to peasants and villagers at the local level that might facilitate that emergence? No, both Marx and Lenin consciously avoided using local structures, relying on a theoretically based social design, and on the manipulation of economic and political variables without regard to local structures, to achieve the changes they sought. In their view, local structures could safely be used only *after* revolutionary reconstruction had taken place. This refusal to work from the begin-

ning with the social materials at hand was certainly one of the failures of Soviet communism. We will see in the next section how differently various revolutionary utopian efforts dealt with preexisting traditional structures.

Buber takes the position that no revolution can succeed unless it has
already happened—that the taking of power by a new group can only be the
formal legitimation of a process that has already taken place.[23] He focuses on
the preexisting traditional structures in every case and shows how the richness of those associational structures determines the capacity of a society to
engage in participatory change that is responsive to local situations and local
needs while fitting into a larger societal picture. The *panchayat, kolkhoz,
ejido, ujamaa, tauhid, shramadana,* and many other traditional village associational forms are all potentially agents of revolutionary change when
brought into full participation. Anarchist Kropotkin emphasized the importance of the fluidity and spontaneity that localism makes possible.[24] As we
will see, the centralist-localist dialectic is important in all macrolevel utopian
experiments.

### The Development of the New Human for the New Society: The Restructuring vs. the Reeducation Debate

Another major issue is the formation of the new human being who is to
function in the new society. Again, we see the familiar division between the
mechanists and the organicists. The mechanists place their faith in structural
redesign to create the new type of human being. When oppressive conditions
are removed and humanly facilitative conditions created, individuals will au-
tomatically engage in constructive and desirable behavior. Essentially, this
theory presupposes the "innate" goodness of humans. The organicists take
the position that humans have to evolve along with the society. If they belong
to the "transformation happens of itself" school, nothing has to be done to facilitate individual transformations. Some organicists, however, see reeducation as an important part of the evolutionary process, involving spiritual,
intellectual, and emotional development. Generally it is the religious utopianists who take seriously the reformation of the individual. Their attention to
this process has clearly paid off in the longevity of many religious utopias.

The educational experiments of many secular utopianists have not been
successful. One could argue that this is because of an inadequate understanding of the human learning process. Even the behavioral modification
techniques of the Walden Two experiment in Twin Oaks[25] do not seem very
successful, although in part this is because of hesitation in applying them.

Squabbling and greed destroy most "organic" utopias. The restructured societies on the mechanistic model are notorious for failing to produce the desired behaviors, even though educational systems are, in theory, included in their design. Political power struggles swamp altruistic behavior every time. The significance of human functioning for both types of utopia is matched only by the inability of any model *qua* model to produce people who can function effectively in it.

### How Utopianists Have Dealt with Their Conceptual Dilemmas

As we look in turn at macrolevel and microlevel utopian efforts to design and implement utopias, we will see how differently various experimental groups have dealt with the tension between the passion for order and the longing for the spontaneity of organic processes; between the desire for central control and the recognition that locality has its own competence; between the desire to destroy all traces of oppressive structures and wipe the slate clean before beginning anew and the impulse to nurture the seeds of the new within the shell of the old, trusting that gentleness, not violence, will free the goodness in humans; and finally, between the urge to redesign structures and the hope to produce new kinds of human beings to achieve the new society. We will see that macrolevel utopias have generally placed less faith in organic local processes, but where they have, they have been more successful. The microlevel utopias, favoring the organic, have tended to fail in terms of order. But neither group has been able to confine itself to one set of strategies or the other, and what we will be observing in the descriptions that follow is a variety of strategic mixes. Because the emphasis in this chapter is on utopian solutions in the real world, theory and action are more closely linked in what follows than is normally found in writing on utopias. Utopias that never reached the praxis stage, of which there are legion, are not discussed.

### Macrolevel Utopian Experiments

In this section we will look at society-wide efforts to institute revolutionary utopias. By their nature, they have a political component that micro-utopias do not, since they are working at the level of the nation-state. This political component both reduces their degree of freedom to experiment and makes them more answerable to the public. The failure of a local utopian commune is not considered a major event, but the nation-state utopian experiment is watched keenly by the rest of the world. There is a strong desire on the part of most observers to cry "Failed!" when the experiment runs into trouble. But, surely, no macrolevel experiment should be pronounced an ir-revocable failure as long as it is continuing to develop, modify, and change its mode of operation. The word *experiment* itself is crucial here; indeed, every political leader in a socialist utopian state emphasizes the experimental na-ture of the venture.

An important point to keep in mind is the statement made by both Marx and Lenin that no one can really know what a fully socialist society will look like. Buber calls this an irresponsible refusal to fantasize, to explore the future directions in the mental experiments so strongly recommended by Weber,[26] but that refusal can also be seen as reflecting an openness to what the future may bring.

***The Soviet Experiment.*** Marx himself would have been horrified to have the Russian socialist experiment called utopian. However, by our broad defini-tion, which includes both designed and evolved utopias with varying degrees of historical readiness for the experiment, the Russian experiment is utopian. Marxist theory gives much attention to the economic and political forces that will have to be controlled in order to construct a socialist state. The early So-viet leaders tried to compensate for the fact that Russia did not have a suffi-ciently well-developed industrial proletariat for revolutionary purposes. The irony is that, by Buber's standards, many of the preconditions for social revo-lution were there. A number of autonomous local soviets had been formed, partially built on the village *kolkhoz* model, partially by urban workingmen's associations. Crucial village-urban alliances had been made. But the problem was that these local associations had their own ideas, which did not match the ideas of Lenin and his planners. In *Lenin's Last Struggle*, Moshe Lewin doc-uments how the overwhelming scale of the problems that faced Lenin at the close of World War I—feeding a famine-stricken nation, organizing produc-tion and distribution of energy and goods—repeatedly drove him into the arms of hardened army professionals and bureaucrats from czarist times who were least likely to implement revolutionary goals.[27] At the same time, he turned away from all the local revolutionary associations already committed to socialist goals because they were too spontaneous, too untidy, and could not be dealt with in the time he felt he had available. According to some scholars (although this is in dispute), he realized too late that he had made the wrong alliances, and his final months were a tragedy of realized failures. In this view, Lenin had created a monstrous new bureaucracy, which he was helpless to modify or control.

The Stalin era consolidated all the worst features of the new state, in which the term *Soviet* had become a parody of itself, a controlled mouthpiece instead of an autonomous entity. We have witnessed the turbulent years from Krushchev to Gorbachev to the breakup of the Soviet Union into the current uneasy Commonwealth of Independent States in 1991; and now we are witnessing the dismantling of some centralized planning and welfare bureaucracies, the retention of others, and a confused effort to create a market economy without the necessary infrastructure of democratic local decision making and experience with entrepreneurial initiatives. The resulting unemployment and decline in quality of life leaves many citizens of the former USSR remembering its achievements, especially the massive reconstruction of a system of feudal privilege into a countrywide educational system to give literacy to a hitherto illiterate population and the creation of countrywide health care and child care services, to say nothing of local palaces of culture to encourage artistic expression in former serfs.

Certainly the original excitement, which lasted for some decades after the revolution—an excitement about being the leading edge of what was to be a worldwide revolution—is now gone. (Hobsbawm gives a vivid picture of the dreams, actual achievements, and limitations of the Soviet utopian experiment.)[28] Yet, remembered pride in a society that "cared for everyone" and a sense of contrast with what is perceived to be a set of uncaring capitalist societies may still give rise to future developments reflecting socialist ideals.

***The Spanish Experiment.*** The extraordinary anarchist utopian experiment that took place in Spain in the 1930s[29] actually produced a Workers Republic from 1931 to 1936, until Franco's invasion triggered civil war and a fascist regime. Yet it remains one of the great utopian stories of the twentieth century and affected a whole generation of men and women around the world who came to defend the revolution in Spain as members of the International Brigade. There were many factions in Spain at the time, but it was the CGT (the Confederación General de Trabajo), the only large-scale anarchist union in the world, that actually established anarchist political practice in some parts of Catalonia. The Asturian revolt, in which anarchists joined with communists and socialists to maintain a commune comparable to the famous Paris Commune of 1870, is one example, out of many, of the organizational skills of anarchists.

The anarchist tradition of complete local autonomy and total participation in local communes, and the radical abolition of private property, actually worked for short periods of time in urban industrial areas of Catalonia, as well as in some rural areas where local autonomous traditions were strong. The reason the anarchist model worked at all, although for admittedly short periods of time, was that anarchist communities had high levels of skill. The anarchists of Catalonia were the most skilled workers in Spain and could easily run factories more efficiently than their alien bureaucratic managers. In rural areas, similarly, the anarchists were excellent farmers, with strong traditions of mutual aid, and they could effectively administer resources in common. But as soon as the anarchist groups tried to include people without their skills and training in their political domain, everything fell apart. The lesson in this story is the importance for "utopias" of organizational skills and associational traditions of sharing and consensual decision making. Whole villages and urban areas had developed these skills. Within the confines of their familiar territory, the anarchists could handle complex social operations very efficiently. The problem was that there was no basis (or time?) for translating these skills into cooperative activity with nonanarchists.

The Spanish experiment, however, is still not over. In 1978 a statute of autonomy passed by the Spanish parliament restored autonomous government and a parliament to Catalonia. Today, the *generalitat* of Catalonia, which proudly traces its existence back to 1359, is presiding over an amazing flowering of Catalonian culture—not only art and literature but also science and advanced technological development. Catalonia sees itself as a major player in creating a new Europe of nationalities rather than states; a pioneer in turning violent and aggressive nationalisms, such as those at work in the Balkans, into a peaceful, creative coexistence of cultures in a harmonious, socially progressive and economically flourishing Europe.[30] The unusual and continuing utopian experiments in ethnic autonomy in Catalonia (and to a degree in the Basque country, as well) are in part due to Spain's unique history. It is unlike the rest of Europe in that it had the industrial revolution without a "French Revolution" and, therefore, never developed strong statist structures. Accordingly, Spain is an important source of utopian alternatives for the twenty-first century.

### Utopian Restructuring and Problems of Scale

*The Cuban Experiment.* The Cuban experiment in instant socialist reconstruction repeated the Russian disasters in miniature, yet the Cuban experiment continues to be of interest. Here was a manageably sized island country. Castro seems to have understood (though not acting on that understanding) the importance of strong local workers' associations for effective national functioning. While there has been some devolution of power to the local level since 1970, Castro's strong and charismatic hand on the tiller limits that process. Literacy, health care, and more equitable resource distribution in comparison with the prerevolutionary society has made life better for the average Cuban, but centralization and serious economic problems—due in considerable part to the U.S. embargo and refusal of all trade relations—have propelled a steady stream of Cubans toward North American shores. The rise of a new black middle class in Cuba and increasing trade and cultural interaction with Europe and the rest of Latin America may well lead to continuing positive change in that society. The country's modest size is in its favor.

**The Chinese Experiment.** In contrast to Cuba, the Chinese experiment was heavily burdened by the scale of Chinese society from the start. Yet the revolution was built on a traditional peasant associational infrastructure, including clans and age-old peasant secret societies. Mao Tse-tung, the charismatic leader of the revolution, was in touch with that infrastructure. He first walked the length and breadth of China (metaphorically speaking) well before the revolution, becoming familiar with village life. He later led the Long March into what turned out to be a very productive "exile" with a group of loyal followers who helped turn the tide of the revolution, the tradition of local involvement remaining unbroken. Watching the film of the Long March that was made to honor Mao's eightieth birthday, one realizes that village involvement in an otherwise remote part of China bound the mystique of the revolution directly to the people in a unique way. Unlike other revolutionary leaders, Mao was familiar with local conditions in many parts of China and had confidence in local associational structures. Block-by-block neighborhood committees actively involving every household on the block continue to function in the cities of communist China, although currently overwhelmed by migrations from the countryside. These neighborhood committees have intrigued Western visitors to that country for decades. Repressive recording of women's menstrual cycles to keep families down to one child each exists side-by-side with helpful social services.

But what neither Mao nor anyone else in any country had was the organizational know-how to create a manageable administration for a country that contained one-quarter of the world's population. Because he had complete faith in his own vision, he never consulted with the European-trained experts available to him who might, over time, have helped create a viable transition to communist modernity. His experiments—overnight collectivization of agriculture, backyard furnaces, the Great Leap Forward—were more foolhardy than utopian. When the burgeoning of unworkable bureaucracies produced chaos, he turned to the masses, unleashing the Cultural Revolution and throwing its continuity into local hands. The dark side of clan structures and village life immediately appeared. Terrible things happened, including blood purges. Nevertheless, travelers in China have heard not a few stories from intellectuals who were sent to pig farms for "reeducation"—moving stories about a new kind of learning experience for city-bred intellectuals, a "hands-on" education about the life situation of the poor peasants of their country. The full story of both the Great Leap Forward and the Cultural Revolution is still coming out, piece by piece.

That these violent efforts at localism took place in the context of an authoritarian state that reserved for itself the power of life and death over entire populations makes the experiments both puzzling and interesting. The twin Chinese traditions of active peasant societies at the local level and the mandarin system—one of the world's oldest imperial bureaucracies—at the national level probably have something to do with the fact that large-scale experimentation was possible at all in the world's largest country. The groups left out of that equation—students, the tribal minorities, and occupied Tibet—have suffered severely from the experiments and may become a serious force to be reckoned with in future developments.

However, remnants of the spirit of utopian adventure can still be found in one major element of Chinese society: the huge Chinese Women's Federation. Its organizational beginnings date back to the 1870s. It is a not insubstantial force, since it theoretically reaches into every household in China. The Federation, to a degree, makes up for the deficiencies of the educational system, which falls far short of educating the population to the skill level needed. Until recently, at least, it continued to organize local training and employment opportunities for urban youth who fell between the cracks in the larger system. However, levels of bureaucratic inertia and corruption in that larger system, the refusal to listen to courageous public statements of dissenting youth and intellectuals, and the resistance to giving the Women's Federation an independent hand in the administration of the 1995 International Women's Conference in Beijing may seriously limit those sources of future utopian thought and practice still available in Chinese society.

### Other Two-Thirds World Utopian Experiments

*Tanzania, Mexico, and Iran.* Nyerere's efforts to build a socialist utopia in Tanzania based on the concept of a village economy (the *ujamaa*) ran into serious problems, even though the principle of building on traditional local structures was in theory to be followed. The *maji-maji*, activists in the independence movement, were involved. Nevertheless, many local structures suffered from bureaucratic decision making at the national level, and there was widespread village demoralization. Here is a case of what appears on paper as a very attractive utopian design running into serious economic and political difficulties.

The *ejido* system of communal land ownership, which was revived by the Mexican government in the 1915 land reform, represented a utopian experiment that could not survive the competition of traditional landholding interests and urban-based political power. The *ejido* system is present as a tradition in all Spanish cultures and has Indian equivalents as well. A high degree of knowledge and skill remains in the peasantry, in spite of severe disadvantages, and frequent efforts to revive the *ejido* system are undertaken by rural groups in different Latin American countries; the uprising in Chiapas, Mexico, in the 1990s is a most recent example. In *Relentless Persistence* McManus and Schlabach give a stirring account of such movements and actually hold out hope that there may be major breakthroughs in land reform as a result of widespread grassroots action as the twenty-first century begins.[31]

On still another continent, the Iranian revolution is not usually thought of as an experiment in utopia, but in fact, by Shiite Moslem standards, it was precisely that. The Iranian revolution was an experiment in the construction of an orthodox Islamic republic with the obliteration of church-state distinctions, under twentieth-century world-economy conditions. There is little doubt that the rich associative structures of local mosque communities with local imams facilitated the revolution. It has hardly seemed like a utopia to Western-oriented Iranians, whose lifestyles have had to go underground. Under continuing conditions of economic decline, the sector of the Iranian population that willingly adopted certain traditional practices of devotion — the seclusion of women and the strict ascetic and stewardship practices that *Shia* orthodoxy requires — is becoming less enthusiastic about the new order. The rewards of establishing a vigorous non-Western identity are at odds with the many sacrifices this path entails. The creative rethinking of history and conflicting traditions going on locally and internationally among Muslims in many countries may lead Iran into new developments in coming years.

Islamist movements to institute orthodox Islamic republics exist in a number of Arab countries at present, with varying degrees of political strength. Only a few are associated with violence and terrorism. Over time, less publicized Islamic movements, whose spirituality calls for the strengthening of the civil society and a partnering relationship between women and men, may

46 Historical Overview

well gain more visibility and support. The result may be a new cultural and
spiritual flowering in the Arab world.[32]

*The Indian Refusal of a Utopian Experiment.* If utopian experiments are instructive, so are refusals to experiment. At the time of India's independence
from Britain, there were several revolutionary nationalist movements that had
helped gain that independence and offered local community development
models for India to utilize. Gandhi and Sri Aurobindo were the two revolutionary leaders who had the most highly evolved community development
models, based on years of experiment and practice. Both offered educational
systems that provided for the holistic development of the individual in terms
of intellectual, spiritual, and craft skills; both offered small-industry community development that could serve India's economic needs without denying
the advantages of modern technology. Furthermore, both offered experience
with the traditional *panchayat*, or village councils, and their participatory
mechanisms. The first national parliament was dominated by Congress party
members who had been associated with the Gandhian movement. The first
prime minister was Nehru, a Gandhi associate although *not* a disciple. Yet the
policy India chose was one of intensive urban-based industrialization. The
government rejected a unique indigenous development model in favor of following the Western path. It simply ignored the *panchayat* system and Hindu
traditional methods of education.[33] Education continued to be based on the
British model.

It would be interesting to compare the achievements of China and India in
terms of the relative success of their very different choices. China chose the
utopian experiment; India chose a highly pragmatic westernization. Yet today
India is increasingly seeking to assert its identity as a nation with its own
tradition and its own ways of conducting foreign policy. Its decision not to engage in a utopian experiment, even when all the conditions for that experiment were apparently in place, warrants further study.

*Israel: A Hard Case.* Martin Buber has called the Israeli kibbutzim one of
the world's few successful utopian experiments.[34] The kibbutzim are a
unique invention of the modern era, and the kibbutz way of life, with complete communal ownership of the means of production and communal
arrangements for childrearing and family maintenance, has produced a generation of Israelis who think of themselves as the "new human beings" and
can function productively in the new society—that usually elusive goal of all
utopias. Research indicates that the kibbutz-reared youth (a minority) are

more sensitive to group processes and to the needs of those around them and participate more effectively in group decision making than young people who were not brought up on kibbutzim (the majority). They are also, however, reported to make better soldiers.

The experiment at the state level of creating an ingathering of people of common religious/ethnic heritage who have spread across the globe over the centuries and of constructing a socialist society in which these diverse people can live and labor productively together is an unusual achievement. However, the idealism evoked by the concept of Zion, or the Peaceable Kingdom, was not equally applied to an internal minority—the Arab population that has long been native to the land. The much-heralded peace process that is to give independence to occupied Palestine has, as of the late 1990s, slowed to a crawl. A high level of violence continues in the occupied territories. External relations between Israel and Arab states continue to be fraught with tension.

Often utopias can successfully isolate themselves from the larger world in the short term, but they can rarely do so in the long run. The degree of attention given to the development of crosscutting associational structures inclusive of both Arabs and Jews, both within Israel and within an independent Palestine, and with surrounding Arab nations, will determine the longer-run success or failure of the Israeli utopian experiment.[35]

*Utopia in Western Europe and North America.* Although the United States cannot be technically regarded as a utopian experiment, for many, historically, the United States *was* utopia. As indicated earlier, it was seen as the new Garden of Eden. It, along with Canada, became the home of many utopian experiments that could not take place in Europe because there was not enough room, either physically or socially. If the United States is the home of many utopian experiments at the microlevel, it could be said that Europe has been a prime exporter of such experiments. The United States has always rejected socialism, but its values of individualism have enabled it to give space to socialist, anarchist, and religious experiments of every kind.

Europe has gone much further with socialism, but few states would conceive of themselves as utopian experiments. Sweden is an exception. The Swedish experiment is comprehensive in terms of providing a welfare state without parallel in Europe. At the state level, it has been possible because Sweden has the richest associative structures of any country on the continent. Early in the nineteenth century, it had a countryside adult education program at the village level and village debating forums, which would be the envy of any Western country today. It was those structures that enabled Sweden to develop the first effective, countrywide participatory population control policy in the world. These local structures continue alive and well as Sweden moves into the twenty-first century.

### Microlevel Utopian Experiments

Microlevel utopian experiments are much easier to initiate than macrolevel ones, since the responsibility of the experimenters is only to a limited group of people operating on a small scale. Microlevel utopias are thought of as a Western phenomenon, but, in fact, there are many village-level utopian experiments in the Two-Thirds World. They have a special characteristic: reaching into the past to find traditional local structures that can be redeveloped to make a better life at the village level under contemporary conditions. The *sarvodaya* movement, which builds on the *panchayat* tradition in India, and incorporates Gandhi's ideas of local development using local resources but is also open to appropriate uses of high technology for local betterment, has now become an international movement with linkages to comparable groups on other continents.[36] In Sri Lanka, the counterpart institution is the *shramadana*, village work sharing with a strong spiritual component.[37] The sarvodaya movement has now become a transnational nongovernmental association (NGO), as has the World Council of Indigenous Peoples, with international congresses held in Geneva. These transnational bodies provide support for local experiments and legitimation for non-Western approaches to community development.

Another source of legitimation operating at the international level was the United Nations World Decade for Cultural Development (1988–1997), which encouraged and funded efforts by governments and NGOs to identify indigenous and ethnic communities whose traditional knowledge base relating to their environment and whose traditional practices of cultural transmission, education, and community decision making are at risk through the political and economic pressures of modernization. Long discouraged, these practices, when brought back to life, frequently have the character of a utopian experiment for the people involved.[38] Many of these practices involve women's associations; indeed, women have particularly benefited from reaching into the past to find the utopias of the future.[39]

***Microlevel Utopias in the One-Third World.*** When Charles Nordhoff did his survey *Communistic Societies in the United States* in the early 1870s, he found there were eight societies for the promotion of communes and seventy-two communes that had developed between 1794 and 1852.[40] The oldest had been in existence eighty years, the youngest twenty-two years. (Some are still in existence a century later.) Religiously based (or with a doctrine held with religious intensity), they had differing patterns of communal ownership but a similar work ethic, high craft-skill level, and good basic schooling for their children. The standard of living was generally higher than that in the immediate neighborhood. Communes were peaceable, with a strong standard of morality, and generous in sharing with the local and transient poor. Communal lives were so well ordered that Nordhoff found the communes unutterably dull; the culture seemed very limited, and higher education was not valued. But they were all good farmers! Nordhoff commented that the commune members seemed to enjoy life and find pleasure in amusements that looked tame to him.

What do such communes achieve? A demonstration of a more serene and humane way of life, with a higher level of altruism than in the outside world. These utopias do not set out to change the world; they simply wish to show that it is possible to live differently in it.

Economic forces should not be ignored in considering the founding of this type of commune. Members are often working-class people who frequently have had a hard time making it alone. More new communes are founded during times of economic depression than at any other time. Many single women who could not find a place in the economy joined these communities in such periods and prospered. These religious communities of the 1800s were primarily agrarian.

During this same period, also in the United States, there were forty-seven socialist experiments, studied by John Humphrey Noyes.[41] They all failed in rather short order. Unlike the religious communities, the socialist utopians tried to develop a model that could change the world. Their founders were, as Noyes says, "high-minded, highly cultivated men and women, with sufficient means, one would think, to achieve success." Unlike their religious counterparts, the socialist utopians were rarely skilled farmers. Equally unlike their counterparts, they were highly individualistic. Brook Farm, New Harmony, Nashoba, and New Lanark were among the secular short-lived communities.

The concept of building a working model that can spread to the larger society continues to be sufficiently compelling to attract new utopian efforts in each generation, based on the style of that generation and the needs of the times. Many utopian ventures started in the depression of the 1930s, reminding us again of the relevance of economic forces. Among the most interesting and least known of these ventures are the twenty-two cooperative farms

organized by the Farm Security Administration of the United States government that operated between 1937 and 1942, the year when Congress closed
down the project.[42] These cooperative corporation farms were established for
poor farmers regardless of race. In those where the members psychologically
took ownership of the project (some never did), a much higher level of living
developed; members took reeducation seriously, and there was much mutual
aid and substantial economic betterment. When other factors were held constant, these farms were more productive than the average for the state in
which they were located. This uncelebrated depression experiment on the
part of the U.S. government should be explored further. (Similar ventures
were undertaken during the depression by the governments of Wales and
Australia.)

Other depression-generated utopian experiments included the Quaker
community of Penncraft in Pennsylvania for unemployed workers, the Delta
Farm in Mississippi, the Macedonia Cooperative in Georgia, Saline Valley
Farms in Michigan, Celo Community in North Carolina, Koinonia in Georgia, and the Borsodi back-to-the-land movement.[43] Many of these communities have continued to the present—some with highly diversified activities,
such as Celo, with its school, summer camp, pharmaceutical cooperative,
and various craft products. Catholic urban communities serving the poor also
began in the 1930s. Born of economic necessity combined with strong idealism, these communities have continued as a demonstration of viable alternative lifeways within a capitalist society.

The list of such communities was swelled by the wave of new settlements
founded by the generation of World War II conscientious objectors. They
came out of the alternative service camps and prisons determined not to return to the same old world but to translate their visions for the good society
into experimental communities. Some joined the communities already
founded in the depression. Others founded Quaker, Brethren, and Mennonite settlements or joined existing religious communities, such as the Hutterite
Bruderhof (a group belonging to the older German tradition of Anabaptist
communities, who fled Germany under stress of wartime conditions and settled in North and South America).

Although some of the new communities were short-lived, twenty-seven of
the communities founded in the 1930s, 1940s, and 1950s are still listed as
active, functioning groups in the 1995 *Communities Directory*.[44] What this
unusual set of utopian ventures has achieved has been a continuing associational structure, deeply embedded in the peace movement, which has enabled social dissenters as well as wartime conscientious objectors, their wives,

and their children, and now their grandchildren, to continue sustained peacebuilding activities over a lifetime. This is my generation; many of them are in leadership positions as senior citizens in today's peace and justice movements.

In the 1960s and 1970s came a new round of utopian experiments, often lumped together as the "hippie" or "new age" communities. While a number did indeed disintegrate rapidly, because they were resistant to the social disciplines needed to hold a community together, this was also a period of highly practical experiments in rural and urban group living and the beginning of the ecotopian revolution. Two hundred of the communities founded in these two decades are operational today, their activities described in the 1995 *Communities Directory* mentioned earlier. The Farm, a once-controversial 1,500-person community founded by Stephen Gaskin in 1972,[45] has settled down to solid pioneering in soy technology, solar energy, and development projects in Central America. Each of these 200 communities has developed a viable work discipline and a critical mass of altruistic members with some vision of a society for which they are willing to keep working. This vision includes the abolition not only of militarism but of war itself and (frequently) the end of the nation-state system as we now know it. It includes a sense of social justice, a strong environmental ethic, and a discerning attitude toward science and technology. Many communes are rural because it is easier to live simply and cheaply in such a setting, and not just because of a desire to escape the city. Most have active urban-rural networks. The misuse of power is a major issue with communitarians. They find that leadership is important but insist on a highly participatory process with strong checks against authoritarianism.

If the 1960s and 1970s were the beginning of a new wave, a further swelling of that wave occurred during the 1980s. The 137 communities listed in the *Directory* as founded in that decade have a strong ecological and earth-steward-ship orientation, furthering the land-trust movement, and are also strongly peace activist and family- and child-oriented, favoring homeschooling for their children. Many of these 1980s communities have a spiritual base, not a few centered on Eastern spirituality. The Danish cohousing movement, which provides extended-family relationships for families and individuals who build contiguous living quarters with many shared and cooperatively used facilities and has a pattern of mutual aid and joint cultural activities, got a strong start in the United States and Canada in that decade. The same trends continue in the 1990s, with 131 new communities already reported in the first half of the decade.

The *Directory* listings referred to so far are for North America only. An ad-

ditional very incomplete *Directory* list of 70 communities in 21 other countries includes communities in Europe, Latin America, Asia-Pacific, and
Africa. The community themes and activity patterns are very similar to those
for the North American communities of the 1980s and 1990s.

Spiritually motivated social and ecological innovation characterizes most
of these groups. Because of the brevity of community descriptions in the
*Communities Directory*, we cannot know the extent to which these intentional communities are also participating in the relatively new barter systems
that are springing up to partially replace cash economy in communities
across North America. Examples of these new barter systems (based, of
course, on a very old concept) include LETS (Local Economic Trading System), originating in Canada, and the U.S.-based Time Dollar Network and
Hometown Money Programs, such as the Ithaca Dollar in Ithaca, New York.
Interest in alternatives to a market-based capitalist economy is high, and
many movement newsletters are devoted to this subject.[46]

It cannot be denied that intentional experimental living communities directed toward an increase in peace, human gentleness, justice, and Gaia-
awareness, and toward spiritual attunement to the evolving human condition
are growing in number and sophistication in ways of working for their high
goals. However, we can hardly say that they are major social forces in contemporary society. Relatively few of them do overtly political work, although
the Sojourner Community in Washington, D.C., is an outstanding example
of spiritually based political action.[47] There would seem to be a huge gulf between these very small-scale efforts at human betterment and the state-level
utopian designs discussed earlier. Are they, therefore, insignificant? Or are
they laboratories functioning as laboratories do, providing a more or less controlled environment for discovery? I would argue the latter. However, the
"controlled environment" emphasis on boundaries, the view of utopia as an
island, are misleading concepts because they direct attention away from the
fact that these utopias are connected with the larger society through all kinds
of networks. They are a vital part of the sociosphere. Let us explore these linkage systems.

### Connecting the Micro and the Macro: The Future of Utopianism

One context in which the micro-macro linkage of utopian experiments
should be seen is the rapid development of transnational nongovernmental
organizations in the twentieth century. The more than twenty thousand
transnational nongovernmental networks that bring diverse people together

through common interests and concerns are today a major new set of actors in the international system. Compared to nation-states, they have few resources and little power. Yet most of the world's intellectual resources and many of its craft and social skill resources are concentrated in these organizations, particularly in the scientific, cultural, and human welfare associations. Research on major world problems, such as the threat of nuclear war, environmental deterioration, malnutrition, disease, and climatic changes, is done by scientific NGOs with support from the United Nations and largely nongovernmental sources. Governments would be helpless without the policy recommendations NGOs are able to make, based on their research and experience, although the advisory process is nearly invisible to the general public. Most major policy initiatives at the international level of the UN and governments in recent decades have been based on the work of transnational nongovernmental organizations. Many of the most innovative community development projects at the local level are also carried out by NGOs linked to local grassroots organizations (GROs).

Because NGO networks are information networks as well as face-to-face people networks, local utopian ventures today have a very strong probability of being recorded and transmitted over a variety of channels and eventually being incorporated into policy recommendations. NGOs represent a new level of associative richness potentially connecting local communities everywhere in ways of which we are only now becoming aware.

One NGO in particular, the World Federalist Association, represents a unique micro-macro linkage because its network of local groups around the world seeks the utopia of emerging global governance. The concept of world peace through world law, most brilliantly developed by Grenville Park and Louis Sohn in a book of that title,[48] is diligently pursued by world federalists and by a number of other NGOs oriented toward peace and justice. The World Order Models Project may be thought of as its global think-tank, having generated a number of studies of possible models for a more integrated, more peaceful international system. Many of these studies are described by Richard Falk and colleagues in *The Constitutional Foundations of World Peace*.[49]

The old order was shaped by less than 50 states, mostly of the West. The emerging order is being shaped by 188 states, representing much more of the diversity of human experience on the planet. Accordingly, the range of social experimentation has been extended enormously. More of the new states have tried state-level utopias, blending tradition and modernity in their utopian experimentation to soften the abruptness of the changes experienced in this century. When they fail to do this adequately, and when they fail to make room in the political process for ethnic, tribal, clan, and religious diversity, major violence erupts. Too many such failures have led to bloody civil war in the past decades.

Yet, at their best, many countries of the Two-Thirds World are struggling to forge a creative utopian response to the challenge of the One-Third World out of the very pain and suffering to which colonialism has subjected them. They are dealing with the trauma of finding a machine they don't understand in a garden they no longer own. Their blends of tradition and modernity deal precisely with those persistent dilemmas discussed earlier: mechanistic versus organic change, centralism versus decentralism, violence versus nonviolence, the redesigned robot versus the human being-in-process.

The socialist countries play a special role in utopian experiments in the old "three worlds" terminology, since they are usually given the separate designation of the Second World. They belong to the West, but their social clocks have run at a different speed. Because they faced the opportunities and traumas of modernization later than the rest of the West and have not yet experienced the traumas of "overdevelopment," their images of the future are more like those of the Two-Thirds World than of the One-Third World. In a 1967 study based at the International Peace Research Institute, Oslo, it was found that there was noticeably more optimism and a sense that the future was more open-ended in the non-West than in the West.[50] This was before the more recent world food crises, before general realization of the failure of the World Bank–generated development models imposed on the non-West, before the current high levels of ethnic conflict, and before the breakup of the Soviet Union. It was also before the significance of the nuclear threat and the extent of world militarization was recognized. Most of the optimism recorded in the 1960s is gone now.

Does this mean that it is time to declare all utopias of East and West a failure? The question of success or failure of a utopian experiment may not be relevant to our deeper concerns. If, as Kenneth Boulding says, our most significant learnings are from failure, not success, then each utopian experiment is successful to the extent that learning from its failures takes place. Many of the macro-utopias—the former Soviet Union and its successors, the Commonwealth of Independent States, China, Israel, Cuba—might be considered to be in active learning phases right now. A significant number of the micro-utopias have lasted long enough for much learning to have taken place. Even the very short-lived utopias represent thoughtfully chosen responses to upheaval and change and, presumably, have enabled the participants to move on to other more sustainable responses.

The message about the importance of associative richness as the basis for utopia building on anything beyond the local scale has gotten across to the extent that "networking" is a word almost as common as Coca-Cola. The message about the importance of a focus on learning has not had equal promotion. There is still a tendency to believe that designing the structures will produce the desired behaviors. People may denounce Skinnerian philosophy, but they prefer manipulation by design to venturing out on the uncharted seas of human learning. How does anyone ever learn a really new thing? Since utopias are by definition "new," "not-yet," "other," human beings will be able to function in them in ways that do not throw us back to the old order *only if* we pay enough attention to learning. Wishful thinking about the desired transformation of consciousness as an inevitable historical process distracts us from studying the difficult disciplines that will make transformation possible.

From the perspective of peace culture, both the micro-utopian communities and the macro-utopian experiments represent efforts to develop ways for humans to live together nonviolently, creatively, fulfilling all the potentials that our birthright capacity for visioning the other and better tells us can be realized in the human tomorrow. Historically, peace cultures in every society hand down utopian visions from generation to generation, even if only in hidden spaces. Practically, peace culture values and practices motivate us to keep trying, to keep learning, to keep developing new skills that will help us deal with greed generated violence, impatience, and the desire for power over others. Most urgently, peace culture visioning must keep before the human race the possibility of open flexible structures that can handle large-scale interactions without compulsion and oppression. And peace culture visions must keep reminding us that social compassion begins in the small, the local, but it never ends there—it only opens new paths to the greater whole.

# 3

# Peace Movements and Their
# Organizational Forms
## The Seedbed of Peace Cultures

WE HAVE EXPLORED in chapter 2 how utopian visioning and utopian experiments persist through time as an expression of the human longing for peaceable lifeways. Another expression of that longing is found in peace movements—popular groundswells of opposition to war and violence— accompanied by efforts to demonstrate alternative ways to deal with conflict and injustice. Over time, peace movements develop more specific agendas and take on organizational forms that help them pursue these agendas. In this chapter we will survey the movements and follow their evolution into the organizational forms of twentieth-century peace action, closing with an examination of the linkage system between organizations as a significant component of a transnational peace culture.

Throughout history, peace cultures rooted in communities of faith have had a special role in movements to oppose war and to bring about peace and justice. With the increasing secularization of the One-Third World, there has been an accompanying secularization of Western peace movements as well, but the faith-based sectors of peace movements nevertheless remain strong even today. We are here looking at peace movements as peace*building* movements. Peacebuilding is taken to mean any activity directed towards the replacement of armed violence and physical coercion in situations of conflict by nonviolent justice-seeking behavior. Peacebuilding is seen as creating new kinds of social space in society for new behaviors and new social relations, broadly conceived. Peace movement strategies and tactics have varied widely through history—from demonstrations, marches, strikes, fasts, and mass emi-

---

An earlier version of this paper was written for the U.S. Institute of Peace.

gration; through strategic noncooperation; to education, third-party intervention in conflicts by mediation, conflict resolution, and reconciliation; to the already familiar creation of utopian communities. As we will see, there is some significant overlap between peace movement strategies and experimental utopian ventures.

## Early Faith-Based Peace Movements

We have already noted that the basis for movements to bring an end to war and violence and to find alternative ways to deal with conflicts is present in all religions. The themes of reverence for all living things and compassion for fellow human beings are found in the teachings of indigenous peoples as well as in Hinduism, Jainism, Buddhism, Taoism, Judaism, Christianity, and Islam. They all urge restraint, truthfulness, rectitude, forbearance, temperance, justice, nonviolence—and love.

However, we have also noted that most of these religions also have a concept of holy war divinely ordained on behalf of a righteous cause. Warriors fought for Jehovah, for Allah, for God, for Christ, for Lord Krishna. Christians called such wars crusades; Muslims call them jihad. The holy war was to be conducted according to a carefully constructed code. The means of sustaining and reproducing life were to be spared: trees, crops, women, and children. And always some individuals were called to absolute nonviolence, even in the midst of battle.

Reminders that the nonviolent way is the higher way are frequent in sacred scripts. It is therefore not surprising to find peace teachings being followed under even the most violent of circumstances over the centuries. Pacifism is not a modern innovation. In the history of the Jews, as one example among many, the national crisis that culminated in the destruction of the Second Temple gave rise not only to a war party but to a peace party as well. Rabbi Johanen ben Zakka openly countenanced nonresistance to the Romans. His intercession won the concessions that made vigorous cultural survival possible. The saintly Hillel and the peaceful Essenes belonged to that very early Jewish tradition of nonviolence.[1]

Muslims can recall the example of the Prophet Muhammed before the Hegira, when he struggled nonviolently against enemies of the faith. It is clear in the Koran and in the Hadith that the inner struggle to be in submission to God is the greater jihad, of much higher importance than the lesser jihad of external war. Also, the Prophet gives many injunctions to settle quarrels without violence. The Sufi sect of Islam has taught the practice of the love of God and fellow beings for centuries, including a very specific discipline of nonviolence.[2]

The history of nonviolence in Christianity goes back to the first centuries of the Common Era, with Christians refusing military service. That war is listed as a forbidden occupation by Hippolytes (160–236 C.E.) reflects the pacifism of the early church up to the conversion of the Emperor Constantine in the fourth century. From the time of Constantine on, the Roman imperial diocese became the basis of church organization and set the pattern for the use of force. But as the new Christian aristocracy embraced war, ordinary Christians fled by the thousands to monastic settlements in Egypt, Palestine, Syria, and Mesopotamia in nonviolent protest against the oppressive practices of imperial society. By the fifth century there were tens of thousands of Christians living in monastic settlements of such a scale that they represented collectively one of the largest economic organizations of the ancient world.[3]

The peace traditions of the Christian church, nurtured by monasticism, continued to generate inventive modifications of imperial warfare. Ninth- and tenth-century "Peace of God" declarations that at certain times of the week and year there would be no fighting were grassroots declarations by peasants and town dwellers. The Truce of God was proclaimed by bishops, with similar rules about no-fighting days, to protect the poor in their domains. Later these rules were co-opted and subverted by feudal lords who used them to recruit for the Crusades from 1100 to 1400.

There were large-scale peace movements during the Crusades—movements of voluntary poverty and refusal of arms. The Humiliati, the Poor Lombards, and the Poor Catholics all refused to take feudal oaths, bear arms, or obey church authorities. Lay religious orders for both men and women, such as the one founded by St. Francis, with 1,500 congregations across Europe toward the end of the Crusade era, followed a rule of voluntary poverty, compassionate service, and nonviolence. Penitential processions of thousands moved from city to city, actually conducting peace negotiations between the poor and the aristocracy wherever they went. A popular peace movement of the mid-1200s gathered 400,000 people in Verona on August 28, 1233, for what was called the Great Alleluia, a public demonstration to end a prolonged and bloody civil war.[4]

These movements offered alternatives to the Crusades in the form of peaceful teaching missions. Unarmed mendicants traveled to the Holy Land, North Africa, Persia, China, Armenia, India, and northern Europe, bearing the gospel of peace and the practice of nonviolent conflict resolution. Traveling troubadours recited peace poetry. Many unarmed pilgrims accompanied the first Crusade, but later the crusaders kept them out. From the civil ferment created by the large-scale peace movements of peasants and town dwellers in the crusader centuries came the Reformation and the Anabaptists.

## From the Crusades to World War I

The Anabaptist movement represented a basic defiance of all outward authority and a commitment to live as Jesus lived. Its adherents formed share-the-wealth communities on the model of the early Christians. By refusing infant baptism, Anabaptists effectively removed themselves from parish records and therefore could not be conscripted. Artisans and traders, they supported the peasant revolts of the 1500s against social and economic injustices and came to be considered very dangerous by the authorities. Although violence was not infrequent in the peasant revolts, the Anabaptists tended from the beginning to be nonviolent. Embodying a combination of medieval mysticism with Protestant reform, they represented a third way in a confused age: a strong focus on practice and truth seeking, a rejection of worldliness and the politics of the age, and a commitment to dealing with social injustice without the use of force. Living in scattered communities in the Swiss Alps, in towns along the Rhine, in Holland, in Moravia, and later in the English Midlands, persecuted and hunted, they nevertheless managed to generate a powerful new social-spiritual ethic, as described in the previous chapter.

When a new wave of armed Christian colonizers was mobilized after the Crusades to invade the Americas, it was followed by other, very different colonizers, who crossed the Atlantic with very different intentions: Catholic religious orders and the new Anabaptist communities. The descendants of Catholic religious orders that had already opposed the Crusades followed the armed colonizers to the New World, opposing wars of conquest, slavery, and oppression. The Mennonites, Brethren, and Quakers arrived somewhat later, intending to create the communities of peace and justice in the New World that they were prevented from founding in Europe. They, too, opposed conquest, slavery, and oppression. The social inventiveness and reproductive staying power of the peace churches of post-Crusade Europe, beginning in the Swiss Alps and subsequently spreading (albeit thinly) across the Americas, are amazing, as is the hardiness of the band of Catholic peace witnesses that have traveled an even longer journey through time.

The rules of governance for William Penn's Quaker colony of Pennsylvania led to seventy years of peace with neighboring Native American peoples, a strong contrast to the recurring warfare with the Native Americans in the other colonies. These rules also made a significant contribution to the United States Constitution.[5] The practice of friendly mutual aid with the Native Americans and an ongoing work of mediation between them and continually arriving land-grabbers could not, however, hold back the onslaught of large numbers of armed Europeans. Outnumbered in their own legislature, Quakers and Mennonites gave up the holding of public office as the demand for raising armies carried the day. (Brethren stayed outside of government from the beginning.) But the dissenters continued to press for peaceful settlement of disputes and were, in fact, involved in a reconciliation effort with members of Lord North's government at the time of the American Declaration of Independence—unsuccessfully, as it turned out.

What is important is that the Anabaptist tradition of nonviolent conflict resolution did not disappear but played a continuing role in the developing civil society of America. In the decades before the Civil War, Anabaptists were deeply involved in peaceful abolition efforts. In 1827 there were 140 abolition societies in the South, not a few of them with Quaker leadership, and by 1850 only six percent of southern whites owned slaves.[6] Unfortunately, Quaker and like-minded efforts were inadequate to the task of organizing the Middle Way that could have brought about abolition without war.

From the time of the French and American Revolutions, however, more forces were at work in the West than Anabaptism. These revolutions ushered in the concept of the state as a moral community based on a social contract, creating a new political environment for the development of peace as a citizen's issue.[7] The uneasy relationship between the peace churches and state authority made way for a widely based citizens' movement in Europe during the Napoleonic wars that emphasized the connection between war, militarism, and poverty. The Treaty of Vienna in 1815, ending a quarter century of wars and revolutions, marked the start of a new era of increasingly secular transnational peace movements, with activities throughout Europe, including Russia, the Balkans, Spain, and Portugal.

The first all-women's peace societies began appearing at this time, an offshoot of the general women's movements of the century. Priscilla Peckover of England began a transnational network of women's peace groups that has had some continuity up to the present. The first International Peace Congresses in the 1840s were held in London and Brussels, but the Crimean War and other revolutions slowed down organizational momentum until the late 1860s. Although women were full participants in these congresses, they chose to maintain separate women's peace organizations as well.[8] A new generation of peace activists focused serious attention on economic issues generated by militarism, including the effects of arms races, and began exploring the kinds of institutional mechanisms that would be required to put an end to war. The charismatic leader of the next generation was Bertha Suttner, author of the best-seller *Die Waffen Nieder* (Down with Arms!), who persuaded Alfred Nobel to endow the Nobel Peace Prize. The rise of international socialism during these years put peace in the context of social justice and class struggle.

The establishment of the Interparliamentary Union in 1889 and the International Peace Bureau in 1892 provided a transnational infrastructure, however rudimentary, for the serious work of peace organizations in Europe as they developed concepts of (1) a United States of Europe, (2) abolition of arms, (3) rights and freedoms for the citizenry, and (4) the establishment of a permanent league of states to keep the peace. National peace societies multiplied, and their strong political focus on arbitration is considered to have contributed to the successful binding arbitration between the United States and England after the Civil War (the Alabama Decision). The fact that there were several thousand peace activists in over one hundred national peace organizations by 1889 certainly contributed to the political climate in which the first Hague Peace Conference was held and to the developments that followed it.

The 1894 Universal Peace Congress developed a model arbitration treaty, the Code of International Arbitration, and although the efforts of national peace societies to get the major powers to adopt it were not successful, their activities did help pave the way for the Hague Conference. Peace movement energies and public interest ran so high that states could not afford to ignore the czar's invitation to the Hague, disinclined though political leaders were to take Czar Nicholas II seriously. Cooper writes, "A small army of indefatigable workers—men and women—traveled lecture circuits, published and catalogued libraries of books and brochures, raised money from governments and private donors, confronted politicians, challenged military budgets, criticized history curricula, combated chauvinist and establishment media, lobbied diplomats, questioned candidates for office, telegraphed Congress resolutions to foreign ministries, and held congresses nearly every year from 1889 to 1914 to thrash out common positions."[9]

Between 1890 and 1900 there were 63 successful international arbitrations. Lobbying national governments to accept arbitration, mediation, and third-party good offices in interstate conflicts was a major peace movement activity. The peaceful separation of Norway from Sweden in 1905 in spite of threats of war on both sides was due to the activity of peace movements in both countries.

Arbitration was not the only focus of activity, however. The Freemasonry movement that spread across Europe in the latter part of the century, for example, was strongly antiwar as well as anticlerical. Fourteen thousand Masons marched in the streets of Paris to try to stop the civil war at the time of the Paris Commune. Masons were also involved in the Esperanto movement, which promoted a peace strategy of creating a common artificial language.

The shift from a concept of peace as the absence of war to a concept of peace as a positive, organic process of interstate relations was completed in these years, and women were the largest constituency for the new thinking.[10] An indication of the volume of peace-related nongovernmental activity in these years is that fifteen bibliographies were published of books on economic and political aspects of peace and general peace education literature, in French, English, German, Italian, and Dutch, between 1888 and 1914.[11] The 1910 Universal Peace Congress addressed the basic issues of the need for international law, the right to self-determination, and a critique of colonialism. The 1913 Congress, marking the opening of the Peace Palace in The Hague, proposed an international police force and tried, unfortunately too late, to shift international attention to arms control after having soft-pedaled that emphasis in favor of arbitration for some years. Warnings to governments by the European peace movement of a war to come went unheeded.

Because of World War I, peace movements on both sides of the Atlantic collapsed for a time. However, the nonviolence movement led by Gandhi in India became stronger, serving as a source of inspiration for the West in the postwar period when old and new peace movements came to life again. Gandhi, drawing on the concepts of satyagraha, truth-force, and ahimsa, action based on the refusal to do harm, led a nonviolent independence struggle in India from 1917 to his death in 1948. One unique aspect of his work was a carefully developed sequential methodology of nonviolent action: (1) making demands; (2) educating the opponent and the public about those demands; (3) undertaking deliberate acts of public protest, such as fasting, marching, or civil disobedience, on behalf of those demands; (4) continuing the process of self-examination and search for possible cooperation with the adversary on honorable terms; (5) surrendering no essentials in negotiation; and (6) agreeing fully on fundamentals before accepting a settlement.[12] The creation of ashrams, spiritual communes in which people prepared for the work of satyagraha, helped provide the institutional base for the movement.

The spread of the movement (it is estimated that there were hundreds of groups carrying out satyagraha in India at the time of Gandhi's death) depended in part on its rootedness in Hindu religious traditions and the capacity for self-discipline based on traditional asceticism. It also depended on

Gandhi's skill as a strategist and his personal magnetism, which attracted some of the best minds and most powerful personalities in India to work side by side with him as he worked with the masses.[13] Not least, it depended on Gandhi's opening of the movement to Indian women, who participated by the thousands. Women recruits like Madame Pandit and Sushila Nayar not only helped empower their Indian sisters but also gave charismatic leadership to the growing European women's movement.[14] The enthusiasm of Western peace movements for nonviolent strategies based on such a different culture—one of the unexpecteds of history—is a tribute both to Gandhi and his associates as teachers and to the countries of the West as learners. The Gandhian movement also represented a reintroduction of the spiritual element into more secular Western developments.

Other unique contributions from the Indian subcontinent also relate to satyagraha: the *gramdan* nonviolent land redistribution movement led by Vinova Bhave, which at its height involved nearly 70,000 villages, and the associated Shanti Sena peace brigades, trained at Gandhi centers in disciplined nonviolence for the gramdan movement and for other conflict-resolving projects. (Shanti Sena training, imported to the United States, became an important tool for the Civil Rights movement there some decades later.) A remarkable Islamic nonviolence movement, led by Ghaffar Khan among the Pathan warriors in the mountainous frontier country of India in 1929, resulted in major political, social, and economic reforms in the mountain regions, achieved by the Khudai Khidmatgar, former warriors organized into a peace army pledged to work nonviolently for independence and the well-being of all God's creatures.[15]

## Two World Wars: Discontinuities and New Beginnings for Peace Movements

Peace movements do not do well in wartime. During World War I there was overall a great decline in peace movement activity, but with some notable exceptions. One was a group of Christian pacifists from twelve countries that met in 1914 to declare "We are one in Christ and can never be at war." Various national branches of this group formed during the war, and in 1919 they came together to establish what became the interfaith International Fellowship of Reconciliation (IFOR). Their commitment was to establish a world order based on a culture of nonviolence, and their members were spread across Europe, the Americas, Japan, China, New Zealand, Australia, and Africa. Another wartime exception was a group of women meeting in The

Hague in 1915 to bring an end to war while their husbands were fighting in opposing armies. They persisted throughout the war and in 1919 became the Women's International League for Peace and Freedom (WILPF), a band of feisty social innovators—scholars, activists, and homemakers—working away on the design of a viable postwar organization of states. The American Jane Addams contributed a lifetime of intellectual, political, and spiritual leadership to this outstanding group of women.[16] Other networks had been functioning quietly during the war, including the International Anti-Militarist Association, formed in 1904 in the Netherlands to work against war and all forms of social and economic exploitation. Some members of that group reorganized to become the War Resisters International (WRI) in 1922. Membership rapidly expanded to twenty-four countries by 1933, with a concentration on conscientious objection to military service.

Another category of groups that continued peace work, particularly in support of wartime conscientious objectors, had a new burst of activity after the war: the historic peace churches. Mennonites, Quakers, and Brethren all formed service committees in 1919, first to do urgent humanitarian relief and then to develop peace education and peace-building projects that looked to removing the causes of war and rebuilding relationships between former enemy states.

The peace movements, in short, had not died during the war after all, and a new round of activity was launched in the 1920s. The International Peace Bureau resumed activity and became very involved in the League of Nations' 1932 World Disarmament Conference. Germany's withdrawal from the League, however, and the rise of fascism there and elsewhere made disarmament work heavy going. As the League declined in effectiveness, a coordinating council of about fifty major international nongovernmental organizations took more leadership and focused on the need for peace education and an end to glorification of war in textbooks, even planning an international university. The International School, a secondary school to educate the children of diplomats for a more peaceful world, was founded in Geneva. In the United States a massive Emergency Peace Campaign was mounted by a coalition of peace leaders as European horizons darkened. However, events of 1939 brought coordinating council and peace campaign efforts to an end, leading to the near-dissolution of the International Peace Bureau and many constituent organizations.

World War II was more devastating to secular peace movements than World War I had been. Most of the graduates of the International School were killed in the war, as were many peace movement leaders. It was a battered band that met in 1946 to form the International Liaison Committee of Organizations for Peace with the twenty or so surviving peace organizations, to continue the work of the temporarily defunct International Peace Bureau (which did not come back to life until 1964). They gave their best energies to the support of the newly formed United Nations, which—unlike its failed predecessor, the League of Nations—was supposed to "save succeeding generations from the scourge of war."

The Cold War set in all too soon, taking a serious toll on the efforts of the independent peace organizations. Major energy in Eastern Europe went into the 1949 establishment of the World Peace Council—a body that, to the distress of the independent peace movement, refused to criticize the activities of the Soviet Union and the Warsaw Pact countries. Accordingly, during the 1950s and the 1960s, part of the energy of the independent peace movements had to go into the problem of how to deal with the nonindependent peace movement, while at the same time addressing the new problems of nuclear weapons. The peace churches, which had been able to operate camps and special service projects for conscientious objectors and other pacifists during World War II, were less affected. Because they had greater freedom of movement after the war—in part due to their history of humanitarian service projects in Eastern Europe during and after both world wars—they were able to continue a dialogue across Cold War boundaries.

The sobering context of the Cold War did not, however, hinder fresh waves of peace movement activities. SANE was formed in the United States in 1957 and the British Campaign for Nuclear Disarmament in 1958. For the next several years, thousands participated in the Easter Marches from London to the Aldermaston Atomic Weapons Research Establishment, with similar marches and campaigns in Canada, Switzerland, and Scandinavia, and fewer in France. Inevitably, splits occurred between peace groups. Some were between pacifists and political radicals, some were between longtime peace organizations (like those of the historic peace churches, the Fellowship of Reconciliation, the Women's International League of Peace and Freedom, and War Resisters International) and the more specifically one-issue antinuclear movements that were more concerned with political effectiveness than with a way of life.

The strategies of these movements were varied, ingenious, and manifold.[17] There were peace walks—walks to specific weapons establishments all over Europe, coast-to-coast walks in the United States, the San Francisco to

Moscow Peace Walk, and the Women's Great Peace Journey across Europe. There were vigils and silent demonstrations in front of Red Square in Moscow, at the Pentagon, in various world capitals from London to Canberra, at the UN, in Hiroshima and Nagasaki—and at weapons production sites. There was the solemn holding of the Accra Assembly for Disarmament in Ghana; the nonviolent mobilization of peasants, workers, and students across Latin America that led to the signing of the Treaty of Tlatelolco designating twenty-four states of Latin America as nuclear weapons–free zones; and the peaceful land reclamation movements by Latin peasants and indigenous peoples. In the South Pacific the antinuclear movement of a coalition of religious and civic INGOs that led to the signing of the Treaty of Raratonga by ten states in 1985. In the United States and Canada, there was Women Strike for Peace, which as a housewives' movement spread to Europe and parts of Asia and helped lead to the Partial Test-Ban Treaty. There were student demonstrations on every continent, and teach-ins were invented on college campuses to reshape understandings of security. Japanese housewives took to the streets to demonstrate against the U.S.-Japan mutual security treaty. Protest ships were sailed into forbidden waters at nuclear test sites in the Pacific, and symbolic invasions of nuclear production plants and nuclear testing sites in the deserts of the American Southwest were launched. All this created a sense of tremendous popular will to end the arms race, particularly the nuclear arms race.[18] Yet the waves of activity rose and fell, and weapons production, testing, and deployment by the major powers went steadily on. The Partial Test-Ban Treaty was a weak success in 1963, and the 1968 Non-Proliferation Treaty was actually signed several years after the Campaign for Nuclear Disarmament (CND) movement had lost momentum.

The loss of momentum and sense of discouragement each time a movement peak was followed by a trough was perhaps more apparent than real. The nonviolent Civil Rights movement of the 1950s and 1960s in the United States had initiated major, if slow-moving, changes throughout that society, particularly through desegregation of schools and workplaces. CORE (Congress of Racial Equality) and SNCC (Student Nonviolent Coordinating Committee) mobilized a generation of white and black students for social change. The charismatic leadership of Martin Luther King, who, like Gandhi, was committed to the nonviolent liberation of his people and, like Gandhi, was a great teacher able to surround himself with men and women of outstanding qualities from his own community, helped clarify the connection between the oppression of blacks in the South and oppression of natives in Vietnam. Outrage over a blatantly expanding nuclear arms race that totally ignored the human suffering of Hiroshima and Nagasaki helped generate renewed activity as well.

## Nonviolent Action: Strategies, Not Movements

Nonviolent action, which has received much attention through the movements led in the twentieth century by Gandhi and Martin Luther King, is a special technique that oppressed peoples have used throughout history in conflict situations to achieve ends that could not otherwise be achieved, against powerful adversaries. As Sharp points out, the conflict issues can be highly diverse—economic, living space, identity, ownership, or political power.[19] While nonviolent action tends to be identified with peace movements, it is, in fact, a set of techniques that can be used in a variety of causes. It can be thought of as a collection of discrete procedures for protesting, constraining, and pressuring an adversary in an acute and active conflict—methods that eschew physical violence and destruction. Sharp lists nearly two hundred such methods. Nonviolent action keeps showing up throughout history. When in 494 B.C.E., in protest against the doings of the consuls, the plebeians of ancient Rome peacefully withdrew for some days from participation in daily life to the hill that came to be known as the Sacred Mount, they were engaging (successfully, as it turned out) in nonviolent action.[20]

Precisely because these strategies for protest and change avoid harming adversaries, they can be considered as strengthening the peace culture of any society in which they are used. It is encouraging to realize that over and over through the centuries, on every continent, in situations of injustice social groups rediscover or reinvent nonviolent ways to bring about change. The extent of use of nonviolent strategies historically and in this century is only beginning to be appreciated through the work of Sharp and his colleagues. These strategies hold considerable promise for the future.

## New Developments in Peace Movements

A complex coalition movement launched in 1978 in the United States by Mobilization for Survival—partly a peace movement and partly an antiwar, anticolonialism movement—came into being on city streets and college campuses and in the workplaces of America. It was succeeded by the Nuclear Weapons Freeze Campaign of 1980–82. A new level of technical skill and occupational expertise informed the peace organizations that developed in the seventies and eighties and permanently changed the character of peace

movements domestically and abroad. By the eighties there was general awareness that the issues of militarism, economic maldevelopment, environmental degradation, and human rights were all interconnected. Movements
became more focused, more sophisticated, and less dependent on mass mobilization in the streets for energy to continue.[21] Since peace movements had
already acquired a transnational character in the previous century, these
changes were felt to varying degrees on every continent.

### Women's Movements

Already before World War I, women's organizations with peace platforms
(Women's Christian Temperance Union, Young Women's Christian Association, and, subsequently, the Women's International League for Peace and
Freedom) had been working to increase participation of women in all sectors
of society, to redistribute resources toward women and men in the Two-Thirds
World, and to create transnational infrastructures to further collaborative problem solving on peace, justice, and human welfare issues. By 1973 there were 17
women's INGOs working for international understanding. By 1986 there were
61. The UN gave women an international platform from which to launch the
first and second women's decades. Women's peace groups met through the
early 1990s to prepare workshops for the 1995 International Women's Conference in Beijing. These workshops were intended to provide training in the resolution and nonviolent management of conflict, both in home and public
settings. The linking of customary practices of violence against women in family and community and violence in war has been a major focus of both grassroots and transnational women's groups since the seventies, as has the
development of media skills and organizational skills to present different images of how human beings can conduct their affairs.[22] A group of women
scholars formed the Women and Peace Study Group of the International
Peace Research Association in the early 1970s to contribute to the conceptualization of a postpatriarchal social order in which all forms of social violence
are eliminated.[23] Similar groups of women scholars have since formed in all of
the major social science associations to study gender issues from their discipli-
nary perspectives. Because there has been such an impressive array of creative
peace strategies emerging from women's peace movements on various continents in recent decades, chapter 5 in part 2 is devoted to that subject.

### The Peace Research Movement

Social scientists in Europe, the Americas, and the Asia-Pacific region,
working on issues of disarmament and stable peace among states, were in-

tensely frustrated by the Cold War. Aware of their heritage of close to a century of social science research on the causes and effects of war, they decided early in the 1950s that it was time to launch a concerted effort to build a coherent knowledge base that could assist policy makers in bringing war to an end as an instrument of national policy. Several generations of graduate students in the 1950s and 1960s provided intellectual and psychic energy, and professors began pouring out new ideas. *Fights, Game and Debates* by Anatol Rapoport (1960), *Toward a Science of Peace* by Ted Lentz (1961), and *Conflict and Defense* by Kenneth Boulding (1962) were among the first books from the new peace research community to call attention to the obsolescence of war in the nuclear age; they were followed by an exciting series of essays by Johan Galtung (1975) analyzing the theory and practice of war systems and peace systems and how to get from one to the other.[24] New research institutes were founded: the Peace Research Institute-Oslo, led by Johan Galtung and a group of eager young Norwegian scholars, with its *Journal of Peace Research*; the Center for Conflict Resolution at the University of Michigan, led by Kenneth Boulding, Anatol Rapoport, and a group of equally eager young scholars, with its *Journal of Conflict Resolution*; and the Canadian Peace Research Institute, led by Norman Alcock and Hanna and Allan Newcombe. A new worldwide peace research movement was launched.

Conflict resolution and peace research centers sprang up all over Europe; in the Americas; in India, Japan, and Australia.[25] By 1965 scholars from centers on all continents met in Groningen, the Netherlands, to establish the International Peace Research Association (IPRA) with enthusiastic support from UNESCO. Spin-off regional associations emerged in Europe, Latin America, North America, Asia, and Africa. Peace studies became a new part of the curriculum on college campuses.[26] IPRA's Peace Education Commission, Global Education Associates, and other peace education bodies carried the idea of peace studies everywhere—including to elementary and secondary schools and to peace organizations—as a new tool to use in developing grassroots skills in peace building. The campus teach-ins and student strikes (the slogan "Shut down the war university and open the peace university" was heard everywhere) recruited growing numbers of professors and students to the study of alternatives to a military-based security policy. Governments, responding to a new type of peace movement lobbying, established national peace research institutes; Sweden led the way, followed by the United States, several other European countries, and Australia. Alva Myrdal, the Swedish Ambassador to the eighteen-nation Disarmament Committee in Geneva, gave courageous leadership to the doomed effort to persuade the major powers that disarmament was a wise security policy. Throughout the twelve years the Committee met, she never gave up trying to bridge the gap between national security perspectives and peace research perspectives.[27]

Peace researchers soon moved from the well-plowed field of disarmament studies to the more challenging one of economic conversion and alternative modes of defense, including civilian-based defense. An early study of civilian nonviolent resistance on a national scale in the 1920s through the 1940s by Adam Roberts[28] was followed by a monumental macrohistorical study of political nonviolence by Gene Sharp[29] to usher in decades of fruitful research on the strategies of nonviolence.

In Europe peace researchers played an important role in helping to develop the Helsinki Agreements and the Conference for Security and Cooperation in Europe (CSCE). Peace researchers have helped a number of European governments explore the possibilities of a nonoffensive defense (NOD) strategy, basing a national security system on weapons usable only for defending a country's borders. In the United States, they have served as advisors to state economic conversion programs. ICON, the Internal Conflicts Study Group of IPRA, pioneered the exploration of early warning systems for situations of potential and actual ethnic conflict and in designing systems of conflict mediation. This began in the early eighties, before there was general awareness that internal conflicts would also play an increasingly significant role on the international conflict scene. International Alert is the peace NGO that focuses primarily on such conflicts. In 1990, during the Gulf War, IPRA set up a Commission for Peace Building in Crisis Areas, focusing first on the Middle East, and mobilized an international group of scholars to work with scholars from the Middle East on developing strategies for peace building there.[30] Another group, the Oxford Research Group, has focused specifically on nuclear disarmament.[31] That work is ongoing, and other crisis areas will be addressed similarly as resources become available.

Many international relations institutes around the world are now shifting away from the old national security paradigm to a common security paradigm, aided by a series of independent international commissions on the new world order, most particularly the Palme Commission (1982) and the Brundtland Commission (1987). These commissions and others on economic security (Brandt Commission, 1983; South Commission, 1990) and the MacBride Commission on the New World Information Order (1980) both arose from and contributed to general peace movement dissatisfaction with old defense strategies that were identified as harmful to human and social development.[32] The work of peace researchers contributed to the reports of these commissions.

The Zone of Peace strategy, designating areas that would be free of weapons, is one peace research development that has been very useful to peace movements. ZOP agreements can range from Nuclear-Weapon-Free Zones to completely demilitarized zones, with many variations in between. It was an alliance of the peace research movement and regional coalitions of peace organizations that made the Weapons-Free-Zone Treaties of Tlatelolco and Raratonga possible and the new Zone of Peace activity in the Philippines.[33] Many more ZOP plans are on the drawing boards, awaiting further peace coalition activity in the relevant region.

Another useful tool for peace movements developed by peace researchers has been the Seville Statement on Violence, produced by an eminent group of social and biological scientists at a UNESCO Conference in Seville in 1986, stating that war is not a biological necessity but a social invention.[34] This statement and supporting background information from the fields of biology, psychology, sociology, ethology, and genetics has now been debated by scholars and used by educators and community activists around the world, with the help of a Seville Support Network.

One group of peace researchers has for several decades worked with conflict analysis and third-party intervention through innovative methods of structured dialogue between adversaries. An account of the early use of this approach in three specific conflicts in Asia, the Mediterranean, and Africa is found in John Burton[35] and another in Adam Curle,[36] the latter covering conflicts on these continents and in Europe and the Americas as well. A third innovation is known as elicitive conflict resolution, taking account of existing local practices of dealing with conflict, and also referred to as conflict transformation. This approach has been pioneered by John Paul Lederach[37] and is now increasingly in use.

The World Order Models Project represents still another group of peace researchers, men and women scholars from Europe, Asia, Africa, and the Americas who have worked together since 1966, moving beyond the dynamics of war prevention to exploring "Preferred Worlds" in which the world order values of peace, economic well-being, social justice, ecological stability, and positive identity would be realized.[38] Cochaired by Saul Mendlovitz in the United States and Yoshikazu Sakamoto in Japan, the work of these scholars continues today and has been of great importance in exploring the possibilities of a global constitutional order based on grassroots initiatives.

The story of the development of regional peace research movements in response to unique regional needs is an interesting one. Latin American peace researchers first began mobilizing in Scandinavia in the early 1970s, finally forming the Latin American Council on Peace Research (CLAIP) in 1977 in Mexico to address issues of *dependencia* (dependency), militarization, and land reform. The peace researcher-activist and Nobel prize recipient Adolfo Perez Esquivel gave the kind of charismatic leadership to the nonviolence movement in Latin America that Gandhi had given in India and Martin Luther King in the United States. With the dedicated assistance of Hildegard and Jean Goss-Mayr, International Fellowship of Reconciliation secretaries who took the fostering of the nonviolence movement in Latin America as their life calling, Esquivel and his gifted colleagues across the continent founded SERPAJ (Servicio Paz y Justicia), a multicountry network of national organizations whose continuing challenge has been introducing nonviolence into situations of armed struggle. A more recent organization including peace researchers and leading public figures, the South Commission, is following up on earlier success in achieving the Nuclear-Weapons-Free Zone Treaty of Tlatelolco with a project to conceptualize and develop the institutional infrastructure for a more completely demilitarized Latin America.

Japan and India have been major centers for the Asian Peace Research Association (APRA), with Australia taking leadership in more recent years. Gandhian peace studies centers developed in a number of Indian universities. Research on Gandhi's *sarvodaya* model of grassroots village development through self-help and the practice of nonviolence has continued in the Gandhi centers even while being ignored by the national government,[39] and research reports are regularly published by the Gandhi Peace Foundation journal, *Gandhi Marg*. Research institutes in India, Pakistan, and Bangladesh have all focused on the relationship between development policy, military policy, and peaceful resolution of the conflicts of the region.

Japan, the first and so far the only victim of nuclear bombing, has been the center of international antinuclear movement activity since the early fifties. It has had a strong peace research community since 1963, focusing on peace education curricula for the schools, on protecting the gradually eroding peace provisions of the Japanese Constitution, and on working with Asian colleagues through APRA on denuclearization and disarmament for Japan in a context of alternative security arrangements throughout the larger Asia-Pacific region. Yoshikazu Sakamoto, a former Secretary General of IPRA and founder of APRA, has been a leader in these developments, which involve scholars in Bangladesh, India, Pakistan, Malaysia, Sri Lanka, Australia, New Zealand, and China.

Continent-wide movements are difficult to mobilize in Africa, where intra-continental communication systems work poorly. The first African Peace Research Institute was founded in the early 1970s. The current APRI in Nigeria was "refounded" in 1985, and the African Peace Research Association (AFPRA) in 1988. The focus for collaborative activity has been the denu-clearization and demilitarization of Africa as a whole. South African peace researchers, who have long worked on problems of interethnic conflict, are now coming into closer contact with their colleagues in other countries. The African Centre for the Constructive Resolution of Disputes (ACCORD), based at the University of Durban, has played an important role, together with the Center for Conflict Resolution at the University of Capetown, in the political transformation of South Africa. *Conflict Trends*, published by AC-CORD, reports on important new developments in the region.

A discussion of peace research in the Two-Thirds World should not ignore the Two-Thirds World internal to the Americas. The Inuit peoples of Canada and Alaska have increasing contact with peace researchers in Canada and the United States, and the Center for Arctic Studies at Dartmouth College, New Hampshire, is opening up new opportunities for collaborative research on the numerous boundary and resource issues that involve the Inuit, Canada, the United States, and Russia.

The Fund for the Development of Indigenous Peoples of Latin America and the Caribbean was established by heads of state of the Ibero-American nations in 1993, the International Year of Indigenous Peoples. The chairman is Rodolfo Stavenhagen of el Colegio de Mexico, a globally known researcher on ethnicity and conflict resolution. This promises well for the further development of nonviolent conflict resolution in Latin America. Certainly, the long history of nonviolent action by Native Americans in this hemisphere to reclaim stolen lands and ruthlessly abrogated sovereign rights of peoplehood and individual human rights in economic, social, and political spheres needs to enter the public record.[40]

### Occupationally Based Peace Groups

A less visible part of peace movements is found in the development since the 1960s of peace organizations within specific occupations and professions. This should be noted as a separate phenomenon from the development of sections or committees on peace and disarmament issues formed within existing professional associations, mentioned in the section above on peace research. The 1988–89 *Peace Resource Book* listed twenty-two occupation-based peace and disarmament organizations in the United States, perhaps half of them linked to INGOs with sections in a number of countries.[41] The list includes associations for architects, business executives, computer professionals (two organizations), educators, high-tech professionals, physicians, lawyers (three separate organizations), media professionals, veterans (three separate organizations), nurses, parliamentarians, performing artists, psychologists, social scientists, physical scientists, and writers and publishers. The twenty-two groups each draw on their own expertise and contacts to educate themselves and the public about alternatives to nuclear defense and military security. They also contribute to policy discussions and address the cultural context of militarism. These groups are project-oriented: architects design peace parks; educators design conflict resolution curricula for the schools; lawyers design arms control procedures; physicians and nurses address urgent health care issues; performing artists offer drama, music, and poetry that draw attention to the peacemaking dimension of human experience. In short, they are serious about helping to create a living peace culture that can offer concrete alternatives to war and violence.

In the scientific community the best-known organization is the Pugwash Conferences on Science and World Affairs, founded in 1957 in Canada by scientists from East and West. Its purposes: to address the dangers of the nuclear arms race; to build trust and confidence within the international scientific community; to share research findings on scientific and technological aspects of new weapons, verification technology, possibilities of arms control and nuclear disarmament, and approaches to economic conversion. Pugwash is not a mass movement but has taken care to educate decision makers on arms control matters (though not directly promoting disarmament). The group of atomic scientists who began publishing the *Bulletin of Atomic Scientists* in 1945, concurrently with the establishment of the more issue-oriented Federation of American Scientists, is more directly focused on educating the public about atomic dangers and alternative approaches to security. Hard on its heels came the Council for a Livable World, formed in 1946, also in response to the nuclear threat, and with a mission to educate the public about the need for arms control. The Union of Concerned Scientists, founded in 1969 in response to the "Star Wars" type of security thinking, is even more movement oriented, with a highly effective lobbying wing. It is committed to educating the public about the misuses of science, whether in weaponry or in other arenas that endanger the global environment. It also studies energy technologies, transportation policy, and agricultural practices for safer human futures.

The International Council of Scientific Unions established a commission in the 1970s to investigate the hazards associated with different levels of nuclear military action, from one bomb to an all-out war. Its findings[42] have been very important to peace movements in every country, in raising levels of motivation to work for alternatives to nuclear defense. More information about the current peace work of scientific NGOs will be given in chapter 11.

### Other Peace Movement Organizations

One of the earliest peace movement activities to come alive after World War II was world federalism. In 1947, with widespread support from parliamentarians and the internationally oriented sector of the general public in twenty-five countries, the World Movement for World Federal Government was founded; by the time of the 1950 Peoples' World Parliament in Geneva, the number of participating countries had grown to forty-five. The International Peace Bureau tried to reconvene all peace and internationalist organizations in 1946, but political agendas varied so widely that it was not until 1949 that a coordinating council for international and national peace organizations could be convened: the International Liaison Committee of Organizations for Peace (ILCOP). The War Resisters International participated, as did the World Federalists, Service Civile Internationale, and the International Fellowship of Reconciliation. The formation of the World Peace Council in that same year with leadership from Warsaw Pact countries, including delegates from seventy-two countries, unfortunately launched the Cold War in the peace movement. Continuing attempts to hold dialogues about the need for impartial criticism of the military policies on both sides of the Iron Curtain finally bore fruit fourteen years later with the formation in 1963 of the International Confederation for Disarmament and Peace (ICDP), a body based in Western Europe that was committed to dialogue with Eastern Europe. This made possible the beginning of cautious East-West communication that, while difficult and widely misunderstood by many even in the peace movements of those decades, played a significant role in facilitating the end of the Cold War and such progress as there was in arms control. The twenty-three–member ICDP was representative of the major international peace organizations of the early sixties, including (in addition to the IFOR and WRI) the Ghana-based Accra Assembly, the Sarva Seva Sangh of India, the CND (Campaign for Nuclear Disarmament) movements of Europe and the Asia-

Pacific region, and SANE (Committee for a Sane Nuclear Policy) in the United States.

The War Resisters International, though much constrained in its activity during World War II, never stopped assisting conscientious objectors who refused military and/or alternative service, and it greatly expanded that work after the war, because of the ongoing reality of conscription in Europe and the United States. Its research and publication of information about conscription around the world provided valuable information on the rights of conscientious objectors country by country.[43] WRI has continued to press for the establishment and expansion of those rights. The fact that the number of conscientious objectors globally has continued to expand in recent decades is certainly to a significant degree due to WRI's efforts. The organization has performed a similar service for war tax resisters.[44] In recent years, it has also focused on the culture of militarism by campaigning against war toys and all forms of cultural violence, including violence against women, and by providing nonviolence training for children as well as for adults.

WRI's dream of a nonviolent army goes back to the Shanti Sena activities of its Indian members. At its 1960 triennial in India, years of discussion about the Shanti Sena bore fruit in a spontaneous declaration of a number of participants: "It's time to form an international peace brigade!" Shortly afterwards, the World Peace Brigade was established near Beirut, Lebanon, with WRI participation. It also functioned in Tanganyika and Kenya in the context of the independence movement of Zambia. An abortive march from Delhi to Peking in 1963 to bring the India-China conflict to an end was the last effort of the underfunded and underorganized Brigade. Reconstituted, with a firmer base, as the Peace Brigades International in Canada in 1981, it has continued to benefit from WRI participation in its activities in the Middle East, Asia, the Balkans, some states of the former Soviet Union, and the Americas as well. With members and affiliates in twenty-seven countries, WRI also played a prominent role during the Vietnam War protests, internationally and in the United States, where it spearheaded the draft resistance movement.

### The Nuclear Disarmament Organizations

Although there were antinuclear demonstrations from the late 1940s on, it was not until 1958 that the Campaign for Nuclear Disarmament was formally launched in Britain, in response to the spontaneous mass demonstrations of the 1957 Easter March from London to the Aldermaston Atomic Weapons Research Establishment. It was estimated that by the fourth day of that march, 8,000 people were marching. The following year there were 100,000 at the final Easter March Rally. The movement stayed strong until 1964, after the Partial Test Ban Treaty was signed, and then exhausted activists either returned to private life or took a new breath and joined the movement opposing the war in Vietnam. The CND had strong counterpart movements in West Germany, Scandinavia, Switzerland, Canada, and the United States (somewhat fewer in France), as well as in Japan, Australia, and New Zealand. The emotional intensity and relatively long duration of the Campaign for Nuclear Disarmament at its peak—from 1957 to 1964—contrasts with its relatively modest achievement in the 1963 Partial Test Ban Treaty. As has already been pointed out, the Non-Proliferation Treaty was not signed until 1968, several years after the nuclear disarmament activities had faded away.

Another round of large-scale demonstrations in Europe began in 1980 with the formation of European Nuclear Disarmament (END) in protest against NATO decisions on deployment of new missiles in Europe. Massive marches of hundreds of thousands were staged across Europe. Although the demonstrations continued for several years, the missile deployments held, and the movement once again died down.

A significant part of the European peace movement with its own unique environmental focus is the Green movement, best known through the Green party of Germany, founded in 1979. Its political platform in the early days when there were Greens in the German parliament included not only ecological awareness and environmental conservation but also opposition to nuclear weapons and unilateral disarmament. Leaders like Petra Kelly were spiritually rooted pacifists.[45] They brought a fresh wind into the musty house of parliament through a new style of political discourse, a radical pacifist policy orientation, and the delightful practice of carrying green plants into the halls where parliament assembled. Inevitable splits between the realists and idealists weakened the party for a time and caused the loss of its seats in parliament, but in 1999 the Greens became part of the government coalition, and the idea of Green political parties has spread. Greens are now a small but significant part of the political spectrum in France, Britain, Scandinavia, the United States, Canada, and Australia.

### The Mass Movements vs. the Longtime Peace Organizations

It should be clear that organizations like the WRI, WILPF, and other member organizations of the ICDP did not disband when the protestors went home. Theirs was a lifetime and lifeway commitment, and as mass movements waxed and waned they continued their activities and adjusted their priorities to the resources at hand. They never counted on those movements to accomplish the tedious work of getting serious consideration of alternative security policies and a re-formed social order, but they welcomed the extra bodies when they became available. Above all, they welcomed the increased visibility for the peace cause that a mass movement provided. Their rock-bottom, not-to-be-shaken optimism is well described in *Failure to Quit* by Howard Zinn.[46]

One important consequence of the mass movements was the slower but more profound mobilization of citizens in their workplaces, producing the new professional, occupation-based peace research initiatives by social and physical scientists described above. These groups were lower key and less likely to suffer from burnout. They contributed to the steady growth in number of people with a lifetime commitment to peace. The number of peace activists continuing to be available *after* peak protest eras is a significant indicator of civic capability for peace work; this number continues to grow even while people are complaining that the peace movement is "dead."[47]

In the United States, the Committee for a Sane Nuclear Policy (SANE) and the Committee for Non-Violent Action (CNVA) were started the same year as the British CND, 1957. A number of new peace groups formed between 1958 and 1962, and the CNVA and the new and old women's organizations (WILPF, Women Strike for Peace, and other women-for-peace groups) contributed some dramatic public actions of going into forbidden places on land and sea in those years. There were also mass public antinuclear demonstrations in the United States (for example, in New York in 1982). SANE remained a durable group, merging with other groups to stay alive as a political voice for nuclear disarmament, and is alive to this day, although modified and renamed the Campaign for Global Security and, more recently, Peace Action.

From 1965 to 1975 various new organizations emerged in opposition to the Vietnam War, working separately or with the older groups, and a number of new student organizations were formed. The combination of emphasis on grassroots organization, constant demonstrations and activity on college campuses, and effective political lobbying of peace groups in coalitions had its effect on national elections and on the final United States withdrawal from Vietnam in 1975. (We professors became very nostalgic for the liveliness of the antiwar years as college campuses quieted down after 1975.)

After a breather, a new antinuclear effort, the Nuclear Weapons Freeze Campaign, had a vigorous political life in the early 1980s. In spite of getting serious attention in the policy community, it never halted research and development or production of nuclear weapons. In 1987, SANE and the Freeze movement merged for mutual survival. Yet the United States peace movement was far from inert. The 1988–89 directory of the Institute for Defense and Disarmament Studies listed 306 different national peace groups with active ongoing programs (58 of them faith-based) and 6,600 local groups.[48] Most of them were engaged in lobbying and community education.

With the "end" of the Cold War, the breakup of the Soviet Union and Yugoslavia, and the rise of serious ethnic conflict both in older industrialized states and in more recently formed states of the Two-Thirds World, the peace organizations that have survived the peaks and troughs of the postwar decades are exploring new directions, as we shall see in chapter 11.

## Two-Thirds World Peace Movements

Although in terms of formal structures, the bulk of peace organizations are located in Europe and North America, in terms of sheer numbers of participants, we must look to the Two-Thirds World. Asia, for example, has suffered much violence in the second half of this century, to a significant degree generated or worsened by the activities of the One-Third World, yet it has also produced great and prophetic peace leaders who have spiritually empowered mass peace movements in their own countries without the aid of Western technologies of communication and organization. Among them are Thich Nhat Hanh of Vietnam, A. T. Ariyaratne of Sri Lanka, Sulak Sivaraska of Thailand, Aung San Suu Kyi of Burma, and Maha Ghosenanda of Cambodia.

We know Vietnam as the home of a strong monk-led peace movement. Throughout the civil war that became the "U.S. war," many of the 80 percent of Vietnamese who were Buddhist stayed nonviolent. Courageous Thich Nat Hanh never took sides between North and South Vietnam and continues to work for reconciliation from his place of exile in France. Few westerners realize what a great variety of nonviolent strategies the Buddhist peace movement undertook in wartime.[49] Villagers sought to stop tanks and troops by placing their sacred family altars in the path of oncoming armies, and there were mass fasts involving thousands of villagers. Prayers for peace for a divided land were printed by the thousands and distributed all over both North and South Vietnam. The Buddhist School of Youth Social Service trained and sent out multitudes of young men and women to do community development service in North and South. The sacrificial self-immolations by monks and nuns that received so much attention in the West represented only a tiny part of the total community-level peace activity that went on and still continues. Continuing activities have included Buddhist workshops held in the United States for American veterans traumatized by the war and comparable training provided in Vietnam to help both sets of veterans to become a listening presence for healing and reconciliation.

Sri Lanka is another Buddhist country that has experienced much violence in recent decades, resulting in the division of the country along Buddhist versus Tamil Hindu lines. The peace-oriented Sarvodaya Shramadana movement led by A. T. Ariyaratne, drawing on deep Buddhist values of awakening and sharing, had by 1986 held Shramadana camps in over 8,000 of the 23,000 villages in Sri Lanka to build the "psychological infrastructure of peace" and has worked with Tamils to recreate the spiritual value system and the social skills in both groups that will eventually enable the peaceful reconstruction of Sri Lanka as a society. The tools used have been a national conference of all faiths and ethnicities, producing a joint Peoples' Declaration for Mutual Peace and Harmony, and the development of Shanti Sena (peace brigades) in which young men and women of Sinhala and Tamil communities are paired and trained to work together in villages of both North and South.[50] Many other peace groups, both Asian and East-West groups, support similar activities.

Thailand is a third Buddhist country that has experienced violence and military rule in post–World War II years. Sulak Sivaraksa, a Nobel peace prize nominee, has been a strong public voice for nonviolence and human rights, creating a number of institutions and networks of a peace-building nature, including the Network of Engaged Buddhists, which links Buddhists on all continents who are doing peace work.[51] His speaking and writing bridges East-West thinking in peace and development studies. In and out of prison for his beliefs, he has been an important teacher for the youth of his country.

In Cambodia, the country of the Killing Fields, contingents of high-ranking monks led by Maha Ghosenanda, the supreme patriarch of Cambodian Buddhism, have been taking part in peace negotiations in Pyongnang and Phnom Penh since the 1970s. Ghosenanda, known as the Gandhi of Cambodia, also organizes and conducts peace walks, or *dhamayietras*, through heavily mined areas, and also right through militarily contested areas, setting up training opportunities for monks, nuns, and villagers in nonviolent action.[52]

Burma's nonviolent leader Aung San Suu Kyi (a Nobel prize recipient) was under house arrest for five years after her election to the post of prime minister in 1990, an election unfortunately followed by a military clampdown. Her political practice and religious philosophy are both rooted in nonviolence, and though her movements continue to be severely restricted, she may yet succeed in leading Burma into a more peaceful future.[53]

Buddhism has also generated an important peace movement in Japan. Soka Gakkai, a Mahayan Buddhist group basing its teachings on the Lotus

Sutra, is active in both social and political spheres. Under the leadership of Daisaku Ikeda, it has created a university (Soka) and a network of schools and peace research institutes focused on the development of a more peaceful world. Its many local groups of followers in Japan and around the world are actively engaged in work for peace, social justice, and environmental restoration.[54]

In Tibet and in the Tibetan diaspora, the Tibetan Liberation Movement under the leadership of the Dalai Lama (heading a government in exile in India) seeks nonviolently to regain autonomy in its homeland and to transform it into a Buddhist Zone of Peace.[55]

In India the Jains, dating back several centuries before the birth of Buddha, were the first religious order to make ahimsa, the doctrine of harmlessness, their central tenet. While most Jains have through the centuries lived as holy ascetics disengaged from the world, a contemporary activist leader of Jainism, Acarya Tulsi (1914–1997) began spreading the Jain principle of nonviolence to a wide audience not only in India but internationally. Today Jain influence is felt in peace and environmental movements well beyond India.[56]

Gandhi developed his ahimsa teachings from Jainism, and today in India there are two dozen or so Gandhi Peace Foundation centers struggling to meet the need for trained practitioners of nonviolence to work in the midst of the Hindu-Moslem violence in the Kashmir and elsewhere. They administer nonviolent training programs on college campuses, in special youth camps, and at their community centers, as well as maintaining rural development programs and environmental activities generated by the Foundation's new "Environmental Cell." An all-India Shanti Sena was reactivated in 1985 by Sarva Seva Sangh after some years of divisions and splits. Another peace-related movement in India focuses primarily on nonviolence toward nature. Mass demonstrations seek to stop the building of dams that would greatly increase flood dangers. Indian farmers protest the damage the Green Revolution is doing to soils and seeds.[57] Village women have been going into their forests for years to protect them from would-be strippers and despoilers, as in the Chipko movement. Women's movements continue to try to bring an end to endemic levels of violence against women, including bride burning and the killing of female infants.

Another development in India has been the "Dhamma revolution," a Buddhist mass-conversion movement among the "Untouchables," to bring education and human and social development in a Buddhist framework to the most oppressed classes of India.[58]

Nonviolence movements for social change in Islamic countries, unfortunately, do not get the attention that extremist Muslim violence gets in the media. The Fellowship of Reconciliation has done its best to counter that tendency in its publications.[59] An important recent book by Crow, Grant, and Ibrahim[60] documents Arab-Muslim cases of nonviolent struggle in this century, including the nonviolent independence struggle against the British by Egyptians after World War I; the Pathan nonviolent struggle against the British that lasted from 1919 until Indian independence;[61] the Palestinian general strike of the late 1930s, and nonviolent uprisings in Iraq and Iran and Druze nonviolent resistance in the Golan Heights in recent decades. A nonviolent protest by Thai Muslims against the killings of Muslims by the Thai army in December 1975 led to the January 1976 removal of the persecuting Buddhist governor and his replacement by a Muslim governor. The story of a group of Arab intellectuals who created a new vision of Arab culture and nationalism in the second half of the twentieth century is movingly told by Fouad Ajami, in *The Dream Palace of the Arabs.*[62]

Although the four-day nonviolent revolution in the Philippines of February 1986 was most visibly led by Catholics, Muslims have played an important role in the strong Anti-Bases movement that led to the withdrawal of the United States military base there. They have participated in the creation of the Coalition for Peace, a group of twenty-three activist groups that helped bring about Regional Peace Councils; they have been involved in the development of peace studies programs on college campuses; and they have been a strong presence in the Zone of Peace Movement that has led to the establishment of five Peace Zones: in Kalinga-Apayao, Bituan, Naga City, Sagada, and Cantonmanyog.[63]

The weapons of Islam, writes Sufi teacher M. R. Bawa Muhaiyaddeen, are inner patience, contentment, trust in God, and praise of God. "Once we understand what the true weapons of Islam are, we will never take a life, we will never even see anyone as separate from ourselves."[64]

On the African continent the story of the nonviolent struggles of indigenous peoples against colonialism, slavery, and the destruction of fragile environments, and of the role of traditional faiths and values in helping Africans maintain authentic peaceful lifeways, has not yet been told. That story will be found in the villages of Africa, in the creation of groups like the 6-S, a unique African peasant organization spread across nine Sahel countries to help one another deal with the dry seasons. The hardships the peasant men and women face are matched by their spiritual strengths. "The feet do not go where the heart does not go first," say the villagers.[65]

The Accra Assembly, a forgotten part of the antinuclear movement, was another African creation. Its organizers initiated an all-African conference on the nuclear threat in Accra, Ghana, that evolved a plan for nonviolent action to stop French nuclear testing in French West Africa in the early 1960s. The Assembly, in fact, did send teams to the region, but the teams were not successful in stopping the tests.

In South Africa nonviolent action was reinvented by blacks over and over again for fifty years as they struggled against the merciless march of apartheid. Steadily increasing white violence finally led to the African National Congress supposedly giving up nonviolence, although nonviolent actions, in fact, never stopped. The story of those fifty years[66] and the recent campaign to reemphasize nonviolence through local activity based on the National Peace Accord during the transition to a free democratic South Africa demonstrate that faith in the power of nonviolence has not been lost even under the most extreme conditions of oppression.[67] The full story of the new forms of civic organizations and popular groups rooted in the rich soil of religious faith that came into being during the long years of state-sponsored racism is beginning to emerge.[68]

Latin America has been home to two of the most written-about faith-based nonviolence movements of the latter part of the twentieth century: the base community movement[69] within Catholicism and SERPAJ. Servicio Paz y Justica is an eleven-country network of peasants, workers, priests, and middle-class activists who have worked to bring the poor and dispossessed into full participation in the economic, political, and social life of their respective countries through nonviolent repossession of land and of the fruits of their labor in mines, fields, and factories.

The base community movement arose in response to the lack of priests to serve in local churches. The training of lay villagers to give leadership in local churches achieved the *conscientization*—a mental, social, and spiritual awakening—of thousands of formerly illiterate poor. The most visible leaders of these twin movements were Archbishop Dom Helder Camara of Recife, Brazil, who initiated the campaign of "liberating moral pressure"; Paulo Freire of Brazil, who developed the pedagogy of the oppressed; and Nobel prize–winning Adolfo Perez Esquivel of Argentina, founder of SERPAJ. In another sense, the most visible leaders have been the thousands of mothers, such as the Mothers of the Plaza de Mayo in Argentina, who continue their courageous demonstrations and fast and pray outside the doors of oppressive military governments, demanding information about the multitudes of "disappeareds"—husbands, sons, daughters killed or imprisoned by these oppressive governments. Latin America has had its share of violent revolutions,

its men and its women guerillas. However, given the high levels and long
duration of violence experienced by the masses, the extent of commitment
to nonviolence, known in Portuguese as *firmeza permanente* or relentless persistence, is impressive. The five commandments of nonviolence that
emerged from one of the early struggles in Brazil (they rhyme in Portuguese)
are: "Never kill; never wound, in deed or word; always be alert; always remain
united; always disobey the orders of His Excellency (the state governor)
which would destroy us.[70] There are striking parallels between the strategies
of Gandhi and of the Latin American movements—no accident, because his
work was studied and revered by Latin American leaders.

## Peace Movements and Peace Cultures

There is a core element of social excitement in the very concept of peace
*movement.* Deep feelings about human oneness surge forward, and people are
mobilized for action. But without social forms in which to express the oneness,
the feelings fade away. The paradox is that the social forms, i.e., peace organizations themselves, depend on continued fresh infusions of enthusiasm, yet
the very demands of organizational activity dull the vibrancy of intention, setting in motion the peak-trough cycle we have noted. Furthermore, the social
context for both movements and organizations keeps changing. New challenges, new conflicts arise within and between societies as environmental
ecosystems change and social and physical technologies evolve and develop,
while an underlying constant current of migrant populations on the move ensures that different lifeways come in contact with one another. Cultures—
those complexes of historical identity, values, know-how, and ways of
behaving—also change, but much more slowly. The significance of the periodic fresh upwelling of human caring and of the organizational forms that
channel that caring into specific strategies of peace building lies in the combined impact of feeling and form on the culture of the societies in which the
movements arise. They contribute to the peace culture of the larger social fabric, enriching the attitude-value-behavior complexes of peaceableness.

This historical overview of peace movements has brought us to the very
threshold of the present. In part 2, we will see the hidden peaceableness of
much of daily life in today's world, including the inventive peaceableness of
women and children as well as men. We will also follow the new social movements that are focused on changing the relationships among women, men,
and children as a basis for changing the exploitative character of many of our
social institutions as we move into the twenty-first century.

*Part Two*
*Peace Cultures in Action Today*

# Introduction

In PART 1, we looked at how human aspirations and human behaviors in relation to peace have fared in the past, beginning with the historians' tendency to present history as the history of wars won and lost. We discovered another history, the history of efforts to imagine and create alternatives to war, both the utopian experiments and the recurring social movements seeking new strategies for dealing with the conflicts that might lead to war. We identified these efforts as rooted in continuously evolving peace cultures in various parts of the world but did not explore peace cultures as such. In part 2, we will focus on contemporary peace cultures in action, beginning in chapter 4 with an examination of everyday peace behavior in societies that have been identified (by anthropologists and other social scientists) as peaceful. This is followed by a study of feminist contributions to contemporary peace cultures through inventions in peacemaking in chapter 5. The last two chapters of part 2 explore the reconstruction of gender and age roles necessary for a peace culture: first, the reconstruction of men's and women's roles; and next, the reconstruction of adult and children's roles, with examples of how the new roles are emerging in a postpatriarchal, partnership society.

# 4

# Peaceful Societies and Everyday Behavior

LET US BEGIN by remembering that there is no such thing as a conflict-free society. Conflict is ubiquitous. That ubiquity stems from the basic fact of human individuality and difference in the context of limited physical and social resources. Conflict itself should not be confused with violence, which is taken here to mean the intentional harming of others for one's own ends. The differences in wants, needs, perceptions, and aspirations among individuals and among groups, stemming from individual uniqueness, require a constant process of conflict management in daily life at every level from the intrapersonal (each of us has many selves), to the family and the local community, and on to the international community. What keeps this unceasing process of conflict from degenerating into the war of each against all is the equally ubiquitous need of humans for one another, for the social bonding and nurturance without which no society could function. From this perspective, there is no society without significant elements of peaceableness.

Hans Hass has undertaken a remarkable documentation of the universality of human responsiveness to other humans.[1] Traveling around the world with his camera, he has photographed a series of expressive human gestures — smiling, greeting with glad surprise (eyebrows raised), comforting another in grief by having the griever's head resting on the comforter's shoulder, reaching out to protect a child in danger — in settings as far apart as Kenya, Samoa, and France. In cultures that practice disciplined control over such expressive gestures, one finds their fullest expression in children who have not yet learned the discipline.

Hass points out that children learn early how much a smile can do. Why do we humans smile so much? "Because we are not, basically, unfriendly

An earlier version of this chapter appeared as "Peace Behaviors in Various Societies" in *From a Culture of Violence to a Culture of Peace* (Paris: UNESCO, 1996), 31–54.

creatures. Thus our smile is a means of eliciting contact readiness with others and of conveying our accessibility to contact."[2] A smile serves as a social bridge builder.

This universal need for bonding can be thought of as the key to the survival of the human species. It is what draws humans toward negotiating with one another in the face of conflicting interests, needs, and perceptions, whether in settings of family, neighborhood, workplace, or public institutions. The very existence of war and social violence, however, tells us that negotiation is not the only response to conflict. In fact, we may think of responses to conflict as falling on a conflict-management continuum from destruction of the adversary through a range of mediating-negotiating behaviors to complete union with the other.

**Fig. 1. The Conflict Continuum**

## Peaceful Behavior in Everyday Life: Cultural Concepts

Some societies tend toward the aggressive end of the conflict management continuum in their behaviors, others toward the integrative, with many societies falling somewhere in the middle. The historical reasons why different groups pattern their responses to conflict differently lie beyond the scope of this chapter, but we have already noted in chapter 1 that former warrior societies have been known to change and adopt more peaceable ways. We have also noted that warrior societies of the past have all had images of living in peace. The wars of ancient China did not prevent Chang Huen-Chu from writing: "Heaven is the father and Earth is the mother . . . wherefore all included between Heaven and Earth are one body with us and in regard to our dispositions, Heaven and Earth should be our teachers. The People our brothers and we are united with all things."[3] This theme of being kin with all peoples and with earth itself is rooted in a basic experience of the social bonds of kinship and intergroup alliances and the need for mutual aid systems in order to survive, whether in inner cities or on over-stressed farmlands. The peaceful elements of religious teachings strengthen that social bonding. The women's culture also strengthens that bonding, sharing with the religious culture a primary-level responsibility for the well-being of a people. Women's cultures everywhere are an important source of the work of nurturance of a society; a reservoir of experience and knowledge in the bearing and rearing of children; in the healing of the sick; in the growing, processing, and actual serving of food; and in the providing of clothing and shelter. Traditionally, women have had the more difficult role in marriage partnerships through the widespread practice of the woman's moving to the male partner's community and being expected to serve as communication channel and conflict resolver when differences between the communities arise. It is very often, therefore, women who have had the most experience in doing the background work for negotiation and mediation.

The role of infants and young children in the gentling of the human species is often understated. Adults everywhere tend to respond to infants with smiles and modulated voices. Watching small children discover with delight the most ordinary and humdrum items of daily existence literally refreshes adults, as does seeing children at play, creating a wondrous imaginary world that has no purpose but itself.

Through most of human history people have lived in rural settings and in small-scale societies. Just as each familial household develops its own problem-solving behavior, so each social group has developed its own strategies of conflict resolution over time, uniquely rooted in local culture and passed on from generation to generation. Similarly, each society has its own fund of adaptability, built on the knowledge of local environment and lifeworld and the historical memory of times of crisis and change. Such knowledge and experience are represented in familial households as they are organized into communities. The knowledge is woven into religious teachings, into the music, poetry, and dancing of ceremonies, celebrations, and play. It is present in women's culture, in the world of work, in traditional decision-making assemblies, in environmental lore, and in the memory of the past. These are the hidden peacebuilding strengths of every society.

As societies become more complex and elites become differentiated from "common people," center-periphery problems based on mutual ignorance develop. Elites not only cease to share locally based knowledge but cease literally to share a common language with locals. Traditional conflict resolution methods then break down, and new ones are slow to develop during prolonged periods of transition. Since in this last decade of the twentieth century there are only 188 states in the world and "10,000 societies"[4]—ethnic, religious, and cultural groups with significant historical identity—this breakdown of communication and lack of common conflict management practices between ethnies and the larger states of which they are a part is one of the major problems contributing to current levels of intrastate as well as interstate violence. Rediscovery of the hidden strengths of local cultures is one important aspect of peace building for this painful transitional period in contemporary history.

Given the diversity of negotiation and conflict-resolving behaviors that go on every day in every household and every community in the 188 states of the present international order, how can everyday peace behavior be illustrated? This will be handled here in two ways. First, the character and dynamics of everyday peace behavior will be highlighted by choosing societies that set a high value on peaceableness and examining how they go about their conflict management/avoidance interactions as adults and how they train their children to such behavior.[5] Next, we will take a look at peace behaviors to be found in societies in general, common elements underlying wide differences in cultural patterns. The advantage of beginning with societies that are known to be peaceful is that this approach offers behavioral specificity. It highlights the strategies and skill-based nature of peaceful behavior and its dependence on an explicit set of values about nonaggression. Only after that will we go on to see how families in every society, in fact, give some degree of skill training to children to achieve the accepted norms of conflict resolution behavior, whatever they may be. This is the basic process of socialization at work.

In this pursuit of local strengths in peaceableness, we will examine peace behaviors in two types of societies that are alive and functioning at the present time: (1) small preindustrial societal groups that maintain a distinctive identity and yet also have some degree of contact with the larger world and its urban centers and (2) interfaith Irish and North American Anabaptist "peace church" communities that function actively within industrial core societies but have distinctive lifeways that mark them as separate subcultures within those societies.

## The Behavioral Dynamics of Peaceableness in Selected Contemporary Societies

The societies selected here set a high value on nonaggression and noncompetitiveness and therefore handle conflict by a variety of nonviolent means. The four tribal societies to be examined are the Inuit of the Canadian part of the circumpolar North, the Mbuti of the northeastern rainforests of Central-African Zaire, the Zuni of the desert Southwest of the United States, and the mountain-dwelling Arapesh of New Guinea. Each has a distinct and sensitive relationship with its bioregion. Each has distinctive ways of childrearing that produce distinctive adult behavior, but they vary in the degree to which these skills are conflict-suppressing or conflict-resolving, and in the degree to which the skills are based on a strongly dichotomous ingroup-outgroup way of thinking in relation to neighboring peoples. Where there is a strong dichotomous sense, people are free to be aggressive with outsiders and are expected to be peaceful only in their own community. Where attitudes are more inclusive of other peoples, peaceful behavior is extended to outsiders.

## The Inuit

The Inuit live in the circumpolar North, spread out from eastern Siberia through Greenland and Canada to Alaska. They survive a harsh and unforgiving winter cold through cooperation and social warmth, a warmth that extends to the baby animals that children bring home from the icy outdoors to cuddle. Violence and aggression are under strong social prohibition. The social values are centered on (1) *isuma,* which involves rationality, impulse control, thinking problems through calmly and being able to predict consequences of behavior, and (2) *nallik,* which is love, nurturance, protectiveness, concern for others' welfare and total suppression of hostility.

The distinctive childrearing that produces these rational, compassionate, controlled adults revolves around what Briggs calls *benevolent aggression.*[6] This involves an unusual combination of warm affection for infants and a complex kind of teasing that creates fear in children and then teaches them to laugh at their fears. The title of one of Briggs's studies, "Why Don't You Kill Your Baby Brother?" suggests the extremes to which teasing goes, seen from a Western perspective. That it works — in the sense that it produces people with both *isuma* and *nallik,* and a remarkably peaceful society — I would ascribe to the fact that young children are far more socially perceptive, far more sophisticated in their assessment of social situations, than adults usually give them credit for and that they very early figure out what is going on and learn to respond creatively.[7] Although it is a tricky kind of socialization that one can imagine going wrong with some individuals, it does make children self-reliant problem solvers with a well-developed sense of humor, who are affectionate and acutely aware of the disciplined anger-control processes going on inside themselves and others. Girls and boys get the same type of socialization, and Inuit men and women are equally resourceful. There is also a parallel process of much fondling of infants and baby arctic animals, much food sharing and communal eating, much laughter and playfulness. This unusual combination of affection and teasing seems to lead to a high level of conflict awareness and an equally high level of skill in problem solving. The skill of handling conflict playfully, as in song duels (or drum matches) between offended parties, and other similar rituals, produces enjoyable public events rather than battles.

There is no basic we-they, in-out dichotomy, so the conflict management skills are in theory extendable to conflict with non-Inuits. Conflicts with less aware parties such as the Canadian government suggest limits to this. In recent years the Inuit have suffered much from forced government resettlement projects and now have their share of problems with unemployment and accompanying dysfunctional behavior. However, it is also noteworthy that an Inuit, Mary Simon, was chosen as Canada's first circumpolar ambassador. With her colleagues in the Council of Arctic Peoples she has shown the hidden strengths and resourcefulness of traditional Inuit culture by applying them to the protection of the fragile arctic environment and the creation of new spaces for reconstructed lifeways to enable Inuits to maintain a viable society.[8]

### The Mbuti

The Mbuti are hunter/gatherer, rainforest-dwelling Pygmies in northeastern Zaire (now the Congo) who have long had periodic contact with Bantu villagers; they have been movingly described by Turnbull.[9] The basis for their peacefulness is their relationship to the rainforest—their mother, father, teacher, and metaphoric womb. The family hut is also symbolically a womb. Children grow up listening to the trees, learning to climb them early so they can sit high above the ground, listening to wind and waving branches. Mbuti is a listening culture but also a singing and dancing culture, as adults and children sing to and dance with the trees. *Ekimi*, quietness, is highly valued, as opposed to *akami*, disturbance. This preference for quietness, harmony, is reinforced at every stage of life, yet does not preclude children's rough-and-tumble play and a lot of petty squabbling among adults, which tends to be controlled by ridicule. Although children are slapped to control forbidden activities and nuisance behavior, they are also taught interdependence and cooperation. Adults seem to enjoy horseplay and noisy dispute. Semihumorous "sex wars" in which men and women line up for a tug-of-war between the sexes serve as tension dissipaters—the tugs-of-war break up with much laughter. They are also an indication of the companionable equality between women and men. Most groups have a "clown," one person whose antics also help keep conflicts from getting out of hand. For all the squabbling, disagreements rarely get serious.

The contrast between the forest as womb and the love of the silences of the forest, on the one hand, and, on the other hand, the frequency of arguing and the use of joking and ridicule to keep it under control, is an interesting one. The Mbuti themselves value "letting it all hang out" (in modern parlance), not letting conflicts fester. There seems to be a nature-based social equilibrium here, based on a combination of listening, singing, dancing, and squabbling that is not easy for Westerners to understand.

The Mbuti, like the Inuit, have faced a modernizing national government that is destroying their environment and requiring adaptation to the limit of their capability. Worse, their forest home is being overrun by soldiers and guerrillas. Nevertheless, the Mbuti "we" is an inclusive *we*. This suggests potential for some degree of long-term survivability as they link with other rainforest peoples in the new transnational indigenous peoples networks, but the destruction of their lifeways as a by-product of widespread civil wars in the Great Lakes region of Africa is a very serious threat.[10]

### The Zuni

The Zuni live in the arid mountain canyon country of western New Mexico in the United States, many of them on a Zuni Indian reservation. A matrilineal society noted for its peaceful lifeways, its arts and crafts, and its antipathy to overt violence, the Zuni are well known through the writings of Ruth Benedict.[11] As with the Mbuti, the love of harmony is based on a sense of oneness with nature and a sense of place, yet that love of harmony does not preclude habits of gossip and quarreling.

The war gods that once ensured tribal survival in a period of warfare are now thought to be channeling their sacred energy into the peaceful well-being of the Zuni. Earlier ingroup-outgroup attitudes that kept the warfare going are no longer salient. The culture devalues authority, leadership, and individual success. No one wants to stand out. There are rituals for sharing, for healing, for conflict resolution, which help children to learn appropriate group behavior. Problem-solving skills are highly developed but without any counterpoint of individualism. There is continued skill transmission of the remarkable environmental knowledge that enabled a rich Zuni culture to develop in a very arid environment, including traditional agriculture and irrigation practices that are only now coming to be understood by Westerners as representing a very sophisticated technology.

Children, after a very permissive nurturant infancy, are disciplined by masked demons who make an appearance to scold them for fighting. Sudden withdrawals of goodies by adults prepare children for social obedience and nonaggressive behavior. Zuni youth therefore do not respond well to the incitements to individual achievement and competition in use by Anglo teachers in Zuni schools, although group performance levels are high. The economic, social, and political influence the Zuni have been exposed to in the past half century have heavily stressed the Zuni value system and have increased local conflict levels. However, the traditional Zuni skills of cooperation are reasserting themselves in very interesting tribal developments, including the launching of a comprehensive Sustainable Development Plan built on a combination of traditional knowledge of the desert environment and new scientific knowledge, which it is hoped will initiate a renaissance of the Zuni way of life.[12]

### The Arapesh

The mountain-dwelling Arapesh are one of the many tribes living in the highly diverse archipelago of New Guinea, an area divided by successive colonial occupations and now consisting of independent Papua New Guinea and an Indonesian-claimed province, West Irian. Much has changed since Margaret Mead's study of them in 1930,[13] so it should be noted that it is the 1930s Arapesh being described here. These people had in common with the North American Zuni a distaste for standing out, a preference for conformity, and a rejection of violence in the community. This rejection, however, was accompanied by actual hostility towards outsiders, and little emphasis on dealing with conflicts in a problem-solving way.

Arapesh children grow up experiencing cooperation as the key mode of life. All tasks are group tasks. Any one household will plant many yam gardens, each with a different group of households. (We now know that this represents a very sophisticated adaptation to a region with great diversity in soil quality and many microclimates at different altitudes in a bewildering variety of microecosystems. Spreading the risk of poor crop yields over many garden plots planted in different locations at different times during the year ensures that there will be some food at all times.)

For the children, every person in the village is thought of as a relative. Everyone is to be trusted, shared with, loved—children are lent about in a world filled with parents. Children are taught to express anger without hurting anyone and are never allowed to hit a person. This means that conflict is not addressed. The only need for leadership is for ceremonial feasts. The person chosen to be a feast giver (someone already recognized as having regrettable but useful aggressive tendencies) gets special training for his role by the community and has a feast-exchanger partner in a neighboring clan. This is the one accepted competitive relationship, and competition between feast givers from different clans can be fierce and aggressive. The feast giver does not, however, enjoy his role (at least is not supposed to) and is allowed to retire into gentleness when his oldest son reaches puberty. Although feast givers are generally men, there is a minimum of sex-role differentiation or dominance patterns. There are, however, certain culturally allocated specializations. Color painting, for example, is done only by men.

The major negative factor in the society is fear of sorcery, which is thought to come from outside enemies who have somehow gotten hold of an individual's personal "dirt." Even nature-caused crop failures are thought of as sorcery-induced. There are no gradations in social relations—only friends (insiders) and enemies (outsiders). The Arapesh, thus left without any patterns for incorporating the other, the different, the stranger, into their lives, are very vulnerable in the turbulent struggles between tribes, against present and former colonial authorities, and against powerful mining companies destroying mountain environments through open-pit copper and gold mining.

In the four peace-valuing societies we have looked at so far, we have seen a pattern of bottom-line nurturance and sharing behavior experienced from childhood. Sex-role differentiation has been minimal. However, there has been considerable variation in the ways conflict is managed, from avoidance and suppression, as among the Zuni and Arapesh, to acknowledgment of and socialization for managing conflict, was with the Inuit and Mbuti. But all the societies, at the times their behavior was recorded, were living in relative isolation from the urban and industrial centers of their respective countries. Now we turn to two cultures located within politically modernized states; the rural Irish of Northern Ireland and the Anabaptist cultures of the historic peace churches in the United States, both rural and urban.

### The Rural Northern Irish

Some of the rural communities of Ulster exemplify the possibility of nonviolence emerging from violence. The extremes of physical aggression experienced in urban areas are rejected by both contending parties—Catholic and Protestant—in some rural areas. In the communities described in Bonta's collection of studies, the Protestants have abandoned their former "superior" socioeconomic statues for a more egalitarian stance *vis-à-vis* the Catholics, and communities of both faiths work very hard at developing many joint activities.[14] They deliberately form nonsectarian groups, so as to prevent the religious polarization prevalent elsewhere in Ulster. They have very self-consciously chosen bridge building across cultural and religious differences. Joint activities for children and youth as well as adults are carefully planned. Hostile behavior is quickly dealt with in the interests of community harmony. Social, economic, and cultural functions that involve cooperation of Catholic and Protestant farmers and business people are given high priority, and people strongly value good-neighborly relations. When violence does occur, it is blamed on outsiders. While locally inclusive in their peacebuilding, they are threatened and vulnerable in the face of the larger-scale violence taking place in the region. The success of current negotiations in the 1990s between the two parts of Ireland and Britain may depend on the extent to which other areas are willing to accept peaceful interfaith communities as role models for relations on a larger scale.

### The Anabaptist/Historic Peace Church Communities

Anabaptism has its roots in fifteenth- and sixteenth-century movements—partly originating in the Swiss Alps—to defy all outward authority (including infant baptism, which forcibly incorporated each newborn into the local religious power structure). These movements, described in chapter 3, produced a type of early-Christian pacifism as they spread through Europe. In the seventeenth century (and later), many of these Anabaptists migrated to the Americas in search of religious freedom and freedom from military service. The three main communities presently active in the Americas, known as the historic peace churches, are the Brethren, the Mennonites, and the Quakers. Other smaller communities include the Amish, the Doukhobors, the Moravians, and the Hutterites. We will focus here on the three major Anabaptist communities. Traditionally abstaining from political action because of their rejection of military service[15] they have nevertheless become increasingly involved in various types of pubic activity to remove social and economic injustice and to bring and end to war as an instrument of state policy. In the Second World War, the three faith communities in the United States cooperated to administer Civilian Public Service Camps for their own young men and other conscientious objectors as an alternative to military service.

All three communities hold to the testimonies of simplicity, gender and racial equality, and personal and social nonviolence, yet find themselves an increasingly urban and middle-class that stands in contrast to the communities' more rural origins. Their challenge is not only to develop strategies for living their witness; increasingly, in the twentieth century, they have sought to find ways to work for their vision of a "peaceable kingdom" on earth and to rear their children to carry on efforts for social transformation of an increasingly violent larger society.[16]

The three faiths differ in degrees of hierarchical authority, with the Quakers as the most egalitarian, having no "hireling shepherds" (as ministers are traditionally referred to among Quakers).[17] All three faiths stress democratic participation of all members, including women, and decision making at the local level. Quakers, however, in the absence of authority figures, developed a special consensus approach to decision making based on the "sense of meeting," as members sought divine guidance on what was to be done in the face of conflicting views of participating individuals. The refusal to use voting procedures and majority rule meant that decisions could not be taken until either all members reached agreement or dissenters were willing to "stand aside."[18] What is particularly interesting about the consensus method is that it respects the presence of conflict and allows for the full airing of differences. It also depends on a disciplined spiritual maturity of members of the community, a common acceptance of collective inward illumination of the group, and great skill in intellectual discernment and interpersonal and intergroup communication. This is a tall order for any group, and therefore great importance is given to the religious education of the children of a Meeting. They must be prepared not only to carry on the consensus process within their Meeting but also to carry Friends' testimonies into the larger society in an active pursuit of social and economic justice and peace. Although consensus is specifically Quaker, the educational practices described here are also common among Mennonites and Brethrens.

Anabaptist testimonies begin in the home. While individual families certainly fall short of the ideal, spouse relations (based on a full and equal partnership) and parenting are taken seriously by both parents. An important part of parenting is the cultivation of the divine seed in each child, so times of silent worship in the home, as well as discussion and reading, help prepare children for their responsibilities. Explicit training in nonviolent responses to conflict and alternative ways of dealing with conflict are emphasized. Conflict suppression is not encouraged. Rather, children are urged to "work things out." All this is in the context of an affectionate family life and a nurturant local Meeting. "The chief enjoyment of Friends is connubial bliss," wrote an eighteenth-century observer of Quakers, and although divorce takes its toll in every religious community today, Anabaptist families on the whole have an enjoyable family life. On the other hand, Anabaptist adults—and children too—also carry a certain load of guilt. Given their acceptance of responsibility for peace and justice in the world but the reality of the huge gap between what any individual or family or Meeting can do and what is needed, guilt is inevitable. A healthy family and a healthy Meeting keep a sense of humor about this. Laughter is an important safety valve. So are imagination and skill in organizing useful local service projects that can absorb individual energies creatively.

An important institution in the local communities of all three faith groups is the Sunday School (by Quakers called the First Day School), where adults of the congregation do their best to supplement the work of the member families by preparing children and young people spiritually, intellectually, and in terms of social skills, specifically for peacemaking. Community history and the stories of Quaker, Mennonite, and Brethren heroes and heroines are an important part of this education.

While the forms of worship of the three faith communities are different, all three have a strong emphasis on family life, individual spiritual development, and training for social service and peacebuilding. All three have developed remarkable service bodies that do peacebuilding around the world, and Brethren and Mennonites are particularly strong in nonviolence training for their youth in preparation for giving a year or more of service in their own country or abroad. The Children's Creative Response to Conflict Program, now used in elementary and middle schools in a number of countries, was first developed by Quakers to help children deal with conflict.[19] A similar program, Alternatives to Violence, was developed to prepare prisoners for life after prison. Each faith supports outstanding schools and colleges that educate young people who seek an active and participatory learning experience.

Because all three Anabaptist communities are committed to the work of social transformation towards peace and justice for all people, "enemy" concepts are not used nor is the language of fighting. There can be no enemies, only strangers with whom a relationship needs to be developed. Peacemaking is seen as building bridges across differences, finding solutions to the problems of all disputants in ways that injure none, and reframing disputes so common interests can be discovered.

The world sometimes overwhelms the sense of faith-based identity, and callings can weaken. Also, individuals can feel hopelessly compromised by the world they are trying to change. To deal with these problems, the three historic peace churches formed the coalition "New Call to Peacemaking" several decades ago in order to strengthen each other's resolve to carry on

peacemaking activities. Currently they jointly support the training and deployment of unarmed peace teams in situations of serious violence in Africa,
Central and Latin America, and the Middle East.

## Peace Behaviors that Can Be Found in Any Society

Microsocieties such as we have been examining, which take peace and nonviolence as primary organizing values of their lifeways, are rare in the closing
years of the twentieth century. Most of humanity lives in societies marked by
increasingly high densities of weaponry, from handguns to bombs to the terrors of chemical and biological weapons. But underneath the layers of violence each society, without exception, has its peace behaviors, precious
resources that can be available to help bring about new and gentler forms of
governance locally and on a larger scale in the next century.

Where do we find these behaviors, these peace culture resources? In the
recurring cycles, rhythms, and rituals of human celebration, with its feasting,
singing, dancing, and sharing of gifts. In the reproductive cycles of human
partnering, of birthing, of family maintenance as the years go by, and the
completion of dying—in the cycles that bind people together across kin
groups. In the succession of woundings and healings of human bodies as they
move through life's dangers in those cycles. In the labor to produce sustenance from the earth. In the daily round of trade, the barter and exchange of
goods and services. And, perhaps most wonderful of all, in human play—the
playing of games, the play of artistic creation, the play of the mind in the pursuit of knowledge. Let us explore each in turn.

### Partnering and Reproduction

The familial household is the most adaptive of human institutions, expanding and contracting through history according to changing social conditions from individual units consisting of a single person or a couple to the
200-person multifamily commune, the *frèrèche* or *zadruga* common in parts
of medieval Europe, or the monastic households of monks or nuns. Different
social patterns develop in different times and places. While the human capacity to love is not necessarily the basis for partnering, that capacity to love
mellows many a marital companionship over time, whatever the nature of
the original marriage arrangements. The newborn infant depends on that capacity to love for survival; for the little ones that do survive, love can multiply
as mothers and infants interact. Love can multiply as fathers and infants in-

teract too, and it is noteworthy that in all the peaceful cultures described earlier in this chapter, fathers played an active role in parenting the young. Infants and children have a gentling effect on adults everywhere, as the Hass
photographs show, but this gentling effect can be enhanced or reduced by
childrearing customs. There are societies where fathers ignore children until
they reach the age of six or so, and then suddenly reach in to remove little
boys from their all-women's world and put them in an all-men's world, to be
raised to be fierce and manly. The attention that fathers give to their sons
under these conditions hardly has a gentling effect on either generation.

How some societies become harsh and punitive, or withdrawn and fearful,
rather than peaceful and trusting is beyond the scope of this chapter. However, one significant step toward a gentling society is the creation of social
arrangements that provide for both parents to spend more time with infants
and small children. Another is giving skill training in handling interpersonal
conflicts, again as we have seen in the societies already examined. Such training has a multiplier effect on peaceableness in a society, since the interpersonal skills learned in families are then used in the community as well. The
limits to the skills of diplomacy and negotiation exercised at the intergroup
and international levels are set by each society in the family arena where they
are first learned.[20]

### Production and Sustenance

In societies where nature is both parent and teacher, where a close attunement to the environment patterns the ways of obtaining food and other resources, the skills of listening to nature and the skills of listening to fellow
humans are closely related. Because nature is unpredictable, human interdependence and resource sharing means survival in times of drought, flood, or
earthquake. Finding ways to make that interdependence a visible reality in
complex societies where rich and poor do not interact, and finding ways to listen to the natural environment on city streets, is a challenge for the inhabitants of industrialized states—and a challenge that peace activists accept.
They are constantly seeking ways to dramatize the reality of human interdependence for the basic necessities of life.[21]

### Celebration and Ritual

Celebrations are the play life of a society, occasions for embodying the experienced beauty of both inner and outer lifeworlds in song, dance, poetry,
and the creation of symbolic imagery. They are also occasions for reaffirma-

tion of identity and social values.[22] At their best, feasting and gift giving emphasize sharing and reciprocity, a sense of the community as one family. When sharing and gift giving have a character of spontaneity and exuberance, and singing and dancing are freely and widely participated in, then celebration is a powerful reinforcement of peaceful and caring community relations. It becomes a time of letting go of grudges, of reconciliation among persons whose relations may have become strained. To the extent that there is a clearly defined articulated basis for the celebration, patterned in ritual, it also becomes a reconnection with creation itself, a reminder of the oneness of the cosmos and all living things. It becomes a time for the making of vows to undertake difficult tasks to serve the community. Celebrations mark the rites of passage from birthing to childhood to puberty to adulthood. They mark wounding and healing, and they mark dying. They also mark the great historical moments of the remembered past, and the great traumas.

The quality of the peace culture in any given society can be found in its art forms. The visual, the kinetic, and the audial arts are interpenetrating expressions of the joys, sorrows, and spiritual intuitions of humans as they participate in the lifeworlds of the planet and beyond. Art forms that enhance the capacity of the human senses for experiencing and relating to those lifeworlds are part of the very core of a society's peace culture. Art forms that constrict the capacity to relate to those lifeworlds reflect, on the other hand, a culture of violence.

In short, when celebrations lose their playfulness, when art forms constrict the capacity for relationship, when gift giving becomes carefully calibrated exchange, when performing becomes competitive, then they lose their character of replenishing the human spirit and are a poor source for general peaceableness.

The role of religious belief and practices in building the habits of peace in daily life has already been discussed. When those religious rituals that emphasize a loving, forgiving God and loving and forgiving relations among humans are given primacy, when women and men are seen as partners with equal voices in a community of faith that seeks social and economic justice for all people, and children learn nonviolence, then religious practices and rituals will contribute to peace. Yet most contemporary societies have a diversity of religious communities, including some that emphasize holy war and strong exercise of patriarchal authority. It can certainly not be said that all religious groups will be oriented towards peacemaking.

## Trade and Exchange

The words "nurturance" and "caring" have been used a great deal in this chapter. It must be recognized, however, that nurturance and caring do not have to characterize all social interactions in order for them to be regarded as contributing to social peace. The establishment of trade relations with neighboring and more distant social groups contributes to the mutual well-being of participants when each has something the other wants—even in the absence of other elaborating behaviors (as in the famous anthropological examples of silent trade). What is necessary is that each party see the exchange as fair and reasonable, as mutually beneficial. In fact, much gift giving is actually exchange in this sense, as Mauss makes clear.[23] Sahlins points out that the practice of trade became a creative alternative to simply raiding one's neighbors—a habit that, unfortunately, can easily lead to more or less continual warfare.[24] By the same token, trade has a quality of fragility about it—if either party is dissatisfied, there is always the possibility of reverting to war. Ceremonial gift giving lies at a point somewhere between the trade that is a substitute for war and more spontaneous sharing.

The line between ceremonial gift giving, which is a periodic redistribution of wealth that keeps a certain balance over time of giving and receiving, and gifts given more spontaneously and without mental calculation about future benefits is impossible to draw, and the effort probably makes no sense. A response of spontaneous gratitude on the part of the recipient of a gift may also have incalculable value and be considered in itself a return "gift." The fact that we speak of "exchanging gifts" at certain holiday seasons suggests that, for the most part, some degree of exchange is assumed in gift giving. In fact it is worth noting that marketplaces often have an air of festivity about them even when all transactions are apparently commercial. What actually happens in many situations involving human exchanges, whether of service or goods, is that a reciprocity multiplier effect is at work.[25] Each person throws in a little extra for "good measure," whether the extra quarter-ounce of meat on the butcher's scale or a warm smile to the clerk at the checkout counter. It is the reciprocity multiplier effect that ensures that trade will further continuing goodwill among the parties involved and helps them deal resourcefully with conflicts when they do arise.

## Play of the Imagination

Celebrations have been referred to as society at play. But play by its very nature performs a serious creative function for each community, as Huizinga has pointed out.[26] Taking place outside the realm of everyday life, play nevertheless creates boundaries, rules, and roles ("let's play house—you be the daddy and I'll be the mommy"), and structures spaces within which children can create their own realities in fantasy. Mary Reilly emphasizes the importance of play in learning nonviolence and self-control.[27] Watching infant monkeys at play, she comments on "the conversion of aggression into social complexity" as the monkeys learn control over their movements in the course of rough-and-tumble activity. When children's rough-and-tumble play dissolves into tears because a child is hurt, the same learning can take place.

The fact that play space is also space in which children can practice grown-up activities does not take away from the fact that play is done *for its own sake,* "for fun." This makes "playing" important for adults, who tend to be excessively tense and serious about many of their activities. Competitive sports and spectator games may work against the spontaneity of play, for both players and watchers, but the rudiments of play survive as the popularity of spectator sports suggests. Yet there are other, less obvious forms of play. Some are highly developed: the mind at play in science; "the muse" at play creating poetry, music, painting, sculpture; the body at play in song, dance, and drama. Play goes on at the grassroots level in the folk culture of each society, and it goes on among the elites as well, but the play of each tends to take separate forms in terms of style, language, and content. It is time to rediscover all the different forms of play, including artistic and scientific play, and find ways to release them into a shared celebration of play in public spaces. We cannot ignore that some art, and some sports, have become so violent that they have lost their character of play. The recovery of play as fun, a basic heritage of every society, is the best answer to that violence.

One way to think about play is that it allows the imagination to fantasize alternatives to everyday reality. These alternatives maybe thought of as images of possible futures. A society that encourages the play of the mind encourages the exploration of other and better ways of ordering life ways. We have already mentioned Polak, the Dutch historian who discovered through his macrohistorical studies that societies tended to be empowered by positive images of the future. The visions themselves could act as magnets, drawing forth behaviors that could bring the envisioned future into being.[28] Polak wrote *The Image of the Future* in 1950 for a war-paralyzed Europe, as a call to begin imaging how things could be, to create visions that could inspire actions. A half century later we have once more reached a state of social despair, in countries of both the North and the South. What are the possibilities for the twenty-first century? The task of shifting the cultural balance away from violence and toward nonviolence is a challenge for all—whatever one's walk of life, one's age, one's gender, wherever one lives on the planet we call home. The range of human activity that can be retuned to contribute to peace building is vast. The only limitation on that retuning is the willingness to liberate our own imaginations.

5

# Breaking New Ground
## Feminist Peacemaking

THE STEREOTYPICAL VIEW of peace as women's business and, therefore, not important in real-life public affairs hides from view the extraordinary creativity women have shown through time in creating not only public spaces for peaceful interaction in the midst of violence but also new ways of thinking and acting. Precisely because women are marginal to public decision making in the existing social order, they are freer to develop new approaches. They have few vested interests to protect. These peacebuilding activities of women have been touched on in chapters 3 and 4, but now we will examine the specifics of that creativity more closely.

The modern women's movements have their roots in nineteenth-century industrialization. This produced a new middle class of educated, though still dependent, women whose leisure enabled them to join elite women in an awakening to the victimage of the poor around them and the violence associated with that victimage. It did not take them long to realize that dangerous working conditions, bad housing, low wages, low skills, and poor health and the anodyne of alcohol were creating a vicious cycle of poverty for urban and rural poor, and that war was the overriding destroyer of the quality of life for all. As women began spending time in poverty-stricken neighborhoods, they came to realize the peculiar entrapment of their poorer sisters, how unevenly the burdens of poverty fell on them. After some decades of activity among the urban poor, middle-class women finally realized that they too were help-less—they could not act independently against economic and social injustice and war because they had no civil status, no decision-making power. The sense of sisterhood that emerged from this realization, though genuine, was

An earlier version of this paper appeared as "Feminist Inventions in the Art of Peace-making," *Peace and Change* 20, no. 4 (Oct. 1995): 408–38.

limited in scope, and even today it has yet to transcend the barriers of race, class, and culture.

The rise of the suffrage movement in the One-Third World of the North meant for many women the narrowing of the broader focus on social ills to the wrongs suffered by women. This left standing in the wings, so to speak, the women reformers who had been galvanized by the evil effects of war, colonialism, and unbridled capitalism on the world as a whole. Children came to be seen as part of the social burden unfairly borne by women rather than as small human beings to be liberated from the double trap of patriarchal violence and maternal exhaustion.

What I wish to emphasize here, however, is that social or humanist feminism,[1] with its commitment to a more holistic view of social pathologies, preceded the development of the narrower equity feminism. Since the roots of social feminism were secure in a more transcontinental soil, that broader feminism did not fade away. Social feminists were busy in the last decades of the nineteenth century helping to invent a new social form within, yet beyond, their traditional sphere of maintaining the civil society: the nongovernmental organization (NGO). The new phenomenon of transboundary networks of citizens' groups concerned with human welfare on a planetary scale had already given rise to a number of women's transnational groups in the 1880s and the 1890s. The World Young Women's Christian Association (WYWCA), the World Women's Christian Temperance Union (WWCTU), the International Council of Nurses, and the International Council of Women were already formed and at work in Asia, Africa, and the Americas, as well as Europe, before the twentieth century. Their members worked for the education and welfare of women and children as part of a larger effort to bring an end to arms races and establish conditions conducive to the creation of a peaceful and just international order.

Each decade brought new internationally oriented groups into existence. The World War I gathering at The Hague of activists and professional women from the countries then at war, resulting in the formation of the Women's International League for Peace and Freedom (WILPF), has been mentioned in chapter 3.[2] By the 1930s farm women, midwives, doctors, lawyers, and a number of other interest groups had formed NGOs, and their numbers have continued to expand through the twentieth century.

It is this inventiveness of women in the sphere of the civil society that is our focus here. The constraining effects on women of their relegation to the household and the private spaces of society have been overstated. What tends to be ignored is the historical reality that women's work of feeding, rearing, and healing humans—building and rebuilding communities under conditions of constant change, including war, environmental catastrophe, plague, and continual push-pull migrations—has produced resources and skills within women's cultures that have been critical not only to human survival but to human *development*. My argument here is not an essentialist one, that women are biologically predisposed to nurturance and peacemaking. It is, rather, that women's knowledge and experience worlds have equipped them to function creatively as problem solvers and peacemakers in ways that men have not been equipped by their knowledge and experience worlds. This, obviously, can change. More sharing of experience worlds between women and men will be an important next step in human development.

Women's understanding of the social systems in which they live has been profound and often pathbreaking. A discussion of the many contributions women scientists and futurists have made to peace culture through that understanding of social systems—contributions of women such as Danish economist Ester Boserup, Italian futurist Eleanora Masini, American environmental systems modeler Donella Meadows, Anglo-American economist Hazel Henderson, Kenyan biologist Wangari Maathai, Indian physicist Vandana Shiva—would take a chapter in itself. For this, readers are referred to my broader study of feminist inventions in peacemaking.[3] However, two women who have been my own mentors must be included here, particularly because they have been of great importance to the women's peace movement: Margaret Mead and Alva Myrdal.

Margaret Mead cared deeply about the state of the world as a whole, in all its diversity. Her *Cooperation and Competition among Primitive Peoples* was a very early contribution to the new field of peace research; and after World War II, she worked hard to convince her colleagues to do more work on the dynamics of cooperation and peacefulness.[4] She also encouraged early curriculum developments in peace education for elementary and secondary schools.

Mead also played a special role in early initiatives for what became the Women's Decades by vigorously speaking on behalf of an early 1960s "housewives project" that became International Cooperation Year in 1965. The Year was originally conceived as a project of women visiting women around the world to see the different ways in which basic tasks of caring for families and communities were carried out. This was a period of transitional consciousness-raising for women, and Mead encouraged them to think of themselves as

the "world's housekeepers"—a big step in those days. International Cooperation Year was the precursor of International Women's Year and all that has followed, and Mead's global vision enabled her to be one of the first to see the
possibilities in the housewives project. Because she herself lived in a web of
global interconnectedness, there is hardly a social movement of the
post–World War II decades that she did not personally touch. She was enthusiastically supportive—but also penetratingly critical when critical discernment was needed.

Alva Myrdal was also of Margaret Mead's generation. A Swedish family sociologist, child development specialist, and leading disarmament expert, she
understood social systems "from inside" as she struggled with the demanding
triple task of rearing three children while partnering a world-renowned economist (Gunnar Myrdal) and both researching and actually creating the kind
of local institutions and services that a society would need to produce peaceful citizens in a humane world. The unique contributions that both Mead
and Myrdal have made in their own autobiographical sharing of their experiences of weaving childrearing into professional life, supplemented by the
vivid accounts of that process shared with the world by their respective daughters,[5] make it possible for us to translate the concepts of transformative systems change into the dailiness of "growing up human."

Over time, Myrdal's systems analysis expanded in complexity from child,
family and nation[6] to the international realm of diplomacy, first as Sweden's
ambassador to India and then as its minister of disarmament.[7] Her analysis
grew ever more multidimensional without ever losing its organic character.
She kept finding new entry points for social change even as the world continued to become more dangerous. Her words in 1980 were, "Giving up is
not worthy of a human being." She founded new organizations right and
left, both governmental and nongovernmental. A particularly noteworthy
and enduring one was the Swedish International Peace Research Institute.
Her main hope for change, however, lay in civil society and nongovernmental institutions.

Mead and Myrdal are exemplars of the role of women in creating new understandings of the social systems in which they live in order to open up these
systems to transformative change. The role of feminist thinking in the field of
peace studies, for example, is of particular importance. Here the feminist
analysis of power as power *with*, or *empowerment*, rather than power *over*, provides the key to the transformational modeling of the postpatriarchal system
in which violence has no place.[8] At the same time, it points to a primary in-

tervention point in the patriarchal system for achieving system change: the daily practice of violence against women and children in the family. This violence stunts the growth of problem-solving and conflict resolution capability in every other part of society and increases male dependence on the very capacity for dominance that cripples men as human beings. Paradoxically, this dependency generates military forcing systems in modern states that drive societies helplessly to war out of sheer inability to engage in sustained problem-solving behavior.[9]

### The Invention of Global Sisterhood: Adventures in Networking

Over time, as the density of transnational women's networks increased and grassroots women began interacting with urban women, a movement sense of the "women's problematique" emerged with surprising speed.

Networking at the local level is, of course, the oldest tool of the human sisterhood, and the nineteenth- and twentieth-century development of women's NGOs brought that networking to the international level. However, a new phase in women's networking began with the establishment by the United Nations Economic and Social Council (ECOSOC) of the UN Committee on the Status of Women that eventually led to International Women's Year in 1975. Through the new, less formal and primarily nonhierarchical women-to-women contacts between continents fostered by International Cooperation Year in 1965, the realization grew that development policies imposed by the patriarchal structures of the United Nations and its member states were pushing the Two-Thirds World societies into unprecedented poverty and dependency. Information and action networks began proliferating, linked both to traditional women's groups at the village level and to the more formally structured NGOs, but with a life and purpose of their own. Five of these networks will be examined here, chosen because they are networks of networks. Two of them came into existence in relation to the 1975 International Women's Year Conference in Mexico City: ISIS, which prepared for the conference by holding an International Tribunal on Crimes Against Women in Brussels in 1974, and the International Women's Tribune Center, which came into being to facilitate communication among NGOs during the conference.

ISIS, founded by European women, had its first offices in Rome and Geneva, but soon moved to its present coordinating centers in Manila and Santiago.[10] It networks with over 50,000 individuals and organizations in 150 countries, from grassroots groups to policymakers. Its purpose is empowerment of women to shape their lives and their societies through networking, information, and skill sharing in every arena in which women need to work. In recent years, having noted poor health as one of women's major hazards, ISIS has developed strong regional women's health networks in the countries of the Two-Thirds World. Its main resource centers maintain libraries, bibliographies, and information on human resources and data bases. Up-to-date information is shared through monthly bulletins, the quarterly journal *Women in Action*, and a women's *Health Journal*; all are published in both Spanish and English. The center also offers hands-on assistance in networking and training in the use of new information and technologies. *Women Envision*, created to inform all constituencies about preparations for the 1995 Women's Forum in Beijing, provides comprehensive information about all other conferences and campaigns of potential interest to women.

The Women's Tribune Center, located across the street from the UN in New York, performs a similar function, with more emphasis on UN resources, activities, and special agendas affecting women, with how-to information on the utilization of NGO mechanisms to achieve specific goals.[11] It has the same commitment to grassroots and Two-Thirds World women as ISIS. It publishes the *Tribune, Women and Development Quarterly*, with analyses and case histories of women's development activities around the world. It also puts out special bulletins that are calls to action on specific issues, such as the successful campaign to place violence against women on the agenda of the 1993 UN World Conference on Human Rights. The Women's Tribune Center also publishes periodic conference calendars with information for local groups on how to get involved in decision-making sessions of importance to them. All these publications are brimming over with strategies for using United Nations and other gatherings to further women's issues. They are toolkits for undertaking projects in social and economic development: they give instructions in the use of new technologies and in the media development, and they also offer strategies for human rights and campaigns.

GROOTS (Grassroots Women Operating Together in Sisterhood) is more specifically directed to local grassroots organizations. It was formed during the third World Conference on Women in Nairobi, Kenya, in 1985. Appreciating the diversity of women and cultures in their forty-country network, they use workshops, forums, focus groups, community conversations, surveys, open letters, and questionnaires, so that women themselves identify their abilities, needs, and priorities. They exchange strategies across national and regional boundaries, publishing their own national and regional analyses. Non-hierarchical and bottom-up, GROOTS' international task force has representatives from nine world regions, north and south.[12] Another women's network that was formed to respond to the new level of activism represented by GROOTS was the Global Fund for Women, which came into being to help fund the new local activism of women, with a particular emphasis on the needs of African women.[13]

WEDO (Women's Environment and Development Organization) began organizing women's caucuses at United Nations conferences during the PrepComs for the UN Conference on Environment and Development in Rio in 1991. It works to make women more visible as participants, experts, and leaders in policymaking on international affairs and in formulating alternative, peaceful solutions to world problems. It continued the caucus process at the Cairo Population and Development Conference in 1994 and the World Summit on Social Development in 1995, building an ever-stronger global network of women and publishing a primer series on Understanding the Impact of the Global Economy on Women and the Environment.[14]

The fifth network, known as the Huairou Commission on Women and Habitat, was founded at the 1995 Women's Conference in Beijing and is itself a coalition of coalitions.[15] From its office at the United Nations, it coordinates information from seventy women's networks and information centers around the world, with twelve key networking NGOs serving as focal points. Its purpose is to empower women as activists and decision makers to create sustainable communities at the grassroots level, to be heard by governments, and to advise the United Nations and intergovernmental agencies on the development of peaceful, sustainable communities. The central participation of women in every aspect of community building, from local to global, is the guiding principle of this coalition of coalitions.

All the bulletins and newsletters published by ISIS, the Women's Tribune, GROOTS, WEDO, and the Huairou Commission are full of contact information. They contain names and addresses (and now, increasingly, fax and e-mail codes) and project summaries that enable women to know as never before what is going on in the international sisterhood. It is difficult to convey the excitement and sense of empowerment that comes from tapping into this information and activity flow, into this worldwide process of reflection, envisioning, analysis, and concrete action for change. It is almost like a new life-form, encapsulating everything that scholar-practitioner-activist women of the twentieth century have worked to achieve, in an actual systems transformation. What is brought together here is the best of new science and technology woven into social structures and relationships that model the feminist postpatriarchal world, complete with well-marked points for system change.

The link with peace, however, is more implicit than explicit. Nevertheless, side by side with this inventive networking, another set of explicitly peacebuilding inventions have come into being. We will turn now to selected examples from a large field of women who saw themselves as peacebuilders and were imaginative and adventurous in the way that they went about their peacebuilding work.

## Inventive Practitioners of Peacemaking

### Kamaladevi

Kamaladevi was extraordinary even among all the extraordinary women of the Gandhi movement in India. When I met her in the 1980s, she was a regal, distinguished public figure known and loved for her passionate lifelong advocacy of community development involving craftwork, the skills of community peacebuilding, and the participation of women in public life—all based on her youthful apprenticeship to Gandhi himself.[16] In her student days she joined a group that she herself built up into the *Seva Dal*, Gandhi's "Peace Army." She was a key organizer of the *Dal* in villages across India, especially its women's brigades in bright orange saris. She gained the experience for doing this by working with a group of forest-dwelling women doing Chipko (save-the-trees) action and message carrying in the early days of the Indian independence movement in the forests of Karnatka. The *Seva Dal*, forerunner of the *Shanti Sena* organized after Gandhi's death, never achieved the mobilization of the hundreds of thousands of 16- to 45-year olds envisaged when Kamaladevi took over the organizing, but there were *Dals* in villages from one end of India to the other. In theory, each member was to receive rigorous physical and psychological training for three kinds of tasks: (1) recruiting and leading *satyagraha*, nonviolent actions like the famous 1939 salt march to the sea; (2) doing community development; and (3) stepping into the middle of riots and calming people down.

Although few *Dals* actually had intensive training, the volunteer community groups formed under that name involved energetic community activists, many of them women, who were committed to the nonviolent independence movement. The remarkable self-discipline shown by the villagers in the large-scale *satyagraha* actions was to a considerable degree due to village-level leadership of these *Dals*. One of Kamaladevi's tasks was to mobilize community support for these *Dals* so that they always had food and clothing as needed when engaged in full-time action. Otherwise, every *Dal* member was self-supporting. Although massive *Dal* actions were noticed internationally only in the 1930s, *Dal*-type activity had already begun in 1914. There had been years of local experience before the great salt march.

Kamaladevi could think in terms of complex wholes and never miss a detail. Many women and men were involved in putting together this amazing and little-known nonviolent organization of community social change agents, but it was Kamaladevi's organizational skill, imagination, and daring that made it work. Of upper-class background, through her life she moved easily among the very poor and the very rich, among the powerless and the powerful, in and out of prison. She was at home everywhere, always keeping to a disciplined, deeply spiritual personal simplicity. As far as I know, there has been no organizational movement comparable in scale to the *Seva Dal* since the *Dal* itself was banned by the British in 1942. After independence, Kamaladevi herself turned to the massive task of resettling refugees from Pakistan after partition, to mediating communal violence, to developing craft centers at the village level to counter excessive governmental emphasis on industrialization (she refused to serve in the government when asked), and always to increasing educational opportunities for women and improving their civic status.

## Marjorie Sykes

An Englishwomen from a Yorkshire coal-mining village who settled in Gandhi's Ashram at Sevagram, Marjorie Sykes had already been thoroughly trained in *sarvodaya* and *satyagraha* when in 1957 Vinoba Bhave decided to revive Gandhi's dream of a *Shanti Sena*, a true nonviolent peace army.[17] To bring it into being, he appointed an all-women's committee with Marjorie at its head to create the organization and a pattern for training and service. Again, the vision was, as in the case of the *Dal*, to mobilize hundreds of thousands of volunteers, of Sainiks. As the *Shanti Sena* developed, Marjorie found the scale too ambitious and found that training young people in large numbers rendered the training itself inadequate. So she established an alternative model of small village centers for training small groups and linking the training with doing agricultural work locally. At her own center in Kotagiri, she would take eight or nine people at a time for one month's intensive training in nonviolence to do reconciliation work. That model has been carried over into the training program she came to the United States to develop for the Peace Brigades International, the Western successor to the Indian *Shanti Sena*. Her skills as a mediator and as a practitioner of nonviolence who also worked with the soil led to a three-year stint of working with tribal peoples on India's northeast frontier with China. She also responded to many calls for help in training for the practice of nonviolent conflict resolution in Asia. In its way, Marjorie Sykes's insistence on developing the *Shanti Sena* in small groups and keeping to small-scale, in-depth projects has been as important a contribution in its time as Kamaladevi's India-wide organization of *Dal* was in the earlier years of the independence struggle. Each met a pressing social need, and each reflected the social vision and the inventiveness of its shaper.

### Muriel Lester

Muriel Lester left her upper-class English home as a young girl to live a life of voluntary poverty, first in the Bow District of London's East End.[18] Here she founded Kingsley Hall, a settlement house as unique for England as Jane Addams's Hull House was for the United States. In the mid-twenties, she joined Gandhi in India. Then, when another Englishwoman, Maude Royden, and two male colleagues announced the formation of a Peace Army to be put at the disposal of the League of Nations to stand between the armies of China and Japan in Manchuria, Muriel became a traveling representative of the Peace Army, negotiating with heads of state as easily and naturally as she sat and worked with the poorest village women of India and London. The Peace Army never grew beyond eight hundred recruits, training never got properly organized, and the League of Nations never accepted its offer of interpositioning in Manchuria. However, the concept stayed alive, and Muriel Lester remained the most visible of a group of Peace Army mediators who traveled back and forth between Japan and China, and then around the Middle East throughout the 1930s.

Muriel's unique brand of people's diplomacy gained a hearing with high government officials wherever she went. Her shuttle diplomacy between India and Britain as Gandhi's ambassador on behalf of Indian independence has few parallels in contemporary international relations. From 1934 her official title was Traveling Ambassador for the International Fellowship of Reconciliation; in that role she left no continent, no conflict untouched. The peace movement has never had, before or since, a people's diplomat so welcome in the world's foreign ministries, so attentively listened to, and with such a reserve of energy for constant travel. Unfortunately, her skills could not prevent World War II nor keep her out of prison when her Latin American peace mission ran afoul of key European interests. But neither did her high-level diplomacy distract her from her identification with the poor, with racial and ethnic minorities, and with aboriginal peoples, nor keep her from spending "equal time" among these peoples in their own settings in every country she visited. When I met Muriel Lester in 1947, she was sixty-two, a radiant, queenly presence but at the same time as simple and unaffected as any of the eager young peace activists she was meeting with that summer's day in Syracuse, New York.

Of all the creative peacebuilders I might have described, I chose three who worked in one way or another with the concept of a peace army. This concept remains alive and well today—and also as elusive and difficult to operationalize as ever and as needful of women's inventiveness. We will return to the peace army theme in the next section on group peacebuilding inventions.

## Peacebuilding Inventions of the Women's Peace Movement

Again, I will choose a few examples from a great abundance of peace movement inventions, to give the flavor, range, and variety of women's inventiveness.

### The Peace Education Movement

Is peace education an invention? For a secularized, modernized world, it is, and contemporary peace education is, to a significant degree, the product of the work of many different women's groups—teachers, social workers, and peace activists—who worked steadily from the 1840s to the founding of UNESCO in 1945.[19] What were they doing? Developing the kind of education that would be needed for a demilitarized world in which disputes would be settled peacefully. Their century of work in curriculum development; in the study of child development from the perspective of how children can learn to be peaceful with one another; in starting international schools, training teachers, and developing a vision of what a peaceful international community could look like—in all this, women helped to lay the groundwork for the establishment of UNESCO. Marie Montessori of Italy was one of that legion of peace educators whose name stands out because of the theory and practice of peace education she developed in the 1930s. Starting with the individual child and focusing on the release of the unique capabilities of each child into concrete activity of a peacebuilding nature, the Montessori approach has become the basis for a whole system of education. Not only is it practiced in contemporary Montessori schools, but this approach has also helped to shape the present field of peace education.[20]

It was the combination of vision, theory, and practice that brought peace educators into a leadership role within the new discipline of peace research that developed in the 1960s. It was peace educators who insisted that peace research should not only undertake general systems analysis of intergovernmental relations but also conceptualize the interrelationships of peace, security, economic and social development, environmental issues, human rights, and the participation of women and minorities as the central problematique of human learning. The record of the effects of this emphasis on peace research itself can be seen by reading through the issues of the International Peace Research newsletter from 1965 to the present.[21]

### Peace on the March, Peace on Strike, Peace Journeys

Women have walked, sailed, ridden horseback, and otherwise traveled in public spaces for peace since the beginning of the colonial era, but the peace walks and marches of the post–World War II era had a special flavor and flair.

A new level of women's activity was reached in 1961 with the Women Strike for Peace movement, which began in North America and quickly spread to Europe.[22] The concept of the strike—of noncompliance with the basic duties of homemaking as a way of protesting nuclear testing and preparations for war—immediately exploded into a very active women's invasion of public spaces, from court houses to parliaments, and made the idea of a *women's agenda*, based on women's understandings of the meanings of security, a new force in politics. This not only brought a new style into political discussion that included humor, laughter, and flowers, it brought a new wave of women candidates for public office, from local to national, into the public arena, a wave that has continued unabated into the 1990s. This movement has taken place in all regions, though unevenly in Eastern Europe, where women face a unique set of regime transition problems.

Already during the meetings of the Disarmament Commission headed by Ambassador Alva Myrdal in Geneva in the 1960s, women's groups were visibly present, insisting on audiences with ambassadors and ministers of foreign affairs and heads of state. Women for Meaningful Summits, a group based in New York, became a logical extension of this earlier activity, as did other evolving women's networks. Women's Action for Nuclear Disarmament (WAND), for example, was founded by Dr. Helen Caldicott in the early 1980s to empower women to act politically, to reduce militarism and violence, and to redirect military resources toward human and environmental needs. In the 1990s, WAND became Women's Action for New Directions, with a strong legislators' lobby to dramatize in inventive ways—both to state legislatures and the national Congress—the need for drastic change in national security policy.[23] Over time, women's voices have become steadily more articulate and more experienced in what it takes to affect summit diplomacy.

The group with the longest experience in all these types of activity, the Women's International League for Peace and Freedom, carried out a particularly dramatic public exercise when it undertook, at the initiative of the Swedish Section of the WILPF and with cooperation of many other groups, the Great Peace Journey.[24] Between 1985 and 1988 internationally composed delegations traveled first by bus to twenty-five countries in Europe, and then to countries of the Pacific, South and East Asia, the Americas, and large parts of Africa and the Middle East—visiting ninety states in all. In each country, the delegation put five questions to heads of state and senior officials in foreign ministries regarding national defense policy and willingness to use peaceful means of dispute settlement, subsequently reporting the responses to the secretary general of the United Nations and to the representatives of each national mission at the United Nations. The grand finale, a global popular summit at the United Nations in 1988, consolidated four years of dialogue with governments and gave new saliency to the United Nations as a place where the peoples of the world could face a general assembly of their governments seeking clearer articulation of new dispute settlement practices.

### Peace Colonies

In contrast to the adventurous journey across continents stands another type of invention: encampments, guardian sites, and zones of peace. Women established encampments at munitions storage and testing sites at Greenham Common, England; Seneca Falls, New York; Frauenfeld, Switzerland; Cosimo, Sicily; Kita Fuji, Japan; Neve Shalom, Israel—and elsewhere. Living in tents right up against the barbed wire of military bases, Greenham Common women and their sisters in various places practiced nonviolence, harmony with nature, participatory democracy, and mutual nurturance within encampment communities, trying to model the world they sought to create.[25]

The Zone of Peace movement also represents a type of claiming space for peace. What women have uniquely added to the macro concepts of regional nuclear-weapon-free zone agreements, like the Treaty of Raratonga in the Pacific and the Treaty of Tlatelolco in Latin America, has been to persuade local towns and cities to declare themselves zones of peace. Once a community has made such a declaration, it immediately becomes possible to develop a wide range of peacebuilding activities in the community: sister city projects between continents, conflict resolution curricula in the schools, public peace gardens, up to and including economic conversion projects that wean local manufacturers from military contracts to civilian types of production. Beyond that, the variety of festivals and peacebuilding community events is limited only by the social imagination of the community itself and particularly of its women.

Another example of the creative use of the imagination to solve critical peace-threatening problems locally is Joanna Macy's innovative proposal to establish guardian sites at decommissioned nuclear reactors and waste facilities for site monitoring, research, nuclear education, and the development of disciplines of mindfulness and devotion to the well-being of future generations.[26]

### Global Peace Services

Another invention born in the minds of Swedish women in the 1980s was the idea of a women's global peace service. Originally intended to train all-women teams to do work similar to that of mixed peace teams such as Peace Brigades International—interpositioning between parties in combat; protective accompaniment for endangered locals in high-violence situations; creation of safe spaces for normal activities like farming, education, and care of children; help for refugees; and humanitarian provisions of health and food services in the midst of war—the group has expanded to include men but still has strong women in leadership.[27] The project is based on the concept of forming partnerships with local women and men in areas of conflict to support these locals in their own peace efforts and to bring them additional resources and conflict resolution and mediation training from the international network as needed and desired. Because Global Peace Services does not act unilaterally to form international teams to intervene in local conflicts but is committed to the prior development of partnership relations, the networking process to achieve this in various regions is a slow one. Furthermore, the resources needed to do this kind of work go far beyond what the peace NGOs alone can muster. Coalition building with other women's and men's NGOs and with the UN itself to achieve new levels of capability is a new challenge.

## Other Women's Initiatives

Three points regarding women as contributors to peace culture should be clear from this chapter. First, women's experience worlds and their traditional social responsibilities help shape their peacemaking skills. Second, women are less bound by conventional definitions of security and military necessity and are, therefore, more free to imagine different ways of doing things and more free to use the skills they have in creative ways in public spaces. Third, when women have access to support groups, networks, and opportunities to learn new skills, they can—and do—become more active participants in dealing with militarism, oppression, and violence.

The concept of training for global peace services mentioned above has been translated into a number of regional projects in the world's hot spots. An important example is the Center for the Strategic Initiatives of Women, founded in 1992 to give leadership training to local women's groups in the Horn of Africa countries to break the cycles of violence in situations of ongoing civil war.[28] Their work is to bring new perspectives and peacebuilding skills into local and national decision-making bodies. Such women's groups have sometimes been able to disarm local guerrillas in situations where United Nations peacekeepers have been unable to act. Because of the new level of networking among women's groups, these conflict-resolving and disarmament skills are spreading, but, unfortunately, this phenomenon is not being well reported. Women peacemakers are very active, for example, in the Balkans, but one would never know it from press coverage of the conflicts there. The Women Peacemakers Program of the International Fellowship of Reconciliation does a great deal of training for women in situations of violence in the countries of the South as well as in Europe and strongly supports women's groups in Muslim countries, including Afghanistan (which has three different national women's NGOs).[29] The intensive consultation and training event held in 1998 by the Peacemakers Program in India for women from eleven Asian countries is an example of the communication and skill sharing that is going on at an increasing pace among women's groups facing serious violence. Another emerging development of this kind is "Women Waging Peace," a global initiative of Harvard University's Women and Public Policy Program that plans to bring together various United States–based conflict resolution resources as a form of technical assistance for women in major conflict areas around the world.[30]

## Women and Peace Culture

I have used the term *inventiveness* in this chapter to emphasize the ability of women to find new and unexpected ways of changing mindsets, behaviors, and social institutions that support practices of dominance, violence, and war. Some are primarily symbolic, but many are practical, like the guardian site solution to disposal of nuclear wastes and peace services training to bring about local disarmament. It could be said that the women's movement is claiming public space for the *practice* of peace culture. Since that public space has not been traditionally available to women, they have had to be inventive about claiming it, as well as inventive in demonstrating what the quality of human relationships can be in a society that chooses the ways of nonviolence.

Creative examples are of little use in isolation, so the development of women's networking in recent decades may in itself be the best invention of all. What women learn from each other they bring home to their own communities, making new relationships possible between women and men, adults and children. Those new relationships will be explored in the remaining chapters of part 2.

# 6

# New Partnerships—Women and Men

WOMEN'S CREATIVE THINKING, inventive strategizing, and networking for a more peaceful world described in the preceding chapter has all taken place in a male-dominated world—the same world in which women have struggled for equality and fought against oppression and violence. How was that possible?

Two reasons stand out, among a variety of contributing factors. First, women have always been able to create some significant space for action in every society—both hidden, private space and public space—as my *Underside of History: A View of Women Through Time* documents.[1] Second, there have been peaceable men, and men who have been peace leaders, in every age, and most of the historically acknowledged prophets and teachers of peace have been men. It follows that there are sensitive, caring men in every society who are responsive to women's creativity and enjoy working with women in a partnership relationship. The women I described earlier all worked with men who respected them as equals, even though these same women have also experienced their share of obstacles generated by patriarchal institutions and behaviors.

This should not surprise us. Historians and archaeologists who have tried to reconstruct sex role patterns in early human societies have suggested that egalitarian relationships between women and men predated male dominance. (Many references to these studies will be found not only in the *Underside of History*, mentioned above, but also in Riane Eisler's *The Chalice and the Blade*.)[2] Furthermore, such egalitarian societies can still be found today, as I indicated in chapter 4. The rise of turf-consciousness, the physical

Parts of this chapter are drawn from "Changing Gender Roles in Familial, Occupational and Civic Settings," which appeared in *Society as Educator in an Age of Transition*, ed. Kenneth Benne and Steven Tozer (Chicago: Univ. of Chicago Press, 1987).

accumulation of goods, and the warrior state to protect both came later. By a process too complex to describe here, the institution of the patriarchal family emerged as a property-holding device enabling men to control women's productive and reproductive capacities in the service of a male-dominated state. That control included giving the power of life and death over women and children to male heads of household. That life-and-death power, combined with the absence of independent juridical status for women and their subjection to physical punishment to ensure obedience, was enshrined in the legal codes of most states right up to the twentieth century. Women's movements worldwide are still struggling to remove the restraints on women's autonomy and freedom of movement, restraints that continue to exist in practice, even when removed by law.

Law and custom, however, could not change the fact that women and men are of the same species and have, apart from their differing reproductive equipment, similar ranges of talents and capabilities. Fortunately, women have exercised these capabilities in the spaces they could create, or human development would have come to a standstill long ago. But the social, political, and economic patterns of male domination, even though no longer universally embodied in law, are alive and well in both public and private spaces in the culture of male dominance. What we are experiencing today is a very uneasy, and often violent, era of transition from a culture of male dominance to a culture of partnership and equality between women and men. As has already emerged in various ways in the previous chapters, such a partnership lies at the core of the concept of a peace culture. It is therefore useful to explore how this transition is coming along.

The story of women's struggle, particularly in this century, to combine family roles, work roles, and civic roles in a world that still expects women to take full responsibility for home and children, with other activities as "extras," has been well documented. If partnership means an evening out of responsibility so women do not carry a double or triple work load, what are men's movements contributing to the development of the partnership, and to the gender identity of men and women, in the process?

## Men's Movements

The first thing one becomes aware of in reading current writing about the situation of men in today's world is how much pain men are experiencing. This is somewhat unexpected. What, these macho, competitive, impatient, and often violent and abusive men who dominate our cutthroat market economy, run the machinery of governance, hog the public civic scene, hold the purse strings for art and culture and rule the family roost with an iron hand—these men are in pain?

Psychiatrists who specialize in therapy for men write of their rapidly expanding and almost overwhelming caseloads of suffering men.[3] What do their patients report? A loss of vitality in love, work, and play. An underlying sense of humiliation and failure. Loneliness. Lack of a sense of direction. A terror of being thought weak and womanish, a longing to become "real men." And so many social forces seem to be arrayed against the embattled male wage earner: the Civil Rights movement, floods of Two-Thirds World immigrants entering the job market at a time of economic uncertainty and widening wage gaps, the threats of poverty, rising crime, and violence. And on top of it all, an angry women's movement.

The message is becoming increasingly clear that many men do not enjoy their assigned macho roles. During childhood and youth they experience a forced socialization into an aggressive style of male dominance through athletics, as described by Sabo and Runfola in the thought-provoking *Jock: Sports and Male Identity*.[4] Yet as adults they may prefer a quiet niche in the workplace where not more is asked than they feel they can handle. Even for men bursting with energy and self-confidence, the race to the top is not necessarily fun. Once, these achievers wrote poetry and dreamed dreams. But now a part of them is atrophying, shriveling up, and many would like to break away from the insistent high-pressure demands of work. They may get little pleasure out of their men's club activities, traditionally the prized secret center of the male world, and as Pleck describes,[5] they resent their dependence on the women in their lives (who have their own secret world). They *must* work or they will have no identity. The only thing they were ever expected to be was breadwinner. If a man becomes unemployed, he is literally nothing.

If anything, men's work role situation is more complicated than women's in this transition era. A man is in the situation of competing at work—his only source of identity—with women while at the same time he feels emotionally dependent on women in his private life. He can't turn for nurturance and support to other men as women can to each other, because male talk is not "personal" talk. He hurts and he can't cry.

Men have a variety of ways of responding to their dilemmas, and few of these give any hints of their underlying pain. The most widespread response is abusive behavior toward women and children. Uncontrolled violence toward women by male partners has been one of the most serious and widespread by-products of patriarchy as a social formation. Such violence erupts in more than 50 percent of all marriages in the United States, and in one out of four marriages physical abuse is chronic — monthly or more often.[6] This violence is found in all countries, on all continents. In times of social upheaval, economic depression, and war, the practice of such violence assumes horrific dimensions. Once started, it usually escalates, and one-eighth of all homicides are committed by spouses killing spouses. Similarly, rape and child abuse are widespread, and also increase in times of social upheaval.

Another way that men choose to deal with their dilemmas of uncertainty and incomplete personal identity is to join the men's militia movement. This "new war culture," which began about the time of the fall of Saigon and the defeat of the United States in the Vietnam War, creates a fantasy land in which men become warriors preparing for heroic battle against enemies of society. Three types of imaginary war zones are created by this highly energized warrior culture, according to Gibson: (1) the widely played National Survival Game and its many variants; (2) the annual Soldier of Fortune convention, where militiamen from all over the country gather to celebrate the warrior culture; and (3) elite combat schools and firing ranges.[7] While police also attend the combat schools, as do some military officers, the participants are mostly paramilitaries, men entirely separated from traditional state-sanctioned police and military structures and organizations. A fourth type of war zone might be added: the survivalist camps that dot the mountains of the western United States. The new war culture has been accompanied by a sharp rise in the sale of military weapons to civilians. As far back as 1989, the U.S. Bureau of Alcohol, Tobacco and Firearms had estimated that twenty-three million military-style rifles had been sold in the United States since the Vietnam War.

The militia tend to be all-male tribes, without mothers, without girlfriends, without nurturant mentors. (Occasionally a few warrior women seek admission.) There is no concrete image of a new and better world being fought for. Blood sacrifice itself is sacred. There is a great deal of anger and obsession with vengeance. Who are these tribals? They come from many backgrounds and may be bankers, professionals, factory workers, or postal clerks. All normal social boundaries are transcended.

On the basis of his experience as a participant-observer in this movement, Gibson has been able to describe how this culture has made its way into every sector of American society; into the media, governments, schools, the economy, and the extreme religious right. Entitling his book *Warrior Dreams*, he asks how these would-be combatants can be helped to wake up from their

warrior dreams. He points to the deep underlying insecurity of the participants, and their need for a new definition of masculinity—a masculinity
that includes fathering and makes room for a new type of socially creative
adventuring.

A third way of dealing with masculine insecurity is to seek a more inward
and mythopoetic approach to male identity. Bly calls it the recovery of male
energy, or the "wildman" within, using the symbolism from the Brothers
Grimm's fairy tale about Iron John.[8] Men gather together "in the woods" and
use drumming and other rituals in the journey to renewed manhood. Such
gatherings are sometimes seen as putting down women, but this is not necessarily so.

The fourth and most promising approach to men's woundedness is found
in that part of the men's movement that seeks wholeness—not only through
a new relationship with other men in support groups, but also through new
relations with women in nurturant partnership and with children through
nurturant parenting. This is a complex, multifaceted, and still developing
movement.

If the 1963 publication of Betty Friedan's *Feminine Mystique* marked the
beginning of the contemporary women's movement, then 1974 might be
thought of as marking the beginning of the contemporary men's movement.
Nineteen seventy-four was the publication year of Fasteau's *Male Machine*,
Farrell's *Liberated Man*, and Pleck and Sawyer's *Men and Masculinity*, studies rounded out a decade later with James Doyle's *The Male Experience*, in
1983.[9] Nineteen seventy-four was also the year in which the National Conference on Men and Masculinity held its first conference. That conference
eventually evolved into NOMAS, the National Organization for Men Against
Sexism. Helped in its birthing by the women's movement, NOMAS has consistently supported equal rights for women. Over the years, however, the
men's movement has multiplied into a variety of groups and refined its con-
ceptualizations of masculinity.

The 1990s discussions of masculinity, building on the experience of several
decades, include thoughtful examination of the socialization process, such as
*Constructing Masculinity* by Berger et al. and Buchbinder's *Performance Anx-
iety*. More political approaches include Kemmel's *Politics of Manhood* and
Messner's *Politics of Masculinities*.[10]

A key part of the men's movement has focused on men's recovery from the
practice of abusive violence. MENSTUFF, the national Men's Resource
Center in Anselmo, California, maintains an online listing of "alternatives to

violence" centers for men in the United States.[11] In the fall of 1998, in California alone the listing contained 210 centers. A strong nationwide network of support groups for abusive men now exists. Their goal is to help abusers control their own behavior. RAVEN (Rape and Violence End Now) in St. Louis, EMERGE in Boston, and AMEND (Abusive Men Exploring New Directions) in Denver are examples of the kind of men's groups that have come into being in local communities. These are usually organized on an all-volunteer basis.

The volunteers in these self-help projects for men show a skill, sensitivity, and dedication that is awe-inspiring. They also support childcare and women's shelter projects. *Learning to Live without Violence: A Handbook for Men Who Batter*, by Sonkin and Durphy, is an outgrowth of the RAVEN project.[12] In addition to this crisis-oriented work, the National Men's Resource Center helps a broader network of men's consciousness-raising groups stay in touch with one another. As Pleck and Sawyer summarize its goals, men's liberation involves (a) closer friendships with men; (b) a freer showing of emotions; (c) recovery of psychic energy; (d) fuller relations with spouse; (e) fuller relations with children; (f) more social skill and trust, less violence and competition; and (g) a change in values, with less need for dominance.[13] These goals are slowly being realized. Although the women's movement helped the men's movement get started, many women are not aware of the great supportive efforts on behalf of women carried out by the men's groups described here.

NOMAS is of particular interest because it developed from a loose-knit, spontaneous social movement in the early 1970s; went through a period in the 1980s as the national organization for Changing Men (NOCM); and finally, in 1992, became the National Organization for Men Against Sexism, with national task groups in the following areas: Men's Studies, Ending Men's Violence, Homophobia, Eliminating Racism, Men's Culture, Men and Mental health, Men and Spirituality, Pornography and Prostitution, Men and Prisons, Bisexuality, Child Custody, and Adult Supremacy. As this is being written, NOMAS is announcing with pride its twenty-fourth National Men and Masculinity Conference, to take place in Pasadena in 1999. NOMAS ranks today as the oldest and most politically progressive network of men who share a hopeful perspective about men and masculinity.

However, the men's movement has many faces and many special orientations. One such group is Stay at Home Dads (SAHD), a support group for fathers who choose to stay at home with children while their wives maintain outside employment. In these families both parents believe someone should be home with the small children, and the 1991 U.S. Census reported that 20 percent of children younger than five were cared for by fathers during the mother's work hours. A recent report on SAHD points out that "stay-at-home dads express a sense of pride and power in a role to which this society generally affords little prestige. Still, they admit it's one tough job."[14] Quite a different face is represented by the Promise Keepers, an evangelical Christian men's group founded by an evangelical football coach in Boulder, Colorado, in the early 1990s. While conservative in its approach to political issues and adamant that women's place is in the home, it also holds men to a higher standard of behavior as husbands and fathers, calling them to a more attentive and listening relationship to their families.

Some men's groups have been in existence for decades; others are more recent or have recently expanded into new activities. MOVE (Men Overcoming Violence) originally worked with adult males but now has a program for young men ages fourteen through nineteen called Youth MOVE.[15] MAP (Men Against Pornography) was founded in 1984 but has recently developed an online anthology, "Quitting Pornography," in response to the increasing tendency of men to browse the World Wide Web for sexual satisfaction. MIPE (Men's International Peace Exchange), founded at the start of the Gulf War to build a worldwide community of peacemakers who would help men become more peaceful, now publishes a quarterly newsletter, the *Peace Exchange*, with subscribers in about twenty countries.[16] Newsletters and the Internet are becoming increasingly important in the men's movement (as in all movements) as new local men's centers form and new ideas and programs develop in this growing sector of contemporary peace culture. That these men are seeking a voice is exemplified in the new name of the former *Valley Men Magazine* of the Men's Resource Center of Western Massachusetts: *Voice Male*.

In fact, there are many voices, and national events to make the voices heard, in which various local groups participate. Brotherpeace, an annual event each fall in various cities in North America that involves vigils and demonstrations against men's violence in all its forms, is one of many examples. The Canadian version of Brotherpeace is the White Ribbon Campaign. Wearers of the White Ribbon during the designated month—November or December—are pledged never to commit or condone or remain silent about violence against women.

Another face of the men's movement should be mentioned here, one that has gone more in the direction of men's rights—in divorce, in child custody, in paternity. The National Congress for Men, founded in 1981 as a coalition of several thousand fathers and men's rights groups around the United States, focuses on the issue of exclusion of men from the household except as provider (and after divorce, as visitor).[17] If the gentle gender groups define their tasks largely in relation to feminism, the "Free Men," as they are sometimes called, lean toward a reformist version of the traditional male bond. Both groups are struggling to define what the men's community should mean for men.

While the men's movement in the United States has received particular attention, the movement itself is found on every continent, often linked to related concerns for peace, the environment, and alternative lifestyles that lead to living more gently on the earth. In terms of mythic symbols, Iron John of the Europeans must take his place beside god/goddess Shiva of the Hindus, the universal progenitor who is at one and the same time the wild huntsman and the giver and teacher of the arts and the sciences, the one who dances creation. And there are many more mythic figures to symbolize the complexity of the male-female journey. More recent versions of the men's movement around the world are reported periodically in *Women in Action*, a journal published by the international feminist organization ISIS. One issue reports on the Korean "Group of Wish-to-be-Good Fathers," founded in 1992 in Seoul, now with sections all over Korea and also in Los Angeles, as well as on "Fathers of Students Preparing for the Entrance Exams," founded in 1994.[18] The names of these organizations speak for themselves. In Australia we find Men Against Sexual Assault (MASA) and Men Against Patriarchy (MAP). In Thailand we find Men for Gender Awareness (MEG). An anonymous member of MEG, explaining the function of such groups in a number of countries, points out that men find it easier and therefore more effective to accept suggestions and criticism from other men. In order to feel comfortable taking action on gender issues, they need a men's support group. Men in such organizations generally share the belief that patriarchy is a root cause of many problems in their society.

Invoking the word *patriarchy* to account for male violence is an oversimplification. However, the fact remains that there is an omnipresent cultural symbolism of the male head of household that evokes an ancient warrior imagery of little use in dealing with the complex problems of the modern world. That imagery dictates a reality that leaves parenting to the mother, produces generation after generation of mother-reared children, recreates the battle of the sexes in every cradle, and leaves a residue of permanent infantilism in the character of every adult man and woman.

Our era owes an enormous intellectual and spiritual debt to Dorothy Dinnerstein, who had the wisdom and courage to point to mother-rearing, the very foundation of the household pattern of social reproduction, as a major source of human maldevelopment in society as we know it.[19] For the first year of an infant's life, it is the mother who is the sole fulfiller and frustrator of all those intensely felt infant needs. That fulfiller-frustrator role continues throughout the childhood and early youth of boys and girls alike. The father stands aside from that intense double role, aloof and apparently powerful. As boys grow older, they discover how powerless the fulfiller-frustrator is and make the shift to identify with the person they see as the source of real power—the father. Girls cannot do this. They are trapped in the helplessness of their own mother.

In reality, everyone is trapped. Boys grow up without real autonomy because they only know how to be served, not how to serve others. They are dependent on women. Girls grow up without real autonomy because they know they *must* serve. And so men hate women even while they love them, because they feel caught in their own dependency. Women hate men, even while they love them, because man care is a lifelong burden, and a lonely one. Each retreats to their own gender community, men pretending independence in the safe bravado of the male bond, women taking solace in the only nurturance they may ever get, in the female bond. Yet the male-female bond persists, full of hope and longing, for there is much for men and women to share with one another. Love, frustration, pain, and ambivalence alternate in a never-ending cycle as men and women turn first toward each other, and then away to their own gender community. Out of that cycle comes much social violence.

It doesn't have to be that way. Through their own lives, and through their involvement in parenting and other relationships with children, members of the men's and women's communities—both heterosexual and gay/lesbian, as individuals and in social movements—are affirming that it doesn't have to be that way. They are beginning to break the vicious cycle. For families with children this means joint parenting from birth or alternating the stay-at-home role between partners. For childless households it means planned involvement of adult members with young children.

Breaking the link between mothering and total frustration/fulfillment for the young, sharing those basic frustration/fulfillment experiences between spouses—and, for single care-givers, with friends—will enable male and female children to grow towards autonomy as they realize that frustrations and fulfillments are part of the nature of human experience on the planet, rather than a sequence tied to a giving and a withholding on the part of women.

One arena of social movements that is making an important contribution to the redefinition of gender roles toward a fuller recognition of the potentialities of both women and men consists of the gay and lesbian communities mentioned above. Although some same-sex relationships play out conventional dominance-submission patterns, a significant sector of these communities develop domestic partnerships—women with women and men with men—that are not caught up in gender-defined dominance-submission relationships.[20] These women and these men can more easily achieve love with autonomy, work sharing with dignity, and nurturance without infantile dependency. At their best, these one-gender households represent the ideal of what man-woman relations could be; however, we shouldn't be surprised when they fail to achieve this ideal in their own households, since they have been as exposed as the rest of us to the poison of sex-role dominance.

It is ironic that both gays and lesbians, particularly those who are part of peace and social transformation movements, are subjected to a great deal of violence. Gays suffer the most, since they represent a different kind of masculine identity, which is very threatening to the carefully cultivated male image of machismo. Not surprisingly, gays and lesbians have in recent decades been forming their own communities—a special type of the utopian experiments described in chapter 2. The 1995 *Communities Directory* lists eleven such communities in North America, in locations from coast to coast, but predominantly located in the southwest of the United States.[21] Many, but not all, are spiritually based. Most religious denominations also have gay/lesbian fellowships, often embattled within their own faith community. Themes of an inward calling to a more holistic personhood, and of living simply and gently with other humans and with the earth itself, are common to both secular and religious groups and communities.

Both heterosexual and gay households are likely to have children to nurture. Shared parenting not only breaks negative cycles of excessive dependency, it opens up to men what has been closed to them: those gentling and sensitizing experiences that allow them a fuller development of hidden capacities and social skills, a more complete personhood. By the same token, it opens up to women the broader range of activities the old double role denied them. Conflict, frustration, anger, and rage will not disappear, but they need not be gender-linked.

Will men and women become more alike? More likely, they will become more different, because with shared parenting, a fuller individuation of each personality will be possible. Whatever biological potentialities are present in individuals will have freer play with the fuller maturity that comes from sharing nurturance and service roles between men and women. The link between gender and occupationally defined social roles will have been broken. Nor will the three types of gender communities I have been speaking of disappear. What we have learned from the study of groups of women-identified women and men-identified men is that same-sex relationships have special qualities that can unleash creativity and joy. Women do not have to be lesbian or engage in sexual relations with their kind to enjoy women, any more than men have to be gay and engage in sexual relations with their kind to enjoy men. The greater freedom to move back and forth between male bonding, female bonding, and male-female bonding will further enhance individuation.

With greater individuation, gender identity will evolve dimensions now hidden under the facade of occupational stereotyping, and false stereotyping of gender roles will no longer need to be upheld. But there are pitfalls for men in the backlash to the women's movement, in that their search for a more holistic identity must come from within rather than in response to feminist pressure. One young advocate of Bly's approach sees past Bly's apparent antifeminism to the deeper issue of human autonomy, both male and female. Jim Cypser writes:

> a man who *concedes* to be sensitive to others' feelings, to forgo the luxury of violence, to do a fair share of housework, or to respect women in authority *because of the "demands" of women* is faking it. A man who does these things *of his own masculine will because he perceives they are right, or acts of love,* is not faking it; and his actions may change the world. Such a man should and commonly will rebuke his unliberated peers when they object to his habits. He will do so with words or actions forceful enough to communicate to them that he is not a fake; rather than being under the sway of women or femininity, he is acting from his own masculine impulses.[22]

There are pitfalls for women, too, in the feminist backlash against the idealization of domesticity. Distinctions need to be made between false and authentic nurturance. False nurturance is the phony coddling of men and the habitual practice of self-abasement and soft compliance with arbitrary and unreasonable demands. The hidden side of false nurturance is deception and calculation. Authentic nurturance is based on clearheadedness: it requires a strong sense of self-respect as well as respect for the other; it affirms strengths and acknowledges weaknesses of the other and is supportive of the other's needs, both personal and social. The nurturing woman, like the nurturing man, is acting from her own best and deepest impulses. False nurturance is, indeed, to be rejected, but authentic nurturance in both private and public spheres is essential to a healthy peace culture.

## Public Nurturance Roles for Men and Women

In speaking of nurturance roles, both for men and for women, the emphasis has heretofore tended to be on interpersonal interaction in familial settings. And certainly this is where the sensitive awareness of the other and the capacity for empathy, so essential to nurturance itself, is developed. However, in a peace culture, nurturant behavior crosses the boundary from the privacy of the home into public spaces, and so we can speak of public nurturance. In practical terms, what does public nurturance mean?

It means to foster settings and styles of interaction and rules for mediating conflicts of interest that release the most positive and creative and mutually affirming responses in all participants. It means turning public interaction to the interests of the widest possible community. It means a passionate concern for the welfare of human beings of all groups and conditions in all nations. The language of public nurturance is, in part, the language of human rights: It is a declaration of love for the human species translated into the language of international law. More specifically, it is a declaration that cancels the biological labeling involved in the concept of the gender-based division of labor. According to the UN Declaration of Human Rights, women and men have a publicly acknowledged right to a social and international order in which our finest potentialities as humans can be realized. Dominance skills cannot achieve such an international order for us. Neither can bargaining skills alone. Only an appropriate combination of nurturance, competence, and love—in a working partnership of women and men—will get us there.

Developing the skills of public nurturance is not easy for either men or women. Both have to learn new ways of interacting that have not been part of traditional gendered behavior, but both also have resources in traditional patterns that can be reframed for new ways of working in the public sphere.

Men, in giving up traditional dominance behavior, have their experience in team sports to draw on—the careful observation and constant adjustment to the movements of teammates—and they can use their own everyday negotiation skills, reframing these behaviors to approach both male and female coworkers in a partnership mode rather than an authority mode, yet without giving up their essential identity as men. Two good examples of male public nurturers are Andrew Young, former United States ambassador to the United Nations, and Jimmy Carter, former president of the United States, both of whom have done outstanding peacemaking work in situations of great tension.

Women, in giving up traditional "serving" behavior, can draw on their own unacknowledged social systems understanding of how things work, based on years of negotiation with various parts of the local community on behalf of the household. (Increasingly, they are also having the same training as men in team sports.) They can also draw on their years of experience in organizing their time to accomplish multiple tasks simultaneously—a daily "must" for homemakers with young children—and their psychological insight into the needs of those around them. Women can reframe these behaviors without giving up their essential identity as women. They don't have to become "female men." Examples of women's public nurturance include the work of Alva Myrdal, Swedish ambassador to the United Nations Disarmament Commission, and that of Aung San Suu Kyi, the long-imprisoned leader of Burma's National League for Democracy, who, on being released from prison in the summer of 1995, immediately took up a creative nonviolent political leadership role untainted by any hint of revenge.

"Partnership" is a word less seen than heard. Yet behaviors are changing, if slowly. The increase of women in the workplace is more visible than the increase in fathering and domestic roles for men, stay-at-home dads not withstanding. A Detroit area study compared hours spent in housework by employed wives and their husbands in 1965 and 1975 and found that over the decade, men had increased their housework time by only 6 minutes.[23]

In 1979 a two-generation study showed that sons felt fathers should be more actively nurturant and less active as providers than their own fathers reported. The differences were not large, but there was a trend.[24] The trend towards involving husbands not only in birth preparation classes but also in birth itself has in fact produced a new generation of fathers who delight in intimate contact with their children from infancy onwards. Fathers carrying infants in snuggles (infant carrying packs) are not a frequent sight, but they are becoming less rare. In the 1970s the Rapoports, themselves a husband and wife research team, studied what they call coordinate marriages, in which career responsibility and parenting and homemaking responsibility are equally shared between men and women. Studies in Britain, Norway, and the United States all documented high marital satisfaction in such marriages.[25]

A five-year longitudinal study conducted in the 1980s at Boston University, following couples through early pregnancy into early parenting, found that happy fathering and a good marital relationship were strongly related to a balance between feelings of affiliation and feelings of autonomy on the part of men.[26] That balance, for both men and women, is the key to a stable partnership. "Let there be spaces in your togetherness," says Khalil Gibran in *The Prophet*. Betcher and Pollack point out that just because men have not been fathered in their own childhood does not mean they cannot discover fatherhood in relation to their own children, and give examples of the happiness that can come with such belated discovery.[27] We can expect a continuing surge of fatherhood literature in the near future.

## Adventurous Partnering for Peace

A fully developed peace culture depends on the linking of women's knowledge and experience validated in microspaces to men's knowledge and experience in macrospaces. Women can bring to those macrospaces that kind of authenticity, spontaneity, and variety of response styles that characterizes their interactions in less public arenas. When women are added to all-male working groups in more than token numbers, they bring with them an expressiveness and capacity for flexible, cooperative activity that is widely appreciated, and they bring an ability to listen to and relate to people of different ages, temperaments, backgrounds, and needs. What men bring to the partnership is a zest for exploring new territory, trying new things—a spirit of adventure and an enjoyment of risk taking. Thus women and men can each bring out the most creative traits of the other.

This should be thought of as a zesty, adventurous partnership at a time when mounting social problems cry out for a sharing of male and female experience worlds. Many hazards lie ahead as the twenty-first century dawns. Since men and women assess risks differently because of their different social experiences, and thus arrive at different judgements about response to situations of danger, their partnership allows for more seasoned but also more flexible responses to those dangers. It has, for example, been frequently documented in studies of public opinion regarding arms policy that women have almost always favored less armament and more attention to nonmilitary approaches to security. In situations where families are exposed to serious environmental pollution, such as Love Canal and Three Mile Island, women are more apt to make the choice to leave the environment, taking the children with them, than are men. This leads to the prospect of increasing numbers of broken families in precisely those situations of stress where family members need one another most. Although individual perceptions are to be valued, men and women urgently need to develop *some* common perceptions of the possibilities and dangers before us, particularly in relation to the welfare of the next generation.

Detachment is needed as well as empathy, attention to details as well as the big picture, an appropriate sense of timing, complex spatial visualizations, "downstream thinking" in terms of possible consequences of present decisions—all these approaches vary between men and women as well as within gender groups. Never have women and men more urgently needed to listen to each other's judgments, or needed more urgently to dialogue about the differences.

We are at the beginning of such listening and dialoguing. Jessie Bernard writes of tipping points in social process beyond which there is no turning back.[28] Perhaps we are approaching such a tipping point in American society today with regard to women's active roles in the public sphere. Large numbers of young women now in professional training will bring the two experience worlds of the public and private spheres with them into their working life and into their civic life. They will seek out men who are prepared to do the same.

The sheer need for a greater diversity of competencies, plus the power of caring itself, will enable younger women and men to work together in spaces from which women are now excluded. After all, it is not as if society has enjoyed the threat and dominance games that have been played for so long. Men and women are both miserable with threat behavior.

The image of the mounted warrior that has always captured the imagination of historians needs to be exorcised. Public parks are still filled with equestrian statuary testifying to our fondness for this image. The initial encounter between mounted pastoralists and urban foot soldiers many centuries ago made clear the advantage in power that derived from being mounted, from looking down on others from on high. We have never, since those early times, been able to let go of our attachment to that idea of the power of being up high, the power to dominate. The steed the air force pilot mounts is far deadlier than the nomad's horse, and can be directed against the planet itself, so the romance of dominance is somewhat diminished now. We face today two opposite trends with regard to dominance—particularly in its extreme form, militarism. More and more men, either through indifference or through an active interest in the pacific arts of nonviolent conflict resolution, are refusing the soldier role, while more and more women are choosing the soldier role as an opportunity to succeed in new spaces.[29] If there are still to be battlefields, then it can certainly be argued that these battlefields should also be shared experience worlds until women and men are both ready to go another way.

The great humane nurturer-leaders of the past have always come walking. They do not sit either on thrones or on horseback but engage in dialogue at eye level. The other important characteristic of the great nurturer-leaders is that they have always sought solitude and privacy in alternation with their work in the public arena. The capacity to nurture is ultimately matured in private settings. We cannot always be in public, for high rates of social interaction drain us of our capacity for openness and for listening. We need places of retreat. One such place is the familial household, be it of the two-parent family, the one-parent family, the singles' dwelling, or the monastery. It may be any one of the forms of communal household that have been reinvented in this century, reflecting the need for islands of relationship in troubled times. It may be the solitary hermitage, such as my own Rocky Mountain retreat, where in the past I have often sat thinking, meditating, or writing, with only animals and birds for companions. In emphasizing the public sphere for those who have been forcibly privatized, we must not forget that in private spaces we are able to develop understandings that will be precious to our society. Men have been as deprived of the opportunities for reflection that the private sphere affords as women have been deprived of the opportunity to help shape the civic order. It is a mutual sharing of spaces we need to move toward, not an exchange of spaces. The social policies that derive from such sharing of men's and women's worlds will allow new developments of the human possibility in each of us and will be far less costly to maintain. Such policies will need no armies to implement them, at home or abroad. The new model of the warrior will derive from traditions retold by the elders of many Native American tribes—that the warrior is one who helps make things work for the welfare of every man, woman, and child in the tribe; who deals with enemies through problem solving in song and by games of counting coup (having touched the enemy) rather than killing. These revisioned warriors will walk side by side with their sisters, as in the old Homeric dreams of the Elysian fields, "while fresh singing breezes blow from the sea to renew the human spirit."[30]

# 7

# New Partnerships—Children and Adults

T HE CONCEPT of partnership between women and men no longer seems alien or strange to us, given the emphasis in recent decades on stories of women's creativity and inventiveness, and their increasing public visibility as determined actors working for a more humane world. But where are the comparable stories of the creativity, inventiveness, and determined action for change on the part of children and youth—the six-to-eight to eighteen-year-olds? Who even notices them? Like women, they also have a hidden history of remarkable achievements in private spaces. Unlike women, their entry into public spaces in recent decades has been neither recognized nor acclaimed. The heavy hand of patriarchy still weighs on them. They are minors by law and voiceless by custom.

Yet the century began differently. This was to be the Century of the Child, and of the child-centered society. It was discovered that children were not just miniature adults, but small human beings whose physical, social, emotional, and intellectual development gradually unfolded over the first two decades of life until they became fully adult in their twenties.[1] This insight, however, has had some unfortunate consequences. In the One-Third World, it has produced whole industries that have grown up around "the child," producing not only elaborately designed clothing and toys, but specially designed children's spaces. It has also led to an increasingly complicated set of social arrangements that leave children so finely age-graded that they are rarely exposed to others than their age-mates from preschool on, except in their own families. Somewhere between the ages of eighteen and twenty-one, this age-

Some materials in this chapter first appeared in *Our Children, Our Partners*, the 1996 James Backhouse Lecture (Kelvin Grove, Queensland, Australia: Margaret Fell Bookshop, 1996).

segregated youth is abruptly tossed into the adult world and expected to take on those very adult roles from which they have been so carefully segregated.

This practice of exclusion from adult civil society is based on three concepts: (1) children are weak, unformed human beings who need protection from environmental hazards and exploitative adults; (2) children's experience and knowledge worlds are so limited that they have no information or skills of use to adult society; and (3) society is so complex that only specially demarcated spaces staffed by professionally trained adults can prepare children to live in it. The underlying view is that children must be protected from victimage. In the UN Declaration of the Rights of the Child, only three out of ten principles refer to children's *rights*. The other seven refer to constraints and protection against possible harm. (However, it is also true that the 1989 Convention on the Rights of the Child goes further and recognizes that the child has claims and rights equal to those of adults.)

The irony is that harm against children has grown exponentially in the very century that was supposed to be dedicated to the creative flowering of human childhood. Children are indeed victims. They are subject to increasing levels of violence within the family itself—the one place in which we would like to think they were safe. And in every world region there are growing numbers of street children, many of whom have no families at all. The latest UN reports tell us that children are sinking deeper into poverty on every continent. Closely related is the continuing ruthless exploitation of children in field and factory, particularly (but not only) in the Two-Thirds World. The rates of social violence in neighborhoods and between neighborhood gangs are rising, along with increased rates of participation of children in drug traffic. Schools, too, are combating violence within their walls—often, ironically enough, by increased use of physical punishment. Shoot-outs in schools are becoming a horrifying new reality in the United States, where children have relatively easy access to guns due to lax public regulation. Over all the other violence hangs the great dark cloud of war—guerrilla war, civil war, interstate war. Land mines and indiscriminate bombing and shooting in countries saturated with weapons result in far more deaths of children than adult soldiers wherever there is war. Perhaps the saddest deaths of all are the deaths of child soldiers—children recruited into guerrilla armies as young as four and five years old.

And still we continue to try to develop and maintain age-segregated spaces for children: in education, from preschool to the university. In churches and temples, communities of faith strive to replicate that age-grading in the name of quality religious education. Children's clubs, services, and special programs are all age-graded right through the teens. The habit persists: we have social groups for young adults, for young parents, for middle-years folk, and on through the "Golden Age" years. This is not to decry age-old practices of ritual initiation of age groups into the next stage of life, practices that celebrate arrival at each new stage of responsibility for self and society. And certainly there are sequences of learning that are useful for children, and identifiable sets of common needs in different stages of life. The problem is that the practice of social grouping by age has been carried to an extreme, leaving very few common social spaces in which child-adult friendships can develop. Think, reader, if you are under eighteen, who your over-thirty friends are. If you are over thirty, think who your under-eighteen friends are. Many preteens and teens have never had a serious conversation with an adult who was not a relative, a teacher, or someone else with special responsibility for the young. There are exceptions, of course, to the practice of segregation, particularly in rural areas where farm families interact across generations in both work and play. Religious and ethnic groups also create space for intergenerational activities, especially in times of celebration.

Nevertheless, there is an underlying attitude, particularly in the One-Third World, that contributes to the pervasive separating out of children and adults, an attitude of disrespect for children and their capacities, masked by the provision of much specialized attention in carefully designated settings. Some of this disrespect comes from patriarchal authority patterns, some from a dislike of the unexpected—something children can be guaranteed to introduce into adult settings—and some from a basic social denial, a refusal to face a future different from the present, a future that will belong to and be shaped by those who are now children.

## The Knowledge and Experience Worlds of Children and Youth

The challenge for those of us who are older is to open ourselves more fully to the actuality of the rich and multidimensional knowledge and experience worlds that children and youth inhabit (unless they belong to that sadly deprived group who live glued to a television set or computer screen). This is the only possible basis for better cross-age partnerships, whether at the interpersonal or the societal level. If we search our own childhood memories, we will remember our own frequent frustration over the behavior of uncomprehending adults. How could we forget what we once knew?

Who knows how different today's world would be if an older generation had started listening to young people such as the students at the first International School in Geneva, children of the diplomats serving in the new League of Nations in the 1920s and 1930s. The youth who participated in that early inspired effort at education for a new and more peaceful world were all killed in World War II. Not one graduate survived.

We do not lack evidence of the value of listening to the young. A 1979 study by geographer Robert Kates and associates, of hazards for children, involved consulting a multiracial cross-class group of three to six-year-olds. These children could not only identify all the adult-listed hazards in the experimental room in which they were placed, including "dirty air," but went on to identify hazards that the adult participants in the experiment never noticed.[2] They also gave more realistic hazard ratings for each problem than the adults did. How could this be? For one thing, three to six-year-olds live at a different eye level than adults and therefore see things adults never see. Living at different eye levels becomes a powerful metaphor for what children see that remains invisible to adults.

The young not only have their own keen powers of observation, they respond to what they see and help change their environment, help deal with problems in ways adults rarely notice. They are in fact co-shapers of their families and of their society, noticed or not. In my studies of the memories of college students about how they nurtured their parents through difficult times, I found that they remembered devising strategies to help suicidal mothers and fathers through serious depressions. They thought of ways to help fathers who had lost their job and self-respect to feel loved and needed. They comforted mothers grieving over the loss of their own mother. Some of these memories went back as far as the age of four. Rarely did the parent being helped have any idea of the actual role their child was taking on.[3]

The mistake adults make is to fail to appreciate the complexity of the knowledge and experience worlds of even very young children. In the first couple of years of life they have observed and taken in information about their physical and social environment at a staggering rate; their "learning curve" might be thought of as a straight vertical line. The learning rate gradually slows down in the pre-teen years. By the time we are adults it is more like a learning crawl than the high-speed intake of the very young.

Compare, for example, adults and children at a lakeside or ocean beach in the summer. Many of the adults (not all!) are sprawled in the sun in a stupor or have their eyes fastened to a book. The children are creating magic worlds in the sand at the water's edge, collecting every conceivable kind of shell, pebble, bits of debris, and seaweed to decorate their miniworld, perhaps engineering small streams around towers and walls. Of course it's great to relax in the sun, but respect the world-creating play of those children!

Anyone who seriously observes children at play in neighborhood settings would not underestimate what they know; but in our ordinary life we don't observe children that way. When Roger Hart did a two-year study of children in a small Vermont town, getting permission from the young ones themselves to be with them in their own spaces, he found that the children had a competence in mapping and knowledge of local land use that considerably exceeded adult knowledge of the same terrain.[4] These were working-class and middle-class children. The same types of observation made of street children in the big cities of the Americas, Asia, and Africa indicate that their knowledge of how to survive in an extremely hostile and sparse environment is awesome.

Precisely because of the complexity of children's experiences and their cognitive processing of those experiences, stage theories of cognitive and moral development such as those of Piaget and Kohlberg oversimplify the maturing process. Children's thinking and social responsiveness are not that different from adult thinking and responsiveness, except for the actual difference in the storehouse of happenings in their lives.[5] Although the significance of the accumulation of lived experience must not be underestimated, neither should we underestimate the capacity for reaching sophisticated and mature judgements on the basis of whatever knowledge store is available. In short, we must respect the capacity of children to *think!*

It is useful to remember how arbitrary our demarcations of childhood, youth, and adulthood are. In general, the term *children* is used for those under twelve or fourteen, *youth* for those from age fourteen or fifteen to twenty-one or twenty-five. This means that in some societies youth become legally adult with full citizen's rights at age twenty-one, in others not until twenty-five. That is a long time to wait to be heard. However, rites of passage in most societies honor milestones along the way for children in their acquisition of know-how for living. In Tibetan Buddhist cultures, children go through a Shambala rites-of-passage ceremony at age eight, when they formally take on responsibility for the feeding of animals and other work relating to care of the earth and provision of food. A second ceremony comes at age sixteen, when they take responsibility for the spiritual and social well-being of others—in other words, civic responsibility. These ceremonies have become very important in the lives of American Buddhist families, and I have been moved by the solemnity of the ritual for eight-year-olds.

A more common practice for most social groups is that the first rite of passage comes at puberty and the second at marriage. In most Western societies the puberty rite involves very limited recognition of a new stage of responsible participation in society. Bar mitzvah for Jewish youths and baptismal and/or confirmation rites of Christian churches are not usually followed by giving children or young people a specific voice in church decision making.

The amazing thing is how much responsibility and how many worries children young people carry, in spite of the care we take to protect them in segregated spaces. Children and youth in any society have many problems today. A recent study of youth concerns in seventy-five communities in Colorado by the Department of Human Services lists the following most frequently reported concerns:

| Concern | Fraction of Youth Reporting |
| --- | --- |
| substance abuse | 76.5% |
| youth violence/gangs | 53.0% |
| teen pregnancy | 53.0% |

High school programs for fourteen-, fifteen-, and sixteen-year-old mothers to complete their education, and also learn child care and job skills, is now one of the major features of many high schools in urban areas of the United States. The teaching of aikido, a set of physical techniques to be used in case of unprovoked attack, involving nonviolent deflection of blows, is rarely taught in schools but is increasingly available in special training centers.[6]

An encouraging number of youths do not live passively with their fear. They do form partnerships with adults to make problems visible and work for solutions. One impressive example of such partnership based in the United States is the Children's Express. I quote from a recent report:

> Created in 1975, Children's Express (CE) is an international news service reported by children and teenagers for audiences of all ages. For almost 20 years, reporters (8–13) and editors (14–18) have examined critical children's issues and brought them to national attention. CE news teams . . . traveled on assignment all over the United States, and Cambodia, Thailand, Hiroshima, Chernobyl, Israel, Zambia and post-war Kuwait, reporting with the zeal and honesty of youth. Its young reporters and editors (over 3000 to date) . . . have interviewed senators, congress members, presidents, and prime ministers, as well as high school dropouts, homeless youth, cancer survivors, and children of war.[7]

They are advised and financed by a far-seeing group of distinguished editors and publishers who understand the importance of intergenerational work. One Children's Express publication, *Voices From the Future* (1993), is a moving series of interviews by young reporters with gang members, skinheads, homeless teens, and otherwise "at risk" teens. Many of these teens have found ways to develop safe places and support systems for each other, with the help of caring adults, that will make a better future possible for themselves and their peers.

Generally, adults waiver between accusing youth of being indifferent to the world they live in and condemning them for raging at it with whatever weapons they have at their command. Sometimes youth are indifferent. Sometimes they are murderous. But how do we explain the courage for change in street children that Children's Express interviewers found, the courage that all those who work with children and youth in the most violent settings do find? And how do we explain the 110,000 young people who not long ago poured into Paris from thirty nations in Europe, East and West, North and South, Catholic and Protestant, to meditate and pray with the ecumenical monks of the Taizé community who arrange this youth prayer periodically—filling five huge exhibition halls for five days of devout, intensely spiritual search? "We need this. At home we are at the end of our rope. All we hear is war," said a young Serbian participant after a night of prayer with fellow Serbs and Croats.[8]

How do we account for Iqbal, the Pakistani child sold into slavery at age four by his parents, who after six years of being shackled to a carpet-weaving loom most of the time, tying knots hour after hour, was freed with the help of the Pakistani Bonded Labour Liberation Front. Where did he find the strength to help lead the crusade against child labor that brought him to Sweden at age twelve to address an international labor conference in 1994? What was going on in his mind, and in his spirit, in the years from age four to ten when he was chained to the loom, and where did he find the words to speak of it?

How do we account for the fact that Indian-born Satish Kumar, one of today's outstanding teachers and practitioners of nonviolence and Director of Programs at Schumacher College in England, knew at nine years of age that it was time to leave home and become a Jainist monk, undertaking one of the most rigorous spiritual disciplines that any human being of any age could undertake?[9] Yes, we underestimate the young.

The miracle of this child-segregating century is that so many children manage to grow up socially and spiritually whole. They somehow find nurture in what appear to be social deserts. They can see beyond surfaces, and find hidden caring when it is there, including the caring of an often out-of-control and abusive parent. That capacity for in-depth seeing on the part of the abused child becomes a resource for breaking the often vicious cycle of abused children becoming abusing parents.

The inexplicable keeps happening—there are the young who apparently live in utterly barren and loveless settings, yet there is a seed that comes to flowering as the child matures. Somewhere in that barren life, kindness has entered. With kindness, the seed can flourish in barren soil, like the tree that takes root in a rocky crevice of a steep mountainside. The tree will grow toward the sky, nourished by the barest minimum of crumbled forest debris that winds have swept into the crevice, and by occasional trickles of water from passing storms.

Robert Coles, the psychiatrist who spent a lifetime studying and working with seriously troubled children, came to see after thirty years of this work that he had been ignoring a profound spiritual sensitivity that kept coming through in children's responses to his very secular questions about their lives. Realizing that he had been missing something basic about how they were dealing with their lives, he then devoted several years to interviewing eight to twelve-year-old Muslim, Christian, and Jewish children, as well as children with no religious identification, about their faith and belief. These were all youngsters with serious problems. Discovering an awesome spiritual maturity and self-insight in their answers to his questions about the meaning of life and their views of God, and of good and evil, he came to understand that children coped with their lives at a far deeper level than psychiatric analysis alone could reveal.[10] They were being nurtured by sometimes very fragmentary sources the adults around them would not have been aware of.

### Examples of Youth-Adult Partnering

In the glimpses just given of the knowledge and experience worlds of children, I have emphasized not only cognitive ability and skill, but the capacity for nurture and empathy. The concept of partnership involves an assumption of significant two-way sharing of responsibility and problem-solving capabilities, and also mutual empathy. However, we face a huge gap in moving from rhetoric to reality about youth-adult partnering because there is so little social awareness of how much children and youth know, how much they have to contribute in terms of social problem-solving. There is also a comparable gap in social awareness of how even very young children actually *nurture* the adults around them. Teen *insensitivity* to adults is legendary in the Western world (though not in the non-West), and few adults come to perceive the levels of concern and caring, the downright anguish beneath the "hip" teen facade.

Yet large though these gaps are, significant numbers of children, youth, and adults are bridging them and forming deeply meaningful partnerships based on a common concern for humanity and for the earth itself. Since each age cohort views the world through the lenses of formative social events of their early years, whether assassination of key leaders, wars, depressions, environmental catastrophes, or positive events of peacemaking and the creation of new socioeconomic and political forms, each age cohort has enhanced sensitivity to certain aspects of society and decreased sensitivity to other aspects. Accordingly, children, teens, and adults literally experience different worlds. Cross-generational sharing of these differently experienced worlds is essential for holistic problem solving.

In terms of youth-adult partnerships, what adults contribute is a greater accumulation of life experience with political, economic, and social institutions of society—with "how things work"—more access to communication systems, and much more access to resources. What children and youth contribute is based precisely on their different age perspectives and includes a penetrating set of counterobservations about how things *really* work that highlight important aspects of daily social transactions that adults overlook or become blind to. (It was a child, remember, who called out, "The emperor has no clothes!") Also, unjaded by life, they have more energy for trying new strategies.

Partnering, whether among adults or between adults and children, is on the basis of shared responsibility and shared respect, in a relationship of equality that does not preclude alternating roles of leading and following, teaching and learning. A good partnership relation implies mutual nurturance, whether the relationship is marital, parent-child, work-related, or civic. Before we turn to some examples of partnership, let us consider the shared spaces available for intergenerational interaction. Faith communities are increasingly realizing that they need to give more time to family gatherings in church, temple, synagogue, and mosque. Schools and local governments are promoting the concept of peer mediators, which brings those young people trained as mediators into contact with adult authorities as equal participants in important conflict-resolution processes. Service learning, which existed in

Scout troops long before the term came into educational usage, brings school children into many community projects as equal participants with adults. Not all community spaces are age-segregated.

In considering the specific examples of nurturant partnership between adults and children/youth to follow, let us bear in mind that there have always been adults who have instinctively related to children in a nurturant partnership of mutual respect—in every age, in every culture, no matter how age-graded or patriarchal or authoritarian the society. But as I have already indicated, the developments of this century have largely been in the direction of one-way care and protection rather than cooperation in a spirit of mutuality. The 1989 UN Convention on the Rights of the Child, going beyond the original Declaration on the Rights of the Child, has done for children and youth what United Nations conventions on women's rights have done for women. In both cases the United Nations has provided a platform for the public working-out of concerns related to a fuller participation by these traditionally excluded categories of persons in the societies of which they are a part—concerns that would have otherwise been ignored. From the United Nations side, this has been facilitated by the 1979 International Year of the Child as well as the World Youth Assemblies of 1970 and 1980, the 1985 International Year of Youth, the 1990 World Children's Summit, and the 1998 World Youth Forum. The 1998 Forum is of special interest because it preceded the first-ever World Conference of Ministers for Youth Affairs in Lisbon, Portugal, and youth delegates were able to present their conclusions directly to the government ministries that needed to hear them.

From the side of emerging global civil society and the world of international nongovernmental organizations (NGOs), we have witnessed a dramatic increase in the number of NGOs relating to children and youth. The 1993–94 *Yearbook of International Organizations*, volume 3, lists 859 NGOs focused on children, 47 on adolescents, and 458 on youth.[11] However, when we ask which of the children's NGOs involve actual *participation* of children as members and initiators of activity, only 22, or 6 percent, fall in that category. In the case of NGOs focused on adolescence, 10, or 21 percent, involve their direct participation; for youth NGOS, 191, or 42 percent, are fully participatory. This means that most of these organizations are *advocacy* organizations *on behalf* of children and youth. Certainly, advocacy has an important role to play, especially in dealing with the suffering of the young. Nevertheless, in terms of developing actual intergenerational partnerships for social change, the NGO world has a long way to go.

On a grassroots level, however, things have been happening in terms of children and youth activities with adult partners, particularly since the 1960s. Since older youth already have a long history of organizing, I will focus here primarily on the preteens and younger teens. By the 1970s that extraordinary musical theater format, the Peace Child, had evolved. Peace Child productions involved taking a musical score (produced by adults) around the world and having local children, preteens, and teens create their own play about peace in their own language, built around the musical score.[12] Thus, hundreds of versions of the Peace Child were performed by children on every continent for several decades, with the help of peace activist adults. These productions served to conscientize and to mobilize both adults and children, not only against war but for a greater visibility and participation of children in public life.

Other initiatives arose in various countries, and by 1990 the Coalition for Children of the Earth was in its early stages, a development made possible by a high level of networking activity among children and youth and their partnering adults. The deteriorating condition of the earth itself aroused children on every continent. The resulting children's movements were a startling demonstration not only that children were more aware of the condition of their immediate environment than many of the adults around them but also that they were able to project in their own minds what this meant for the world. Young Carolina Garcia Travesi in Tamaulipas, Mexico, was nine when she first started worrying about the contamination all around her in the air, soil, and water of her town. She started a local ecology club with her classmates and by fifteen, when I met her at a conference on the environment in Boulder, Colorado, had become one of a new generation of team leaders in youth initiatives to save the earth. She was one of hundreds of children who, by sheer determination and ingenuity, got to the Rio Conference on the Environment in 1992; her energy, imagination, and articulateness attracted the adult partners (including her own rather surprised parents) necessary for the development of continuing organizational structures and communication networks.[13]

Many parallel initiatives emerged independently and then became interlinked as groups found out about each other. The Peace Child organization gave birth to Rescue Mission Planet Earth in response to the tremendous opportunities for networking at Rio and began publishing *Global Network News* to help connect children and young people.[14] The newsletter reports on conferences and projects, such as the European Youth Parliament for the environment. The Youth Parliament considers findings from youth gatherings in seven European states on the four following issues: (1) implementation of *Agenda 21*, the priorities-setting document that emerged from the Rio Conference on the environment; (2) school waste projects; (3) energy use and savings projects; and (4) the organization of a Europe-wide competition for the most pro-environment school on the Continent. Many other gatherings and projects are also reported. Rescue Mission's own in-house *Action Update* newsletter publishes letters from elementary and secondary school youth about local environmental projects they have initiated in their schools and communities. It is important to note that children are learning how to work with teachers and local school authorities to institute both in-class and after-school activities that the schools would not otherwise have considered. Sharing and teaching skills of how to work with adults and with school systems has been a not inconsiderable part of Rescue Mission's work.

The Peace Child successor organization has published an attractive and highly readable version of *Agenda 21* prepared by children under the title *Rescue Mission Planet Earth* and also collected manuscripts from its young members for a history of the United Nations entitled *The World in Our Hands*. To give an idea of the magnitude of the networking for the United Nations history project: 30,000 young people from 120 countries submitted material for the book. After a substantial culling and editing process, the book was printed and presented to the United Nations on its fiftieth anniversary. Among more recent projects is the preparation of a Rescue Mission Cabaret modeled on the Peace Child project—scripts to be created locally around a core set of songs. All of this is done by young people from eight to nineteen years of age, with Peace Child founder David Woollcombe serving as a key adult partner.

Rescue Mission Planet Earth also works with Voice of Children, an international network started in Norway in 1991 with children aged twelve to fifteen, to promote the civic participation of children in local, national, and world governance. A memorable civic event in Sydney in the early 1990s, when thirty-five young Australian members of the Voice of Children gathered in Parliament House to tell the listening politicians, business leaders, and media what they were concerned about, is typical of Voice of Children initiatives.

The European Youth Academy, based in Villach, Austria, has since 1993 brought together young people and their teachers from various countries who have worked locally on problems and opportunities common to all and then come together, first regionally and then all together for annual, week-long events at Villach. One emphasis is on creating regional zones of peace, a concept that is most highly developed in the Alps-Adriatic region (northern Italy, Slovenia, Croatia, western Hungary, and Austria). Supported by the Council of Europe, the European Youth Academy is creating pan-European youth networks that can continue into the future as Europe struggles with creating new peace-building activities across all borders and cultures.[15]

These and other international networking groups such as Lifelinks, which works on school twinning between continents, all cooperate in the very loose Coalition for Children of the Earth to promote an Annual Day of Access around the world for children to discuss with local, national, and international officials and leaders their thinking about threats to human survival.[16] Children who gathered at the 1995 World Summit of Children in San Francisco prepared a request to the UN General Assembly to declare an Annual Day of Access. They also presented a proposal for an ongoing General Assembly of older children and youth of nonvoting age, to provide a voice at the United Nations for the nearly 45 percent of the world's population that are legally "minors." In the International Keeping the Promise Document of the Children's Summit, the young drafters point out that "children are not partial human beings, humans-in-progress. They are full citizens and members of the Human Race."[17]

All this youth networking bore fruit at the historic Hague Appeal for Peace Conference in May of 1999, an NGO worldwide mobilization to call attention to the failure of states to act on the commitments of the 1899 Hague Peace Conference to bring an end to war. A Hague Appeal youth newsletter that reached youth groups on every continent during the year before the conference helped mobilize young energies by carrying stories of preparatory gatherings of students and young people in Africa, Asia, Europe, and the Americas. The five-day Hague Conference itself, packed with sessions reporting local youth peace action around the world as well as skill-training and project-development workshops, lay the groundwork for a new level of local-global youth linkage.[18]

Youth are not waiting for the United Nations to act. With the help of adult partners, through the Voice of Children and other organizations, they are learning how to hold hearings on important social issues in their local communities, preferably in the local town hall.[19] Reports indicate attentive audiences of local and state councils and legislators, business people, and media. Many towns in Europe already have a Day of Access when young prevoting age citizens join local governing councils for the day and speak of their concerns.

The examples of partnering given so far have involved the creation of transnational networks to support civic action of children and youth at the local level in their own communities. Although the networks have included youth from all continents—with Asia, Africa, and Latin America well represented—many of the initiatives began in Europe and have tended to reach children with schooling and with supportive families. Another type of partnership has developed, as street children—children displaced by poverty, war, and environmental degradation—have found adult partners to help them create new lives for themselves and their communities, in both the One-Third and the Two-Thirds World. In the U.S., for example, Kidspeace is a coalition of centers working with kids in crisis, and Global Kids focuses on how to deal with violence.[20]

### Street Children Networks in the Two-Thirds World

Street children, ranging from two-year-olds to teens, either have no family living quarters at all or come from homes that are too crowded or too abusive to make space for them—factors that drive them to life on the streets. They are among the most savvy children in the world. At best, they become family to each other, managing to earn enough from odd jobs and scrap collection to survive and, not infrequently, to bring money to a destitute single mother in another part of town. At worst, they are victimized by drug dealers and beaten and killed by police. The more fortunate ones develop street enterprises and find adult partners who help them with skill training and modest capital for their enterprises.

In New Delhi a group of street children between the ages of seven and seventeen had the idea of opening a restaurant "so we will always have enough to eat." They found support from street workers affiliated with the NGO Caritas to rent space in a bus terminal. Here they first underwent an intensive ten-day training in cooking, nutrition, cleanliness, serving customers, and bookkeeping. They now have a modest restaurant in the bus terminal, with a room in back in which to sleep, and two hours a day of schooling arranged by the local Caritas street workers groups known as Butterflies. There are many hundreds of stories like this from the streets of Asia, Africa, and Latin America; and stories from the cities of Europe and North America are now adding to this saga of the world's street children.

In Brazil, where police killing of street children drew international media attention, two hundred citizens' organizations already working with street children formed a national movement. This adult coalition made possible the holding of a street children's congress in 1986. Over forty ragged and barefoot street children between the ages of eight and sixteen were helped to get to Brasilia to tell the government and the public what street children need: chances for education and work. Now there is less killing and more education and employment for street children.

From continent to continent, street children are the recyclers of urban waste, picking up every kind of scrap and carrying it, often over considerable distances, to recycling centers. They earn enough to eat, but not much more. One study of street gangs describes a twelve-year-old gang leader in Manila, the Philippines, who "looks after" his gang of children, six- to twelve-year-olds, by organizing their labor of begging, scavenging, and pushing carts for other vendors to ensure that all get enough to eat. The gang has its own moral code. Members look out for each other—and even have time, says a nine-year-old member, to play! They enjoy running, skipping, and chasing cars. With no adult partners, however, there is little possibility of any education in their future.

A group of street children in Nairobi, Kenya, who scavenge in garbage dumps for recyclables were luckier. They found adult partners (the Undugu Society) who arranged for special short-term courses for street children in local slum schools. Thus the children could learn to read and write while continuing their salvage work each day and would have a chance for vocational training once they were literate.

Girl street children live mainly by "survival sex." The only way out is for girl gang leaders to connect with adult partners who help them find local schooling space and teachers so their gang members can learn other skills.

Street children survive as well as they do because they help each other. Older children take responsibility for younger children. Girl children often have babies to look after before they are fifteen. When adult partners become available, this pattern of taking responsibility for each other translates into opportunities for education, training, and employment as well as the possibility of homes and "real" family life and civic life. Transnational organizations like Street Kids International, based in Canada; Child to Child Trust and Streetwise International, both based in England; Childhope, affiliated with UNICEF and working mainly in Latin America, and Outreach, a Nairobi-based UNEP-affiliated NGO network for providing learning materials for street children all provide streetwise and caring adults to partner street children in creating better lives for all.[21] It must not be forgotten that the heartening record of good outcomes is possible because street children have already been family to one another in the streets and have shared survival skills with one another. Adult intervention alone could not produce these outcomes.

Children who have been traumatized and brutalized by war may have had less opportunity to help one another than street children. Often change comes more abruptly into their lives—sudden devastation of a village by guerrilla warfare, sudden loss of home and family. Nevertheless, here too the work of healing, which must both precede and accompany any effort to help such children rebuild their lives, begins among the children themselves. The older children help the younger children in the centers where they are gathered to be fed and housed. Child to Child Trust has been particularly active in encouraging this child-to-child nurture. The heightened awareness of the impact of armed conflict on children, including their being forced to become child soldiers, has been substantially aided by the publication by the United Nations of Graca Machel's report on this subject.[22]

## The Self-Empowerment of Children and Youth

Many of the youth-adult partnerships described in the previous section have relied to a significant degree on adult leadership and adult access to resources, although the *substance* of the activities has been the creative work of children and youth. Now we will turn to an arena in which children and youth are the self-empowered initiators, selectively seeking adult partners in their highly individual learning quests and community action projects. I refer to the self-schooling movement, which began as an identifiable preteen and teen movement in the early 1970s, not the older homeschooling movement, which has traditionally been a parents' movement to replace the relatively bureaucratic learning systems of public schools with family-based learning, parents serving as teachers. The difference between the two movements lies in the role of the parents. In the established and legally recognized tradition of homeschooling, the parents plan the curriculum, procure the necessary learning materials, and do the teaching. In self-schooling, the young person sets her education goals, identifies the resources needed, and negotiates with potential teachers where needed in fields like the sciences and the arts. Her parents serve as consulting partners. In her search for learning spaces, she will come to know the community far better than many adult residents. She will know its museums, libraries, theaters, craft centers; she will find its hospitals and clinics, its laboratories, repair shops, mom and pop stores, local markets, and local farms. She will trace its labyrinth of governance structures, its regulatory and helping services. At times she will seek more, at other times less, assistance from her parents. But however much or little assistance she seeks, it is a child-parent partnership because there is mutual respect for the process within the family. There is a united front presented to school authorities, and a caring responsiveness within the family if and when problems arise.

While at the extremes the difference between parent-initiated homeschooling and self-schooling is very noticeable, most homeschooling has large components of self-schooling in it. Generally, when the homeschooling movement is referred to, it covers both kinds, and differences tend to revolve around the relative emphasis given to the respective roles of parent and child in the educational process.

The basic assumption of the "unschooling" movement is that classroom teaching often de-motivates children, and that too much school time is devoted to organizational matters, too little time to "on task" learning. Proponents of homeschooling point out that roughly 1,100 hours a year are spent in school, and only 220, or 20 percent, of these consist of "on task" learning. In short, 80 percent is seen as being devoted primarily to organizational matters.[23] In the 1990s there were at least eight organizations and newsletters in the United States devoted to homeschooling, self-schooling, or "unschooling" in general.

No one knows exactly how many teens and preteens have entered upon such adventures in learning. However, most self-schoolers keep a journal (handy evidence for local school inspectors), and some of them publish informal newsletters as a means of communication with other self-schoolers in different regions. Since many of them write very well indeed, there is by now a considerable published literature by self-schoolers about their journeys of discovery. Grace Llewellyn's *Teenage Liberation Handbook* is a gold mine of information about books, journals, newsletters, and networks devoted to self-schooling.[24] The book is addressed to teenagers, not to parents, but parental partnering roles get full play in it. Unorthodox though young people's self-designed curricula may be, records indicate that they score very high on scholastic aptitude tests. College admission has not been a problem for homeschoolers.

The zest for knowledge, love of life, and determination to make the world a better place that we find in self-schoolers suggests that these seekers are already contributors to the culture of peace this book is about. (*Homeschoolers for Peace and Justice* is the title of one newsletter published by a homeschooling family in California.) Self-schoolers develop finely honed social skills in their search for adult teaching partners and often become adept community organizers. Experienced at barter—offering babysitting or yard or house work in return for learning opportunities—they can even be thought of as pioneers in the LETS movement (Labor Exchange Trading System), which builds community relations through barter.

Transnational self-schooling networks are in the early stages of development. For years, each issue of the recently defunct *TRANET*, a transnational publication devoted to alternative and transformational movements, carried a section on "Youth and Learning," in which homeschoolers, self-schoolers, and alternative schoolers wrote from various countries about their learning projects and asked to correspond with others with similar interest.[25] So far, however, the networks seem to be largely Euro–North American. Homeschooling, both parent-led and child-initiated, certainly exists in every country, not only where national public education systems are still rudimentary but also where they provide universal access. Wherever homeschooling is found as a movement, it offers a voice of creative dissent, aiming for a higher concept of human and social development in the societies of which it is a part.

Another important self-empowerment movement for children and teens is the Youth Section of the Re-Evaluation Counseling movement. An all-ages movement that now has groups in nearly sixty countries on all continents, it offers a peer counseling process that frees people from past distress experience to become self-confident social change agents in the world around them. It has active preteen and teen groups with a strong "youth liberation" emphasis. These groups, working locally, nationally, and internationally, are demanding a voice in the civic affairs and decision making of their communities. Internationally, RC, as it is known, is organized into "biennial" age groups. The youngest international group consists of thirteen- and fourteen-year-olds, and a group for eleven- and twelve-year-olds seems to be emerging. There is a special youth magazine for preteens and teens, *Young and Powerful*, published in England.[26] There are "liberation reference persons" for youth in various world regions whose names and addresses are widely publicized. RC can be considered an adult-youth partnership movement in that it gives strong emphasis to adult backing for youth-initiated action.

## Youth-Age Partnership and Peace Culture

It is estimated that by the year 2000 one-half of the world's population will be under twenty. Many of these youth will have experienced unprecedented violence and brutality—to say nothing of serious malnutrition—since their early years, yet they will be moving into the ranks of full citizenship and decision making at a very rapid rate, beginning in the first decade of the twenty-first century. Current practices of segregation by age and social class will leave these young people ill-prepared for their new responsibilities.

For this reason, social movements based on the concept of youth-adult partnership for social change—movements addressing the issues of peace building, environmental regeneration, human and social development, and human rights—will have an increasingly important role to play in making the crucial transition that lies ahead. This is the transition *from* a world ordered by age and gender dominance systems that suppress much human know-how and creativity and continuously sow new seeds of violence and war. It is a transition *to* a world ordered by mutually respectful problem-solving partnerships across ages and between genders, which sow the seeds of gentleness with the earth and peace with one another.

We have seen that many new partnering networks between preteens/teens and adults have been forming in recent decades—nationally, regionally, and globally. While the language and strategies of the partnering networks differ, there are strong commonalities. Take a moment to consider the Coalition for Children of the Earth groups, such as Rescue Mission Planet Earth, Voice of Children, and Lifelinks, all working with and through the school systems of the countries in which they are active; then call to mind the international networks of street children groups making do with the resources that poverty itself generates; finally, consider their more economically blessed sisters and brothers similarly engaged in self-schooling, self development and community development entirely outside the highly organized school systems of their respective countries. All these efforts are characterized by a high degree of youth initiative and creativity, with respectful, supportive participation by adults in a partnering mode and a shared vision of a more humane world in which life will be better for everyone.

These new networks overlay older communities, groupings of both indigenous peoples and more settled farming peoples, that have long practiced more traditional youth-age partnering in gathering subsistence from Mother Earth. These peoples know a pattern of intergenerational work, play, and

community worship that has not completely disappeared, though urbanization and industrialization have destroyed much of it. Where those patterns
still exist, in each world region, they should be recognized and honored. The
new networks have much to learn from older practices.

What can we expect from the new movements in the twenty-first century?
Can we envision a future in which there is a preteen and teenage member of
every city council, every local citizen's committee, every state legislature, and
every national house of parliament? Will communities of faith support teen
participation in decision making? Will school systems shift to a more community-based, apprenticeship-focused mode of education? Will families hold
democratic family councils? Will youth and age dance together, sing together, play together? If that is what we want, we must dare to imagine such
a world, and then begin making choices to bring it about.

*Part Three*
*Conflict Structures and*
*Their Transformation*

# Introduction

IN OUR SEARCH for evidence that peace cultures exist, we began in part 1 by exploring human history, contrasting the prevailing image of the past as the story of wars won or lost with the persistent recurrence of peace movements through time and the persistent experiments, whether in real life or in the imagination, to develop utopias—egalitarian colonies of peace—as alternatives to societies ordered by hierarchy and domination. In part 2 we looked at peace cultures in action in our own time, beginning with a sampling of actual societies characterized by creative nonviolent behavior in everyday life. Then we looked at social change movements specifically focused on developing new, creatively nonviolent human relationships. The area of feminist social inventions was considered first, followed by movements pioneering new and gentler roles for men and new, egalitarian relationships between women and men. The concluding chapter of part 2 explored the development of new activist roles for children and a new partnering relationship between children and adults.

Throughout parts 1 and 2, the concept of structural violence—the patterning of social institutions that results in violence, oppression, and injustice for victim sectors of society, whether locally, regionally, or globally—has been the implicit backdrop for each exploration of actual peaceableness. Now comes the hardest part: examining the structural bases of violence in today's world and considering the transformational potential within each of the interrelated sets of structures for movement toward viable cultures of peace. Since my own lifelong focus as a sociologist has been on human behavior at the local level, seeing how people create and are created by their biosocial environments, it happens that my knowledge of the interfaces of the local and the global has been largely limited to the tracing of transnational networks of peoples' associations, utilizing only the most general conceptions of the interaction of these networks with global economic, political, and information/communication structures.

Understanding how all this fits together in the sociosphere-biosphere totality of Gaia herself is a daunting challenge, yet one I dare not ignore. Why? Because despair over existing forces of destruction unleashed by the social and physical technologies of the postindustrial earth-ravaging age is a major obstacle to the creation of new structures that can birth a peaceful and compassionate future. We cannot work for what we think is impossible. So, ill-equipped as I am, I will do my best to outline some of the structural transformation potentials in some major arenas of human activity. Reader, please see this as a joint enterprise between us, and carry on your own further exploration of transformational potentials.

The term "paradigm shift," referring to a basic reconceptualization of "how things work," has been heavily used and overused in recent decades, but for understandable reasons. The term offers a way to apprehend the magnitude of the shift in our thinking required to break out of failed patterns of organizing how we live on the planet. A basic background theme of the domination of the weak by the strong has lurked insistently throughout parts 1 and 2 and must be addressed in part 3 as a failed response to an omnipresent set of apparently conflicting human needs in any social order. These are the need for autonomy, individuality, one's own social space, on the part of individual human beings, in contrast with the need for bonding with others, the need for social support, the need to love and to be loved. The adversarial or domination model of human relations addresses only the need for autonomy and social space, with winners and losers. But, as we have noted from time to time, there is another model, the mutuality model, which takes into account both the need for space and the need for bonding in a relationship that seeks positive outcomes for all parties in a conflict situation.[1] The mutuality model is thus a problem-solving model (a win-win model, for those who like this terminology) that has a positive multiplier effect, in that each social problem resolved to the mutual advantage of the parties concerned creates the basis for more problem-solving behavior in future conflicts.

The predominant theme for governance and systems of law, for economic activity and its associated use of natural resources—and even for our information systems, particularly at the macrolevel—is domination and control. And yet there are mutuality elements in each system, or societies could not have survived. Continued survival is, however, seriously in doubt, given current extremes of militarism, resource depletion, and economic and social injustice. What elements, what social movements are available for further development away from dominance and toward cooperation, toward mutual problem solving, toward a highly diversified but sustainable global peace culture?

We will begin this search by looking in chapter 8 at the state system and its problem-solving inadequacy in the face of the thousands of ethnic and other cultural identity groups sprawled across all national borders around the globe, in homelands and in diasporas. New political autonomy concepts and institutional arrangements in the problem-solving mode will be explored as possible modifications of existing state systems. Next, we will consider in chapter 9 the workings of global corporations and their environmental and social impacts on the One-Third and the Two-Thirds Worlds, and new movements for ecodevelopment and coexistence with the more-than-human world that are based on different understandings of relationships between humans and the ever-changing bioregions of the planet. In chapter 10, the old/new "information orders" of the planet will be considered, including their different impacts on the One-Third and Two-Thirds Worlds. Here we will address both the media itself, including different types of control of the media, patterns of schooling, and the effect of living in cyberspace on the human creativity and social skills of those who inhabit it. The reclamation of local communication cultures will be considered in the cyberspace context.

Chapter 11 will explore the structure of the global military system in its One-Third and Two-Thirds World components, and the role of NGOs and grassroots movements in its transformation through processes of demilitarization; resocialization of guerrillas, terrorists, and soldiers; and creative approaches to the challenges of swelling communities of refugees and displaced peoples.

The closing chapter will look at the peaceableness of the planet from the perspective of the 200-year present: Where were we at the beginning of the twentieth century, and where might we be by the end of the twenty-first century, in terms of a creative, evolving, and biosocially sustainable complex of peace cultures for the planet?

# 8

# *Peoples and States*

A MAJOR OBSTACLE to the practice of the peacemaking skills that actually exist in every society is the tension between the 188 states of the international system and the "10,000 societies," ethnically, linguistically, or religiously based identity groups sprawled across all state boundaries.[1] Modernization theory assumed that each state would assimilate all identity groups within its borders in the course of building the polity, yet supposedly disappearing ethnies (peoples claiming a common cultural heritage and lifeways) are rapidly reasserting themselves. Furthermore, new ethnic communities form as migrant streams from the Two-Thirds World settle in the One-Third World, generating new hybrid cultural identities, such as British-Sikhs in England or Hispanic-origin citizens in the United States. Diasporas and the creation of new hybrid ethnicities through migration are of course as old as the human experience of migration itself, and are further testimony to the enduring importance of ethnicity, broadly defined, in the contemporary social order

Strong ethnic identities are today frequently seen as a source of social disintegration, violence, and terror—a retrogression to a less evolved social condition. Yet over most of human history, as well as in the present, different ethnic, cultural, linguistic, and religious groups have coexisted peacefully on common or adjacent terrains. The current revival of communal identities in all states, from the most to the least "developed," and even the creation of new mythical identities with no real historical foundation, suggests that these

---

Parts of this chapter are taken from a longer study prepared for a festschrift (in Japanese) for Kinhide Mushakoji: "Ethnicity and New Constitutive Orders: An Approach to Peace in the Twenty-first Century," in *From Chaos to Order*, vol. 1, *Crisis and Renaissance of the World Society*, ed. Hisakazu Usui and Takeo Uchida (Tokyo: Yushindo Publishers, 1990).

identity groups may have an important function to serve in sustaining the social order. The resurgence may in fact be a response to the failure of the modern nation-state to meet the needs of its diverse populations—not only the need for the equitable distribution of resources and opportunities, but also the need for meaning and a sense of self-worth. The widening gap between One-Third and Two-Thirds World countries, between North and South, has been well documented, and may in itself be a demonstration of serious inadequacies in the organizational forms of the state.

We will look at identity groups (also referred to as communal groups, or ethnies) as resources for dealing with some of the structural problems of the modern state: (1) the problem of scale, with the center unable to manage its peripheries effectively; (2) the problem of adequate knowledge of local terrains, where many of the resources for problem solving are located; and (3) the problem of relevant skills for the issues at hand. From this perspective, industrialized countries may suffer from social and cultural underdevelopment to the extent that they have applied more or less forcible assimilation policies to numerically significant ethnic/cultural groups within their borders. Frequently economically disadvantaged, these minorities are sometimes referred to as the Third World within the First World. Communal groups are to varying degrees storehouses of folk wisdom and technical problem-solving skills that increase the chances of survival for their members within polities where they are disadvantaged. These skills include conflict resolution skills for use both internally and with outsiders and knowledge of how to use environmental resources, rural or urban. That wisdom/skill complex may undergo distortion and even degeneration in interaction with an indifferent or hostile state.

The United Nations World Cultural Development Decade (1988–97) and the 1993 Year of World Indigenous People represent efforts to examine that uneasy diversity of world cultures as precious resources for human and social development in a period when the social inventiveness of modernizing forces seems to be at a very low level. However, since such decades and years are programs of member states of the United Nations, participation of actual ethnies in decade/year activities is uneven. A 1994 proposal from a citizen's commission to establish by treaty a General Agreement on Culture and Development involving indigenous, tribal, grassroots, and community action groups was dropped under pressure, but the plan still exists and may be revived in the future.[2]

The magnitude of the multiethnic reality for contemporary states is suggested by a survey I undertook in the 1970s of 159 countries.[3] This survey revealed that only four states (three of them European, one Asian) were mono-cultural, having one shared ethnicity in the entire country, and twenty-four states were monolingual. Ninety-one states had between 100 and 3,000 ethnies (India and Indonesia had the most), each ethnie also being counted as a linguistic community, though neighboring tribal groups would probably be able at least to understand one another. Given the rates of migration from Africa and Eurasia to Europe and North America in recent decades, the ethnic counts for Euro–North America will be higher today.

The awareness of the multiethnic character of most contemporary states is heightened by the fact that most post–World War II wars have been intrastate rather than interstate. However, it must be borne in mind that there were only 51 independent founding states of the United Nations in 1945. This means that of the 188 member states of the United Nations today, 137 came into being after the United Nations was founded. Many of these have been going through a series of internal power transitions in the decades since. The reason for these power struggles can be traced directly to the two to four centuries of occupation by European colonizers (in some cases preceded by Arab colonizers), who ruthlessly ignored traditional economic, political, and cultural systems and lifeways of the numerous ethnies within any given colonial administration. The preferential treatment given to some ethnies over others for the convenience of the colonizers created inequalities and resentments that continue to fuel present-day conflicts. These antagonisms are *not*, however, age-old, but have a specific, relatively recent origin. Afro-Asia and the Americas were certainly not utopias in the eras prior to Western colonial expansion, and expansionist kingdoms go back a long way in history. Nevertheless, most tribal groups had functioning conflict resolution practices internally and with neighboring tribes, practices that have in many cases continued "underground," so to speak, into this century. Often, however, they are found in such weakened form that they have not been able to cope with post-independence power conflicts, particularly when these have been sustained by weapons supplied by states from both sides of the Cold War. The efforts to rebuild fragile states that have undergone genocidal warfare, such as Somalia, Sri Lanka, and Rwanda, include efforts to rebuild traditional institutions for mediation and dispute settlement.[4]

Clearly the melting pot theory that assumes the creation of one supernationality within each state does not correspond to reality, and a world system made up of such states does not offer a viable political future for the twenty-first century. The possibility of future peace cultures will depend on a new constitutive order substantially different from the present state system—one that permits much wider participation of identity groups, with all the cultural, skill, and knowledge resources they represent, in shaping the polities of which they are a part. The intense and continuing efforts to evolve new constitutional formats in countries with strong communal groups, like Canada, Switzerland, Belgium, Spain, and the United Kingdom, are suggestive of the new forms of autonomy that will continue to arise, albeit in some cases with great pain, in coming decades. How countries like those of the former Soviet Union and the former Yugoslavia, where there have already been so many brutal forced movements of ethnic populations in recent memory, and countries like Nigeria, Sudan and India, currently paralyzed giants seething with tribal and religious turmoil, will find their way is harder to tell. In the end, one must hope that ingenuity, imagination, and a longing for peace will generate solutions.

Ethnicity has many meanings. Ethnic groups have sometimes been studied as oppressing elites (as, for example, in South Africa). They may also be studied as nationalities, cultures, or linguistic groupings. Sometimes the ethnicity is, in fact, a religiously based cultural form. I will use the term *communal group* (sometimes called *identity group*) to refer to all groups that have some sense of common history and common fate, recognizing that the common history may be at least in part mythical. Communal groups may or may not be territorially based, and most of them spill over the boundaries of several states. Historically the best-known nonterritorial communal groups have been Gypsies and Jews, who can be found on all continents. Now, however, more and more identity groups have subgroup settlements in both hemispheres. The boundaries of communal groups are fluid and change over time, as the consciousness of historical roots and common fate heighten or fade according to social conditions.

However, there is one set of identity groups that are more clearly demarcated in space: indigenous peoples. Unlike those ethnies that have a long history of more or less active struggles for autonomy, indigenes have made their way into public awareness more recently—although their sufferings go back to the beginnings of colonialism on every continent. Indigenes are a special category of communal groups because every aspect of their way of life depends on their relationship with the specific ecosystem of which they are a part, be it desert, forest, jungle, mountain, or riverine plains. Their identity, religious beliefs, social customs, and means of subsistence are intimately linked to a particular territory, and each group may be said to have a unique two-way communication with their environment. As large-scale industrial logging, mining, and creation of military reserves and nuclear storage areas have been with increasing rapidity destroying their homelands, indigenous peoples have been organizing national, regional, and transcontinental networks and councils to work for recognition of their rights and special relationships to their tribal territories. Since most of them have never been out of their homelands, and their culture is an oral culture, not literacy-based, this global movement is a triumph of indigenous ingenuity, helped by a new generation of college-educated indigenous youth and a number of partnering NGOs from the North.[5]

Ironically, the World Bank in the 1980s suddenly woke up to the fact that there were 200 million tribal people on the planet (the 1995 estimate was 300 million), roughly 4 percent of the world population, and that they possessed among them uniquely useful knowledge of how to live in fragile ecosystems.[6] That knowledge will now turn out to be critical for the survival of the very industrial societies that have been busy, with help from the World Bank, destroying their own ecosystems and those of the tribal peoples. Now the race is on between those who want to work with indigenous peoples and learn from them and those who are bent on continuing to mine, log, and otherwise exploit and destroy their lands.

When the United Nations declared 1993 to be the International Year of Indigenous People, the declaring body refused to use the term *peoples* with an *s*. This was, in fact, a refusal to recognize that each tribal group has its own communal identity, with related rights and responsibilities. It also suggests what a rocky road these now actively mobilizing peoples have ahead of them. Member states that refuse to use the term *peoples* are skirting the issue of autonomy for indigenous communities. While there are now more than thirteen UN Conventions dealing with the rights of ethnic and other minority groups, the concept of a Permanent Forum at the United Nations for indigenous peoples, and an Assembly of Autonomous Peoples to include all the unrepresented people of the planet, is still a long way from being accepted. The good news is that at least there is a process under way!

### Ethnies and Indigenous Peoples as a Resource for Conflict Resolution and Problem Solving

Communal groups can be thought of as trust groups, minisocieties in which there is mutual respect, some degree of social equality, mutual aid, and regular intergenerational communication. Group practices celebrate a shared history, strengthen communal identity, and provide meaning for life as lived in the present, as well as some degree of predictability for the future. Most communal groups provide the opportunity to their members for regular sharing in neighborhood and locality, although some groups may have members living in widely scattered locations.

Kin relations, actual or fictive, and the family unit, however defined (it may be single-sexed, as in monasteries and in lesbian/gay communities; it may be one-, two-, or three-generational) are important to communal groups. The commitment to nurture and support across generations, the recognition of the individuality of each person and his/her special place in the family unit, the care taken of children when these are present, and the ever-present necessity for conflict resolution whenever human beings live in close proximity to each other produce in each culture unique patterns of intrafamilial and community interaction. Except under conditions of great threat and hardship—and sometimes even then—these patterns have certain characteristics of peaceableness. Challenges from the larger environment, when they are not overwhelming, generate creative, problem-solving behavior.

The matter of scale is critical here. The intimate knowledge of local terrains possessed by members of folk societies has been discovered only recently by modern science. Today there are intensive efforts to study agricultural practices, aquaculture, pisciculture, sylviculture, medicinal knowledge, and varieties of traditional crafts, all representing more or less sophisticated knowledge systems, developed in some cases over thousands of years. It is not just traditional technologies that are important, however. Wherever indigenous communal groups are located—whether in forests, mountains, deserts, islands, or modern cities—they develop adaptive practices that enable the group not only to survive but to contribute to the functioning of the larger society. This adaptiveness and creativity, released within a social structure small enough to give feedback about how its members are doing, supports people economically and psychologically through failures as well as successes. The state does not do this for its citizens—neither the old industrial states nor the newly "developing" ones. In theory, every state provides a safety net, but the holes are so large, in both market and centrally planned economies, that nonmainstream populations fall through the net. Identity groups help their members to survive the fall.

Every ethnie has its wise elders, its peacemakers, its negotiators. It also has its troublemakers and violence-prone elements, which a horrified Europe is now witnessing in the massive ethnic warfare that has broken out in former Yugoslavia and in republics of the former Soviet Union. When an ethnie is healthy and in some kind of balance with the larger society, it contains aggression and violence within limits, since violence is clearly self-damaging. But oppression of ethnies is increasing; injustice piles on injustice, to the point where the twentieth century has been called "the bloody century." Violence cannot always be contained in the face of escalating wrongs. That is why it is time to explore a new constitutive order, with a place for communal groups as co-shapers of their polity.

One of the most difficult aspects of contemporary life with its continuous stream of migrants and refugees from continent to continent is that individuals and groups are continually having to interact with others who are strangers to them, in contexts where little or no possibility arises for the development of trust. Michael Barkun describes how acephalous or leaderless societies are able to live at peace with one another without formal structures to facilitate that peace.[7] He points out that interactions with neighboring groups develop slowly over time, so that familiar routines can be established with the stranger and the necessary minimum of trust created. If societies are thrown too rapidly into too close a contact with neighboring societies, new habits of interaction cannot be developed fast enough and violence results. That is the plight of every modern society, industrial or not. When Tönnies wrote about the transition from the *Gemeinschaft,* or community-based society, to the *Gesellschaft,* or contract society, he warned that it would be necessary to continue to develop *Gemeinschaft* relationships within the contract society—for contractual relations cannot bear the full weight of human needs for recognition and support.[8]

Communal groups, ethnies, to the extent that they are able, still practice the traditional trust-establishing ways of dealing with the stranger, and there is no reason why these should not be more widely recognized, and made room for, as an aid to society at large in dealing with diversity. The Bedouin, meeting a stranger in the desert, gives food first and asks no questions until an interpersonal relationship has been established through conversation. Some tribes have the practice, when a stranger appears on the horizon, of sending out one person to engage in a dialogue about places and people until some contact point through mutual knowledge of a person, place, or event has been established. If none can be discovered, the two in dialogue create a fictive point of contact. The point of contact once established, the greeter brings the stranger back to the group for introduction and welcome as a distant relative, a member of the larger tribal family. Anyone who has been welcomed as a stranger into an ethnic enclave community in any city anywhere in the world knows the warmth of this type of welcome. Such practices are an important resource in an anomic world.

With the current rise in ethnic warfare, there is little danger of romanticizing ethnicity, but its positive functions need to be understood. Nonetheless, it is certainly true that many have fled ethnic communities because they felt smothered in their embrace. Such communities may also practice their own cruelties, and women in particular often suffer from severe discriminatory and abusive practices—a situation hardly less likely in modernized than in traditional societies. Creative interactions with the larger society, however, limit, modify, and will eventually erase these cruelties. That is what the worldwide human rights movement is about. Even so, many in the South see the Universal Declaration of Human Rights as Eurocentric, overemphasizing individualism and not including the concepts of group rights, such as communal rights to land and the right of identity groups to evolve and change *as groups*.

Having explored the concept of identity groups, we shall now look at what has happened to the modern state itself, examining the problems to which identity groups possibly can contribute a solution.

## The Modern State: A Vision of Peace and Justice?

The Hague Peace Conference that ushered in the twentieth century affirmed a world in which nation-states would no longer use war as an instrument of diplomacy. Not only war was to be abolished, but also poverty and disease, as the American Andrew Carnegie optimistically instructed his board in 1911 when the Carnegie Foundation for Enduring Peace was established. World War I was seen as a "regrettable error," but the vision in the 1920s was once again of a world of peace and justice for all, specifically affirming the self-determination of nationalities. The problem was that for the Eurocentric people holding this vision, there was a failure to recognize fully the ethnic diversity of even Europe itself. As for the South, this was a vast blur of land to be colonized, resources to be used and peoples to be eventually civilized for the advancement of (European) prosperity. There was no awareness of the realities of autonomous nationalities, cultures, and civilizations, either at home or abroad. The universalism of that era was a false one.

The second "mistake" of European culture, World War II, was fought to a not insignificant degree on the peripheries of Europe by soldiers of the colonized South for their European masters. In its aftermath there was a discovery of the South as peoples with their own agendas. The new human rights concepts delegitimized colonialism, so the old colonies were turned into states by definition, regardless of the crazy patchwork of nationalities inhabiting each former colony. Coalitions from the South, including the Non Aligned Movement and the Group of 77 (now 120 states), found a voice and a forum in the United Nations, and kept calling attention to more and more peoples who should be liberated—the island colonies, the trust territories. This they did while nevertheless holding on, as now-legitimate states, to their own patchwork of nationalities. Thus, for example, the existence of Kurdistan, spread as it would be across the borders of more than five Middle Eastern countries, was outlawed. The minority nationalities of Europe and the Americas were similarly ignored by states of the North.

Conventional political theory declares that the long journey from primitive, fractious tribalism to the highly evolved modern nation-state, in which tribalism has been absorbed into a new type of citizenship guaranteeing rights, security, and welfare for all, has in Europe and North America been essentially completed. If the newer states of the South are still troubled by tribalism, in time they will assimilate their populations as the industrial democracies have done. The emerging modern world system, already at peace in a temperate zone triangle including Australia, Japan, North America, and Western Europe,[9] will be able to relinquish a highly technologized national military alliance system as soon as the transition to a world market economy has been completed. We are moving toward a world at peace.

The reality that shadows this optimistic picture is that there have been more wars in the twentieth century than in the eighteenth and nineteenth centuries combined. There were 127 armed conflicts from World War II to 1990, and 30 ongoing armed conflicts in 1998 alone. Most of these wars have involved ethnic disputes exacerbated by involvement of the Great Powers. This means that the world political map has been in more or less constant upheaval during this period. The Eurocentric triangle never was really free of it, but now the struggles are physically entering home territory as barriers between Eastern and Western Europe are breaking down.

Not only has the modern state system been unable to reduce the havoc caused by war, it has been unable to close the poverty gap. The 25 percent of the global population estimated by Gurr and Scarritt to be members of minorities at risk,[10] peoples experiencing serious deprivation in relation to fellow citizens of a given state, provide a rough indicator of the failure of the state to reduce poverty, victimization, and oppression within its borders. When we learn that 44.9 percent of the population of Africa south of the Sahara come from minorities at risk, no one is surprised—these are not yet "developed" states. But what of the twenty-one minorities in thirteen West European countries, 7.8 percent of the total population, who are at risk? What of the eight minorities in four North American countries, 15.8 percent of the population, who are at risk?

As migrant populations move from one region to another trying to escape poverty, and as the growing refugee streams seek to escape ethnic and political victimization, the number of identity groups needing accommodation on the planet will increase.[11] Referring to them as minority groups is misleading, as it suggests they are groups that happen not yet to have been successfully assimilated but will eventually be absorbed into the national societies where they are settled. It also suggests that there are ethnic groups, as opposed to nonethnic mainstream populations. A more realistic approach would be to think of "minority" groups as differentially treated communal groups in a universe of 10,000 communal groups—recognizing that everyone belongs to an ethnie (sometimes more than one). Majority or mainstream communal groups such as Anglo-Saxons are ethnies too, with various subcultures (such as WASP, a categorization used mainly by non-Anglos), but no longer identify their own ethnicity because they think of themselves as "the people" of their country.

The fluidity, shifting character, and sheer numbers of communal groups make it difficult to discuss them in well-defined analytic categories. To a considerable extent they are self-defined, and many of them are primarily oriented toward cultural identity and the protection of their rights as a group to share in the benefits of the state in which they live. However, an increasing number are seeking various forms of political recognition and political autonomy as the state fails to respond to their needs. Whether it is the nationalist movements in the Celtic fringe of Britain—Scotland, Wales, and Northern Ireland[12]—or the Celtic and Basque fringes in France and Spain, the Sardinians in Italy, the Saami (Lapps) in Norway, the native peoples in the Americas, and the French in Canada, or the host of now-warring ethnic groups in Eastern Europe and the former Soviet Union, the story is always the same: each group is being denied some of the economic, social, and cultural opportunities available to other populations in the state in question. If the trend were toward a diminution of the number and activity levels of alienated identity groups, one could say that the state is evolving in the direction of more effective functioning to provide more equal opportunity for its member populations. The trend, however, is in the opposite direction—toward an increase in the number and intensity of alienated, disaffected groups. In his stunning critique "And When the Bombing Stops?" Anthony Judge of the Union of International Associations castigates legal theorists, international relations specialists, and students of complex systems for their failure seriously to work on the visualization of alternative arrangements to existing territorial boundaries and the concepts of sovereignty they involve.[13] The founding of the Association for the Study of Ethnicity and Nationalism in 1990, and its journal, *Nations and Nationalism,* indicate that reconceptualization of the international system is, in fact, going on.

## The Search for a New Constitutive Order and Local Autonomy

What is not generally recognized is that a few states, both old and new, are realizing the impossibility of effective administration at the national level of very heterogeneous populations, cultures, and ethnies. These countries are, accordingly, engaged in various efforts to modify their constitutional structures to maintain the boundaries of the existing state while recognizing the right of certain numerically significant member populations to make decisions concerning resource allocation and social welfare of their own people. This means shifting the locus of authority downwards to regional and local units, following the principle of subsidiarity. Subsidiarity calls for decision making to be exercised as close as possible to the locus of the actual activity being decided. I shall give some examples of these constitutional explorations on each continent, beginning with Europe. It will be apparent that an enormous amount of effort is required to achieve modifications of this kind, involving protracted negotiation and continuing conflict resolution. There are no easy alternatives to dispute settlement by military force. Yet to achieve the high goals set for the world by national leaders at the beginning of this century, this path of protracted negotiation is the most likely path to a peaceful world order.

## Constitutional Status of Nationalities in Europe: Some Examples

Before discussing initiatives concerning national minorities undertaken by individual states, I should note that the Council of Europe in 1995 adopted what is known as the Framework Convention for the Protection of National Minorities. This Convention gives such minorities the right to "maintain and develop their culture, and to preserve the essential elements of their identity." Further, states can no longer engage in practices "aimed at assimilation of persons belonging to national minorities against their will."[14]

The examples that follow represent state initiatives and include political entities that were once old states or empires and became modernizing states that were expected in the nineteenth century to merge older ethnic identities in a new state identity. They have been chosen because each has felt compelled to undertake some constitutional modification to deal with communal entities within their borders. They are only examples, not a complete listing. The United Kingdom, for example, which is currently working on the issue of the necessary constitutional modifications to deal with autonomy aspirations in Northern Ireland and Scotland, is not included. Those European countries that have differentiated communal groups but have not as yet seriously considered constitutional modification in relating to them are not discussed. Neither are two other categories of differentiated communal groups, migrant workers and refugees.

### The Former Soviet Union

It is useful to begin with the now-dissolved Soviet Union. Until recently it was considered one of the newer modernizing states of Europe; it also happened to be one of the most multiethnic states in the world. It was founded on a principle of "socialist federalism" embodied in successive constitutions that described the Soviet Union as a union of nation-states. The 15 union republics also "contained another 38 national-territorial formations at three different levels (mostly within the Russian republic): 20 autonomous republics, 8 autonomous regions and 10 autonomous districts."[15] Since at the most recent estimate there were 128 ethnic groups in the now-disbanded Soviet Union, clearly many of these did not have representation in the federation. That 27 "new" peoples had been registered since the 1979 census is an indication of the continuing pressure to recognize more ethnies.

As is well known, the principle of subsidiarity was never practiced in the Soviet Union. Tishkov comments that "the rigid command-administrative system established in the 1920s and 1930s, with its vertical bureaucratic structures and omnipotent center destroyed any possible practice of federalism."[16] Even before the recent dissolution, this entire system was being rethought, and Tishkov among others called for a new conception of the primary rights of peoples to existence as collectivities to be put into the Constitution. Pointing out that the original Declaration of Rights of the Peoples of Russia of 1917 was a visionary statement of the right of self-determination indicating a very different road from that taken by the Soviet state, Tishkov once suggested that the Soviet Union might still lead the way in developing a creative constitutional format for ethnic-cultural and political autonomy. (This, of course, did not happen.) Because of recurring ethnic hostilities between peoples within a number of the republics, plus not only demands for more autonomy on the part of existing formations and units at various levels but also the increasingly strong secession movements of the Baltic Republics, the new Soviet administration was already engaged in intensive negotiations on many fronts well before the actual dissolution. The tragedy is that constitutional change moved far too slowly and was overtaken by events. Today interethnic and interstate hostilities within the former Union are so intense that creative restructuring of relationships remains a possibility only in the long run.

### The Consociational Democracies

Consociational democracy, as contrasted to majority rule democracy, depends on the segmentation of society into vertical groups, which are thus not constantly rubbing shoulders over issues that could generate conflict.[17] Only the leaders of the different groups interact, on the basis of an overarching consensus. Power sharing and divisions of jurisdiction are key characteristics of the consociational model.

*Switzerland* is often referred to as the prototype of this model. The Swiss confederation of twenty-three sovereign cantons (of which three are divided into six half-cantons), with four official languages, has its origin in the Middle Ages. It took centuries of warfare and ethnic hostility to achieve the present Federation, which has limited powers in relation to the cantons and fairly frequent national referenda, yet the Federation has played a very important role as a neutral country in this century. The level of negotiation, village by village and canton by canton, required to make the Federation work is very high, but one in which the Swiss take pride. Equality of economic status, a continuing issue, has been dealt with more or less successfully through regional specialization. Currently the French-speaking Jura district within the bilingual Bern canton, feeling discriminated against by the German majority, is asking for its own canton, so the process of building the Swiss constitutive order still goes on.

*Belgium*, an independent country since 1830, has struggled for a century with Flemish-Walloon separatism, stemming from what is economic deprivation for the Flamands in comparison to the French-speaking Walloons. Three cultural community regions have been created over the past twenty years through constitutional engineering, altering profoundly the institutions, jurisdictions, and responsibilities of the state. Citizens must now be a member of a Dutch, French, or (minority) German-speaking community; regional governments function in Flanders, Wallonia, and Brussels. Current ethnic power-sharing agreements of a very complex nature require constant negotiation, bilingual Dutch-French conduct of all government affairs, and careful respect for each identity group's needs. The fact that Belgium has had thirty-two governments since World War II indicates how difficult the coalition process is. A recent reversal of the previous economic advantage of the Walloons over the Flamands is currently requiring a whole new set of negotiations to redress new imbalances.

In *Spain*, whose predominant identity groups are Spanish, Basque, Catalan, and Galician, the Basques and the Catalans have had autonomous regions since 1979—the result of long and, for the Basques, violent autonomy struggles. Economic difficulties have been met by carefully planned educational and cultural development in each province, carried out in the national language. Catalonia in particular has a very intense economic, social, and cultural planning and development process under way, and publishes an English-Catalan magazine, *Catalonia*, to describe the autonomous region's achievements. It will be interesting to see whether these efforts, accompanied by increasing regional pride and economic initiatives, will solve the problems that the central government of Spain failed to solve. Success depends, in fact, on the cooperation of the central government with the region's development plans. How cooperative the central government will be is not yet clear.[18]

*Italy*, dealing with a well-organized autonomy movement in the South Tyrol, first created an autonomous region in 1947. In the face of vigorous local campaigns, including terrorism, the national government repaired the inadequacies of the 1947 arrangement with a revised autonomy statute in 1972. The economic provisions of the revised statute, bolstered by educational and judicial autonomy, have been particularly important in freeing local initiatives for economic development. Full bilingualism has not yet been achieved, however, and the long process of negotiation between the autonomous province and the Italian government continues.

*Norway*, slow for a long time to respond to the autonomy movement of its northern Saami people, could hardly continue to ignore the Saami when they hosted the Sixth General Assembly of the World Council of Indigenous Peoples in Tromsö in 1990. By 1993, after much lobbying, the Norwegian government recognized a separate Saami parliament with certain limited powers, and negotiations continue for broader recognition of Saami rights.[19]

In each of the examples mentioned, the constitutional modifications to meet the needs of communal groups within the country's borders have been undertaken in a context of increasing the viability of the state itself. The state has been able to maintain the allegiance of these communal groups through providing them with the means to take more initiatives to shape their life conditions. Far from heralding a regression into communal warfare, these modifications have made it possible for a diverse society to establish some minimal common identity while giving space for the diversity of its members.

A particularly interesting example of an autonomous region linked to another country but not within its borders is Greenland, a noncontiguous part of Denmark. The Greenland Home Rule government was established in 1979 with its own parliament, by agreement with Denmark. Greenland has long provided leadership for the peoples of the Circumpolar North, some of whom have had various forms of local self-government since 1971.[20] It is also Greenland that made a formal proposal at the 1993 World Conference on Human Rights held in Vienna, for a permanent Forum for Indigenous Peoples to be established within the United Nations system. This will probably take several years of negotiation to achieve.

### South Asia

The states to be discussed here were all colonies of modernizing European states in the nineteenth century. The new states' horror of communalism as a basis for political organization is based to a significant degree on the doctrines of the European colonizers. Communalism and tribalism were seen as the great enemies of modernization and political maturity. As the colonies became independent, each state tried to establish a national identity, based on colonial borders, into which communal identities could be assimilated, regardless of the preexisting geographical distribution of the communal groups. The complexities of the political situations that followed can barely be touched on here. In the worst cases, all-out communal warfare has replaced earlier patterns of coexistence and is threatening to destroy the postcolonial states. In the best cases, older patterns of coexistence have been translated into negotiated intercommunal political coalitions with some promise of stability. It is useful to remember that in general the European states have had much longer to negotiate their coalitions. (It took centuries for Switzerland.)

At the time of its independence from Great Britain in 1948,[21] *Sri Lanka*, it has often been noted, was thought to have the best prospects of any Asian nation for developing a peaceful, prosperous civil order. Hindu and Muslim Tamils predominated in certain areas, Buddhist Sinhalese in others. Vastly different languages and cultures notwithstanding, there was enough mutual respect to make the prospect of peaceful coexistence in the new state likely. Minority northern Tamils, through the advantages of missionary education in the English language, represented the majority of the Western-oriented elite of the country. The Buddhists, on the other hand, were a 75-percent demographic majority who were not Western-oriented. The Tamils were nervous about the Sinhalese majority, and indeed the first election after independence brought precisely the feared majority into power. The new government promptly made Sinhalese (which Tamils do not speak) the official language of the state, and the percentage of Tamils allowed in the universities was reduced. In general, the Sinhalese sought to eradicate the colonial heritage, which meant eradicating what advantages the English-speaking Tamils had. The 1972 constitution exacerbated Tamil fears by mandating special protection for the Buddhist religion. The Sinhalese government, recognizing the problem for Tamils, had tried to address their concerns by devolving state power to the provinces (Tamils were the majority in the northern and eastern provinces). But Sinhalese public opinion and powerful Buddhist groups strongly opposed these efforts. Ethnic hostilities increased to the point that by the early 1980s a full-blown war of secession was going on—a war that has so far resisted all attempts at outside mediation and internal negotiation. There has been such a fractionation of Tamil groups, and such a hardening of positions on all sides, that experienced negotiators do not see any resolution of this conflict in the near future.

*Malaysia* came to independence as Malaya in 1957 (becoming the Federation of Malaysia in 1963) as a deeply divided multiethnic society with 50 percent Malays, 37 percent Chinese, 11 percent Indian, and 2 percent "other." Ethnic cleavages are compounded by linguistic, religious, and cultural differences. The Malays consider themselves the indigenous inhabitants, and the Chinese have traditionally dominated major sectors of the economy. There has been communal violence at regular intervals since 1945. However, an expanding economy brought a degree of prosperity from the 1950s on, and there has been room for Malays to do well without making inroads on Chinese economic turf. Wise management of ethnic confrontations in the 1950s and emphasis by the British on educating an indigenous administration to manage health, education, and community services left the newly independent country with competent administrators in 1963, and much experience in interethnic compromise. Although the Malays had the numerical majority, the Chinese were a significant part of the electorate, and a permanent multiethnic coalition was developed even before independence. The Malays, the economically disadvantaged group, realized very early that they could not get what they wanted without the help of the Chinese, and vice versa. Unlike the Sinhalese, who wrote Tamil participation out of political life, the Malays drafted a language act providing for continued use of English, Chinese, and Tamil. The Chinese, in turn, were willing to support an augmentation of Malay economic resources. A combination of luck and some good negotiating skills created a direction that led from ethnic violence to relative ethnic peace. Continued negotiation is very important in maintaining the present political stability. Pressures and hostilities are not absent, but they are more or less contained in skillful political coalitions.[22]

### India-Pakistan-Bangladesh

Nowhere in the world has the colonial imprint on traditionally multiethnic societies created a more continuously contentious situation than in the region of pre–World War II British India—now the three states of India, Pakistan, and Bangladesh. The initial partition of India into India and Pakistan in 1947 was bathed in blood from the start, and at the time of this writing another war looms between these states over the disputed areas of Kashmir.

Independent *India* was a determined modernizer. It reorganized the 560 native states that entered the new India, either merging them with adjacent provinces, converting them into centrally administered areas, or grouping them into unions of states. By 1956 another reorganization abolished the unions of states and merged all formerly native states either into one of fifteen states, or into one of eight centrally administered areas. In 1962 a sixteenth state was created, and in 1966 the Punjab was partitioned into two states, making a total of eighteen states; the annexation of Sikkhim in 1975 made nineteen. These arbitrary reorganizations resulted in economic, social, and political disadvantages for the majority of communal groupings thus swallowed up. The religious divisions (83 percent Hindu, 11 percent Muslim, 3 percent Christian, 2 percent Sikh) don't even scratch the surface of India's ethnic, linguistic, and cultural identity groups. The forced assimilations did not succeed. India's commitment to liberating East Pakistanis from West Pakistan by military might (in what is now Bangladesh) destroyed the possibility of a solid negotiating relationship with Pakistan. Thus the land of Gandhi has a poor track record of negotiation of differences, internally or externally, since his death and has faced frequent communal rioting in the 1990s. Grassroots movements to resolve communal differences may in the long run succeed where the government so far has failed.

*Pakistan* also has a bad track record, but it has only three major communal groups challenging the domination of the majority Punjabis. The problem is that these three communal groups (Baluchi, Sindhi, Pushtun), while only 30 percent of the population, claim 72 percent of the land as historically theirs from ancient times—reaching back 5,000 to 10,000 years.[23] So far, the claims are simply dismissed; for the Punjabis, there can only be one unitary state. Only the Baluchi, however, consider a war of secession. The other two groups would settle for substantial political and economic autonomy. At issue for these minorities is the need for a larger share of the royalties from natural resources extracted from "their" land, and control over outside entrepreneurial and governmental economic enterprises.

The only hope for either of these two states, and for impoverished Bangladesh as well, hinges on two large reforms that are needed. First, there should be more constitutional compromise within each state. Second, the current win-lose stance in bilateral relations should be rejected and replaced with a willingness to negotiate outcomes that will advantage all parties instead of only some.

It is not that bargaining cultures do not exist in these societies, but rather that they never had a chance politically in the particular historical context of the India-Pakistan partition.

The numerous smaller tribal groups of South Asia have long struggled against national development policies that are destroying their lands, and have formed many local and national councils that pursue both courtroom processes and more dramatic strategies, such as the courageous Chipko or Hug the Trees movement of India. A few become internationally known, such as the people of East Timor seeking independence from Indonesia, but all are struggling year in and year out to save their lands. Violent liberation movements get more attention, but nonviolent struggles are widespread and persistent. People do not give up.

## Africa

*Nigeria* is an instructive example of a multiethnic society that went through civil war and came out the other side, determined to arrange a constitutive order that would keep the state together within its colonial-defined borders.[24] This most populous state of black Africa is a "nation of nations," with from two hundred to four hundred ethnic groups, depending on how one counts them, and ten major groups accounting for 90 percent of the population. Since independence in 1960 it has developed structurally from three regions to the present twenty-one states, alternating between central-ized military rule and decentralized civilian rule. A three-year civil war ended in 1970 with the successful reintegration of the secessionist Ibos into the Fed-eral Republic. Because of the strength of the traditional emirate subculture, there has been in place an effective capacity for local government linked to federal structures in a complex linkage system with both vertical and hori-zontal components. While there has been much political creativity in Niger-ian society, there has also been and continues to be much conflict. The new constitutive order that was to have been implemented in 1992 with a return to civilian government was upset by a military coup. Although the election of 301 local government authorities for a transition period did take place, au-thoritarian rule is for a time muffling further development.

Nigeria's strength had been that its westernized elite and traditional tribal leaders mingled in ways that did not happen in other former colonies. Many traditional tribal leaders have been given a share in the national economic pie, and traditional tribal titles are still valued. This means that at least until the present impasse, there were many cross-ties between ethnic groups and between federal and local authority holders based on access to a combination of traditional and modern statuses and roles. The role of tribal elders in con-flict resolution, widely recognized locally and nationally, has made possible Nigeria's continuity as a nation of nations through a succession of military and civilian governments. Multiple legal systems have on the whole been flexibly administered and have served to supplement the informal tribal elder system of conflict resolution. The 1990s crisis of military rule has weakened those systems, but Nigeria remains a multiethnic society commanding atten-tion as it struggles towards its postponed new constitutive order.

*Sudan*, the largest country on the African continent, rich in resources and traditions, has been in the throes of civil war for most of the years since its in-dependence in 1955.[25] A superficial look suggests an industrialized Arab North exploiting an undeveloped tribal South, but the reality is much more complex. The exploitation is real enough — mineral resources from the South fuel the factories of the North. However, populations of both North and South are highly diverse. There are one hundred languages and about forty different cultures, with an Arab admixture in both regions. The education level in the English-speaking South is as high or higher than in the Arab-speaking North. The South, which had been "protected" from Arab incur-sions during the colonial era, entered independence expecting to share equally with the North under a new constitution. However, the earlier period of protectionism left the North looking down on the South and unwilling to share power on an equal basis. Efforts on the part of an authoritarian northern leader, Nimeiry, to enforce Islamic law on the entire nation was not in fact a true northern issue, since many northerners rejected the Islamization of the Sudan, preferring a secular state.

The longest civil war in Africa is destroying much of the country's infrastructure. Since the range of ethnic diversity is similar in North and South, and there are educated elites with common interests in both North and South (contrary to appearances), it has been suggested that serious negotiation would reveal those common interests and enable the construction of a constitution providing for multiethnic power sharing. However, the sheer dynamics of protracted conflict and internal power struggles in the South has weakened the negotiating capacities of the society. The hope remains that new leadership will rescue the country's potential as a viable multiethnic society.

The indigenous peoples of Africa have become increasingly active as development policies have been destructive of their homelands. In North and West Africa, tribal groups are politically active but do not have strong intertribal associations. A complex situation of bloody civil strife in the Great Lakes Region of West Africa is endangering the very survival of the forest dwellers and causing great instability for even the more stable states of the region. In Central Africa, however, there is a well-functioning Central African Forest Peoples Association, and in East Africa the Maasai have organized the Maasai Development Organization for all Maa speakers. These organizations enable member tribal groups to negotiate with national governments and seek help from the United Nations and from NGOs.

In the Asian and African countries we have examined, we have seen that a plurality of cultures is not in itself an obstacle to the formation of a stable state—if these cultures are recognized, respected, and brought into active power sharing on the basis of continual negotiation. When historical circumstances erode mutual respect and when negotiating relationships to achieve an appropriate constitutive order cannot be maintained, the state is not viable.

### The Americas

A very instructive effort to create a new constitutive order is going on among the ten states in the Canadian Federation at the present time.[26] The principle of the multiethnic state was affirmed some years ago with the establishment of a ministry for multicultural affairs. However, the formula for the constitutive order, whether in relation to native peoples or French-speaking Quebec, continues to elude lawmakers. The Meech Lake Accord, a complex amendment to the 1982 Constitution designed to meet demands of a secession-minded Quebec, was rejected by a number of provinces in the Federation, including Quebec itself. A second effort with a painfully redrafted amendment has also been rejected. Furthermore, secession has also been rejected several times by the Quebecois themselves. The next steps are unclear as of this writing. Considering how many years of negotiation have been required to work out arrangements satisfactory to all parties in European plural societies, and how much negotiation is required to sustain new arrangements once agreed upon, it was probably unrealistic of Canadians to think they could romp through the process of a constitutional amendment quickly.

The *United States* is still characterized by a melting pot outlook and is a long way from being prepared to modify the constitutive order to allow, for example, for bilingual instruction in bilingual states (such as those of the Southwest, with substantial Hispanic minorities). Only Louisiana, with its French Acadian heritage, has recognized a second language, French, to be taught in state elementary and secondary schools as a part of the state's ethnic heritage. The Federal Bureau of Indian Affairs, while dealing with the rights of native peoples, is hardly an example of power sharing. Treaty rights negotiated by native peoples with the United States government in the previous century are continually being abrogated or ignored, and are the subject of more or less continuous litigation.[27]

One of the interesting findings from U.S. census data over recent decades is the stability of reported ethnic identity by region—a stability that sometimes goes as far back as two hundred years. Asian, Hispanic, and North European identities all show this kind of stability. (Surprisingly, 83 percent of all census respondents report another ethnic origin beyond simply American.)

In the case of Native Americans, a different but not unrelated phenomenon is evident. While there are 173 identifiable American Indian tribes, nations, and bands in the United States today, the sustained efforts of the United States government to eliminate tribes as political and social entities led to a widespread nonreporting of Native American tribal identity through the 1960s. From 1970 to 1980, however, there was a 70 percent increase in people listing their race as American Indian.[28] This clearly represents a cultural phenomenon, not a population explosion, and parallels the activities of the World Council of Indigenous Peoples to establish a status under international law for the indigenous peoples of North America and other continents. Since the rates of poverty, unemployment, illiteracy, and limited life expectancy are higher for Native Americans than for other ethnic groups, it is not surprising that the resurgence of ethnic identity is accompanied by vigorous efforts to increase educational levels and employment opportunities for Native Americans. One aspect of this phenomenon is the appearance of a new generation of Indian colleges and Native American journals blending rediscovery of traditional knowledge with modern science and technology.[29]

Today it can be said that mutual aid systems of Hispanic, Asian-American, African-American, and Native American communities are becoming stronger and more sophisticated. The story for smaller identity groups is more uneven, depending on economic and social circumstances. The more equitable power-sharing arrangements that must inevitably develop in the twenty-first century in the United States may be as much at state and regional levels as at the national level, given the existing federal system. Some substantial modification of the existing practice of simple majority rule will probably be required in order to achieve this.

The native peoples of Central and Latin America have become increasingly active since the 1980s in organizing national councils of tribal peoples within states and bioregions. The world conference of indigenous peoples, ecologists, and environmentalists organized by the Coordinadora of Indigenous Organizations of the Amazon Basin in 1990 signaled a new level of Latin American mobilization and political activity, strongly felt at the United Nations Conference on Environment and Development (UNCED) in Rio in 1993. Given that the World Conference of Indigenous Peoples founded in 1982 holds biennial General Assemblies in different world regions, a gradual strengthening of regional indigenous organizations can be anticipated in the years ahead. The draft treaty on indigenous peoples that the UN Commission on Human Rights has been struggling over for several years will eventually contribute to the strengthening of the role of indigenous peoples at the United Nations itself, but the process is a slow one.

## Plural Societies in the Twenty-First Century

Pluralism, diversity, and pressure to change constitutive orders will increase, partly for the reasons already suggested—that communal groups provide identity, meaning, and a sense of self-worth to their members; that they offer a more manageable scale of management of human affairs; that the knowledge of local terrains makes such groups more effective in problem solving; and that their cultural knowledge stock and special skills offer problem-solving and conflict resolution capabilities that are not available at the national level.

This increasing pluralism will be furthered by the continuing development of human rights concepts and norms, including group rights. The UN World Cultural Development Decade and a hoped-for Decade of Indigenous Peoples can provide opportunities for heightening levels of awareness of the cultural, ethnic, and biosphere diversity of the planet's many lifeworlds. Research, teaching, and a new level of active participatory involvement of the "10,000 societies" will give further positive meaning to communal identities as sources of cultural enrichment for a more interactive world of the future.

The structural arrangements we have briefly examined have involved either territorial federations or a variety of formulae for proportional representation giving opportunity for political participation of all parties/communal groups having a specified minimum size within the state. It would appear that a parliamentary system facilitates power sharing in a way that presidential, majority-rule systems do not. However, not all pluralistic societies have formal power-sharing arrangements. Some arrangements are informal but seem to work. Sometimes the demands for participation by communal groups are met by cultural councils, such as territorial councils for guest workers in certain European countries.

No one set of conditions or arrangements guarantees a more participatory power-sharing world. Economic prosperity may help, but is not critical; the absence of a strong dominant group helps, but also is not critical. What does seem to be critical is the willingness to negotiate, to respect the other. Patience and the willingness to take the long view, to spend lots of time on process, is a key factor.[30] Industrial societies do not have much of a culture of patience, and another set of major actors on the world stage not discussed in this chapter, the multinational corporations, do not contribute much patience either.

There is one encouraging aspect to the contemporary scene, however. The roles of state and corporation alike are being increasingly modified by the growth of NGOs, now 20,000 strong, and their grassroots counterparts, the much larger networks of GROs, which are local to each country. These developments offer both horizontal and vertical linkages for peoples within and between countries, independently of the action of the states they span. They act in the human interest, on a human scale, and are already actively engaged in community education, dialogue, and negotiation in many areas where there are serious communal conflicts. In fact, as far back as 1978, there were already 65 NGOs with branches in 44 countries whose primary purpose was to support separatist or cultural autonomy movements.[31] A 1994 *List of Indigenous Organizations* contains entries for 200 separate bodies.[32] The World Council of Indigenous Peoples and the International Work Group for Indigenous Affairs (IWGIA) are good examples of NGOs that provide a global network to support native peoples in their local settings around the world. It might be said that the world's polities are coming full circle from tribal-local to global-local formation.

Over time, the states of the twenty-first century will not only be characterized by a greater variety of constitutional arrangements for participation of diverse identity groups within their borders, but they will work more interactively with NGOs. They will also work with intergovernmental organizations (IGOs) and with new political forms, such as the European Union, as well as with the many UN bodies that also crisscross national boundaries. With more vertical and horizontal linkages across borders, and more emphasis on local initiative, one can hope for a gradual transformation of states from instruments of military force to facilitating partners in developing a global network of peoples' cultures of peace, fully interactive with the lifeworlds of the planet.

Not only are states changing, but the corporate forms of what is now thought of as the global economy are also changing, as is the technosphere of which they are a part. In chapter 9, we will examine both the destructive aspects of these changes and emerging potentials for a new pattern, that of ecodevelopment.

# 9

# Gaia, the Technosphere, and Development

## Gaia: An Overview

We have looked at the needs of the "10,000 societies" for their own cultural spaces within and across state boundaries as a condition for states and peoples to live in peace with one another. But peoples and states are not the only actors in the story. There is that larger entity of which peoples and states are only a part—Gaia herself, that great body of interacting systems of the lithosphere, hydrosphere, biosphere, and atmosphere in a process of continuous adaptation and change.[1] Our own species, very late arrivals in the gaian biosphere, have lived comfortably with the biosphere's multitudinous life-forms for most of the 100,000 years that *Homo sapiens* has existed on the planet. The sociosphere, social networks among humans, developed very gradually, and by 30,000 years ago, humans had found their way to every continent. With the beginning of agriculture 12,000 years ago, the sociosphere began changing some features of the biosphere of which it was a part. This environment-changing process was accentuated by early urbanization and the eventual rise of empires and civilizations. By the time humans were developing increasingly sophisticated technologies for reworking the materials around them, they had stopped thinking of themselves as part of gaia, instead considering the planet as an environment to be utilized and reshaped for human convenience. Today it is primarily indigenous peoples who speak of "all our relations"—meaning all life in the biosphere. Industrial (and now postindustrial) society, busy building its technosphere, is mining the lithosphere, exhausting its soils, and destroying large parts of the biosphere, including forests, plant life, and the uncountable creatures, large and small, that see to the biometabolic processes that keep earth alive and livable. (Recently, economists have condescended to label these processes as "ecosystem services.") Further, unrestrained human reproduction is in itself overwhelming earth's carrying capacity.

In the last century of the second millennium of the Common Era, all this technosphere building has taken place in the name of development and is seen as progress. Unfortunately, the concept of development, which was originally conceived as human and social development, was captured by technospecialists and narrowed down to economic development, measurable by gross national product (GNP) alone, with little reference to quality of life, relationship to the earth, or equity in distribution of resources. GNP-based development planning led to a widening of the gap between rich and poor, not only between countries of the North and South, but within countries of the North as well.

Even while this technodevelopment is threatening the survival of life as humans have known it, a slow change in human consciousness about our relationship to the planet is beginning to take place. The development of geosphere-biosphere studies, with the encouragement of the International Council of Scientific Unions and UNESCO's Man and the Biosphere Program, are producing a radically new understanding of the planet as an ecosystem.[2] As awareness grows that natural and social processes are tightly interwoven, the thinking about development is changing. Phrases like "alternative development," "sustainable development," and "ecodevelopment" have begun to appear in both local and international discourse.

Before looking at the state of the technosphere, it will be helpful to consider the geobiosphere itself. First of all, oceans cover more than two-thirds of the earth's surface, a part of Gaia that we are only beginning to explore. Of the land surface, 11 percent consists of polar and high mountain regions, 18 percent tropical/subtropical/temperate regions, and 70 percent humid biotic regions (the regions of forest canopy containing most of the biologic diversity of the planet). Most human populations are concentrated in the tropical/subtropical/temperate regions, and much mining of surface and subsurface resources takes place in the humid biotic regions.

The land surface can be thought of as a mosaic of landscapes, or bioregions, the "givens" of nature. Bioregions are regions with natural characteristics of flora, fauna, water, climate, soils, and landforms that make them distinguishable from surrounding regions. There are macroregions, sometimes referred to as ecoregions, of considerable size, such as the Sonoran Desert in the southwest of the United States, and georegions, such as the watersheds of major river systems. Smaller bioregions may consist of specific river basins. The significance of bioregions from the human perspective is that, historically, human populations have developed distinctive lifeways based on the physical resources of the area they inhabit. Each local community can then be thought of as a small bioregion of interacting life-forms, complexified by the built environment contributed by humans.[3]

Before the development of agriculture, humans were simply a part of earth's metabolic processes. With the advent of agriculture came technometabolism, inputs and outputs of materials and energies from technological processes. Metallurgy and the production of cement were practiced in the ancient civilizations of the Middle East, and technological inventions came apace through the centuries—but it was not until the nineteenth and twentieth centuries, with rapidly increasing food supplies, industrial productivity, and modern sanitation systems—that human populations themselves began pressing heavily on the carrying capacity of the earth.

Since farming economics first came into existence, the human population has increased 1,000-fold, one-half of this increase in the last thirty years. There has been a 10,000-fold increase in the intensity of resource and energy use and waste production by humans. Three-fourths of this increase has occurred in the lifetime of today's senior citizens. In the 1990s about half of those resources have gone into military buildup and weapons production, leaving an insecure world awash in weapons. Soil degradation is outpacing increased food productivity, so serious worldwide food shortages lie ahead. Greenhouse gases released by combustion of fossil fuels is affecting the planetary climate, both through global climate warming and through the increasing instability of local weather patterns—meaning more violent hurricanes, floods, and droughts. Environmental pressures, in turn, leave states more conflict-prone than ever.[4]

Once, the planet was humanity's school. Its forests and meadows, mountains and deserts, the fellow creatures who crawled, walked, swam, and flew were teachers for early humans of how to live sustainably in the many different niches the ecosystems offered. Today, the people of the One-Third World inhabit man-made shells and the world outside is their toxic wasteland. Their knowledge comes from video screens filled with images and data, but their ears are deaf to struggling Gaia, pushed beyond her capacity to adapt and adjust. The ones who hear her cries are the people of the Two-Thirds World (except the few who dwell in sheltered outposts of the technosphere). Clinging to the barren mountains, denuded forests and deserts, and edges of the wasteland, they can do little more than try to keep themselves—and her—alive from year to year. What happened to bring us in less than two centuries from being obstreperous but manageable parts of the biosphere to our present potentially planet-destroying role? And can the damage be undone? Can humans and the biosphere be reconciled?

## Problems of Scale and the Rise of the Corporation

In looking at the mismatch between state boundaries and the distribution of peoples—of ethnies, in chapter 8, we saw repeatedly that states did not have the knowledge of local terrains necessary to safeguard the lifeways of people living productively in the microregions they inhabited. The far-off centers of decision making were totally out of touch with the local on-the-ground realities. This same phenomenon of increasing size and scale of operations has been even more striking in the economic sphere. Production units have swallowed each other so that fewer than 500 corporations now control more than 70 percent of global trade, and 47 of the top 100 economies in the world are actually transnational corporations. Agribusiness is now part of that corporate world, and there is little room left for family farms and community production enterprises. The overwhelming trend is toward economic globalization: the ever faster moving of money, factories, and goods around the planet by corporations searching for cheaper labor, cheaper raw materials. *Globalism*, once a term indicating that we are one human family sharing one fragile planet and trying to share and cooperate for a better life for all, now has sinister connotations, as does the concept of economic development itself. It will be our task here to explore the contradictions between different concepts of development and highlight alternative development, or ecodevelopment, as the path to a humane and peaceful future.

The economic dimension of human life can scarcely be ignored. It has to do with the utilization of earth's resources to meet human wants and needs, with the work life of human beings involved in the processing of those resources, with ways of sharing what is produced through market and nonmarket mechanisms, and with the activity of consuming what is produced. The verb "to economize" means doing all this with thrift, prudence, and the avoidance of waste.[5] We will, therefore, hold that the economics of a culture of peace involves living gently on the earth, in tune with the planet's regenerative capacity (usually referred to as "sustainability"); and that it also involves taking joy in labor and in sharing the fruit of labor—and pleasure in using those fruits in moderation.

The megasystem of production, distribution, and consumption in the current world market economy has more to do with economic warfare than peacefare, and there is a vast uneasiness in both the One-Third and the Two-Thirds Worlds about the predatory character of economic life. The rate of displacement of workers due to technological advances in automated production is surging, not only in the production of goods but in human services. While there is a vast media rhetoric about the joys of consumption and the leisure society, opinion polls more often report how stressful the heavy emphasis on consumption is for the hardworking and unremittingly courted consumers.

The rediscovery of the joy of work, and particularly of labor-intensive work and voluntary simplicity in lifestyle, are central themes in a growing social movement that rejects prevailing concepts of economic development as economic growth. The movement brings together concern for the health of the more-than-human planetary ecosystem, for planet-centered "sustainable" development (i.e., ecodevelopment), and concern for peaceful problem-solving behavior among peoples and states. It is becoming clear not only that the quality of family life and community life is closely linked to the quality of work life, but that the failure to provide supportive conditions for the non-waged work that sustains families and communities in relation to their environment marginalizes the most essential of all human activities. These ecodevelopment movements will be explored in the last section of this chapter.

A serious division in the world today, far more serious than the Cold War communism/capitalism divide ever was, is the divide between the One-Third and the Two-Thirds Worlds (with a corollary divide between rich and poor inside the One-Third World). This divide has become, in the eyes of the Two-Thirds World, "The Dominance of the West over the Rest." A recent book bearing this title provides a stunning distillation of an increasingly articulate critique, by leaders of thought in the countries of the South, of Western values, intellectual discourse, and social and economic practice.[6] Western behavior is seen through the prism of postcolonial dominance. This dominance is perceived as the imposition of inappropriate economic models that serve Western corporate interests and are enforced by World Bank policies and Western military power. These models have been exceedingly destructive of fragile ecosystems and have obliterated traditional knowledge, skills, and practices evolved over centuries to conserve those environments. Further, the non-West has suffered the imposition of an incomplete formulation of human rights standards selectively and hypocritically applied by the West. An added insult from the perspective of these leaders is the West's complete failure to understand the richness and complexity of cultures and civilizations that have evolved over millennia, long before Western culture and science arrived on the world scene.

Since mutual respect based on mutual listening and learning is a precondition for peaceable relations between peoples, the failure of the colonizing West to respect the lands and peoples it colonized is perhaps the single greatest obstacle to future peaceful cooperation. Two-Thirds World economists and historians find the technological and economic dominance of the West particularly infuriating because the civilizations of Asia, the Middle East, and Northern Africa had generated spectacular scientific, technological, cultural, and spiritual achievements in the first millennium of the Common Era and halfway into the second, and were the teachers for a backward Europe.[7]

An example of Western failure to learn is its ignorance of the *orature*, the oral traditions, of Central and West Africa. The Ifa system is a literary system, based on 256 categories of knowledge dealing with history, religion, medicine, philosophy, and science. It is a corpus of traditional African knowledge and an academic system in itself.[8]

Scientists of the South particularly deplore the mindless use of technology by the West with the onset of industrialization. When we consider that this industrialization has polluted the air, soil, and waters of the planet, added to climate instability, and destroyed forests—the earth's "lungs"—we may have some sympathy with the technological conservatism of Emperor Ch'ien-lung in receiving an embassy from King George III of England. The Emperor's reply to the display of wares and offers of trade was "there is nothing we lack. . . . We have never set much store on strange or ingenious objects, nor do we need any of your country's manufactures."[9]

With this overview of dissenting views on development, we will now turn to the Western model of development as it unfolded in what might be called the Maldevelopment Decades.

## The Maldevelopment Decades

The story of economic development in the twentieth century begins with the missionary zeal of the West to foster social and economic development around the world in the nineteenth century. Partly religious, partly scientific/technological/industrial, partly economic, partly cultural, these images of development helped generate a multifaceted colonization movement with the theme "new ideas must be implanted to replace the old." Increasingly, the scientific paradigm became central to this movement: the objective pursuit of knowledge about the physical world and its phenomena through observation and experiment, accompanied by systematic formulation and testing of hypotheses. This knowledge produced a stream of applications that enhanced human control over the environment. Through harnessing new energy resources and increasing production efficiencies, it increased food supplies and created physical infrastructures, including sanitation, that made high-density urban agglomerations possible. The population explosion that accompanied these developments was welcomed as fueling continued economic growth. Development came to mean increasingly capital-intensive technological sophistication in the production processes and the generation of more capital and income. In other words, economic growth itself was seen as development. The scientific search for truth and the religious-humanistic quest for the good life for human beings lent legitimation to this economization of what was understood as development, considerably assisted by the so-called Protestant ethic of disciplined hard work. Western culture was seen as having a unique synthesis of science, economics, and religion to produce a qualitatively new way of life thought of as "modern."

The Malthusian specter of the previous century—that population would always expand to the limit of subsistence—was apparently exorcized by new agricultural technologies that increased food supplies and by the fact that reproduction rates were decreasing dramatically in industrialized societies.

## GNP and Development as Economic Growth

A key factor in the contemporary pursuit of development was the phenomenon of national income accounting practiced by governments toward the end of the 1920s. This involved the collection and publication of information about national income and productivity, its sources and distribution, summarized in the concept of gross national product, or GNP (now referred to as GDP, gross domestic product)—the dollar value of finished goods and services for the state as a whole. The existence of a number representing GDP made it possible to measure progress toward that passionately desired goal, economic growth. The limitations of this measurement were ignored. Is thus everything that is produced, by definition, good? Indeed not. There is no distinction between costs and benefits, between productive and destructive activity. A dramatic example: "The nation's central measure of well-being works like a calculating machine that adds but cannot subtract. . . . By the curious standard of GDP, the nation's economic hero is a terminal cancer patient who is going through a costly divorce."[10] Earthquakes and floods cause money to change hands. So do toxic waste dumps, crime, divorce, and watching TV.

All add to the GDP. But all the unpaid work of nurture and civic caring, the labor of the volunteer in family and community, contribute nothing.

The ultimate deception of the GDP is that it tells nothing about how wealth is distributed in a society. No problem! The heady experience of watching the GDP rise year after year was enough to assume progress for all, since "rising waters lift all boats." The founding of the United Nations appeared to offer an instrument for extending this Eurocentric monetized culture to the rest of the world, and the Development Decades became the specific mechanism for that extension. Voices warning that there was more to development than bringing in new projects from the West (as were heard at a UNESCO North-South Conference in the early 1950s) were ignored. Because development aid was based on replacing existing infrastructures and traditional knowledge with new structures and new knowledge, that aid never connected with the social and economic realities of the target countries. By the middle of the second Development Decade, drought and depletion of soil and forest resources as side effects of inappropriate development technology added famine to the other burdens of the South. GNP growth rates turned negative in a number of countries, including states with "good" development prospects, like Ghana and Nigeria. Neither the much-heralded New International Order, adopted by the United Nations in 1974 with the goal of equalizing economic opportunity for the South, nor the efforts of the Group of 77 to break the resistance of the North to a program of development-as-equals for the South, with eventual redistribution of the world's resources, made any difference.

Development Decades have continued into the 1990s, but the North has lost interest, and few states have ever provided the development aid first promised in the 1960s. The Two-Thirds World debt stock grows by almost $100 billion each year, and southern debt service regularly exceeds new lending. The net outflow of resources from the South to the North creates a crushing burden for the South. The World Bank and the International Monetary Fund have used that debt burden to force countries of the South to undertake widespread structural adjustment programs (SAPs) in their economies. Each SAP demands economic and social policies that channel the country's resources and productivity into debt repayments and "enhanced" transnational competition and away from the needs of its own people, while privileged elites live in a luxury that only a few can know. There are apparent exceptions to this sad story, particularly the Newly Industrialized Countries (NICs) of Asia. Although NICs have, to some extent, succeeded in industrializing while preserving traditional social structures and culture, as

Japan has also been able to do until recently, corrupt lending practices have built up financial edifices that do not have a correspondingly productive economic base. As a result, the world has now entered a prolonged economic crisis and the gap between actual wealth and paper money stands revealed.

Maldevelopment was for some time considered to be a disease of the South, but by the mid-1980s the gap between rich and poor in the North was widening and technology-induced unemployment and/or underemployment continues to increase. The phenomenon of giant corporations began toward the end of the nineteenth century with the development of new information technologies, and now at the end of the twentieth century economic globalization threatens the well-being of workers on every continent. Over the past decade and a half, the number of transnational corporations has skyrocketed from 7,000 to more than 35,000, and a mere one percent of the transnational corporations (TNCs) on the planet own half the total stock of foreign investment. At the same time, they shed labor heavily, and small enterprises cannot take up the slack. The General Agreement on Tariffs and Trade (GATT) and the North American Free Trade Agreement (NAFTA) promise more of the same. Now the monster of the North is also devouring its own children. One little-understood form of that monster is found in transnational crime syndicates, which have been called one of the major threats to the world system in the 1990s and beyond.[11]

The sheer visibility of inner-city poverty and homelessness, the rising tides of violence and drug addiction spreading out from the cities, the less visible decay of rural areas, combined with increasing complaints by the middle classes of being stressed by the burdens of consumption and a high-speed life are problems enough. On top of these, the very high visibility of downsizing of major corporations—leading to either unemployment or reemployment at lower salary levels for both skilled workers and mid-level managers who thought they had lifetime job security—have acted as the last straw, bringing about a major questioning of the doctrine of social betterment for all through continued economic growth. There has been at the same time a longer-run shrinking, first of the agricultural sector and then of the industrial sector, that has also played a part in sending workers into poorer-paying jobs while corporations move their production sites from the One-Third World into the Two-Thirds World with its cheaper labor. The accompanying merger mania of large corporations has finally focused attention on the role of megacorporations in the decline in quality of life for the general population. The sheer size of such corporations is now being seen as a major factor in this decline. So what happened to the ideology of growth?

## Critique of the Pursuit of Economic Growth

An early questioning voice was Kenneth Boulding, whose *Organizational Revolution* appeared in 1953.[12] Correctly predicting that new information technologies would produce a new leap in the size of corporations, he pointed out that the limiting factors on organizational growth were an increasingly unfavorable environment and an increasingly unfavorable internal structure (the larger the organization, the more grades in the hierarchy, the greater the gap between top and bottom), and that the larger an organization becomes, the more harm it does if it fails to function properly. Kenneth Boulding was also noted for his critique of "cowboy economics"—behaving as if the earth's resources were unlimited. Here was an early questioning voice.

In 1972 the Club of Rome published *Limits to Growth*, by Donella and Dennis Meadows and colleagues, which pointed out the limits to the carrying capacity of the earth and the dangers of a constantly expanding population and expanding use of natural resources for continued growth in economic output.[13] Thus the debate began between those who recommended economic and social policies based on a recognition of limited resources and the technological optimists who said continued economic growth was essential to human betterment and human inventiveness would overcome resource limitations. The debate was often loud and angry.

Then came the gentle voice of E. F. Schumacher in 1973, telling us that *Small Is Beautiful* and that the answer to resource limitations was the application of "intermediate" or small-scale labor-intensive technology to the production of food and other human necessities and a more frugal approach to living on the planet, based on an "economics as if people mattered."[14] Next, in 1976, came *Rio: Reshaping the International Order*. This report to the club of Rome was coordinated by Jan Tinbergen, building on *Limits to Growth*.[15] In 1980 the MacBride Commission produced *Many Voices, One World*, calling attention to the diversity of cultures and lifeways on the planet and the swamping of their voices by the North's control of communications media and dramatically pointing to the role of the media in the drive for economic growth.[16]

There followed a series of independent international commissions, consisting of major scholars and public figures from both the South and the North, which pointed out the serious problems with the West's profligate use of natural resources. These commissions called attention to the hitherto ignored intellectual, cultural, and knowledge resources of the South as well as the need for not only more partnership and mutual respect in pursuit of development, but also more attention to human and social development. The Brandt Commission's *Programme for Survival* came out in 1980, and the second Brandt Commission report, *Common Crisis North-South: Cooperation for World Recovery*, in 1983. Attention to the ways global militarization was endangering development led to the Palme Commission's *Common Security: A Blueprint for Survival* in 1982, and awareness of how development was degrading the environment led to the report of the Brundtland Commission on Environment and Development, *Our Common Future*, in 1987.[17]

None of these efforts was well understood—or approved of—by the major powers in either of the superpower blocs. Instead, there has since then been a rejection of the United Nations, which provided the arena for these dialogues, by some of the major founding powers. Multilateralism is now in decline, and the countries of the South are increasingly having to deal with the major powers on a bilateral basis.

However, the international women's movement, from the time of the first International Women's Year in Mexico City in 1975 to the present, has provided an increasingly articulate voice for a human-centered concept of development, based on the worldwide experience of women as farmers and shapers of community development at the local level. This voice has become even louder and clearer since the 1995 International Women's Year UN Conference in Beijing, which also drew to Beijing the largest NGO gathering ever held. As a people's corrective to the formal deliberations of governmental delegations, the Beijing Declaration and Platform for Action is a powerful statement that development is far more than an economic matter. It has become increasingly clear that one of the reasons for the failure of the development decades was that development planners—all men—had failed to notice that the bulk of farming in the Two-Thirds World is done by women. As a result, resources and credit failed to reach the very workers who could make the best use of them. It was a female agricultural economist, Ester Boserup, who led the way in reeducating the planning community. The United Nations itself was learning the "new" on-the-ground realities well before member states were ready to accept them.[18]

The importance of the pioneering work of UN agencies—such as the UN Development Program (UNDP), the UN International Children's Emergency Fund (UNICEF), and other UN bodies concerned with development—in alerting the world to the problems of bad development theories and policies cannot be overestimated. The turning point in public recognition of this work came with the UN World Summit for Social Development held in Copenhagen in 1995. A major contribution to that Summit was a report by the UN Research Institute for Social Development (UNRISD), *States of Disarray: The Social Effects of Globalization*. Another notable contribution was the report of a preparatory seminar held in Bled, Slovenia, *Ethical and Spiritual Dimensions of Social Progress*. As a result of these activities of the 1990s, a whole new language for discussing development has emerged, and NGOs have played an important role in encouraging that change.[19]

Although NGO momentum had been building for a rethinking of development for several decades, the year 1990 proved a turning point in the mobilization of civil society in support of United Nations efforts. Joint activity by NGOs and grassroots organizations has given new life to the critique of development policy. The South Commission, under the chairmanship of Jules Nyerere of Tanzania, published *Challenge to the South,* calling on the countries of the South to get their own act together and define their own goals and ways of working—and particularly to stop allowing the North to dictate their policies.[20] In that same year, the UN Development Program published its first Human Development report, combining national income (GNP) with two social indicators—adult literacy and life expectancy—in a Human Development Index (HDI). This represented a significant step beyond the purely monetary measure of national development. A process of reconceptualizing development was under way. Countries that ranked high in GNP frequently ranked lower in the HDI index, which takes into account the health and knowledge of the population, and some low-GNP countries ranked much higher than expected on the social indicators, showing that their limited resources were well used. The 1991 *Human Development Report* adds a Human Freedom Index. The 1997 report broke new ground with a Human Poverty Index that measures the extent of deprivation in health, education, and overall economic provisioning and a gender-related development index that adjusts the Human Development Index downwards for gender inequality. Clearly, the process of refining the concept of development will continue, with new surprises in rankings as new indicators are added. Another United Nations contribution to this process was UNICEF's 1995 publication of *The Progress of Nations*, which ranked the states of the world according to their achievements in child health, nutrition, education, family planning, and progress for women. Again, GNP ranking does not predict rankings for these social indicators.

Growth is the shibboleth that is so difficult to destroy at the close of the growth-worshiping twentieth century. Historically, growth is an aberration. A steady-state economy is the norm. Only in recent centuries has growth seemed like the normal condition for human economies. Facing a steady-state economy means facing problems of inequality, of poverty. The rich can no longer keep getting richer while the poor get poorer—injustice stands revealed. Herman Daly, who has been a consistent voice in the wilderness about the problem of poverty, points out that limits must be set on inequality; but this the contemporary market society cannot accept.[21]

Efforts continue to work on the problem of growing inequality and a more in-depth understanding of what "Progress" means. Currently, an NGO, the International Forum on Globalization, is supporting the development of the Genuine Progress Indicator (GPI), which includes social costs as well as additions to well-being. The GPI is arrived at by using data in the following categories: (1) crime and family breakdown, (2) household and volunteer work, (3) income distribution, (4) resource depletion, (5) pollution, (6) long-term environmental damage, (7) changes in leisure time, (8) defensive expenditures (to deal with misfortunes), (9) lifespan of consumer durables and public infrastructure, and (10) dependence on foreign assets. The summary GPI figure is arrived at by subtracting the costs and adding the benefits, unlike the GDP, which counts all expenditures as benefits.[22] The formation in 1990 of the International Society for Ecological Economics, which since 1996 has been publishing the *Ecological Economics Bulletin*, is another example of the rethinking of development processes.

Clearly, the reconceptualization of development and the critique of economic growth as a good in itself is well under way, but in the meantime, what is happening to the growth-hungry corporations?

## The Continued Growth of Megacorporations

As the previous section indicated, megacorporations are growing like Topsy. How is this possible? It all began in the days of the "robber baron" industrialists in the 1880s and 1890s. In 1886 the United States Supreme Court ruled that a private corporation is a natural person under the United States Constitution (though the Constitution makes no mention of corporations) and is thereby entitled to the protection of the Bill of Rights, including the right to free speech and other constitutional protections extended to individuals. This ruling has meant that corporations can claim all the rights enjoyed by individuals but at the same time be exempt from many of the responsibilities and liabilities of citizenship. The merging of industrial empires began. The 1901 amalgamation of 112 corporate directorates under the Northern Securities Corporation of New Jersey, according to David Korten, put "the heart of the American economy under one roof, from banking and steel to railroads, urban transit, communications, the merchant marine, insurance, electric utilities, rubber, paper, sugar refining corporations, and other mainstays of the industrial infrastructure."[23] Thus the equation of the freedom and rights of individuals with market freedom and property rights opened the door for the megacorporations of the end of the twentieth century and made a way for corporations to practice externalization—a shifting of the costs of their economic activities—to the rest of society.

Perhaps the most troubling of the many exploitative activities of global corporations are those pursued by the pharmaceutical and seed industries, which involve the identification and patenting of items from indigenous peoples' storehouse of medicinal knowledge and seeds (and even their DNA). As a consequence, what has been the traditional subsistence base for native peoples now "belongs" to corporations and must be bought from the corporations by the peoples whose ancient birthright it was carefully to draw on such stocks with respect for the rights of all forest life.

The rise in the power of the corporations has been paralleled by the decline in the power of states to regulate them. Since markets are "blind" to social values and guided by money flows, only the government and civic sectors can take on the roles of promoting equitable distribution of ecosystem resources. Yet governments have lost this regulatory power, and the civic sector has not been strong enough to restore that power through citizens' pressure on individual corporations, though efforts continue. However, we have already noted another global phenomenon of the twentieth century: the rapid multiplication of transnational NGOs, from a few hundred at the beginning of the century to about 20,000 in the 1990s. The resulting citizens' efforts to bring about regulatory systems for the transnational corporations have played an important part in recent developments. One focus of the NGOs has been the United Nations itself. Because it is also in the interest of states to be able to exercise some control over the activities of the corporations within their borders, the combined efforts of NGOs and governments generated support in the UN Economic and Social Council (ECOSOC) for the creation of a UN Commission on Transnational Corporations in 1974. This commission, with assistance from the UN Center of Transnational Corporations, was to draft a UN Code on transnational corporations that was to protect both the rights of states to regulate corporations within their borders and the rights of transnational corporations against arbitrary seizure of property by states. After long labor, a draft was circulated in 1986, but a final code was never agreed upon by member states—unsettling evidence of the power of corporate voices both at the United Nations and in member states.

Another approach to globalization of corporations has been taken by bodies such as the Coalition for a Strong UN and the Global Commission to Fund the UN. A proposal to tax foreign exchange transactions (i.e., transborder money flows) opens the way for tracking and eventually regulating what has come to be called the "global casino." Such a tax, known as the Tobin Tax, introduces a new and practical way to fund the United Nations itself while also strengthening its governance capacity. (It is not generally realized that the United Nations functions with a world staff that is smaller than the civil service of the city of Stockholm.) This in turn would strengthen the capabilities of the UNDP, now strongly focused on local needs, and assist in the transformation of other United Nations–related development activities around the world.

In the longer term, a new concept of the "civil economy" is emerging, which may have an important humanizing effect on local, national, and international economic institutions. As described by Severyn Bruyn, a civil economy is a commonweal of self-governing markets. In its ideal form, it is "a system of exchange that is responsible to stakeholders, organized with systems of accountability and various kinds of self-governance [that] evolve through the development of social capital and the shared power of mutual governance."[24]

Some NGOs are already part of this new development, such as Business for Social Responsibility, the World Business Council for Sustainable Development, and the International Forum on Globalization, as well as longstanding NGOs such as Rotary International. Other citizens' groups are exploring strategies to shift rights and powers from corporations back to people, communities, and nature.[25]

## Eco-Awareness and Alternative Development

The mounting social, economic, and political frustrations associated with the United Nations Development Decades have gradually been channeled into the alternative development movement and TOES (The Other Economic Summit group). For several decades, TOES meetings have been held in counterpoint to the annual Economic Summits of the leading industrial powers. During these same decades, the global environmental movement has taken off with explosive energy. The 1992 UN Conference on Environment

and Development in Rio not only brought world attention to the environmental movement, it also brought new life to the alternative development
movement. These two movements began a serious coalition-building process
that is now being felt in every country and in the United Nations itself. What
is happening is both a change in consciousness and a change in practice.
Whether the change is called the Great Turning or the Next Reformation or
the New Paradigm, it represents an epochal shift from an industrial growth
society, dependent on accelerating consumption of resources, to a life-
sustaining society sharing the planet with all living things. One of the most
important groups in building awareness of the dangers to Planet Earth of
present human lifeways is the Worldwatch Institute of Washington, D.C.,
which has been publishing annual State of the World Reports and special-
topic reports since 1984—environmental alerts with a focus on the kinds of
policy changes needed to move toward sustainable lifeways.

There is a reflective quality to this new ecodevelopment movement because it involves a new recognition of the interdependence of the human
species and other living things, a new sense of Gaia herself. This recognition
is most clearly expressed in the Earth Charter, a document that began evolving at the Rio UNCED Conference, with strong support from environment
and development NGOs and religious groups representing the major faiths.
It is now planned that the Charter will be presented to the UN General Assembly in the year 2000, with signatures from millions of individuals around
the world. The 1997 version circulated by the Earth Charter Commission
bears close study because it brings together all the values and practices that a
twenty-first century culture of peace would embody.[26] Beginning with the
statement, "Earth is our home and home to all living beings," it goes on to articulate a series of principles to serve as guides to action for the peoples of the
world. Briefly summarized, they include:

1. Respect Earth and all life.
2. Care for the community of life in all its diversity.
3. Strive to build free, just, participatory, sustainable, and peaceful societies.
4. Secure Earth's abundance and beauty for present and future generations.
5. Protect and restore the integrity of earth's ecological systems, with special
   concern for biological diversity and the natural processes that sustain
   and renew life.
6. Prevent harm to the environment as the best method of ecological
   protection and, when knowledge is limited, take the path of caution.

7. Treat all living beings with compassion, and protect them from cruelty and wanton destruction.
8. Adopt patterns of consumption, production, and reproduction that respect and safeguard earth's regenerative capacities, human rights, and community well-being.
9. Ensure that economic activities support and promote human development in an equitable and sustainable manner.
10. Eradicate poverty, as an ethical, social, economic, and ecological imperative.
11. Honor and defend the right of all persons, without discrimination, to an environment supportive of their dignity, bodily health, and spiritual well-being.
12. Advance worldwide the cooperative study of ecological systems, the dissemination and application of knowledge, and the development, adoption, and transfer of clean technologies.
13. Establish access to information, inclusive participation in decision making, and transparency, truthfulness, and accountability in governments.
14. Affirm and promote gender equality as a prerequisite to sustainable development.
15. Make the knowledge, values, and skills needed to build just and sustainable communities an integral part of formal education and life-long learning for all.
16. Create a culture of peace and cooperation.

Caring for the earth requires recognition of the extent to which industrialization, urbanization, and population growth have damaged it. Because of deforestation, mining of the land and sea, and agribusiness practices of monoculture with intensive fertilization and irrigation, soils and waterways are being degraded. Crop yields, which have steadily increased over the past century, will begin to decline as a result not only of exhausted soils and toxic waste accumulation but of the increasing climate instability associated with global warming. Droughts, floods, and changes in mean annual temperatures result in changes in what can grow where. Having experienced several centuries of climate stability, humans and their crops are ill-prepared for these changes. The money flowing through the global casino (over 90 percent of computerized global financial trading is speculative) can do little to deal with the food crisis.

Since the changes, although global in scope, will be felt locally, the adaptive capacities of local communities will be tested to the utmost. When there are no longer any food surpluses in the world food bank, global policies can do little to generate immediate aid for local communities. Thus, alternative development policies emphasizing locally based initiatives will receive increasing attention. To some extent, this need is starting to be met by the autonomous development approach, now being most actively explored in Africa. An "Expert Consultation on the Role of Autonomous Funds as Intermediaries in Channeling Money for Social and Economic Development in Africa" recommends the establishment of such funds as linkage systems between governments and NGOs, with a strong emphasis on decentralization and respect for local knowledge and initiative in development planning.[27]

The alternative development movement emphasizes even more strongly the role of local grassroots initiative in development, and it is to this type of activity that we now turn.

### The Redevelopment of Local Economies

In sharp contrast to the fascination with the global casino, we find increasing awareness both among planners and the general public of what is variously called the "hidden economy" or the "informal economy": the vast array of goods and services that are produced outside the accounting system of the GDP. The value to the economy of the unpaid work of women in domestic labor, including child rearing; the value of the volunteer labor of women and men in civil society; and the unpaid labor of children add up to at least half of society's total productivity. In spite of the efforts of the feminist movement and other civic groups to call attention to this hidden sector, the unpaid labor of a society is systematically devalued by the market system.

The development of local small-scale lending and bartering systems builds on the hidden productivity of the informal economy and increases the quality of social life as well as economic well-being in local communities. From the Grameen Bank in Bangladesh to the Local Employment Trading Systems (LETS) in Canada, these systems enable participants, especially the poor and marginalized, to develop and use skills and resources that improve the quality of life for everyone. They reverse the effects of centralized banking, the accompaniment of industrialization and urbanization, which has, over time, disempowered the poor in every country by generating rapidly growing cash economies in rural as well as urban areas without meeting the credit needs of the poor.

In Bangladesh, the Grameen Bank was started specifically for the poorest sector of the population and now has thousands of borrowers' groups throughout the country, three-fourths of them women. A network of roughly 8,000 "bankers on bicycle," each trained by the Grameen organization, covers many areas of Bangladesh, and the Grameen principle has now spread to other Asian countries, to Africa, to Latin America, and most recently to North America. Further loans to a borrowers' group depends on repayment of previous loans, and repayment rates average 98 percent of all loans, with women having consistently higher repayment rates than men. Once a women's group has successfully completed its first round of loans for land for farming, or for livestock or tools, they often expand their activities to building schools, clinics, and needed local production facilities. Studies of Grameen find that the incomes of borrowers' groups in Grameen Bank villages are 43 percent higher than that of borrowers in non-Grameen villages. This is a tribute both to the Grameen method and to the business acumen of women borrower groups.

In the United States, Grameen Banking is now found side by side with local credit systems such as the Local Exchange Trading System (LETS)[28] and the Ithaca Dollar. These systems involve the development of local scrip that can be used to buy food items, construction work, professional services, health care, and handicrafts. Since the alternative development movement also includes groups committed to voluntary simplicity—those who choose to live simpler lives, use less of earth's resources in their daily lives, to live more lightly on the earth—the development of barter systems and local currencies is very attractive to this essentially middle-class group as well.[29]

## Other Examples of Alternative Development

While the lumber industry worldwide is busy cutting down the earth's forests, environmental groups are developing increasingly sophisticated strategies for slowing down this process and supporting the creation of sustainable local economies in the remaining forested regions. Sometimes the efforts of local communities bring new inspiration to the international NGOs, and the Chipko movement of India offers a striking example of local effort.

A moving description of a specific action follows:

In a remote village in Northern India called Reni, nestled in the Garwhal mountains of the Himalayan range, a group of women and children were doing an unusual thing. Hugging trees. They were resorting to Chipko, which means to hug, to prevent trees from being felled. With their arms wrapped around the trees, the women and children cried: "The forest is our mother's home, we will defend it with all our might." The women and children stopped about 70 lumberjacks from the forest contractors who were ready to fell the trees.[30]

With country after country selling off its forests to multinationals, not only displacing forest-dwelling people and removing their source of sustenance but destroying the very lungs of the earth and thereby endangering the entire ecosphere, the Chipko movement has spread from village to village and country to country. It is mostly women's work to gather the rich supplies of forest plants, roots, berries, and tree fruits to feed their families and sell surpluses in the market for modest cash returns. It is their careful pruning of trees for firewood that provides the only fuel for cooking. Therefore women know they must be the protectors of forests. They also know that trees help store water in the soil—that both water and the quality of the soil itself will be lost when land is stripped of tree cover. And they know that financial resources needed for local development are in danger of being siphoned off to create roads and other infrastructures for an export-dominated economy, leaving the village poorer than ever. Already, women in the Garwhal area had to walk five to ten miles a day to collect firewood and fodder for cattle, bent double under heavy baskets.

In the local village councils, the leaders and decision makers are men, and these initiatives by women have startled them. Some villages are proud of their women and support them. Others know they are doing what is needed but feel that it is men who should be leading the way. (Only they don't.) Although there have been some sharp disagreements between women and men at the village level, the women have been able to sustain the courage of their convictions, supported by educated urban women like Vandana Shiva, director of the Research Foundation for Science, Technology and Natural Resource Policy in Dehradun, India. Shiva has been an articulate voice linking care for the environment to a model of alternative development. She insists on the importance of building on grassroots capabilities that will lessen the gulf between rich and poor.[31] The village women now know they have a voice, and that voice is beginning to be listened to locally, nationally, and internationally.

In Kenya, the Green Belt movement for reforestation is responding to a different phase of the same environmental crisis that the Chipko movement is responding to. The trees of the Rift Valley in Kenya are already gone, and the land is undergoing soil erosion and desertification on a large scale. The Green Belt movement brings the women of local villages into tree-planting activities in order to rebuild seriously degraded soils and also to provide the foods and fuel wood that a well-cared-for forest can generate. The plan is very simple. The women of each village plant a community woodland of at least 1,000 trees, a green belt. They prepare the ground, dig holes, provide manure, and then help take care of the young trees. The inspiration for this movement came from a Kenyan woman, the biologist Wangari Maathai, who saw that the natural ecosystems of her country were being destroyed.[32] As she has pointed out, the resulting poverty was something men could run away from, into the cities, but the women and children remain behind in the rural areas, hard put to provide food and water for hungry families. Working with the National Council of Women of Kenya, Professor Maathai went from village to village to persuade women to join the Green Belt Movement. Green Belt by now has involved more than 80,000 women and a half-million school children in establishing over a thousand local tree nurseries and planting more than 10 million trees in community woodlands, with a tree survival rate of 70 to 80 percent. This revival of local ecosystems has made fuel available, and family kitchen gardens are once more viable. Furthermore, women have been empowered to develop more ways of processing and storing foodstuffs that were formerly vulnerable to spoilage.

This movement, like the Chipko movement, has also spread to other countries. In Kenya, as in India, educated urban women were in close enough touch with their village sisters to be aware of their needs. The basic development issue at stake, says Professor Maathai, is food security, without which no country can have any meaningful development. Women helped introduce the food security concept to development professionals.

In Chapter 8 we saw how political concepts of modernization and development led to a state system ill-adapted to meeting the needs of the diverse ethnies inside state boundaries. In this chapter we have seen how economic concepts of modernization and development have similarly failed to meet the needs of local populations. Centralization of administration by states and globalization of enterprises by corporations have created problems of scale that divorce decision making from local knowledge and do irreparable harm to the biosphere. The gradual coming together of the environmental and alternative development movements, much accelerated by the Rio conference, have crystallized a new understanding of the interdependence of environments and development, and of the broader interdependence of all living systems in the biosphere. The term *gaia* to refer to that complex of living systems was used at the beginning of this chapter to emphasize the organic nature of the planet, with all its interrelated spheres.[33] The popular use of the word *gaia* represents a change in consciousness that is taking place at both the metaphoric and the analytic levels, and we can be grateful that the work of J. E. Lovelock has helped to provide an empirical grounding for this new conceptualization of the earth as a living system.

The responses to this new understanding are complex and take place at many levels. The evolution of United Nations efforts from the Development Decades to the UNCED conference in Rio has been described and the new awareness of the civil economy within the corporate sphere, with accompanying emergence of new NGOs to enhance accountability of corporations to states and the civil society. At the grassroots level, we have seen an emerging set of values and practices that have created working alternative models of development based on local knowledge and resources but linked by grassroots networks to each other around the world. The process of getting the support of peoples from around the world for the Earth Charter—for a covenant with Gaia—in a way brings together developments at every level in a common commitment to the socioeconomic and ecological dimensions of a peace culture for the twenty-first century.

# 10

# Information, Communication, and Learning

Turning information into knowledge and communicating it, through the various modes available to a society for passing on that which is known and valued, are processes that lie at the core of every culture. In a peace culture these are creative two-way processes in which every sector participates—scholars, teachers, workers, artists, faith communities, activist groups of the civil society, and adventurous youth exploring new domains. We can find this creative two-way flow in microsocieties of our time—among indigenous peoples, in states that have eschewed militarism, in peace-minded subcultures such as have been described earlier. But these highly participatory flows are the exception, not the rule. On the one hand, technological developments associated with the rise of industrialism, global corporations, and modern warfare have so transformed information flows and modes of communication that our age is called the Information Age. So-called information highways make it possible for individuals to sit before computers and TV screens, sending and receiving messages from around the world by electronic means. Work, learning, social interaction, and play are all possible at the screen. On the other hand, when information is communicated electronically, human relationships and human interaction with the biosphere are electronically mediated; this is second-hand information. At best, it is formulated, sent and received by individuals with an active social awareness and concern for the quality of the world they live in. At worst, it is packaged as a commodity by global corporations.

## Information Flows

The general intoxication with the waves of information that flow from screen to screen has led many to believe that a new stage of human development has been reached. They have forgotten that well-developed communication systems existed long before literacy itself. Oral history preserved by griots and bards, music, dance, drawings, pictograms, drumming, signal fires, and long-distance runners preceded books by thousands of years. Books themselves go back thirty centuries, and story-telling and reading aloud are shared human experiences that continue to this day. Traditionally, communication has been interactive and relational.

The appearance of printing presses slowly changed this situation, but printing on a mass scale did not begin until the 1800s and was a process dominated by the colonial powers. Books created reading audiences, recipients of a communication process, with a relatively small elite determining what would be communicated. The Associated Press started in 1848, and Reuters in 1851. Radio became an important source of news by 1910 (the first global broadcast was from Britain in 1930), TV by 1950; and by the late 1970s transmission by computer began the informatics revolution, which continues to this day. Has this revolution liberated humanity from isolation and ignorance, or has it created new forms of domination, whether by authoritarian states or global corporations?

It has done both. The media and information issues of today revolve around questions of how to empower people in communities to share the rich diversity of language, culture, and knowledge of the planet and its humans in two-way communication flows around the world; to replace the one-way flows that threaten to create a homogenized culture reflective of only one small part of the Western world, a built world separated from nature. In the last decade of the twentieth century, a few transnational publishing houses have swallowed most medium-size publishers, TV networks have swallowed all but the smallest independent enterprises, and computer conglomerates threaten to swallow all of the above. At the same time, disparities between rich and poor in both the One-Third and the Two-Thirds Worlds have increased, since the empowering effects of communication technologies are not available to the poor. Without access to that technology, they cannot develop relevant new skills and their stories are not heard. The use of the media by powerful states to demonize adversaries and whip up fervor for nationalist causes is another example of the inequities generated by the revolution in communications technology.

Efforts to deal with these inequities go back to the 1860s and 1870s, when the first international communication agencies (the International Telecommunications Union and the Universal Postal Union) were formed, continue to the present. The 1948 Universal Declaration of Human Rights by the then recently formed United Nations states in Article 19: "Everyone has the right to freedom of opinion and expression; this right includes freedom to hold opinions without interference and to seek, receive and impart information and ideas through any media and regardless of frontiers." However, as the rate of information flows steadily increases, so do questions about the inequities. The rise of the Non-Aligned Movement in the early 1960s represented a call for a new regime—a set of rules and procedures that would define the limits of acceptable behavior—for the world as a whole. Out of this Two-Thirds World movement came the call for a New International Economic Order and a New World Information and Communication Order (NWICO) to right communication imbalances between West and Non-West. One important response to the call for NWICO came from UNESCO, which in 1977 appointed an International Commission for the Study of Communication Problems, with members from the United States, France, Zaire, Colombia, the former Soviet Union, Indonesia, Tunisia, Japan, Nigeria, the former Yugoslavia, Egypt, The Netherlands, Chile, India, and Canada. It is often referred to as the MacBride Commission after its chairman, Sean MacBride of Ireland. The Commission began work in a highly contentious social context. Two-Thirds World protests against the dominant flow of news from industrialized countries were construed in the West as attacks on the free flow of information. On the other hand, in some regions defenders of journalistic freedom were attacked as threatening national sovereignty.

The MacBride Commission's recommendations, with their plea for openness to cultural diversity, have become a landmark for serious consideration of the role of communication in the social, economic, and political life of every society. The section on communication policies maintains that:

> All individuals and people collectively have an inalienable right to a better life which, howsoever conceived, must ensure a social minimum, nationally and globally. This calls for the strengthening of capacities and the elimination of gross inequalities. . . . Since communication is interwoven with every aspect of life, it is clearly of the utmost importance that the existing "communication gap" be rapidly narrowed and eventually eliminated.[1]

The recommendations make very clear the importance not only of having every spoken language (about 3,500 at this time), and the cultural experiences of the people who speak that language, available in communications media, but also of every society telling its own stories, communicating its own news, so information about the world is not filtered through the lenses of a few Western-based media enterprises. Communication infrastructures (particularly the press and radio) reaching into every village are emphasized, making available local community news and programming as well as linkage to national and regional networks. In general, the report links communication policy closely to the overall development policy of each society, to universal schooling and lifelong learning, with due attention to the possibilities of distance learning through radio and TV.

The one underlying theme of the report—to replace one-way information flows with two-way flows, particularly a return flow to the West from the Two-Thirds World—was misinterpreted by the United States and England as support for news censorship in states with authoritarian governments (which, in fact, the report explicitly condemned). This misinterpretation occasioned their withdrawal from UNESCO. England has since returned to UNESCO, but the United States remains outside UNESCO in self-imposed isolation.

The importance of the MacBride Commission's report lies in its strong stand for multiculturalism and for the use of the information highway to enrich local awareness of the diversity of the world's cultures. UNESCO has consistently seen the cultivation of that awareness as one of its primary tasks. The World Decade for Cultural Development, 1988–1997, was intended, among other goals, to be a decade for celebrating cultural diversity.[2] The Decade program sought to strengthen national infrastructures for cultural development and improve school textbooks' treatment of other societies and their history and contributions to the present. The United States, unfortunately, did not participate in the Decade, but recognition of otherwise ignored minority cultures was an important byproduct of the Decade in many countries.

The movement to free up communication flows and respect diversity continues, although slowly. While far more honored in the breach than in the observance, certain basic principles of international communication and information law are generally recognized in the international community:

1. Communication media may not be used for war and aggression.
2. Communication media shall not be used to intervene in the internal affairs of another state.
3. States are obliged to modify social and cultural practices, including information and communication activities, that are based on gender or ethnic superiority or inferiority.
4. Media should play a positive role in educating and enlightening the public toward peace.

5. All peoples have the right to develop local information and communication infrastructures without the interference of external parties and to
   establish communication policies for the benefit of their society.
6. The free and unrestricted flow of information is encouraged.[3]

Having considered the international norms for information flow, we will
now look at the major media to see how each contributes or does not contribute to social well-being.

### Books, Newspapers, and Radio

Books are the oldest mass communication medium, but the phenomenon of
widespread literacy to provide a reading audience is about three hundred
years old. The printing of books continues to expand worldwide, but the reading of books is apparently declining. (This is hard to measure, but teachers at
college levels in the United States report that students are less well read than
formerly.) Similarly, newspapers have rising circulations, but newspaper cir-
culation per capita has declined. However, the number of local ethnic newspapers around the world remains steady, matching continuing levels of ethnic
awareness, both local and in ethnic diaspora. Major urban newspapers give
great prominence to news of war, crime, violence, and crises; much less
prominence to the peacefully creative activities of civil society and positive
problem solving among states. This skewing of reporting towards crises tends
to result in newspapers making only minimal contributions to the peace culture of their respective societies, in spite of the importance of their role in reporting on public affairs and developing an informed citizenry.

It should be pointed out that such skewing is more a result of editorial policy than of the work of the courageous in-the-field journalists who try to present accurate accounts of what is happening, wherever there is violence,
injustice, or creative peacemaking. Journalism is a very dangerous occupation. The Committee to Protect Journalists reports that 474 journalists have
been killed over the past decade.[4] Journalist NGOs, such as the International
organization of Journalists and the World Association for Christian Communication, along with Amnesty International and many human rights NGOs,
do their best to protect reporters and to investigate numerous human rights vi-
olations against journalists by authoritarian governments. However, such governments are not the only danger journalists face. In every country, crusading
journalists are, to a degree, embattled, struggling against government censorship and editorial policies of media conglomerates. Defending the lifespace

and freedom to write of those who try to give a fuller reporting of the human condition is a major task for those who work for a culture of peace.[5]

Radio, though the oldest of the modern media, continues to expand its audiences, and the number of broadcasting receivers has doubled worldwide in the 1980s. Unlike television, radio can be—and is—local, whether in the One-Third or the Two-Thirds World. It is equally at home in rural and urban areas. Many programs are in vernacular languages and feature local news and culture. Programs are relatively easy and cheap to make, drawing on local expertise to supplement more elaborate programs from urban centers. With much local participation, radio definitely promotes two-way information flow. Although demagogues use the radio too (most notably with the rise of Fascism in the 1930s), informed public dialogue is the rule. UNESCO supports Peace Radio in a number of countries, as, for example, in Somalia, and supports independent media in ex-Yugoslavia and the Great Lakes region of Africa. UNESCO also makes available, in a number of languages, programs addressing a wide range of issues in the fields of education, communication, culture, and science. The International Center for Humanitarian Reporting administers a radio partnership project to promote greater use of radio in development communications. International initiatives to promote creative and socially useful radio programming are legion, as the global civic society takes responsibility for increasing two-way information flows.[6]

## Television

Television, a relative latecomer to the mass media scene, has, since the 1940s, expanded to reach up to 80 percent of the North American population, with similar figures for Western Europe, but has much smaller and primarily urban-based audiences in the Two-Thirds World (more in Latin America, fewer in Africa and Asia). The United States exports by far the largest number of programs to the rest of the world. Some states in Africa and the Middle East have adopted policies of limiting foreign imports by establishing a percentage ceiling, a way of resisting cultural imperialism. Objections of the Two-Thirds World are not only to the overwhelmingly American cultural themes but also to the commercialization of the media, both in advertising and in the consumer lifestyles portrayed. The magnitude of the one-way information flow from a very small number of sources in the United States and Western Europe has been very troubling to that sector of the global civil society that is committed to human and social development based on a healthy cultural diversity and drawing on the whole range of human knowledge and experience. Unlike radio, television production is too expensive for locals in the Two-Thirds World. The few educational programs that do present a variety of lifeways in different world regions are not widely distributed.

The aspect of television that is most troubling to many concerned citizens, however, is the amount of violence shown daily on television screens, particularly in United States programs. A statement by a former surgeon general, Dr. Jocelyn Elders, on children's exposure to violence points out that, on average, children spend more time in front of the television screen than at school. Between the ages of five and eighteen, they watch 15,000 hours of television and see 250,000 acts of violence. In contrast, they spend 12,000 hours learning in school.[7] A three-year national television violence study conducted by a four-university consortium reported in 1998 that the proportion of prime-time broadcast and basic cable shows with violence has increased since 1994. The study cites previous research conducted over several decades, which has established that exposure to television violence can contribute to aggressive attitudes and behaviors, to desensitization to real-world violence, and to increased fear in viewers. Pointing out that television violence is glamorized and sanitized, the study reports that nearly 40 percent of the violent incidents are initiated by "good" characters, who are likely to be perceived as attractive role models. Concern is also expressed about cartoons with a high violence content that are viewed by young children. Children under seven have difficulty distinguishing televised fantasy from reality and are therefore at increased risk of imitating cartoon violence, the study points out.

Projects to identify "risky" shows by special ratings to keep children away from them do not even touch the problem of the harm so much exposure to violence does to people of all ages.[8] Violence against women continues to be a major problem, both mirroring and accentuating the continuing victimage of women. ISIS and the UN International Fund for Women (UNIFEM) have joined efforts with other women's groups to try to come up with a strategy to persuade advertisers and media professionals to develop a code of conduct relating to the portrayal and coverage of violence against women.[9]

Certainly, well-designed educational programs expand the mental horizons of children and adults alike, but they represent a small proportion of total television. One strong positive example is WETV, whose programs, produced by the Global Access TV Network, are carried weekly by 35 networks in 32 countries in Africa, Latin America, the Caribbean, and Asia. These programs combine education and entertainment to convey important messages about the environment, sustainable development, cultural diversity, and the empowerment of women and youth. WETV's goal is to distribute programs to 100 countries by 2002.[10]

It is, nevertheless, wise to keep in mind that the brain processes images from television differently from the way it processes words in a book; heavy viewing, coupled with little reading, leads to diminished language skills, lower information levels, and limited reading ability.[11]

Although literacy itself is certainly one of the major achievements of humanity, even reading, when it substitutes for interaction with the natural world, actually reduces human understanding of the animate earth, humanity's first teacher. The alphabetized intellect, says David Abrams in his challenging book *The Spell of the Sensuous*, lives in a carefully charted and mechanistically regulated world; it misses out on the participatory, interactive learning about and with the living earth—available for those who listen to that earth. Continued destruction of surrounding ecosystems is the result. Abrams would not abolish literacy, but he would "write words back into the land."[12]

The same applies to television. If used appropriately, television offers a more expressive medium than radio. Combining images and sound, it has a superior capacity for sharing the cultural riches from the world's 188 states and 10,000 societies. Decommercialized television would have many contributions to make to cultures of peace around the world. Two-way hookups that enable geographically separated groups to dialogue on television, each able to watch the faces of the others on the television screen, are increasingly taking place; they have already become an important tool for a variety of international groups (including multinational corporations). An expansion of such interactive events spanning great distances without the expense of international travel will be very important for the 20,000 NGOs of the global civil society as a supplement to the biennial or triennial face-to-face gatherings that can be afforded by only a small minority of members.

Overall, however, it is a matter of concern that twenty-some megacorporations control most of the approximately 25,000 media outlets in the United States and there is comparable domination by a few megacorporations globally. This is a serious obstacle to the free two-way information flow that is so critical for states and civil society alike.

## Computers

Computers have become the centerpiece of the global information society, changing how humans live, work, learn, and play. Since relatively few people in the Two-Thirds World have access to computers except in urban centers and universities, the resource gap between haves and have-nots has widened. It has been estimated that by the year 2000 there will be 10 billion computers—enough for every man, woman, and child alive—but they will be far from equally distributed.[13]

The existence of a worldwide communications web that ordinary citizens can use—not just governments and corporations and elites—opens up the possibility of widespread democratic participation in public policymaking for the first time in history. Already there are many thousands of websites for groups concerned with peace, development, environment, and human rights issues. One of countless examples is GLOCAL, a Global and Local Electronic Communications Network founded by members of the World Association of Christian Communicators to interconnect faith communities, ecumenical organizations, and social movements worldwide to further social action at the local level. There are roughly 800 websites for peace and justice issues, ranging from alternative dispute resolution to social justice activist groups. By topic alone, a recent search on the Internet for entries on complex emergencies generated 64,000 separate items and documents.

More and more journals are going online as well—everything from *Peace and Conflict Studies*, a journal of the Network of Peace and Conflict Studies, to the *Moksha Journal, a Journal of Knowledge, Spirituality and Freedom* put online by Yoga Anand Ashram. Increasingly, books are also being published in online versions. It is clear that the Internet is heavily used. Although class, educational level, and ethnicity tend to determine who gets access, there is certainly a growing effort on the part of NGOs and UN and state development aid programs to make computers available to underserved populations through placing them in village community centers in countries of the South and in inner-city community centers in countries of the North.

Ironically, the technology for the creation of World Wide Web sites arose in the military. In the 1940s and 1950s, the United States government via the Pentagon provided most of the funding for computer research. By 1958 the government had created DARPA, the Defense Advanced Research Projects Agency. This agency worked with universities in Boston and California to develop increasingly sophisticated communications networks. One such network, Arpanet, became the prototype for the development of national information highways, and the United States military continues to be a major customer for information systems research, purchasing a substantial segment of the entire output of computers, software, and services.[14] Colleen Roach writes of the broader Military-Industrial-Communication Complex.[15] This complex, through interlocking military and communication structures, slants media coverage toward the support of military action when intervention policies are being considered, and toward continued high-level military production as a peacetime policy. A comparable military-industrial communication complex exists in each of today's major powers, generating similar biases in each country toward high levels of military preparedness. Peace movements try hard to counteract these biases, but without comparable access to the media, their message is not widely heard.

Another use of the computer today is to play deadly games involving torture and killing of characters in the games, human or nonhuman. This pastime is chillingly attractive to an unknown but significant number of children and adults.

When we consider information as a commodity, we can see a very different kind of bias distorting the information highways. The issuing of patents to corporations, research institutes, and government agencies covering a wide range of physical, chemical, and biological technologies means that corporations and institutes are earning a growing portion of their profits from intellectual property holdings. As Seth Shulman points out in his study of staking claims on the knowledge frontier, information and knowledge are the enduring lifeblood of our civic culture, and an economy of ideas not tempered by a sense of civic-minded purpose is a disaster waiting to happen.[16] With increasing privatization of formerly public intellectual property assets, the marketplace replaces the formerly shared commons. One blatant example has been mentioned earlier, the patenting by pharmaceutical companies of traditional herbal medicines developed by indigenous peoples. A challenge for the twenty-first century is the development of appropriate mechanisms for keeping vital knowledge resources in the public domain whenever possible, for the shared benefit of all.

In spite of the problems that have been mentioned here, the Internet does provide an important information highway for peace, development, and human rights activity. Critical lifesaving information flows over many of the 800 peace-related websites mentioned earlier. Courageous activists, young and old, feed information to the Internet from war-torn areas where violence, rape, genocide, and actual warfare are going on, giving the hidden stories of

nonviolent action in the midst of violence, providing early warning of genocidal activity, issuing calls for help when individuals and groups are being severely persecuted. These websites tell the stories of peacebuilding around the
world that the media ignore and make visible the zones of peace unreported
by the press. Other significant communities that use the Internet include the
peace research scholars sharing databases and findings on conflict and peace
processes, structures, policies, and scenarios at every level from local to interstate around the world. In fact, social scientists and physical scientists are
sharing databases and research institutes are putting their databases online,
making collaborative research among scholars possible regardless of physical
distance and thereby creating new "communities" of scholars. These practices stand in sharp contrast to the drive to patent and privatize knowledge.
In the long run, may the sharing response be the stronger drive!

In an important new development, practitioners developing training mod-
ules for mediation, negotiation, and conflict resolution can, by putting these
on the Internet, enable persons without access to direct training gain skills
they can put to immediate use in the conflict situations in which they find
themselves. Such a program, with special emphasis on accessibility to users
in the Two-Thirds World, is being developed by the Conflict Consortium at
the University of Colorado. Their first online training program is on the constructive confrontation of intractable conflicts. This program "will provide
users around the world with free and virtually instantaneous access to an extensive and highly customizable training program and consulting service focused on the problems typically encountered by people involved in difficulty,
protracted, or seemingly intractable conflicts."[17] Another training manual
*Conflict Transformation by Peaceful Means* (the Transcend Method), prepared by Johan Galtung, is now on both the UN's Humanitarian Assistance
Training Inventory website, Reliefweb, and the Transcend website, a network
of scholars and trainers in peace and development work.[18]

Another unexpected Internet community is made up of monks and nuns
from monasteries around the world, and spiritual seekers, who wish to share
their experiences of the spiritual journey, their research on sages and mystics,
sacred writings, and theological studies. Copies of hard-to-get ancient manuscripts become instantly available on websites like the one maintained on the
English anchoress Julian of Norwich and the fourteenth-century Friends of
God movement—the "mystics' Internet."[19]

Communities of faith have not been slow in discovering the value of the
Internet for community building. Websites are of particular importance for
scattered minority communities that need to support each other in a some-

times hostile environment. For example, an Islamic Internet Consortium is now being formed to provide information and support for Muslims in North America, including access to the Koran and an "Internet Shariʿah," and in general "to provide an island of order in the chaos of the Internet to bring humanity the message of Islam."[20]

Probably the most important use of computer technology is in the modeling of the interactions of the geosphere, hydrosphere, biosphere, atmosphere, and sociosphere to see what is happening to the planet as a result of human activity. Because of the complexity of the interactions and the amount of data involved, such modeling was not possible before computers became available. The information generated by these analyses will make it possible to take corrective action where present practices are clearly demonstrated to be seriously endangering both the earth and its human population. Computer modeling alone will not generate either the information or the political will necessary for changing humankind's relation to the totality of the living earth. However, at least some of the scientists working in the field of chaos theory, which is producing critical new insights about Gaia, also spend long hours walking in the woods, completely absorbed in the interplay between life forms underfoot, at eye level, and in the treetops.[21] Out of chaos itself, as experienced in the interiority of the human mind, on the computer screen, and in the flux of the lifeworld, emerge our deepest understandings of that which is. We can be grateful to the computer for its role in alerting us to the choices we have to make. (One of those choices has to do with how to build computers without generating unmanageable levels of toxic waste, as has, unfortunately, happened in Silicon Valley.)

It is not hard to demonstrate that computer technology can help make the world a better place. But like every technology, its value depends on how it is used. One of the best discussions of the benefits and hazards of computers, focused on how society might live sustainably with their aid, is to be found in a recent Worldwatch paper by John Young.[22] The overriding question is how to use them well.

The computer has affected how we live in many ways, often compounding the effects of other technologies. One effect has to do with the pace at which we live. Although it was supposed to be the ultimate labor-saving device, the computer in fact multiplies our labors. Back in the 1960s we worried about what people would do with all the leisure time the many forms of automation would bring. Whatever happened to leisure? Today everyone rushes around at high speed all day long—except when sitting in front of the television or the computer itself. Face-to-face interaction, except on the run, is disappearing. Telecommuting leads to social isolation, and day-to-day colleagiality with fellow workers is lost. There is some pressure for teachers, from elementary school on, to become classroom trainers in computing skills; subject matter is imparted more and more by the screen, less and less by the teacher. College professors still lecture, but instead of holding class discussions or being available for office hours, it is now not uncommon for professors to tell students to send questions by e-mail and to give tests by e-mail.

Instead of interacting with neighbors, lonely computer addicts spend their time in Internet chatrooms. This activity can assuage loneliness, but often real identities and real problems and needs disappear into carefully constructed chatroom charades. What is happening is a great de-skilling; a de-skilling of the ability to engage in relationships with other humans, a de-skilling of the ability to interact with the planet itself. Online communication does not carry the cues of human feelings that can be read in facial expressions and body language. And television images do not convey the intimate multisensorial realities of the natural world. People are learning to live with two-dimensional instead of multidimensional realities, and "virtual reality" is the most isolating reality of all.

Humans developed as a species with nature as our teacher and partner. The trees and plants interacted with us and taught us. The winged and the four-legged and the swimmers and the crawlers interacted with us and taught us, and all of our senses were involved in the learning partnership. Human infants need to be held, caressed, talked to. If they are left lying in cribs, they experience real sensory deprivation and develop an attachment disorder. In a way, children and adults who spend too much of their time before computers and television screens are also experiencing sensory deprivation. This is not the fault of the television or the computer screen. It is a fault in human choices about how to use television and computers. The recovery of face-to-face interaction in family life, work, school, civic life, and play is necessary for the recovery of peace culture itself. The lack of ability to read cues about how others feel leads to an increase in quarrelsomeness, to a decline in creative dealing with difference and in the skills of cooperative problem solving. Some of those most concerned about this situation respond by throwing out the television set and unplugging the computer—or at least going off the Internet—but this does not solve society's problem of how to live with communications technology.

The study of communication is an academic discipline, and universities house departments of communication. What do these departments teach? Communication theory; development of communication skills, interpersonal and organizational; communication and culture; communication as a social process; the impact of technological developments on communication; and issues of communication and society. The particular university catalogue I am examining as I write gives a strong emphasis to interpersonal communication, nonverbal communication, entrepreneurial problem solving, and group decision making. These are precisely the areas that Internet communication makes problematic, and it is to be hoped that research focused on this arena will lead to a more judicious use of the Internet for learning and problem solving.

The eagerness for technological innovation tends to downgrade earlier communication skills developed over centuries. The assumption that a literate society no longer needs the skills of oracy—of committing knowledge to memory, either for personal use or for oral transmission—is unfortunate. One might say that in much of the West, literacy has now become the great emptier of the mind. We know how to look things up, so we don't need to remember anything. Consciously building up an interior knowledge stock, and learning to play with knowledge combinations in the mind, run our own mental mazes, and test our own mental combinations in the environment seems to be something that many nonliterates can do better than we. There began to be disconcerting discoveries in the 1960s about the superiority of abilities of nonliterates compared to literates in a developing society, in terms of problem solving and keenness of civic judgment.[23] This refinement of mental and intuitive capacities in developing and working with knowledge stocks that nonliterate societies at their best have achieved is very different from the immersion in visual images that has become so attractive in the post-McCluhan age.

Typewriters—and word processors—should not be allowed to replace the skills of penmanship, which provide a special hand-brain connection in the process of writing, and should continue to be used for some types of writing. Radio, which focuses the listening mind in a special way, does not become obsolete with the arrival of television. Communication through pantomime, dance movements, and song also enriches the empathic ability to understand another person. Nor, finally, should the ease of Internet communication replace face-to-face communication. Each communication technology makes its own contribution to the full development of the social persona, and each should have a continuing place in a mature and peaceful society.

Oddly enough, communing with the self in solitude is also an essential form of communication and enriches one's ability to communicate with others. A pattern of alternating face-to-face interaction with other forms of inter-actions, including solitary communion, helps to slow down the frenzied pace of activity that leaves so many people stressed out and alienated from the very life they live.

## Schooling

The single most important institution for the acquisition of information and learning the skills of communication is the schooling system of each society. Among indigenous peoples, in addition to parental teaching in the family, certain elders take the children in small groups to learn the survival skills of the society— food gathering, hunting, craft skills, ceremonial skills, and oracy (the traditional oral history of the society). Parents, designated teaching adults, and skilled craftworkers, healers, and griots taking on young apprentices were the primary means of education for the young up until the industrial era. Temple schools, for the children of elites, that began with the development of writing might be considered an exception. In general, occupational skills were learned through the apprenticeship process. With industrialization, the advantages of literacy led to a multiplication of temple, church, and monastery schools in Europe and its colonies overseas. Also, in urban neighborhoods, literate women would open minischools in their homes to teach local children to read and write.

The concept of universal literacy is very recent, and although the right to education is now considered an established human right, large numbers of children have no access to schooling. In 1990, 100 million children, most of them girls, had no access to primary education. Another 100 million did not complete basic education, and these often remain illiterate. Millions of other children finished elementary school education but did not acquire the skills of literacy. Compulsory education in theory lasts from five to twelve years in most countries of the South, but poverty keeps many children out of school, and the number of illiterates is actually rising in Sub-Saharan Africa, South Asia, and the Arab states. Child labor, often in conditions of near slavery, and child prostitution are widespread as children, like adults, struggle to survive. Economic sustainability is essential in order for schooling of any kind to take place. It is estimated that there will be one billion illiterate adults in the world by the year 2000, 98 percent of them in the Two-Thirds World. Girls have much less chance than boys for whatever schooling is available. There are also serious problems in the One-Third World, where, in spite of school-

ing, it is estimated that 20 percent of the population over fifteen is function-
ally illiterate.[24]

In the industrialized countries, as elsewhere to a lesser degree, children sit
in boxes called schools for ten to twelve years, engaging in book learning that
may have little relation to the multiplicity of lifeworlds outside. This is true in
spite of educational innovations inside and outside the evolving public
schooling process over the last two centuries. On the one hand, acceptance
of the concept of public education as a human right to be available to every
child has been a significant step forward in the modern world, creating the
possibility of a fuller development of the human mind and making the riches
of human knowledge, past and present, in theory available to everyone. On
the other hand, the segregation of young learners inside school buildings,
away from the larger society and the natural world in which it is embedded,
and the emphasis on textbook learning (and now learning at the computer
screen), separates children from the dynamic processes of their society, and
the dynamics of their bioregion, in ways that children were not separated
under older apprenticeship systems of learning. Intergenerational interaction
becomes the exception as age-grading continues into adult life—all the way
to the segregation of senior citizens in their last decades. Farming communities, where schooling was closely integrated into agricultural rhythms that
made up the daily life of the farm family, were the last strongholds of experiential learning until agribusiness began making family farms unsustainable.
Such farms are now an endangered species, and the one-room schoolhouse,
where teachers and students helped each other to learn, no longer exists in
countries like the United States.

Is it significant that today many people who have completed high school,
quite a few who have completed college, and a surprising number who have
Ph.D.'s feel that they never learned how to *do* anything? People of all ages,
not just college students, will tell you that whatever they have learned to *do*—
in the way of directly dealing with people, systems, production roles of any
kind—they have learned outside of formal schooling. The drive to specialize
is the drive to get a little corner on reality, to feel that one can *do* something,
by manipulating that corner. We are all on assembly lines, and the experience
of completion is rare. Even the small but satisfying daily completion of
household tasks that is available to householders is politicized and rejected
because these tasks are usually linked to an oppressive division of labor.

The despairing cry of the graduating senior, "What am I going to *do*?" is
heard by every college teacher annually. Today even teaching is a declining

job possibility, except for a lucky few. The felt helplessness shows up in many ways. It begins with preteen suicide. Teenage suicide rates grow apace, but suicides at younger ages show the greatest rate of increase. We are all aware how the helplessness shows up in escape into the world of drugs and alcoholism. Gang warfare and schoolyard killings are now a major problem in the United States. Homicide is, of course, one of the most pathological forms of helplessness a society can produce. It signifies helplessness both of the murderer and of the victim: neither has found an alternative course of action.

There is something really odd about the widespread feeling of helplessness today. It is found both in those with the most and in those with the least education. We have covered it over with talk about competence and tried to assuage the feeling with a philosophy of competency-based learning. Competence in what? Our capacity for self-delusion is almost infinite. In order to deal with an increasingly comfortless built environment, and inner helplessness, we utilize our technology to project on our mental screens images of a continuous process of social and environmental construction and redesign. We think we are experiencing rapid change—that we are a progressive, creatively adaptive society—when, in fact, it is all done with mirrors, and we are instead becoming increasingly rigid. Plato's cave analogy expresses the situation well. All we see are the shadows on the wall. The reality is somewhere out there, behind us. But we are protected from that knowledge because of the immediately persuasive character of the technologies we are developing. In fact, whether they deal with the prolongation of life, with moving us or our ideas more quickly around the planet, or with making it still easier to clean immaculate middle-class homes, these technologies are about as useful to us in light of planetary needs as the dinosaur's unwieldy skeleton was to her. While alternative small-scale technologies exist that could free us from this skeleton, in fact we utilize technology to develop ever-larger administrative systems and to reduce individual freedom. Will we go the way of the dinosaur?

We don't have to, because community-based learning can be recovered. It was never completely lost. The idea of the neo–village school or the community-centered school, open to the local environment, has stayed alive in experimental efforts in both rural and urban areas on every continent. Gandhian village schools are still to be found in India, Buddhist temple schools and sarvodaya village schools throughout Asia, ujama and other types of village schools in Africa, and Servicio Paz y Justicia (SERPAJ) schools in Latin America. In Europe, creative experiential learning schools on the models developed by Rudolf Steiner, Maria Montessori, and other innovators stretch from Scandinavia to Italy. And in the United States, the alternative school movement has been particularly active since the early 1960s. (A popular book in the 1970s was *How to Start Your Own School . . . and Make a Book*.)[25] In one way or another, most of these schools are incorporated into the local biosphere, and the economic, social, and (often) spiritual life of the communities where they are located.

For example, in the early 1970s in the San Luis Valley in Colorado, some Spanish-speaking populations simply withdrew their children from a public school system that was educating their children to incompetence and failure by systematically forbidding those children to draw on their own native language and hard-earned knowledge stock. Such parents have created their own community schools in which children and adults alike learn the skills they need to function productively, and with self-respect and joy, in the region in which they live. In situations like this, every adult becomes both a teacher and a learner, every child both an apprentice and a teacher of those younger than herself. The school itself becomes a skills center, linked to the community in numberless ways. What would it mean for a larger town or city to recreate its entire educational system along these lines?

Archibald Shaw suggested this in a pioneering proposal entitled "The Random Falls Idea" as far back as 1956.[26] It has never gotten even close to an actual trial, and yet it holds the answer to many of our most pressing problems. His proposal involves turning the school into a headquarters and the entire community into a complex of learning sites. This would mean a substantial redeployment of personnel and resources in our public schools, as well as a substantial redefinition of the relationship between school and community, teachers and community members, adults and children. The school headquarters provides classroom teaching for very specific skills, and the rest of the learning takes place in a variety of apprenticeship situations that are arranged between pupils and every adult in the community at her place of work. Figure 2 diagrams the school-community relationship in terms of learning sites. A substantial part of the school personnel, now engaged in classroom teaching or in-house administrative work, would be developing and coordinating the numerous linkages that would be needed to ensure that every adult in the community spent some time in a teaching relationship with pupils at her place of work.

One unusual example of community-centered education is found in the self-schooling movement. The young self-starters in this movement make their own contracts with adults for the skills they seek, in a variety of occupational settings, creating their own sequence of apprenticeships. The community *is* their school.[27]

There are a number of conflicting crosscurrents in relation to changing the character of schooling, and space does not permit documenting these developments here. The most promising of these developments seek new ways to link school and community. For example, modifications in existing school systems by introducing service learning and Americorps programs for community volunteering as part of the high school curriculum are healthy movements toward experiential learning in the United States—especially if classroom teachers link classroom social studies to what students are learning in the field. Another school-community linkage is found in the movement to

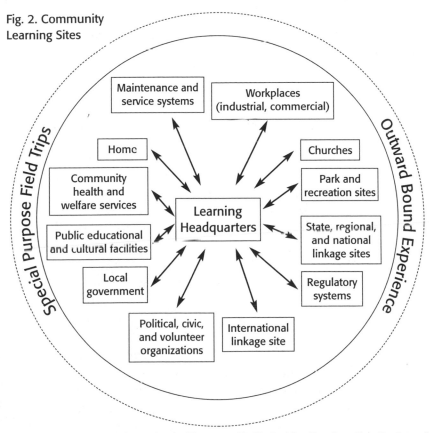

Fig. 2. Community Learning Sites

*Source:* The diagram "Community Learning Sites" first appeared in Elise Boulding, "Learning to Make New Futures," in *Education Reform for a Changing Society: Anticipating Tomorrow's Schools,* ed. Louis Rubin (Boston: Allyn and Bacon, 1978).

teach the biological sciences through study of local woods and waterways and wetlands. In general, dissatisfaction with school and with the quality of community life is leading to wider civic involvement in linking schooling to everyday life. This involvement will make it possible to redevelop the vocational-technical school model from an alternative education for those not college-bound to an experientially based education for all.

Experiential education, in contradistinction to textbook education, is often referred to as an open learning system in contrast to a closed teaching system. Rarely will a school represent a completely closed system and, equally rarely, a completely open system. Most schools are a mixture of the two, with the closed system predominant. However, in general, the verbal-analytic mode of thinking and learning is favored.

Colleges and universities are as bound into the verbal-analytic mode of thinking as the public schools. Professors' lectures often follow a predictable pattern, which is why lecture notes are still a saleable commodity on college campuses. On a personal note, only after several years of teaching did I fully realize what a straitjacket the verbal-analytic mode imposes on the mind. After that, in my sociology classes, from time to time, I gave assignments that required transforming concepts and theories and fact-clusters into a series of other modes, including metaphor, music, poetry, pictures, color, mathematical equations, and diagrammatic and free-form visual presentations. The increase in levels of comprehension, in ability to handle complexity, and in general creativity in dealing with the subject matter was so great that I was myself dumbfounded at the implications for general educational practice.

The development of experiential learning programs in colleges and universities under the rubric of service learning is one of the most helpful developments of recent decades. Service learning itself probably has many antecedents. One is the Outward Bound schools that began in England fifty years ago, training young boys on rescue missions in a community-based approach to education. Outward Bound programs can be found today in academia within schools of education, offering "expeditionary learning." The post–World War I international work camp movement—Service Civile Internationale—might be thought of as another antecedent. Young people in the work camp movement flocked to summer and year-round field service projects in social reconstruction, but usually outside of academia. Training needs for the various national service and Peace Corps types of programs around the world after World War II also played a role in focusing attention on such activities not only as service opportunities but as settings for learning.

However, it was not until the 1970s that serious recognition of service learning as an educational enterprise suitable for college campuses took place in the United States. Many college campuses now have service learning programs as well as administrative facilities available to assist any academic department in establishing a service learning program linked to their discipline, whether in the social or physical sciences or the humanities. There are well over a dozen national service learning clearinghouses to aid colleges in establishing such programs. A recent study of the development of service learning in peace studies programs makes two things clear: there are strong ethical and moral dimensions to such programs, whether they are offered in secular or faith-based institutions, and there is a strong theory-building component in service learning.[28] The traditional assumption that the teaching of theory must rigidly precede practice in real-life situations is shown to be false. The peace studies programs demonstrate that immersion in field situations of conflict and violence can generate theoretical insights and intellectual analysis of conflicts even while cultural empathy with communities at risk and skills of conflict transformation are simultaneously developing.

This type of learning, recalling the Paolo Freire model of teachers-as-learners and learners-as-teachers, involves a profound respect for the capacity of students to respond to the complex challenges of real-life situations. This approach also places a strong emphasis on the personal development of each individual student, particularly through the continuous practice of journaling and reflection. Interestingly, personal development and capacity for intellectual analysis are seen to go hand in hand. Intellectual rigor is emphasized in each program, but so are personal maturity and hands-on peacebuilding skills.

The rapid growth of service learning programs, whether in peace studies or other academic fields, shows an encouraging readiness on the part of students to engage in this more demanding type of learning. The field service elements of these programs are not required; they are entered voluntarily. Because of the triple demands of academic course work, field work with both a research and an action component, and reflective journaling, students in these programs work much harder than in traditional courses of study.

The in-depth exposure to unfamiliar life settings in service learning—particularly situations of violence, poverty, and oppression—invariably has a profound effect on students. They discover very soon that they have much to learn from those they are working with, and that the only viable relationship is one of partnering, rather than of being an outside do-gooder. This experience of partnering will have profound consequences for students' ways of working after completion of their studies.

The larger context for this type of development is the direction that institutions of higher learning will be taking in a rapidly changing world. The idea of universities as nodes in a worldwide web of communities of scholar-teachers and learners in constant interaction with the society around them and with the geosphere-biosphere is beginning to replace the ivory tower concept of higher learning. Yet interdisciplinary communication between university departments locally remains as difficult as intercivilizational dialogue in a worldwide communications web still sadly sectioned into West and non-West, One-Third and Two-Thirds Worlds.

While there has always been a small international community of scholars engaged in a shared search for knowledge, the development of the United Nations University (UNU) within the United Nations system to address pressing environment, development, and peace-building problems of a global nature represents a significant force working to expand the size and effectiveness of that community. With an independent international governing council of respected scholars and ties to UNESCO and to other United Nations research institutes, the United Nations University is creating a community of scholars and graduate students at work in a network of universities and research institutes in each world region, a community with a rich experience of collegial work.[29] The innovative University of Peace in Costa Rica, also recognized by the United Nations, and the newly projected African University of Peace and Development, being planned by the Organization of African Unity (OAU) in collaboration with European and American institutions, will also help strengthen the international community of peace scholars.

The effect of the information age on the quality of human development in the twenty-first century will depend on many things: the technologies of human communication by printed, oral, and visual media, including computers, available in our communities, our schools, and our universities; the choices we make in how to use those technologies; and the extent to which information flows reflect the cultural diversity of our societies and the biodiversity of the more than human world and are equally available to all. Most of all, it will depend on the further development of open learning systems and a culture of reflection rooted in values of human relationship and relationship to the planet. Each part of the human-nonhuman information, communication, and learning enterprise has a potential to contribute to the global flowering of peace culture, but only careful attention to the problems associated with this awesome system will enable that flowering to take place.

# 11

## Demilitarization
### The Hardest Challenge for States and Civil Society

T HE TRAGEDY of the twentieth century is that it began with the promise of
bringing an end to war as an instrument of state diplomacy but is ending as
the world's bloodiest century, with 108 million war dead.[1] (A previous high, in
the sixteenth century, was 1.6 million.) On the eve of the twenty-first century,
the planet is awash with weapons. There are unprecedented numbers of ongoing wars (thirty in 1998), and the threat of nuclear war, whether by accident
or design, still hangs over humanity. Yet, while the planetary environment de-
teriorates and the gap between rich and poor widens, the nuclear weapons
states hang on to their nukes with the tenacity of a small child hugging a security blanket. Five trillion dollars have been spent since the start of the
nuclear age on the development, manufacture, and deployment of this supposedly efficient and inexpensive security blanket since the beginning of the
nuclear age in 1945. At that, nuclear weapons are only one of five categories of
major weapons of war. The other four are chemical and bacteriological
weapons, conventional arms, light and small arms, and inhumane weapons
(land mines). While varying efforts to control the manufacture and distribution of each of these types of weapons have continued over the decades
through a variety of conventions and treaties, the licit and illicit arms trade in
all categories grows in volume. The recent agreement to ban land mines will
limit production of new ones, but existing land mines will continue to be a
menace on every continent well into the twenty-first century. Nuclear waste
disposal sites will have to be guarded for millennia for the safety of humans
and other life-forms.

In the first ten chapters of this book, we have been examining the historical persistence of elements of peace culture even in the midst of war, vio-

lence, and oppression, and how, in our own time, new shoots of peace culture keep emerging from old roots. Is the war culture overwhelming these new shoots after all? Consider a survey of armed conflicts for the period of 1995 to 1997 by the Dutch Center for Conflict Prevention.[2] The categories used in the report are High-Intensity Conflicts (more than 1,000 fatalities), Low-Intensity Conflicts (between 100 and 1,000 fatalities), and Violent Political Conflict (fewer than 100 fatalities). While High-Intensity Conflicts have reduced from 20 to 17 in this period, the cumulative deaths from the time of inception of each conflict are over 14 million. Low-Intensity Conflicts have increased from 30 to 70 between 1995 and 1997, and Violent Political Conflicts from 40 to 74. Ninety percent of the millions of deaths from these conflicts are civilians, and 100 percent of the internally displaced persons and refugees from these conflicts are civilians. Rates of rape of women in these conflicts are not available but are certainly very high, as is violence toward children. Perhaps 10 to 15 percent of the soldiers are child soldiers. To give an idea of the geographic spread of these conflicts, table 1 lists the countries involved in each type of conflict. It is small comfort to point out that only four of the High-Intensity Conflicts are interstate. The intrastate struggles for ethnic and other forms of autonomy are very bloody in spite of or perhaps because of being fought with small, easily transportable weapons. These struggles can also be political triggers for larger-scale interstate wars as neighboring countries feel their own interests are threatened.

Yes, the war culture is very visible, particularly since the communication technologies discussed in chapter 10 bring vivid images of that culture into

### Table 1. World Conflict Map, 1997

| *High-Intensity Conflicts* | *Low-Intensity Conflicts* | *Violent Political Conflicts* |
|---|---|---|
| **Central and South America** | **Central and South America** | **Central and South America** |
| Colombia (FARC) | Brazil (military, police) | Bolivia (Chapare) |
| | Colombia (UP) | Brazil (Para: MST) |
| | Colombia (ELN) | Cuba (exile infiltration) |
| | Guatemala (URNG) | Dominican Rep. (violent protests) |
| | Haiti (neo-Duvalierists) | Ecuador-Peru (border) |
| | Mexico (Chiapas EZLN) | El Salvador (ex-guerrilleros) |
| | Mexico (EPR) | Honduras (Indians) |
| | Peru (Sendero Luminoso) | Mexico (Tijuana cartel) |
| | U.S.-Mexico (border) | Nicaragua (Contras, Re-contras) |
| | | Panama-Colombia (border) |
| | | Peru (MRTA) |
| | | Surinam (Indians) |

## Table 1. (continued)

| High-Intensity Conflicts | Low-Intensity Conflicts | Violent Political Conflicts |
|---|---|---|
| **Western, Central, and Eastern Europe** | **Western, Central, and Eastern Europe** | **Western, Central, and Eastern Europe** |
| Turkey (PKK) | Azerbaijan/Armenia (Nagorno-Karabakh) | Croatia (E. Slavonia) |
| Albania (armed gangs) | Bosnia-Herzegovina (Serbs, Muslims, Croats) | Cyprus (Greece-Turkey) |
| | Georgia (Abchazia) | Daghestan (interclan) |
| | Russia (Chechnya) | France (Corsica) |
| | | Georgia (Ossetia) |
| | | Macedonia (Albanians) |
| | | Northern Ireland (IRA) |
| | | Russia (Cossacks) |
| | | Russia (N. Ossetia) |
| | | Serbia (Kosovo) |
| | | Serbia (opposition) |
| | | Spain (Basque: ETA) |
| **Africa** | **Africa** | **Africa** |
| Congo-Z. (ADFL) | Angola (Cabinda) | Cameroon-Nigeria (Bakassi) |
| Congo-B. (Cobras) | Angola (UNITA) | Djibouti (FRUD) |
| Rwanda (Hutu, Tutsi) | Cameroon (NW prov) | Eritrea (Islamists) |
| Sudan (SPLA) | Central African Rep. (Yakoma) | Ethiopia-Sudan (border) |
| Burundi (Hutu, Tutsi) | Chad (FARF) | Ghana (North) |
| | Comoros (Anjouan) | Kenya (Mombasa) |
| | Congo-Z. (Kivu) | Mali (Tuareg) |
| | Congo-Z. (Bembe) | Mauritania-Senegal (border) |
| | Ethiopia (Oromo) | Niger (Tuareg) |
| | Ethiopia (Amhara) | Nigeria (Ogoni) |
| | Ethiopia (Ogaden) | Sudan (Beja) |
| | Ethiopia (Afar) | Uganda (Tabliqs) |
| | Ethiopia (Harar) | Zambia (opposition) |
| | Ethiopia-Somalia (Gedo) | Zimbabwe (Chimwenje) |
| | Kenya (Turkana, Samburu) | |
| | Kenya (Rift Valley) | |
| | Liberia (NPLF) | |
| | Mozambique (RENAMO) | |
| | Nigeria (PLAN, UFLN) | |
| | Nigeria (Delta state) | |
| | Nigeria (Osun state) | |
| | Nigeria (North) | |
| | Nigeria (Tiv, Jukun) | |
| | Senegal (Casamanche) | |
| | Sierra Leone (RUF) | |
| | Somalia (Somaliland) | |
| | Somalia (interclan) | |
| | South Africa (Kwazulu) | |
| | Uganda (LRA) | |
| | Uganda (WNLF) | |
| | Uganda (ADF) | |
| | Uganda (UYCF) | |
| | Uganda (NALU) | |

(continued)

## Table 1. *(continued)*

| *High-Intensity Conflicts* | *Low-Intensity Conflicts* | *Violent Political Conflicts* |
|---|---|---|
| **North Africa and Middle East** | **North Africa and Middle East** | **North Africa and Middle East** |
| Afghanistan (Taliban) | Egypt (Islamists) | Bahrein (Islamists) |
| Algeria (GIA) | Iran (Kurds) | Libya (Islamists) |
| Iraq (KDP, PUK) | Iran (NLA) | Morocco (W. Sahara) |
| | Iraq (Shiites) | Palestine (intra-Palestinian) |
| | Israel (Hamas, Hezbollah) | Saudi Arabia (Islamists) |
| | Lebanon (Hezbollah, SLA) | Yemen (opposition) |
| **Central Asia** | **Central Asia** | **Central Asia** |
| Sri Lanka (LTTE) | India (Maharashtra, Hindus-Mus- | Bangladesh (CHT) |
| India-Pakistan (Kashmir) | lims) | Bangladesh (Rohingyas) |
| India (Assam) | India (Manipur) | Bhutan (Lotshampas) |
| India (Bihar) | India (Nagaland) | India (West Bengal) |
| Tajikistan (warlords) | India (Punjab) | India (Orissa) |
| | India (Tripura) | India (Madhya Pradesh) |
| | Nepal (Maoists) | India (Andra Pradesh) |
| | Pakistan (Punjab) | India (Tamil Nadu) |
| | Pakistan (Sindh) | India (Mizoram) |
| | Pakistan (NWFP) | India (Meghalaya) |
| | Pakistan (Baluchistan) | India (Maharashtra: Dalits) |
| | | India (Jarkhand) |
| | | India (Sikkim: Gurkhas) |
| | | India (Uttarkhand) |
| | | India-Pakistan (Siachen) |
| | | Uzbekistan (Fergana) |
| **Far East** | **Far East** | **Far East** |
| Burma (Karen) | Cambodia (KR, CPP) | China (Inner Mongolia) |
| | China (Xinjiang) | China (Tibet) |
| | Indonesia (Aceh) | China (Guangdong) |
| | Indonesia (W. Kalimantan) | China (Yunnan) |
| | Burma (Shan) | Indonesia (Java) |
| | Burma (Karen) | Indonesia (East Timor) |
| | Philippines (Moros) | Indonesia (opposition) |
| | | Indonesia (Islamists) |
| | | Philippines (NPA) |
| | | Laos (Hmong) |
| | | North/South Korea (border) |
| | | Papua New Guinea (Bougainville) |
| | | Vietnam (Dong Nai, Thai Binh) |

*Source:* Adapted from European Platform for Conflict Prevention and Transformation, *Prevention and Management of Violent Conflicts, An International Directory,* 1998 ed. (Utrecht: European Platform for Conflict Prevention and Transformation 1998), 43–44.

homes and public gathering places around the world. Further, the military-industrial complex has very effective lobbying and public relations wings, which see to the continued enhancement of those images.

War culture images are images of domination, of the exercise of power over enemies, of destruction of the enemy's lifeways. But war culture itself is also based on fear—the fear of being dominated, destroyed by that same enemy. It is a pathological form of the basic need for autonomy, for having one's own space, and it smothers the other basic human needs for nurturance, empathy, and creative dealing with difference. That pathological fear has driven a century of increasingly deadly arms races. A state can never be strong enough. There is always the danger that it will be overtaken in the race to have the most powerful weapons. This leads to the emphasis on military research and development that has drawn resources away from the social and economic development of the civil society in every state that joins the race. The production and deployment of those weapons further weakens the actual problem-solving capacities of each state as insecurity about the intentions of other states undermines the possibilities of official dialogue. A strangely ambiguous situation results as states come to realize that the arms race itself is dangerous, yet dare not give up lest other states "get ahead." The rise of terrorism further complicates the security picture because the time, place, and weaponry used in terrorist attacks can never be known. This means there are no safe places left on the planet.

Meanwhile, there are those in the civil society who understand that the only real security for any state is a common security for all states, a condition of interdependence based on mutual understanding. While a minority voice, they nevertheless find their opening in the dawning awareness of some policy makers that arms races and continued development of new weapons systems may increase rather than decrease insecurity. The search for a *viable* security system is the meeting point for the war culture and the peace culture. The peace-building sectors of the civil society try to provide new perceptions, new problem-solving capacities, and new confidence-building infrastructures that can maintain peaceful relations without a military threat system. It could be said that what the peace-building sector of the civil society is about is the "civilianization" of security.

We may say, then, that peace culture, all arguments to the contrary notwithstanding, is not fading away. Rather, it is in the process of renewing and updating the efforts of the nineteenth century that led to the Hague Peace Conference itself. In chapter 3, we saw the developments in national peace movements that led to the establishment in 1892 of the International Peace Bureau. Acceptance was growing for the use of arbitration, mediation, and third-party good offices, due to a variety of research, education, and lobbying activities by citizens, which included the development of model arbitration treaties. In fact, between 1870 and 1890, there were sixty-three successful international arbitrations, and the voice of the transnational civil society was sufficiently articulate that states simply could not ignore the invitation of Czar Nicholas to come to a peace conference at The Hague. The time was ripe for new developments in the long, slow emergence of a new constitutive order. The International Court of Arbitration, the League of Nations, and then its successor, the United Nations came into being.

That ripening work, the preparation for new kinds of transnational infrastructure, is a different kind of social process from the very visible public mobilization of large numbers of change-demanding activists at the height of social movements. In the 1990s, with major public peace marches and demonstrations no longer dominating the public consciousness, it is precisely this kind of below-the-surface infrastructure development, which civil society has quietly continued to work for in the century since the Hague Conference, that is now gaining a new momentum. This is the arena in which the peace culture of the international system is found, gathering strength as NGOs, the international civil service of the UN, and creative diplomats from states committed to demilitarization and the peaceful settlement of disputes within and between states work together to achieve these goals. In what follows, we will examine how this peace culture of the international system is functioning at the close of the twentieth century.

Who are the actors in the quiet but essential work of developing alternative security structures that will make demilitarization possible? We will consider states, intergovernmental bodies, the UN system, and nongovernmental organizations (NGOs) as partners in this process.

## States

It may seem strange to start with the behavior of states in describing an emergent peace culture, but we must not ignore that states themselves have been undergoing a long, painful process of trying to negotiate themselves out of the mutual assured destruction trap that the adoption of nuclear defense has created. There are doves and hawks in both nuclear and nonnuclear states. An impressive array of high-ranking officials can be cited arguing for nuclear abolition in each of the nuclear weapons states in spite of the official defense policy. Saul Mendlovitz, director of the World Order Models Project (WOMP), points out that a certain number of peace and justice activists with much transnational experience eventually find their way into government posts in their respective countries, or into the UN, and introduce both a leavening influence and a linkage with civil society that moderates the rigidity and resistance to change of government.[3] Public opinion in the major nuclear weapons states runs counter to state policy; careful opinion polling in the United States reveals a strong opposition to the use of nuclear weapons[4] and a clear preference for a stronger reliance on the UN. In addition, there are strong NGO antinuclear activities in every world region. However, there is a fundamental problem of the utmost gravity: because the major powers are resisting United Nations reform that is in accordance with the existing constitutional process provided for in Article 108 of the current UN Charter, the United Nations is unable to respond to the clear wishes of the world's people. National defense policies are in no way a settled subject.

Table 2, part A, gives a succinct summary of efforts between 1959 and 1996 to limit the use of nuclear weapons. Part B summarizes efforts to control or prohibit the use of other types of weapons. Many thousands of person-hours of government representatives and diplomats have gone into each of the thirty-three agreements listed, in late-night sessions of bargaining, counter-bargaining—and threats. Bargaining and negotiating require listening as well as arguing. (Even threateners have to listen, in order to make sure that their threats are relevant.) Every agreement represents, however weakly, a process in which enough listening took place that a step forward in arms control was achieved, at least by the states signatory to the agreement. This listening, it must be said, was greatly facilitated by the work of concerned NGOs that also spent thousands of person-hours in dialogue with government experts. Also, there is, after all, a kind of peace culture in the international community of diplomats, developed (over centuries of militant nationalism) as a moderating influence on aggressive military strategists. This incipient peace culture in the diplomatic corps of each state is there to be worked with in the demilitarization efforts of the peace-building sectors of the civil society.

At the state level the strongest peace culture is to be found among the middle powers. It was Canada that took the initiative that led to the signing of the Anti-Personnel Landmine Treaty by 145 states in 1998, with the U.S. (along with four other "rogue states") as a holdout state, unwilling to forgo the "protection" land mines might give its soldiers. It was Australia that convened the Canberra Commission on the Elimination of Nuclear Weapons in 1995 that led to public support by 61 former generals and admirals and 117 public leaders for complete nuclear disarmament. An earlier Six-Nation Initiative by the leaders of India, Mexico, Sweden, Greece, Tanzania, and Argentina had increased the momentum for nuclear disarmament in the 1980s. By 1997 the

## Table 2. Arms Control and Disarmament Agreements

### A. Nuclear Weapons

**To prevent the spread of nuclear weapons**

| | |
|---|---|
| Antarctic Treaty, 1959 | 42 states[a] |
| Outer Space Treaty, 1967 | 100 states[a] |
| Latin American Nuclear-Free Zone Treaty, 1967 | 33 states[a] |
| Non-Proliferation Treaty, 1969 | 183 states[a] |
| Seabed Treaty, 1971 | 94 states[a] |
| South Pacific Nuclear-Free Zone Treaty, 1985 | 11 states[a] |
| Southeast Asia Nuclear-Weapon-Free Zone, 1995 | 10 states[a] |
| Pelindaba Treaty, 1996 | 43 states[a] |

**To limit nuclear testing**

| | |
|---|---|
| Limited Test Ban Treaty, 1963 | 121 states[a] |
| Threshold Test Ban Treaty, 1974 | US-Russia |
| Peaceful Nuclear Explosions Treaty, 1976 | US-Russia |

**To reduce the risk of nuclear war**

| | |
|---|---|
| Hot Line and Modernization Agreements, 1963 | US-USSR[b] |
| Accidents Measures Agreement, 1971 | US-USSR[b] |
| Prevention of Nuclear War Agreement, 1973 | US-USSR[b] |
| Nuclear Risk Reduction Centers, 1987 | US-USSR[b] |

**To limit nuclear weapons**

| | |
|---|---|
| ABM Treaty (SALT I) and Protocol, 1972, 1974 | US-USSR[b] |
| SALT I Interim Agreement, 1972 | US-USSR |
| SALT II, 1979 | US-USSR |
| INF Treaty, 1987 | US-NIS[d] |
| START I and Protocol, 1991, 1992 | 5 states |
| START II, 1993 | US-Russia[c] |

### B. Other Weapons

**To prohibit use of chemical weapons**

| | |
|---|---|
| Geneva Protocol, 1925 | 131 states |
| Chemical Weapons Convention, 1993 | 160 states[c] |

**To destroy biological and chemical weapons**

| | |
|---|---|
| Biological Weapons Convention, 1972 | 134 states |
| Chemical Weapons Destruction Agreement, 1990 | US-Russia[c] |

**To prohibit techniques changing the environment**

| | |
|---|---|
| Environmental Modification Convention, 1977 | 63 states |

**To limit conventional forces**

| | |
|---|---|
| Conventional Armed Forces in Europe, 1990, 1992 | 30 states |
| Open Skies Treaty, 1992 | 27 states[c] |

**To register conventional arms**

| | |
|---|---|
| UN Register of Conventional Arms, 1993 | 85 states |
| Wassenaar Arrangement on Export Controls, 1995 | 28 states |

**To control use of inhumane weapons**

| | |
|---|---|
| Inhumane Weapons Convention, 1981, 1995 | 56 states |
| Anti-personnel Landmine Treaty, 1998 | 145 states |

*Source:* Ruth Leger Sivard, *World Military and Social Expenditures, 1996,* 16th ed. (Washington, D.C.: World Priorities Inc., 1996), 29.

[a] Number of signatories are recorded by Arms Control Reporter.

[b] No decision as yet about which state will succeed the USSR as party to this agreement.

[c] Not yet entered into force.

[d] NIS (Newly Independent States) includes all former Soviet republics, except Latvia, Lithuania, and Estonia.

Middle Powers Initiative to Abolish Nuclear Weapons, under the leadership of Canada's former disarmament ambassador, Douglas Roche, was formed to coordinate support from the governments of Australia, Brazil, Canada, Costa Rica, Egypt, Iceland, Ireland, Japan, Kazakistan, Malaysia, Mexico, New Zealand, Norway, South Africa, Sweden, and Ukraine, in collaboration with a group of leading NGOs, to bring the nuclear weapons states into a formal agreement on nuclear abolition.

These activities by middle power governments interacting with organizations from the global civil society have generated information networks, communication processes, and trust-building and problem-solving skills that can be thought of as contributing to that international peace culture that states and NCO participants in the 1899 Hague Peace Conference had hoped to initiate a century ago. While the World Court, the League of Nations, and the League's successor, the United Nations, have, in fact, worked at building an institutional fabric for that culture over this past century, weapons technology has outrun peacemaking capabilities and dulled moral sensibilities.

A less dramatic but important initiative was begun in 1997 by another small state, Norway, to organize a joint international effort to study, control, and limit global production and transfer of small arms. Former Norwegian secretary of state Jan Egeland is the coordinator. Still in its early stages, this activity directly addresses the fact that the wars currently being fought in the Americas, Eurasia, and Africa are being fought with small arms. The enormous accompanying civilian casualties come from small arms. There is no one catchall approach to demilitarization. Every type of weapon must be considered.

It was Ambassador Alva Myrdal, the courageous leader of the UN Commission for Disarmament in the difficult Cold War years, who said, "to give up is not worthy of a human being." That spirit enlivens all current disarmament efforts. The awareness of not only a new century but a new millennium approaching stirred the social imagination of states and civil society alike. As a result, the move by Russia and the Netherlands (conveners of the 1899 Hague Conference) to convene a centennial gathering at The Hague in 1999, with support from a growing number of states, including the 113 states of the Nonaligned Movement, could have provided a chance for a fresh start on specific steps to end war as an instrument of national policy. The UN General Assembly adopted a resolution in 1997 supporting these plans. Instead, a long-simmering crisis in the Balkans erupted into full-scale bombing by NATO of Serbian forces engaged in "ethnic cleansing" of the Albanian majority population of Kosovo. This bypassing both of the United Nations and the OSCE weakened both these bodies, and this has created enormous suffering in Serbia, Kosovo, and surrounding states. The concept of a gathering of states was in tatters, but what was to have been a parallel citizens' Peace Conference on "Time to Abolish War and the Causes of War" did indeed take place. The gathering of 10,000 citizens from all continents picked up the peace agenda the states had abandoned. The UN Conference on Disarmament, with active NGO support, will continue working for stronger treaties on arms control and nuclear abolition. As more and more regions declare themselves to be Nuclear-Weapon-Free Zones (see the next section), the possibility of nuclear abolition grows stronger in spite of the opposition of the nuclear powers. The ruling of the International Court of Justice in 1996 on the moral unacceptability of the use of nuclear weapons may greatly strengthen the case for the abolition of such weapons and further increase the number of zones free of them.

## Intergovernmental Initiatives

### *Nuclear-Weapon-Free Zones*

A significant aspect of state-level peace culture, paralleling the UN General Assembly efforts to limit the production, testing, spread and use of nuclear weapons (see table 2) has been the intense multidecade process, involving regional state groupings, of negotiating the designation of their regions as nuclear-weapon-free. This region-based effort was preceded by earlier negotiations to designate the planetary commons as nuclear-free. The 1959 treaty to prohibit all military use, including nuclear testing, of the Antarctic was the first step in this direction, followed by similar treaties covering Outer Space (1967) and the Seabed (1971). Unfortunately, only the Antarctic Treaty is actually being honored by all member states of the United Nations.

The first regional Nuclear-Weapon-Free Zone, the 1967 Treaty of Tlatelolco in Latin America, was a breakthrough treaty, the first example of the states of a region making the decision to keep their area entirely free of nuclear weapons. This treaty was not easily arrived at, and some states were slower to sign on than others. There was sustained involvement by peace, environment, development, and human rights NGOs of Latin America in the treaty development process. Today, the Treaty of Tlatelolco stands as the model of what states of a region can do to opt out of the nuclear weapons mania. Other regions have followed suit. The Treaty of Rarotonga (in the South Pacific) was signed in 1985; the Bangkok Treaty (Southeast Asia) in 1995; the Pelindaba Treaty (Africa-wide) in 1996. Five states of Central Asia declared their readiness to sign an agreement for a Central Asia Nuclear-Weapon-Free Zone at Almaty in February of 1997, thus preparing to become the fifth specific regional nuclear-weapon-free zone.

The significance of these regional treaties is threefold. First, there are specific and innovative enforcement procedures, including acceptance of full-scope International Atomic Energy Agency safeguards. Second, there is explicit recognition of the step-by-step, region-by-region nature of the denuclearization process. And third, there is recognition by each treaty region that this is a vital early move in a long-range global disarmament process. Foreseeable additional zones currently under discussion include Central and Eastern Europe, the Middle East, and further developments in the South of Asia. Unfortunately, the proposal first made in 1957 by Romania for a Balkan zone of peace was never agreed to by enough states to become a reality. Such an agreement is now further off than ever for this unhappy region. The government of Malta is providing low-key long-term leadership for a Mediterranean zone of peace through its Institute for the Study of Zones of Peace. Since the UN General Assembly has the authority to create forums to facilitate further planning of nuclear-weapon-free zones, it is to be hoped that this authority will be increasingly used in the future.

Many difficulties lie ahead, particularly since the nuclear weapons states are unwilling to place on themselves the limitations they seek to place on others. Recent nuclear testing by India and Pakistan challenges this posture of nuclear power exceptionalism but hardly furthers the denuclearization process. However, the *de facto* existence of clearly delineated denuclearized zones and the core of states that provide leadership for the UN Conference on Disarmament are helping create a new normative order that could make a nuclear-free world possible early in the twenty-first century.

### Small States as Models: Unilateral Demilitarization

In addition to providing leadership for international and regional arms limitation and disarmament agreements and denuclearized zones, some small states have unilaterally declared themselves nuclear-free—twenty-five to be exact (see table 3). Two states actually have peace constitutions: Japan (which is modifying that constitutional provision in practice) and Costa Rica (which is holding firm). Unilateralism has its drawbacks, but this kind of vote of con-

**Table 3. Twenty-Five Nuclear-Weapon-Free Zone Countries (Unilateral Declaration)**$^a$

| | |
|---|---|
| Australia | Nepal |
| Belau (Palau) | New Zealand |
| Costa Rica | Northern Marianas (?) |
| Denmark (?) | Papua New Guinea (?) |
| Faeroe Islands | The Philippines (?) |
| Finland | The Seychelles |
| Greenland (?) | The Solomons |
| Iceland (?) | Spain |
| Japan (?) | Sri Lanka |
| Malta | Sweden |
| Federated States of Micronesia | Switzerland |
| (Ponape, Kosrac, Truk and Yap) | Vanatu |
| Mongolia | |

*Source:* Based on the table "Nuclear Free Zones Around the World," *New Abolitionist,* Mar. 1990, 9, with corrections and additions.

$^a$ These countries either explicitly or implicitly prohibit nuclear weapons by national law, policy, or constitution. (?) means the NWFZ policy may not be enforced.

fidence by a state in the possibility of a disarmed world at least opens the way for others to follow suit and might initiate a more confidence-building dynamic in the international system.

## Other Intergovernmental Resources for Peace Development

There are thousands of treaties binding nations to various cooperative activities in relation to common problems. At best, the treaty process contributes to the development of a common civic culture across geographical distances, national boundaries, and social differences. Treaty making is, by definition, a consensual process in which the interests of all parties must be considered. Treaties can be either bilateral or multilateral. Multilateral treaty making, in which these regional groups are mostly engaged, requires the greatest skill, since the interests of a number of parties must be considered.[5] Studies of treaty partners indicate that diplomatic interaction crisscrosses major alliance blocs and regions and thus creates opportunities for the further development of cooperative civic activity across social and political barriers.

Consensus is an important part of the process that moves nations toward more structured agreements. The Western tradition of majority voting runs counter to the consensual process, so many Westerners are uncomfortable with consensual procedures. Many Third World cultures, on the other hand, find the practice of consensus familiar and comfortable.[6] Western and Two-Thirds World political traditions have thus clashed both in intergovernmental interaction and in the United Nations. The Western mistrust of consensus stems from an awareness that consensus, when improperly exercised, can suppress dissent. When properly used, however, consensus allows for diversity of expression, political pluralism, and an active process of negotiation that can produce, not unanimity, but the willingness to go along with a certain course of action and not raise objections.

Most of these treaties deal with such matters as boundary agreements (boundaries are the most common source of disputes between nation-states); special economic zones and common markets; scarce or potentially scarce resources in the global commons (in space, the world's oceans, the Arctic and the Antarctic); problems of transboundary pollution (acid rain from the United States and Canada falling in Europe and vice versa); and control of drug traffic.

Regional treaty making is one of the major peaceful activities of nation-states. Regional treaty-making groups are legion. The largest, best known, and most widely reported groups in terms of the daily press are the Organization of American States (OAS), the Organization of African Unity (OAU), the Association of Southeast Asian Nations (ASEAN), the Arab League, and the Council of Europe. (The Council of Europe includes, ironically, the Organization for Security and Cooperation in Europe, OSCE, as well as the North Atlantic Treaty Organization, NATO. The latter, as a military alliance relying heavily on nuclear weapons, is the major obstacle to the creation of nuclear-weapon-free zones in the western parts of Europe and jeopardizes the peace-building initiatives of the Council of Europe.) Other negotiation processes go on within more specialized groups, such as the Organization of Petroleum Exporting Countries (OPEC), the Contadora Group (seeking peace in Central America), the African-Caribbean-Pacific group (ACP, concerned with trade and transport), South Asian Regional Cooperation (SARC, trade and development), Gulf Cooperation Council (GCC, developing common services for tiny countries), Cartegena Consensus (eleven Latin American debtor countries), the South Pacific Forum (concerned with common problems of island states), and many more. Different groupings of contiguous states find different common problems, so new associations are constantly forming.[7]

Some intergovernmental structures contribute actively to the development of peace cultures even while maintaining military wings. The Council of Europe is an example. Among its many activities, it sponsors the North-South Centre for Global Interdependence and Solidarity. The Centre describes its organizational structure this way: "The Centre is co-managed by a 'quadri- logue,' a unique four-way partnership that brings together parliamentarians, governments, NGOs, and local and regional authorities . . . providing a framework for European cooperation in public awareness-raising of global in- terdependence and solidarity."[8] It publishes two monthly newsletters. One, *Terra Viva*, copublished with Inter Press Service (IPS), covers global trends, economic and social development, and particularly the impact of interna- tional events on the countries of the South and East—reflecting a redrawn world political map. The second, the *Interdependent*, gives news of meetings and conferences linking European governmental and nongovernmental bod- ies with countries of the South and East in common problem-solving and relationship-building activities. Bodies such as the International Interparlia- mentary Union (IIUP), which brings together members of national parlia- ments to discuss common problems, represent another types of relationship building. A recent proposal by Iranian and Pakistani parliamentarians for the formation of a special section of the IIUP for members from Muslim coun- tries promises to increase levels of understanding both within the Muslin Ummah and across one of the challenging non-West/West religious and cul- tural divides of our times.

## The United Nations

Readers will be familiar with the opening words of the UN Charter:

> We the Peoples of the United Nations Determined

> to save succeeding generations from the scourge of war, which twice in our lifetime has brought untold sorrow to mankind, and

> to reaffirm faith in fundamental human rights, in the dignity and worth of the human person, in the equal rights of men and women and of nations large and small, and

> to establish conditions under which justice and respect for the obligations arising from treaties and other sources of international law can be maintained, and

> to promote social progress and better standards of life in larger freedom, . . .

> Have resolved to combine our efforts to accomplish these aims.

One can sense the intense longing for peace that went into the founding of the United Nations amid the ruins of the old international order represented by the failed League of Nations. This was a longing felt by people who had experienced two world wars already in their lifetime. The United Nations has many limitations, and yet the total UN system has an autonomy of its own: six major operating organs, thirteen associated bodies, sixteen specialized agencies, five regional commissions, and fluctuating numbers of peace-keeping and/or observer missions—plus twenty research institutes, divisions, and special programs, and two UN universities.[9] The UN operates about fifty worldwide information systems and a center in each member state, plus special offices where field programs are located. Since UN personnel are international civil servants carrying special UN passports, it could be said that the entire UN system, in one sense, represents a tantalizing glimpse of what an interstate culture of peace could be. The knowledge, experience, skill, and creativity of those civil servants are a tremendous resource for the world. However, the domination of the Security Council by the major powers, plus the inefficiencies of an inadequately developed international bureaucratic system, lack of coordination, and member-state recalcitrance make the United Nations far less than it could be. Well-thought-out proposals for UN reform are consistently stymied.[10] The enormous efforts that have gone into UN disarmament initiatives over the years—already emphasized in this book—represent painfully slow progress.

Each secretary general in turn has made significant contributions to that progress with the unique tools at his command. Many conflicts have been averted by the use of the secretary general's Good Offices Missions, the sending of skillful conflict resolvers to carry out off the-record discussions with disputing parties. A directive by Secretary General Kofi Annan created a new Department for Disarmament and Arms Regulation to replace the existing, rather weak, Center for Disarmament Affairs, and its head serves as an under-secretary general of the UN. This makes possible a renewed emphasis on arms regulation. There will be a focus on regulating both weapons of mass destruction and conventional weapons, more work on monitoring arms flows (including the harder-to-spot light weapons), and more attention to crisis response.

## UN Educational, Scientific, and Cultural Organization (UNESCO)

In one sense, every UN body contributes to creating the conditions for disarmament, but the UN Educational, Scientific, and Cultural Organization

(UNESCO) plays a special role as the UN body specifically charged with erecting the structures of peace in the minds of human beings. UNESCO has worked determinedly over the years to educate its many constituencies of women, men, and children around the world about the nature of peace culture and what is needed to make it a reality in the world. Major efforts include the bilateral textbook commissions for countries formerly at war; the UNESCO Volumes on World History; the Cultural Development Decade, devoted to a heightened awareness and appreciation of cultural diversity within and among states; the 1986 Seville Statement that war is not biologically inevitable for humans;[11] and the 1994 launching of a UNESCO Culture of Peace Program, which it is hoped will come to full flowering in the UN International Year for the Culture of Peace in 2000 and the UN International Decade for a Culture of Peace and Nonviolence for the Children of the World, 2001–2010. UNESCO is the lead agency in the United Nations System for the Year 2000 activities. Each of these programs has worked with governments and NGOs of member countries to develop grassroots understandings of peace at the local level, and also with national media and educational systems to introduce citizens from every sector of society to conflict resolution and peace-building concepts. Because of limited resources, these programs have so far been a drop in the bucket compared to what needs to be done. Increasing NGO interest in using the 2001–2010 Decade for a Culture of Peace and Nonviolence to develop a climate for demilitarization offers the possibility that this program may generate more substantial activity with wider coverage than earlier UNESCO programs.

### UN Institute for Disarmament Research (UNIDIR)

More specific to the subject of disarmament, UNIDIR (The UN Institute for Disarmament Research), based in Geneva, has conducted a series of major studies on many aspects of disarmament and the dynamics of disarmament negotiations. It has carefully documented problem areas and stumbling blocks to agreement. Its study of the Nuclear-Weapons-Free Zone series of treaties mentioned above will be very important in developing the further strategies needed to get on with both nuclear and general disarmament.[12]

### Blue Helmets

The direct peacekeeping arm of the UN, the "Blue Helmet" peacekeeping forces, were originally seen as a resource for the international community to halt military conflict and bring warring parties to the table for diplomatic solutions. However, special training for UN soldiers in the minimization of violence and in skills of peacekeeping and peacebuilding has been very slow to develop. The line between peacekeeping and peace enforcement, which involves the active use of weapons, has been blurred so that peacekeepers often come to be seen as one more party to armed struggle in a process known as "mission creep." UN commanders are limited in what they can achieve because of the diversity of training of their multinational forces and are also ill prepared to deal with the complex needs of the humanitarian missions that of necessity accompany UN forces to provide relief for suffering civilian populations. In 1998 there were twenty-seven UN peacekeeping missions stationed in Africa, Asia, Latin America, and Europe, some of them in situations of such intense conflict that their very survival was threatened. Observer missions, a special category of peacekeeping, tend to be more successful. Here UN forces may be unarmed and are accompanied by experienced civil affairs officers with problem-solving skills. Overall, the UN peacekeeping system is undergoing a major review at this time.[13]

Serious work is now going on within the UN system with the help of concerned states, such as the Scandinavian states and NGO specialists in the strategies of nonviolence, to develop special training for UN peacekeepers and also to incorporate highly trained, unarmed civilian volunteers into the peacekeeping missions. The undersecretaries general who head the Department of Peacekeeping and the Department of Humanitarian Affairs are cooperating closely in this process.[14] The twenty-first century may well see the emergence of permanent stand-by UN peacekeeping forces well trained in both nonviolence and the minimal use of weapons as a last resort. Such a force could undertake actual disarmament of warring parties as part of a larger process of general disarmament—something they are not at present authorized to do. While some major powers in the UN Security Council tend to oppose this development, future enlargement of the Security Council may make it more open to demilitarized peacekeeping. UNICIVPOL, the UN civilian police force, already demonstrates more enlightened approaches to social turbulence.

An important set of NGO actors at the UN who support a whole range of disarmament efforts is the NGO Committee on Disarmament, which regularly convenes its 220 NGO members both at the UN in New York and in Geneva, to hear reports and give input to specific disarmament measures.

## Nongovernmental Partners in Demilitarization

So far, we have considered the extent to which states themselves, intergovernmental bodies, and the UN contribute to global processes of demilitarization through creative peacebuilding activities that can be considered part of a global culture of peace. Very few, if any, of these developments would have taken place without the active participation of the world community of NGOs. Much of this NGO work, however, is carried out quietly, behind the scenes at intergovernmental and UN meetings. If we look for the more visible signs of NGO activity, one important new theme has created an increasingly popular social movement for demilitarization: millennialism, and the approach of the year 2000.

Millennial fever is the byproduct of the creation of a calendar that counts years and centuries as being before or after the death of Christ. Other calendars, including the Muslim and Jewish calendars, have different major central events;[15] but the once Christian calendar, now secularized as the Calendar of the Common Era, is now generally used as the common international calendar in the modern world. That calendric artifact gives the sweep of a thousand years a great social significance. Historians tell us that at the approach of the year 1000 there was a great deal of millennialist fervor in Europe. People expected great changes, a wonderful new Age of the Holy Spirit.

These are more secular times, but millennial fever is once again abroad. People's hopes for change are now focused on the year 2000.[16] On the one hand, there is already a surge of highly emotional cultic expectations for an apocalyptic break in the accustomed social order. These can be dangerous and must be carefully monitored. However, there is a much more practical and realistic aspect to the temporal significance of entering a new millennium. Many NGOs see a chance to use the emotional impact of entering not only a new century but a new millennium to arouse new social energies for ending war and its attendant social evils.

An important source of inspiration for all these NGOs has been the International Campaign to Ban Landmines, which involved a coalition of 1,000 NGOs. Here was a clear-cut case of grassroots activism making a difference — actually moving 123 states to sign a treaty to ban landmines in 1996, in the face of some opposition by major powers. A second success has followed on the first. Another 1,000-NGO coalition helped bring about the signing in 1998 by 107 states of a treaty to establish an international criminal court, again in the face of some major power opposition. The message: NGOs can make a difference!

## Millennialist NGO Projects for Disarmament, Peace, and Justice

The Hague Appeal for Peace 1999 is a coalition of 600 NGOs that spent several years planning what became a great gathering of 10,000 representatives of people's organizations from many cultures and spheres of society at The Hague to insist on a return to the project of disarmament begun by states at the Hague International Peace Conference in 1899. This is now an ongoing coalition coordinated by the International Association of Lawyers Against Nuclear Arms (IALANA), the International Peace Bureau (IPB), the International Physicians for the Prevention of Nuclear War (IPPNW), and the World Federalist Movement (WFM).

A related movement, Abolition 2000 is a loose coalition of 1,000 NGOs on six continents that calls itself a Global Network to Eliminate Nuclear Weapons. Begun as a caucus at the 1995 review conference on the Nuclear Nonproliferation Treaty, it has as its goal an International Treaty to Abolish Nuclear Weapons, to be signed at the United Nations in 2000. A cooperating group, the State of the World Forum, will hold a State of the World 2000 Conference at the UN in 2000, bringing together leaders of the global civil society to develop new visions and strategies for the twenty-first century. Another important cooperating group in Abolition 2000 is the International Network of Engineers and Scientists for Global Responsibility (INES), whose members work nationally, regionally, and globally to develop workable models of treaties to eliminate nuclear, biological, and chemical weapons and create alternative security systems.

Another group with links to Abolition 2000 is Global Action to Prevent War, a highly focused group sponsored by the World Order Models Project, the Institute for Defense and Disarmament Studies, IALANA, IPPNW, and IPB. Global Action is drawing up a multipurpose, comprehensive program with phased steps to bring states gradually towards general disarmament. Confidence-building measures meant to reassure participating states are built into each phased step. Their model treaty will be an important policy tool to gain support both of states and other NGOs for a year 2000 disarmament initiative.

Jubilee 2000 is a global coalition of faith communities drawing its inspiration from the Book of Leviticus in the Hebrew scriptures, which describes a year of Jubilee every fifty years: social inequalities are rectified; slaves are freed, land is returned to original owners, and debts are canceled. The coalition of faith communities presented "the largest petition the world has ever seen" to the 1999 G-7 Conference in Germany, urging that the debts of the world's poorest states be canceled. The project originated in northern states but is rapidly gaining support from groups in Africa, Asia, and Latin America, both religious and secular. The campaign in the United States grew out of a project of the International Monetary Fund and the Religious Working Group on the World Bank. A number of the NGOs working for Abolition 2000 are also working for Jubilee 2000. It is clear that the issues of war and poverty are linked.

Still another NGO coalition has issued a call for 2001: A People's Conference on Peace. Instead of focusing on one particular theme, this group is trying to bring together the NGO disarmament community and religious, social science, human rights, and women's organizations, as well as social justice and environmental NGOs, to emphasize that war threatens every dimension of life on the planet. The 2001 Conference will devise a platform that addresses all these interrelated threats and redefines security in human terms.

Other 2000 movements focus more on the conditions of peace than the specifics of disarmament but can also be seen as related to the general fervor to end war. One of these groups is the Earth Charter Commission, representing a coalition of five hundred NGOs that originated at the Rio Conference on the Environment and has been growing steadily ever since. In 2000 it will be submitting the Earth Charter to the UN General Assembly as a people's treaty enunciating the principles of respect for all life, care for the earth's ecosystem, sustainable living, the practice of nonviolence, and sharing of resources. What the Commission seeks from the UN General Assembly is an affirmation of the Earth Charter as a People's Charter and the signing of a related treaty, the International Covenant on Environment and Development.

Since the UN General Assembly in 2000 will be held as a Millennial Assembly, a number of major NGO efforts to strengthen environment, development, human rights, and peace programs of the UN and member states will be coming before that Millennial Assembly. The global women's movement will be a particularly articulate voice. The Super Coalition on Women, Homes and Community and its affiliated Huairou Commission will be holding a major Women's Assembly during the UN Millennial Assembly to review progress by the UN and member states in meeting commitments embodied in the Beijing Women's Platform published in 1996. A number of women's groups in Africa, Asia, and Latin America are not waiting for the year 2000. They have been training women to participate in on-the-ground local demilitarization in countries that have experienced major civil war, with help from peace NGOs like the International Fellowship of Reconciliation and special nonviolence training bodies in various countries.

Hundreds of NGOs have collaborated with the projects of the year 2000 as a UN International Year for the Culture of Peace and the decade 2001–2010 as the International Decade for a Culture of Peace and Nonviolence for the Children of the World. The NGOs involved in these coalitions—experienced disarmament and peace activists and professionals—do not expect miracles of disarmament in the year 2000. Rather, they are mobilizing the energies of hope to create a groundswell of world public opinion for specific alternatives to the war system, complete with proposals for specific institutional infrastructures that could make the world a more cooperative and peaceful place in the first decades of the twenty-first century.

## A Supporting Cast from the Scientific Community

The activities of the above coalitions would not be possible without the solid underpinning of scientific organizations such as the Pugwash Conference on World Affairs, which has been bringing scientists from both sides of the Iron Curtain (and from fifty countries) together since the 1950s in annual conferences. At these conferences, scientists share research findings, develop common understandings of national weapons policies, and explore workable proposals for disarmament in every weapons category—including, particularly, nuclear disarmament. They have studied and contributed to every nuclear and conventional arms control agreement listed in table 2 and particularly to confidence-building inspection protocols so necessary to all disarmament agreements.[17] They have operated as a strong independent moral force in the international scientific community, and Pugwash members have received their share of Nobel prizes: most recently, the Nobel Peace Award went to Pugwash itself and to Jusef Rotblat, one of its founders. The more recently formed INES, described above in relation to involvement with Abolition 2000, is another one of a number of important scientific NGOs that contribute to disarmament-relevant research.

In chapter 3 we described the development of the International Peace Research Association, founded in 1965 to advance interdisciplinary social science research into the condition of peace and the causes of war and other forms of violence. (IPRA now has members in seventy countries.) Peace researchers early pointed out the dangers of arms races, the instability of deterrence systems, the superiority of integrative power over threat power, and the difference between positive and negative peace, and introduced the concepts of ecological security, strategic nonviolence, and nonoffensive defense.[18]

Scandinavian peace research institutes in Oslo, Stockholm, and Copenhagen were among the first to build up a body of theoretical, historical, and applied research on disarmament and peace issues. The government-supported Stockholm Peace Research Institute (SIPRI) created a new model for government advancement of disarmament work. This was followed some years later in the United States by the establishment of the U.S. Institute for Peace (USIP). SIPRI is a major source of documentation of conflicts worldwide and the defense policies that sustain them. Needless to say, both SIPRI and USIP came into being as a result of intensive lobbying by NGOs. The International Peace Academy, an independent international institute similarly founded by NGO initiatives, plays a unique role in providing training seminars for diplomats around the world in the skills for conflict resolution and peacebuilding.

The Oxford Research Group, founded in 1982, has carried out a very unusual fifteen-year dialogue with nuclear decision makers in Britain, China, Russia, the United States, and France. Its publications on this dialogue are illuminating.[19] Currently, these states have agreed to work with the Oxford Research Group in addressing the most intractable problems regarding disarmament objectives. The Research Group itself has set a year 2000 date for reporting a possible basis for official agreement on nuclear abolition.

There are many NGOs and institutes that are doing significant research for demilitarization. The ones mentioned here are only a tiny sample of that larger group.

### Other NGO Initiatives

The development of global civilian peace services, originally inspired by the Shanti Sena, or peace armies, that were part of the Gandhian movement in India, has led to a number of NGO peace team initiatives since the 1970s. Peace Brigades International and a dozen other NGOs maintain unarmed, highly trained peace teams in Africa, Asia, the Americas, and Europe.[20] A parallel set of NGOs such as International Alert and the Institute for Multitrack Diplomacy practice preventive diplomacy in areas that threaten to become conflict hot spots. The Swedish Peace Team Forum, consisting of thirty Swedish peacebuilding NGOs, brings together specialists and organizations from around the world in consultations and workshops to expand such peace services. A 1997 conference in Gripsholm, Sweden, cosponsored by the Forum and the Swedish Ministry of Foreign Affairs (an excellent example of NGO-government cooperation), was the occasion for establishing contacts between a new NGO network, the European Center for Conflict Prevention, and similar networks around the world. The European Center's 1998 *International Directory on Prevention and Management of Conflict* is an excellent guide to NGOs supporting peace teams on every continent, as well as to other peacebuilding NGOs.[21] The Center also publishes a valuable quarterly newsletter. Transcend, a computer network of peace scholars and practitioners that offers on-site and in-person training in conflict transformation and was started by Johan Galtung in the 1990s, is another important resource for peace services.[22]

Not to be forgotten are youth peace NGOs, which have been described in chapter 7. Hundreds of young people arrived at the Hague Appeal for Peace Conference in May of 1999, representing local, national, and transnational youth peace groups from every continent. A number of them went on to what was billed as the "First World Summit for Youth Peacemakers" in Phoenix, Arizona, the following week, an event sponsored by the National Conference on Peacemaking and Conflict Resolution based at George Mason University in Fairfax, Virginia. Many new youth networks are now being formed, and youth will increasingly be heard from in the coming decade.[23] One of the most important things that peace movement NGOs can do is to network with the children-and-youth NGOs in a partnering relationship. This is increasingly happening with the older generation of peace organizations, such as the War Resisters League and Fellowship of Reconciliation.

The War Resisters League tried an innovative symbolic demilitarization strategy to celebrate its seventy-fifth birthday in 1998. It declared a "Day Without the Pentagon" and created a dramatic glimpse of such a world by setting up examples of what a demilitarized government would be doing along each of the Pentagon's five sides: a health clinic, a day-care facility, housing for the homeless, a community center, and a peace garden.

Street theater, art, music, and poetry will certainly once again play a growing role in grassroots efforts at demilitarization, as they did in the 1960s and 1970s.

The lowest-key and historically most persistent form of nonviolent practice against war is the peace pilgrimage, an ancient tradition (mentioned in chapter 3) of walking across continents torn by war with messages of repentance, forgiveness, and peace. A current version is the 2,000-mile, three-year Reconciliation Walk, sponsored by a number of Christian groups—across Europe, through the Balkans, and Turkey. It arrived in Jerusalem on July 15, 1999, the nine-hundredth anniversary of the Crusaders' invasion of the Holy City.[24]

The variety and scope of NGO initiatives, of which only a small part have been mentioned here, testify to the creativity, skill, and vision of large numbers of people's organizations around the world.

Now that we have examined governmental and UN initiatives for demilitarization, as well as nongovernmental ones, what are we to think? The number of intergovernmental initiatives for disarmament is both impressive and depressing: impressive for the amount of creative leadership by small- and middle-power states; depressing because of the determination of major powers to cling to nuclear weapons at all costs and because the trade in small arms continues to grow steadily on all continents, unaffected by any treaty process. The UN infrastructure for peacekeeping is inadequate to the demands placed on it, and although substantial improvements are planned, the reluctance of major powers to support an independent UN peacekeeping force weakens every initiative. Can the gradual increase in the overall problem-solving capacity of the international system outweigh the pressures toward maintenance of an anachronistic military defense posture?

Part of the answer will lie in the effectiveness of the efforts of civil society to change that posture. No one group alone can do it. As we have seen in this chapter, new skills and social technologies of coalition building have brought together a great variety of NGO capabilities—scientific, professional, social-political, humanitarian, and spiritual—in the "Year 2000" movements to end war and other social evils. They may unleash a new dynamic at the UN Millennial Assembly and create a new level of commitment to seriously lagging arms control and disarmament efforts. They may, in fact, become a permanent NGO Assembly at the United Nations to complement the UN General Assembly of States.

The NGO activities mentioned in this chapter are part of a large groundswell of civic concern to bring war making to an end for the sake not only of the human race but of the planet itself. That is an achievable goal. Humans are not condemned to endless rounds of violence and counterviolence. But to break that cycle requires much more attention to human development—to the actual quality of the individual human being—at the local level and around the world, as well as to national and regional institutions. This is where peace culture begins.

Will humans make the choices that need to be made to bring about a future world at peace? In chapter 12 we will explore what such a world might look like if we make wise choices.

# 12

# A Possible Future

Having seen the constant, often below-the-surface but steady reaching out of humans to one another over past millennia in spite of the concurrent development over time of social institutions that divide as well as bring people together, that lead to inequality and differential access to resources as well as to the creation of rules of law and principles of justice, what can we hope for in the centuries to come? As a species, we have overrun our niche and deprived countless other species of their habitats. Gaia, that poetic metaphor for a living breathing planetary ecosystem/organism, is struggling to adjust—but damage has been done that may not be easily repairable.

A source of hope lies in the capacity for social learning of individuals, families, grassroots groups, old and new faith communities, NGOs, and of institutions of governance, including states and intergovernmental bodies. Specifically, we can look to the capacity for learning about the interdependence of all living things—what Buddhists call dependent co-arising. The human need for bonding can now be understood as including the need for bonding with nature itself, and the human need for autonomy and space can now be extended to a respecting of the need for space of all living things.

We are in the middle of rough times as I write, and much rougher times lie ahead. The challenge is to draw on the best of the hopes and the best of the learning skills, and the relationship-building, networking, and coalition-forming skills that have developed in this past century, so that the long-term future may yet birth new cultures of peace. In this chapter, we move from what is to what could be.

What follows is neither prediction nor prophecy. Rather, it is an imagined possibility for the next century. Since we can get to the future only from the present (if only there were somewhere else to start from!), I begin with the very difficult situation the world faced in 1999. Without minimizing the difficulties, I offer a hopeful scenario based on the possibility of changing perceptions, wise choices, and positive actions on the part of a variety of actors— local, national, and global—in the coming decades.

## The World No One Wanted: 1999

Two decades earlier the 1980 *Global 2000 Report to the President* had stated, "if present trends continue, the world in 2000 will be more crowded, more polluted, less stable ecologically and more vulnerable to disruption than the world we live in now. . . . Despite greater material output, the world's people will be poorer in many ways than they are today."[1] By 1999 the prediction was proving correct. Climate instability; extremes of flood and drought; slowly rising sea levels; and toxic wastes poisoning land, oceans, and the atmosphere; soil degradation; cementification of productive land in urban areas; and landmines hidden in the countryside of every continent—all were leading to a gradual decline in the quality of human life. It was clear that the earth's harvests would not much longer be adequate to human need, especially considering the great share of those harvests that went to consumers in the One-Third World. Hunger was widespread, and large-scale deaths from famine were being reported.[2] Corporations swallowing corporations, and at the same time downsizing through cumulative technological innovations that were beginning to go beyond the capacity of users to absorb, led to stock market instability and crashes. These crashes were compounded by technological crashes as computers struggled to cope with a multiplication of computer viruses, Y2K problems, and finally with their own hypercomplexity.

Continued internal and interstate warfare in Europe, Asia, and Africa, with constantly shifting coalitions, represented a situation in which neither the major powers nor the United Nations Security Council were in control, and huge spending on weapons, from handguns to missile systems, could not control the increase in terrorist threats and acts. The United Nations peacekeeping forces and humanitarian NGOs were equally prevented from functioning effectively because of the high levels of internal violence, omnipresence of weapons, and severe food and water shortages.

But that wasn't all that was happening. Preparations had been going on steadily among the many NGO coalitions that were working for major commitments to change in the behavior of states and peoples in the year 2000. The rest of this chapter builds on developments already described in previous chapters and offers an imagined scenario.

## The Hoped-For World

There were, after all, grounds for hope. There was the United Nations declaration of the year 2000 as the International Year for the Culture of Peace, and of the years 2001–2010 as the International Decade for a Culture of Peace and Nonviolence for the Children of the World. The 1999 Citizen's Peace Conference at The Hague unleashed a flood of world public opinion demanding serious steps toward ending the arms trade, abolition of nuclear weapons and landmines, and the development of more effective mechanisms for the peaceful settlement of disputes. In spite of transportation hitches and computer breakdowns, there was a steady barrage of gatherings of hundreds of NGO coalitions during 2000 for nuclear abolition and for serious arms control. This was, after all, the International Year of the Culture of Peace. Concrete proposals to reform the United Nations itself to make it a viable vehicle for strengthening peace culture around the world came from the middle powers, from the nonaligned states, and from NGOs. Since under the UN Charter it took only one permanent member of the UN Security Council to block any amendments or changes to the Charter, all proposals were blocked by at least one of the permanent members. In response to this intransigence, preparations were made by the now well-organized disarmament NGO coalitions—jointly with Earth Charter and Jubilee coalitions—for a constitutional convention of the world's people to fashion a new world security organization outside the stalled UN reform process. The new body would consist of an assembly of states supplemented by an assembly of NGOs.

It became clear that the great majority of states would back the new body. After a long period of intense exploration of alternatives by aroused states and an aroused world civil society, major changes did, in fact, come about that did include a world assembly of NGOs. Some groups thought of it as a reformed United Nations; others thought of it as a successor organization. It was called the United Nations to Protect Life (UNPL).

All this activity made it necessary for the still existing United Nations to pay attention to the lack of movement in the Disarmament Commission and the Nonproliferation Treaty Preparatory Committee. The response of states and the United Nations to the outpouring of public outrage evolved slowly, but evolve it did. And similarly in response to the Jubilee 2000 movement, which produced mass demonstrations at key centers around the world for debt forgiveness, control of corporations, and limits to free trade. The Earth Charter movement was quieter and only gradually made an impact as the effect of cumulative citizens' choices regarding lifestyle started becoming visible in the market place.

### Peace Education Initiatives

Thanks to careful preparation by UNESCO's Culture of Peace Program, and the efforts of the International Red Cross/Red Crescent Society, an international coalition of peace education NGOs, including a team of peace educators, interdisciplinary peace researchers, and peacebuilding practitioners, began working together with local colleagues around the world to develop peace education materials for use in local elementary schools. From the beginning there was a particular focus on a course for fifth- and sixth-graders in every country on the theme "Making Peace Where I Live." This age group received special attention because many children, particularly in the Two-Thirds World, did not have schooling opportunities beyond the fifth or sixth grade.

The basic concept was to involve children in interviewing peacemakers in their local communities—elders, healers, leaders in local faith groups, leaders in local market associations, women's organizations and other grassroots groups, and local councils—in short, local residents who could offer diverse models of nonviolent conflict resolution and could speak with children about the various local and cultural resources for dealing with differences peacefully. After understanding the local processes and resources, children were introduced to the political and civic structures of their country responsible for the peaceful resolution of conflicts—as well as support for human rights, economic development, stewardship of the environment, and economic justice. Exercises also helped children explore the international network of nongovernmental organizations and the United Nations system.

School readers and workbooks were prepared to be translated into a number of languages as the program developed, and local workshops for teachers were planned for cooperating states to help local teachers find ways to link traditional peacemaking practices in the area to materials in the readers. The approach was flexible enough to be adapted either to school settings or to youth-oriented community settings, such as recreation programs, scouting organizations, youth clubs, religious organizations, etc. Local women's organizations were very active in helping to organize these workshops and participated in them as well. Thus the peace education and training process became multigenerational, including especially the grandmothers and the wise elders of each community. Local radio and television stations were encouraged to pick up on this material and adapt it to their programs. A special version was planned for men's village councils. An unexpected outcome was the evolution of village peace celebrations with intergenerational pantomimes, singing, and dancing that reflected the themes of listening, mediation, and conflict transformation.

This process went very slowly in countries with heavy internal fighting and guerrilla movements. However, in the Great Lakes region of Africa, and Somalia and Sudan, there had been women's peace groups and village elders trying to do local peacemaking for decades, and these new materials brought fresh life and energy into their peace work. The same was true in the Balkans, and in the states of the former Soviet Union, and also in South Asian countries with a long history of conflict, as well as in Central and South American states.

Because these peace education and training programs began in schools but involved much of the local community, there began to be a new awareness by families of the schools and what children needed to learn that wasn't taught in the usual school curriculum. Local farmers and artisans began inviting classes to their fields and shops, showing children how they worked and talking about concerns such as what was happening to the local environment and what could be done about it. Community service learning projects began to be added to the peace education program. Since in recent decades some countries had been encouraging the establishment of community health clinics in the schools, the issue of health education also began to be woven into peace education. The children and youth NGOs described in chapter 7 became very enthusiastic about these programs and, with the help of UNESCO's school affiliation project, set up a traveling peace education and training network so young people could visit each other's schools in different countries. This brought up the importance of learning different languages. Local immigrants from other countries were brought into the schools to teach their native languages, and learning new languages became a new hobby.

These developments were possible in the 2001–2010 decade because of the commitment of UNESCO, ECOSOC, UNICEF, and large numbers of peace NGOs and foundations to maintain a strong children's peace education and training program. Governments quickly saw the advantage of supporting these activities, since they enhanced the bare-bones educational systems of the poorer states, as well as improving both inner-city and rural schools in the One-Third World. Another set of actors that helped support and expand the peace education programs locally were the interfaith NGOs. The World Parliament of Religions, the International Interfaith Peace Council, the World Conference on Religion and Peace, and the United Religious Initiative all worked together to persuade often-reluctant local temples, churches, and synagogues to study these school readers in their places of worship and come together locally in interfaith gatherings to practice mutual listening and dealing with their differences.

Not only did interfaith groups support the school programs, they added new elements to the study and practice of peacemaking both in schools and communities by linking it to the Buddhist-inspired practice of deep ecology. Local workshops helped people of all ages to reconnect with their often deteriorating environment in the specific context of their personal lifeways.[3]

### The Voluntary Simplicity Movement

In the 1980s and 1990s there had been an increasing articulation of discontent with the fast-paced life of industrial societies and with the pressure to earn in order to consume ever more goods. With the growing gap between rich and poor in both the One-Third and the Two-Thirds Worlds, the burdens of the consumer economy were felt everywhere. As we know from chapter 2 on utopias, there had always been groups who sought to live simpler and gentler lives, more in harmony with the earth, as part of a fuller, more deeply satisfying lifeway. The 1920s, the 1940s, and the 1960s had each produced intentional communities around the world dedicated to voluntary simplicity. The 1992 Rio Conference on the environment put new life into an old yearning, and by 1996, the voluntary simplicity movement in the United States—the most heavily consumerist society in the world—was considered one of the top ten trends, with 10 to 15 percent of Americans practicing participants.[4] David Korten wrote enthusiastically about this new breed of persons, the "cultural creatives":

> They are present in every country, indeed every community, and every race, class, religion, and ethnic group. They include landless and illiterate peasants, retired executives, ranchers, teachers, artists, housewives, itinerant farm workers, small business owners, farmers, janitors, physicians, researchers, corporate drop-outs, local government officials, inner city kids, loggers, wealthy intellectuals with fancy academic credentials, and gang leaders with criminal records. Together, worldwide, they—we—number in the hundreds of millions.[5]

These people had rejected the idea that nonmaterial needs—such as affection, identity, participation, and a sense of creative personhood—could be met by material consumption, and they were aware that the geo/biosphere was hurting from careless and excessive use of its resources. International "Buy Nothing" days became popular.[6]

Living simply, performing meaningful work, and seeking to achieve 100 percent recycling of all materials was their joy. Many, but far from all, were back-to-landers. All had rediscovered their relationship with nature. The number of NGO networks helping people to achieve this new kind of lifeway continued to multiply year by year.[7] Signs of the growing revolt against privately owned automobiles clogging roads and polluting the air became visible in the Global Street Parties that began in 1995 in London and spread all over Europe and the Americas. Such events shut down main thoroughfares in cities and filled the streets with a variety of stalls, music, and dancing. Green Transport Weeks declaring car-free weeks in cities and towns, accompanied by a noticeable decrease in car sales, led to greatly increased public transportation in urban-suburban areas.[8] Slow Food, the International Movement for the Defense of and the Right to Pleasure, founded in Italy in 1986, and with members in 35 countries in 1999, led to the gradual disappearance of fast-food drive-ins around the world, along with the disappearance of cars and increased interest in local agriculture and food traditions.[9]

### The Dawn of the Steady-State Economy

Jubilee 2000 had called for debt forgiveness for the Two-Thirds World and for relevant bodies of the United Nations to take steps toward a fairer distribution of the world's resources. The Jubilee movement continued to grow, strengthened by the voluntary simplicity movement and the growing popularity of how-to books on withdrawing from the pressures of the market economy, such as *Your Money or Your Life*.[10] These movements, plus a generalized dissatisfaction with current lifeways, heralded a long-delayed but finally arrived paradigm shift from the concept of the growth economy to the concept of the steady-state economy. The growth economy had been supposed to solve the problems of Two-Thirds World poverty by achieving economic development in that part of the world. Instead, poverty had increased as enterprises from the One-Third World mined soil, metals, forests, and water resources, polluted environments, and, in the process, caused a decrease in food productivity in poor countries, leaving a legacy of famine.

A major agent of this destruction was a cluster of giant corporations. Economic theory and accounting practices had allowed the transformation by corporations of natural capital into man-made capital without paying the costs of the depletion of the limited supply of natural capital in the geo/biosphere. The consumption of that natural capital was, instead, treated as income by corporations. That "income" would be disappearing as resources disappeared. By 2050, there would be little oil left, for example. This problem had been largely ignored. The cluster of natural and man-made catastrophes on the injured earth, the proliferation of paper money that had no product value behind it, the speedup of economic transactions through the Internet, and an excess of human greed led to a global economic crash and basic rethinking of the concept of development. The planet was not, after all, a magic storehouse of unlimited resources exclusively available to high-tech humans, but a highly complex interdependent ecosphere, its parts irreplaceable. Human activity had already exceeded the carrying capacity of the planet, and hunger was increasing.

How could "development" go forward? With the help of long-ignored economists, like Herman Daly,[11] and a large international community of "alternative development" scholars, practitioners, and activists, and the United Nations Development Agency itself, it came to be generally understood that the only possible economic system for the planet was a steady-state system. Further, it was realized that development needed to be qualitative, not quantitative: oriented to the quality of life of humans and the living biosphere, not to the quantity of consumer goods.

Practice outran theory. By the time the World Bank and ECOSOC came to understand the need to move away from global economic integration, to stop forcing free trade on every state, local communities had already figured out how much the cost of transport of the goods they consumed from faraway places had increased the price of those goods. Where possible (and it was very often possible), they could do better by local production, especially by growing food locally! Imports should be only for what couldn't be produced locally. The new trend was away from free capital mobility and export-led growth and toward a domestic orientation. Developing domestic products for internal markets became the first option, with recourse to international trade only when such trade was clearly beneficial to all parties.

Globalizing capital had weakened national boundaries and the power of the state, that major unit of community capable of carrying out policies for the common good beyond the local. Accordingly, there was now a movement toward the "renationalization of capital," a rooting of capital in communities, for the development of national and local economies.[12] New strict regulation of corporations, accompanied by a redrawing of their charters and removing of their legal personhood, was undertaken by governments, by treaty processes within the changing United Nations system, and by decisions of the World Court. However, corporations were already splitting apart from a combination of social, economic, and natural forces at work. Even the arms industry worldwide was affected. What remained was a hardy group of socially responsible companies, promoting ecological sustainability and responsible corporate citizenship, and groups like the "Fair Trade" movement. This movement had been working for several decades to empower trading by low-income, disadvantaged, and marginalized farmers, artisans, and small producers around the world through a network of producers and buyers fostering inter-local economic relationships.

### The Downsizing of the Military

The tendency to expand military defense systems and to develop new high-tech weapons still strongly evident at the end of the twentieth century could not remain unaffected by the natural, social, and economic catastrophes that enveloped governments. The burdens of recession and levels of social need, including large-scale deaths from famine, clashed with the strong conviction that military strength was essential to deal with terrorism, endemic civil war, and resource shortages. As in the case of the global economy, there was the slow, reluctant beginning of a paradigm shift, both within states and within the already changing UN system. In this case, the shift was away from the concept of national security based on superior military force and toward a concept of common security among peoples and states that was based on the skills of diplomacy, mediation, and nonviolent conflict resolution—a concept long preached but only now taken seriously. The threat of a new round of wars early in the twenty-first century to deal with severe water supply imbalances among neighboring states—a threat as real in the Americas as in Africa, Asia, and Europe—raised the specter of endless water wars in the future and helped to open the way for new thinking. The shift in perception came first among the states that had already been participating in the Middle Powers Initiative in the late 1990s, including especially Canada, Scandinavia, and the Netherlands, backed strongly by the countries that were already in nuclear weapon–free zones in Latin America, Asia, and Africa. Nuclear weapons states held back, but eventually had to go along with the overwhelming demand for a "new UN," now called the UN to Protect Life (UNPL). These trends were reinforced by the rapid development worldwide of the school- and community-based peace education and training systems that put conflict transformation skills in the hands of local citizens of all ages. These programs were already bearing fruit in the local dismantling of guerrilla forces on every continent and the increasing use of mediation instead of guns to end civil wars. These successes were well reported in the media and gave further support to the disarmament movement.

Downsizing and the closing of weapons development laboratories took place in the nuclear-power states, but slowly. The new coalition that brought about the UNPL replaced the old Security Council with a far more inclusive body and ensured the adoption of the rule of the binding triad. This introduced weighted voting in the UN General Assembly based on three factors: (1) one nation, one vote (as existed before); (2) population; and (3) contributions to the United Nations budget. Resolutions passed by majorities in all three of these "legs" would be binding and enforceable.[13] The same coalition brought about concrete action by the nuclear powers, including the United States, to fulfill their obligations under the terms of the Non-Proliferation Treaty to begin the dismantling of nuclear arms (they had already been detargeted in 2000). The Commission on Disarmament was able to get the General Assembly of the "new" United Nations to approve conventions banning small arms, conventions specifying arms reduction in all states, and strict regulation of a greatly diminished arms industry.

All this reduction of armies and weapons availability could not work without major attention to the life transitions being experienced by soldiers and guerrilla groups and the traumas that had been inflicted on child soldiers and raped and tortured civilians. Early UNESCO Culture of Peace Programs and local initiatives had been working with demobilized soldiers, former guerrillas, child soldiers, and women rape victims during the last decade of the twentieth century, and the experiences gained from that work provided models for a rapid extension of this activity. Similarly, the experience of Truth and Reconciliation Commissions in South Africa and elsewhere in that decade led to a deeper understanding of both possibilities in and obstacles to reconciliation processes and a commitment to long-term efforts in this arena. Since these activities were, of necessity, community based—where ex-perpetrators and victims were actually living—they became linked to the peace education and training programs of local schools. The multiplier effect of those school programs was tremendous.

These community-based activities led to a realization of how much violence was being generated by the criminal justice system, the celebrated "rule of law" imposed by western occupying powers on national and local communities during the period of colonial expansion from the 1500s on. A movement for restorative justice had already been evolving both in the West and the non-West, drawing on the most humane of discarded traditional systems of justice, systems and practices oriented to the well-being of both victims and victimizers and answering to the need for healing and restoration of broken relationships. This movement arose in the closing decades of the twentieth century in the aftermath of the traumas experienced by combatants and non-combatants alike during the difficult years of end-of-century wars in Eurasia, Africa, and the Americas. Gradually, courts shifted from a punitive to a healing orientation; prison systems were gradually downsized, and rehabilitation centers came to replace the prisons.[14]

### Creative Initiatives by States

In the description of military downsizing, the states were portrayed as responding to a combination of overwhelming pressure from the civil society and of overwhelmed capacity for dealing with economic and environmental catastrophes. But disarmament did not happen just as a result of these pressures. The coalition of Northern European states plus Canada and the states of the nuclear-weapon-free zones has already been mentioned. This same coalition set up ad hoc commissions to work with regional intergovernmental organizations in exploring problems in each of the major civil conflict zones, particularly in Africa, Central Europe, and the Balkans. It was discovered that in most cases, significant minority groups in one state had closer ties to sister minorities in adjacent states than to their own national capital. In short, arbitrarily drawn colonial boundaries and national governments unresponsive to their minorities were a major part of the problem. At the urging of this friendly coalition, the Council of Europe and the organization for Security and Cooperation in Europe (OSCE) set up special long-term commissions to work with governments and minorities to develop new autonomy structures for ethnies that permitted cross-border joint cultural and economic activities, making national borders more porous. In Europe, much was made of past successful resolutions of such situations as, for example, in the case of the Finland-Sweden dispute over the Aland Islands on the Baltic shores of Finland, and the Germany-Denmark dispute over Schleswig-Holstein, as well as recent developments in the former British Isles, Switzerland, Spain, and Italy. A new openness to such changes gradually developed, including acceptance of the autonomy of indigenous peoples within states, as happened with the establishment of the Saami people's parliament in Norway.

In Africa, the Organization of African Unity (OAU) moved in the same direction, with more attention to the possibility of shifting boundaries, even while making them more porous. In the Middle East, the Arab League and Israel did the same. Constitutional changes in the legal definitions of state boundaries gradually took place on each continent, including North America, with special attention given to indigenous peoples. The creation of Nunavut as an autonomous region for the Inuit people of Canada in 1999 became a model for indigenous peoples on every continent.

These developments honoring indigenous peoples' skills in managing difficult and marginal environments were especially important as water shortages and scarcity of arable land became more serious on every continent, with Africa the hardest hit. Recurring regional famines made equable global distribution of food a contentious issue. To the surprise of the West, the OAU took the lead in drawing on traditional dispute settlement practices between areas of shortage and areas of adequate water and seed supplies and developed models of sharing that other continents adopted.[15]

### NGOs in a Learning Mode

NGOs had been coming in for growing criticism in the last decade of the twentieth century—particularly environment, development, and humanitarian NGOs—for becoming increasingly bureaucratic and removed from the local constituencies they intended to serve. The NGOs that had the most ample funding from governments and foundations tended to be the most criticized. They often were also seen as taking sides in disputes.[16] As funding dwindled and food and water shortage crises increased, two things happened. First, NGOs had to start learning from local grassroots organizations how to function in these new shortage situations, and they came to realize that their global information networks, if wisely used, could help locals communicate directly with one another across geographic distances, so locals could share problems and solutions. This same process affected peacebuilding NGOs, although a significant proportion of them had already adopted a partnering relation with local groups and were usually already working with the peace education and training programs of local schools. They also came to serve as communication channels for local peacebuilding groups to communicate with each other across different regions.

In short, the most effective NGOs downsized to become communication networks for the people they worked with, and only secondarily a source of direct aid. These networks assisted the development of the new localism that had been evolving out of the situation of disrupted markets, transportation systems, and materials shortages. Local grassroots organizations of peasants, youth, and women grew more rapidly in each region as they were able to learn about each other's strategies through available NGO networks. Coulleurs Lomé, an African-Caribbean-Pacific coalition of peasant groups that began at the end of the twentieth century, came to serve as a model for such coalitions and paved the way for grassroots organizations to communicate with regional intergovernmental bodies such as the European parliament.[17]

Although in the twentieth century the NGO movement had largely originated in Europe and spread around the world from there, in the twenty-first century new network-oriented organizations developed rapidly in the 120 states of the Two-Thirds World. In the Arab world alone, civic associations (NGOs and GROs) had grown from 20,000 in the 1960s to 80,000 in the 1980s, and in the 1990s the League of Islamic Universities had issued a fatwa encouraging the use of the Internet by Muslims. This rapid expansion of civic groups continued to take place in Africa, Asia/Middle East, and Latin America. The networking orientation was particularly striking among hundreds of women's peace and development groups struggling to stay in touch during local wars. The International Fellowship of Reconciliation and the International Peace Bureau were important facilitators of that networking, both face-to-face and on the Internet. Indigenous groups grew at a similar pace, regionally and between continents, with the help of the International Work Group for Indigenous Affairs.[18]

An important spin-off from this new growth of NGOs and GROs in the Two-Thirds World was the growing awareness in the countries of the South that the industrial countries of the North were in trouble and lacked the skills for dealing with resource shortages, especially of food and water.

The Network of Engaged Buddhists, which had been conducting trauma workshops for Vietnam veterans in the United States under the leadership of Thich Nhat Hanh since the 1980s, began sending teams from Thailand and Cambodia to conduct dhammayetras, peace walks, through troubled areas of the United States and Europe. These Buddhist groups led local people on walks to neighboring towns and cities to discuss with nearby citizens' groups and local governments how to transport and share limited supplies of food and to help mediate conflicts. Sri Lanka sent teams to hold Shramadana camps in food-short towns to clear vacant lots and unused land, and work with locals to plant food crops, just as they had been doing in Sri Lanka for decades. Gandhi ashrams from India sent sarvodaya teams to towns where there had been widespread factory closings to develop local enterprises using simple technologies to meet local needs, as they had been doing at home in India since Gandhi's time.[19]

Perhaps the most significant help of all came through the good offices of the permanent Forum of Indigenous Peoples, recognized by the UN General Assembly early in the twenty-first century as a United Nations body.[20] Indigenous peoples held special knowledge of so-called wildernesses—savannas, deserts, rainforests, dry forests, and high mountain plateaus—in every part of the world. Aware of that knowledge, and of their skills in food gathering and water conservation while maintaining biodiversity and not depleting the basic local resource stock, the Forum realized that they had a responsibility to share their knowledge and skills with people living in food-short areas who did not know how to use the resources available to them. Local tribes from around the world volunteered teams of their most knowledgeable elders and young people and were assigned to locations that had some relation to the type of land with which they were familiar. They then helped locals develop a new type of agriculture, blending modern and traditional know-how, and introduced their own handmade tools where useful. Because the UN Development Program's alternative development projects were already in touch with many of the most skilled tribal groups, the complex task of assigning teams where they would do the most good was further facilitated. The task of helping to protect indigenous peoples' own lands from hungry resource-destroying invaders was undertaken by Peace Brigades International and other NGOs that supported teams of trained nonviolent activists to partner with indigenous local defenders, and would-be invaders found themselves undergoing a gentle but firm reeducation about land and about sharing.

NGOs like the Malaysia-based International Movement for a Just World, which had long deplored the failure of the West to acknowledge the wisdom and know-how of the non-West, helped Western media understand what was going on and to report it favorably.[21] Muslim NGOs, spurred by the League of Islamic Universities, took the lead as the fastest-growing faith group in the early twenty-first century in sponsoring trust- and confidence-building dialogues in Euro–North America about these new developments.[22] "Everyone has something to teach, everyone has something to learn," was the new saying. Where local interfaith groups were flourishing, they gave strong support to the various teams coming from around the world to empower local problem solving.

Needless to say, all these developments in the NGO sector also enabled the NGO assembly at the new United Nations to be more effective.

### The New Localism

Along with the paradigm shift from the growth economy concept to the steady-state economy concept that was mentioned earlier, there was a shift in thinking on the part of increasing numbers of people toward a preference for developing an alternative life style. Revitalizing earlier traditional agriculture and industry with appropriate and relevant modern knowledge, technology, and skills—thereby creating autonomous self-reliant "rurban" communities—became the focus of the new sustainable livelihood movement. The UNDP had been holding PAPSL (Participatory Assessment and Planning for Sustainable Development) sessions with local villages to help them produce their own action plans for some time, and such local planning quickly became the new norm throughout countries of the South.[23] The term *community-based development initiative* (CDI) came to refer to a related social movement that had begun in the 1980s, representing initiatives taken jointly by NGOs, community groups, and local government to promote people-centered local development with global linkages. NGOs such as Towns and Development, United Towns Organization, and the International Union of Local Authorities helped develop North-South linkages and town-twinning for knowledge and resource sharing that covered all continents. Special coordinating commissions in Africa and Asia made sure that local CDI projects had strong leadership and good linkage systems with relevant bodies in other countries of the South.[24]

Because it was difficult for citizens in Euro–North America to become accustomed to very different patterns of production and consumption, groups like the Global Action Plan International were continually holding workshops on Local Initiatives toward Sustainable Consumption Practices for communities that lacked local leadership and were resistant to change.[25] Many were ready for change, however, and there was a modest but significant back-to-the-land movement, with a proliferation of magazines on homesteading, organic agriculture, and aquaculture integrated into farming—magazines that also included articles on a variety of subsistence skills. One such magazine, *Plain*, had already shifted to typesetting by hand as far back as 1998.[26] Urban agriculture, which had always existed but was ignored as being a sign of underdevelopment in the Two-Thirds World, had received a new boost through the formation by the UN Development Program of the Urban Agricultural Network in 1991. By the early decades of the twenty-first century, urban agriculture became a major source of food for urban populations, making cities to a significant degree self-sustaining.[27]

Money flows and banking underwent painful but necessary changes. However, community banks survived when major national banks closed outlets in small towns and poor urban neighborhoods. The labor exchange trading system (LETS) described in chapter 9 spread like wildfire across Euro–North America, with communities printing their own "time dollars" for use in barter as a supplement to scarce national currency and Eurodollars. In the Basque country and Japan, respectively, the Mondragon Group and the Seikatsu movement performed similar functions, and traditional exchange systems in Africa and Asia were revived.[28]

Although the spread of the localist movement beyond social groups that had already opted for voluntary simplicity was at first a slow and uncertain response to the hardship of global resource shortages, it soon developed a positive dynamic of its own. People rediscovered the joys of community— knowing one's neighbors; getting familiar with local woods, meadows, ponds, brooks, and rivers; doing things with their hands—and spending time with their own families. Work and play could both be fun! Since everyone's efforts were needed, there was an intergenerational mingling, and children were very much *there* and involved. Prisons became obsolete as the earlier-mentioned restorative justice programs came to replace imprisonment for offenders.[29] Community service and reintegration into the community became the rule, and repeat offenders were rare.

### Population-Ecosystem Balance

The crises of the twenty-first century came about because human populations had multiplied to exceed the carrying capacity of the earth and had persisted in ignoring the fact of that limited carrying capacity. Therefore, even with the policy and behavior changes indicated above, the righting of imbalances took time. Between famine and other hardships, by 2030 the human population was below five billion and still falling. Continued population limitation had been widely accepted as a necessary policy. One-child families were the rule. Often, two couples would raise their single children together, and sociability came to be highly valued. Community occasions for adults and children to gather for recreation were frequent. Neighborhood nature walks to observe and listen to trees and plants and animals was a popular new hobby. With the new localism, children were more integrated into the life of the community than they had been in the previous century, and the peace education, training, and service programs that had begun early in the twenty-first century helped make schools major focal points for each community.

Cultural diversity reached new heights, and travel (on foot or bicycle or sail-boat) to learn new languages and discover new lifeways became another favorite hobby. The earlier competitive relations and power struggles in the old corporate, consumerist world made little sense in this new, more local world. Multitudes of small companies flourished where corporations had formerly dominated the scene.

By 2100 the biosphere was beginning to recover from the destruction of the twentieth century, though used-up resources were gone forever. National boundaries still existed for administrative convenience, but regional intergovernmental bodies skilled in conflict management handled disputes peacefully. Mining of the earth's geologic resources had stopped, but continuous recycling kept a supply of previously mined metals available for careful use. With a few carefully planned exceptions for communication and transport, low-technology production prevailed. Communication systems and the successors to twentieth-century computer technology were manufactured in nonpolluting ways. Some of the leisure of the hunting and gathering era of human history had returned.[30] The creative arts flourished, as people discovered new ways to express their inner thoughts and joys and longings. Music, dance, and poetry were part of daily life. The culture of peace initiatives that had begun in the year 2000 had introduced enough creativity and adaptability into local communities to help them and their governments survive the difficult early decades of the century—the period of famine, instability, and dying. The very diversity of this new world gave rise to interesting new conflicts, but since conflict-resolving skills were well developed at every level, from local communities to the now highly evolved United Nations to Protect Life (UNPL), these conflicts provided challenging occasions to use those skills and were followed by the public with great interest.

Humans had learned to listen to one another and to the planet. Life was an adventure. It was a good time to be alive.

*Note to readers:* The above is only one person's imaginings. Now, please stop and enter your own imagination, in the same spirit of recognizing the realities of the present yet making room for hopes for the future that animated what I have written. Reflect, imagine, and write down what you "see."

Elise Boulding

# Notes

## Peace Culture: An Overview

1. Gene Sharp, *The Politics of Nonviolent Action* (Boston: Porter Sargent, 1973).

2. Ronald McCarthy and Gene Sharp, *Nonviolent Action: A Research Guide* (New York and London: Garland, 1997).

3. Gordon Fellman, *Rambo and the Dalai Lama: The Compulsion to Win and Its Threat to Human Survival* (Albany: SUNY Press, 1998).

4. See Chapter 9 for a description of the Earth Charter Movement. A powerful voice for the deep ecology movement is Joanna Macy, whose most recent book (coauthored with Molly Brown) is *Coming Back to Life: Practises to Reconnect Our Lives, Our World* (Gabriola Island, Canada: New Society, 1998).

5. The "10,000 societies" is a term loosely used by some anthropologists. According to Nietschmann, there are "5000 distinct communities in the contemporary world [that] might claim that they are national peoples on grounds that they share common ancestry, institution, beliefs, language and territory." Quoted in Ted Gurr and James Scarritt, "Minorities' Rights at Risk: A Global Survey," *Human Rights Quarterly* 11 (1989): 375. See also Elise Boulding, "Ethnic Separatism and World Development," in *Research in Social Movements, Conflicts and Change*, ed. Louis Kriesberg (Greenwich, Conn.: JAI Press, 1979), 259–81.

6. Eleanora Masini, ed., *The Future of Asian Cultures* (Bangkok: UNESCO Regional Office, 1993), 5.

7. Magorah Maruyamah, *Mindscapes in Management: Use of Individual Differences in Multicultural Management* (Aldershot, Hants, U.K.: Dartmouth Publishing Co., 1994), 57.

## 1. History at Sword's Point? The War-Nurtured Identity of Western Civilization

1. William McNeill, *The Rise of the West: A History of the Human Community* (Chicago: Univ. of Chicago Press, 1963).

2. Arnold Toynbee (1964). *Reconsiderations*, vol. 12 of *A Study of History* (New York: Oxford Univ. Press, 1964).

3. Simone Weil, *The Iliad: A Poem of Force* (Wallingford, Pa.: Pendle Hill, 1956).

4. For example, note E. S. Creasy, *Fifteen Decisive Battles of the World: From Marathon to Waterloo* (New York: Dorset, 1987).

5. Toynbee, *Reconsiderations*, 609.

6. Samuel N. Kramer, *History Begins at Sumer* (New York: Doubleday Anchor, 1959).

7. Bernard Grun, *The Timetables of History: A Horizontal Linkage of People and Events* (New York: Simon & Schuster, 1975). Grun's work is based on Werner Stein, *Kulturfahrplan*, 1946.

8. These points are developed in Carol R. Ember and Melvin Ember, "War, Socialization and Interpersonal Violence: A Cross-Cultural Study," *Journal of Conflict Resolution* 38, no. 4 (1994): 620–46.

9. For a fuller discussion of the two cultures and their impact on social institutions, see Elise Boulding, "Two Cultures of Religion as Obstacles to Peace," *Zygon*, 21, no. 4 (1986): 501–17.

10. Martin Buber, *Israel and the World* (New York: Schocken, 1948).

11. UNESCO, *Peace on Earth: A Peace Anthology* (Paris: UNESCO, 1980).

12. H. Mouritzen, "The Nordic Model of a Foreign Policy Instrument: Its Rise and Fall," *Journal of Peace Research* 32, no. 1 (1995): 9–21. G. Steinsland and P. M. Sørenson, *Menneske Og Makter i Vikingenes Verden* (Oslo: Universitetsforlaget, 1994). *Note:* My vastly oversimplified account here of a very complex history does not even touch on the special qualities of local democracy in Scandinavia once slavery was abolished, on renewed acknowledgment of an older tradition of strong roles for women, on the fostering of community education programs that led to high levels of literacy at the local level.

13. William James, "The Moral Equivalent of War," in *War: Studies from Psychology, Sociology and Anthropology*, ed. Leon Bramson and George Goethals (New York: Basic Books, 1968), 21–31.

14. Quincy Wright, *A Study of War*, 2d ed. (Chicago: Univ. of Chicago Press).

15. Pitirim Sorokin, *Social and Cultural Dynamics* (Boston: Porter Sargent, 1957).

16. These developments are documented in the following books: Charles Chatfield and Peter van den Dungen, *Peace Movements and Political Cultures* (Knoxville: Univ. of Tennessee Press, 1988). Ralph Summy and M. Saunders, "Why Peace History?" *Peace and Change* 20, no. 1 (1995), [Special Issue: Peace History Forum]: 2–38.

17. The UNESCO-sponsored *History of Mankind*, published by Harper & Row, is in six volumes, the last of which, by Caroline Wax, K. M. Panikkar, and J. M. Romain, under the title *The Twentieth Century*, appeared in 1966. The *History of Humanity* series, copublished by UNESCO and Routledge, is still in process; volume 4, *From the Seventh to the Sixteenth Century*, edited by M. A. Al-Bakhit, L. Bazin, and S. M. Cissoko, appeared in 1998.

18. Margaret Mead, "Warfare Is Only an Invention—Not a Biological Necessity," in *War: Studies from Psychology, Sociology and Anthropology*, ed. Bramson and Goethals, 269–74.

19. Raoul Naroll, Vern Bullough, and Frada Naroll, *Military Deterrence in History* (Albany: SUNY Press, 1974).

20. The classic study in this field is Lewis F. Richardson, *Statistics of Deadly Quarrels* (Pittsburgh and Chicago: Boxwood, 1960).

21. These issues are discussed in the following publications: R. L. Garthoff, *The Great Transition: American-Soviet Relations and the End of the Cold War* (Washington, D.C.: Brookings Institution, 1994). R. N. Lebow and J. G. Stein, *We All Lost the Cold War* (Princeton: Princeton Univ. Press, 1994).

22. Major authors here include: Kenneth Boulding, *The Economics of Peace* (New York: Prentice-Hall, 1945). Lloyd Dumas, *Overburdened Economy* (Berkeley: Univ. of California Press, 1986). Ann Markusen and J. Yudken, *Dismantling the Cold War Economy* (New York: Basic Books, Harper Collins, 1992). Seymour Melman, *The Demilitarized Society: Disarmament and Conversion* (Montreal: Harvest House, 1988).

## 2. The Passion for Utopia

1. Fred Polak, *The Image of the Future*, trans. E. Boulding (Dobbs Ferry, N.Y.: Oceana Press, 1961).

2. Frank Manuel and Fritzie Manuel, *Utopian Thought in the Western World* (Cambridge, Mass.: Belknap Press of Harvard Univ. Press, 1979), 1. To capture the flavor of non-Western utopian thinking, note especially the writings of the Chinese sage, Mo Tzu, who wrote eloquently about "Universal Love" and against war; see *Basic Writings of Mo Tzu, Hsun Tzu and Han Fei Tzu*, trans. Burton Watson (New York: Columbia Univ. Press, 1964).

3. Thomas More, *Complete Works of St. Thomas More*, vol. 4, *Utopia*, ed. Edward Surtz and J. H. Hexter (New Haven, Conn.: Yale University Press, 1965).

4. Manuel and Manuel, *Utopian Thought in the Western World*, 10. See also Lewis Mumford, *The Story of Utopias* (New York: Viking, 1962).

5. Karl Mannheim, *Ideology and Utopia*, trans. Louis Wirth and Edward Shils (London and New York: Harcourt, Brace and World, 1952).

6. Robert Boguslaw, *The New Utopians: A Study of System Design and Social Change* (Englewood Cliffs, N.J.: Prentice-Hall, 1965).

7. Everett Mendelsohn and Helga Nowotny, *Nineteen Eighty-Four: Science Between Utopia and Dystopia* (Boston: D. Reidel, 1984).

8. Charles Fourier, *Theory of Social Organization* (New York: C. P. Somerby, 1876).

9. De Fiore's thought is described in Manuel and Manuel, *Utopian Thought in the Western World*, 56–59.

10. Norman Cohn, *The Pursuit of the Millennium* (New York: Oxford Univ. Press, 1957).

11. Herbert Spencer, *The Man Versus the State with Four Essays on Politics and Society* (1884; reprint, ed. Donald Marcal, London: Penguin, 1969). See also Herbert Spencer, *Principles of Sociology* (New York: Appleton, 1896).

12. Arnold Toynbee, *Reconsiderations*, vol. 12 of *A Study of History* (New York: Oxford Univ. Press, 1964).

13. Charlotte Perkins Gilman, *Herland* (New York: Pantheon, 1979).

14. Evelyn F. Keller, *A Feeling for the Organism: Life and Work of Barbara McClintock* (New York and San Francisco: W. H. Freeman, 1983).

15. Lynn Margulis, *Symbiosis in Cell Evolution* (New York and San Francisco: W. H. Freeman, 1981).

16. Charlene Spretnak, *The Politics of Women's Spirituality* (Garden City, N.Y.: Anchor, 1982).

17. These developments are described in Leo Marx, *The Machine in the Garden* (New York: Oxford Univ. Press, 1964).

18. These populist movements are described in John L. Thomas, *Alternative America* (Cambridge, Mass.: Belknap Press of Harvard Univ. Press, 1983).

19. This discussion of the *Magic Mountain* is found in Melvin J. Lasky, *Utopia and Revolution* (Chicago: Univ. of Chicago Press, 1976), 626.

20. Frantz Fanon, *The Wretched of the Earth* (New York: Grove, 1963), 93–94.

21. A description of these arguments is found in Lasky, *Utopia and Revolution*, 626.

22. Sergio Cotta, *Why Violence?* trans. Giovanni Gullace (Gainesville: Univ. of Florida Press, 1985), 1.

23. Martin Buber, *Paths in Utopia* (Boston: Beacon, 1958).

24. Peter Kropotkin, *The Conquest of Bread* (New York: New York Univ. Press, 1972).

25. Kathleen Kinkade, *A Walden Two Experiment: The First Five Years of Twin Oaks Community* (New York: Morrow, 1973).

26. Hans Gerth and C. Wright Mills, *From Max Weber: Essays in Sociology* (New York: Oxford Univ. Press, 1946).

27. Moshe Lewin, *Lenin's Last Struggle* (New York: Pantheon, 1968).

28. Eric J. Hobsbawn, *The Age of Extremes: A History of the World 1941–1991* (New York: Pantheon, 1994). See also C. B. Marshall, ed., *The Communist Manifesto* (Washington, D.C.: School of Advanced International Studies, Johns Hopkins University, 1960).

29. This story is well told in Franz Borkenau, *The Spanish Cockpit* (Ann Arbor: Univ. of Michigan Press, 1963).

30. *Catalonia Culture*, a journal published by the UNESCO Center of Catalonia in Barcelona, Spain, gives a vivid sense of these developments; especially recommended are issues nos. 19 and 20 (1990) and no. 38 (1994).

31. Philip McManus and Gerald Schlabach, *Relentless Persistence* (Philadelphia, Pa.: New Society, 1991).

32. A journal that reports on creative social change in the Arab world is *Civil Society: Democratic Transformation in the Arab World*, which began publication by the Ibn Khaldun Center for Development Studies in Cairo, Egypt, about 1990. The editor is Saad Eddin Ibrahim.

33. For a description of the Gandhian future that Indian leaders rejected, see Bryan Teixeira, *A Gandhian Futurology* (Madurai, India: Valliammal Institution, Gandhi Museum, 1992).

34. Buber, *Paths in Utopia.*

35. The issue of cross-cutting structures is discussed in Elise Boulding, ed., *Building Peace in the Middle East* (Boulder, Colo.: Lynne Rienner, 1994).

36. This phenomenon is discussed in Mahendra Kumar, *Nonviolence: Contemporary Issues and Challenges* (New Delhi: Gandhi Peace Foundation, 1994).

37. The Sri Lanka counterpart is described in Joanna Macy, *Dharma and Development* (West Hartford, Conn.: Kumarian, 1983).

38. Revival of indigenous practices is discussed in Susantha Goonatilake, "Future of Asian Cultures: Between Localization and Globalization," in *The Futures of Asian Cultures*, ed. Eleonora Masini (Bangkok: UNESCO Office for Asia and the Pacific, 1993), 131–59.

39. The role of women's associations is described in Elise Boulding, "The Journey from the Underside" and "Epilogue," in *The Underside of History: A View of Women Through Time* (Newbury Park, Calif.: Sage, 1992), 2: 304–39 and 340–47.

40. Charles Nordhoff, *Communistic Societies of the United States* (1875; reprint, New York: Dover, 1966).

41. John Humphrey Noyes, *History of American Socialism* (Philadelphia: J. B. Lippincott, 1870), 407.

42. These developments are described by Henrik F. Infield, *Cooperative Communities at Work* (London: Kegan Paul, 1947).

43. Ralph Borsodi, *Flight from the City* (New York: Harper & Row, 1933).

44. *Communities Directory, A Guide to Cooperative Living* (Langley, Wash.: Fellowship for International Community, 1995).

45. Stephen Gaskin, *Rendered Infamous* (Summertown, Tenn.: Book Publishing Co., 1982).

46. The summer 1995 issue of *In Context* (no. 41), on the theme "Business on a Small Planet," describes many alternative approaches. The successor to *In Context* is *Yes—A Journal of Positive Futures*, which continues to report creative alternatives. *TRANET* (Rangely, Maine), a bimonthly digest for alternative and transformational movements, was a useful international newsletter that reported on alternatives, but unfortunately it ceased publication in 1997.

47. James Wallis, *The Soul of Politics* (Maryknoll, N.Y.: Orbis, 1994).

48. Grenville Park and Louis Sohn, *World Peace Through World Law*, 3d ed. (Cambridge, Mass.: Harvard Univ. Press, 1966).

49. Richard Falk, Robert Johansen, and Samuel Kim, eds., *The Constitutional Foundations of World Peace* (Albany: SUNY Press, 1993).

50. Helmut Ornauer, with Hakan Wilberg, Andrzcj Sicinsky, and Johan Galtung, *Images of the World in the Year 2000* (The Hague: Mouton, 1976).

## 3. Peace Movements and Their Organizational Forms: The Seedbed of Peace Cultures

1. Descriptions of this tradition are found in Steven Schwarzschild, *Roots of Jewish Nonviolence* (New York: Jewish Peace Fellowship, 1985); Asher Block, *The Jewish Tradition of Peace* (Nyack, N.Y.: Fellowship Publications, 1953).

2. Islamic traditions are described in Glenn D. Paige, Chaiwat Satha-Anand, and Sarah Gilliatt, eds., *Islam and Nonviolence* (Honolulu: Univ. of Hawaii Press, 1993).

3. Early Christian practices are described by Ronald G. Musto, *The Catholic Peace Tradition* (Maryknoll, N.Y.: Orbis, 1986), 50.

4. Musto, *Catholic Peace Tradition*, 84–87.

5. These points are made in Edwin Bonner, *William Penn's "Holy Experiment": The Founding of Pennsylvania, 1681–1701* (Philadelphia, Pa.: Temple Univ. Press, 1962).

6. Anabaptist abolition efforts are described in Louise Hawkley and James C. Juhnke, eds., *Nonviolent America—History Through the Eyes of Peace* (North Newton, Kans.: Bethel College, 1993).

7. These transnational movements are described in Sandi E. Cooper, *Patriotic Pacifism: Waging War on War in Europe, 1815–1914* (Oxford: Oxford Univ. Press, 1991), 5.

8. Elise Boulding, *The Underside of History: A View of Women Through Time*, rev. ed. (Newbury Park, Calif.: Sage, 1992), 2: chap. 3.

9. Cooper, *Patriotic Pacifism*, 61.

10. These developments are reflected in the works cited in Cooper, *Patriotic Pacifism*, and Boulding, *Underside of History*.

11. Developments in peace education are described in Berenice A. Carroll, Clinton F. Fink, and Jane E. Mohraz, *Peace and War: A Guide to Bibliographies* (Santa Barbara, Calif.: ABC-Clio, 1983).

12. The classic analysis of Gandhi's methodology is found in Joan V. Bondurant, *Conquest of Violence* (Berkeley: Univ. of California Press, 1971), chap. 8.

13. Mohandas Gandhi, *Nonviolence in Peace and War* (1942; reprint, New York: Garland, 1971).

14. The history of this movement will be found in Kamaladevi Chattopadhyaya, *Indian Women's Battle for Freedom* (New Delhi: Abhinav Publications, 1983).

15. The story of Ghaffar Khan is found in Eknath Easwaran, *A Man to Match His Mountains* (Petaluma, Calif: Nilgiri, 1984).

16. Jane Addams, *Peace and Bread in the Time of War* (1960; reprint, New York: Garland, 1972). Also see Gertrude Bussey and Margaret Tims, *Women's International League for Peace and Freedom, 1915–1965: A Record of Fifty Years' Work* (London: Allen & Unwin, 1965).

17. Note the following books describing various peace movements and their strategies: Kerstin Greback, Ragnhild Greek, and Ann-Cathrin Jarl, eds., *The Great Peace Journey* (Uppsala: Samhall Upsam, 1989); Barbara Harford and Sarah Hopkins, eds., *Greenham Common: Women at the Wire* (London: Women's Press, 1984); Amy Swerdlow, *Women Strike for Peace* (Chicago: Univ. of Chicago Press, 1993); Louis Menashe

and Ronald Rodosh, eds., *Teach-ins: U.S.A. Reports, Opinions, Documents* (New York: Praeger, 1967); Katsuya Kodama and Unto Vesa, eds., *Towards a Comparative Analysis of Peace Movements* (Aldershot, Hants, U.K.: Dartmouth Publishing Group, 1990); Charles Chatfield, *The American Peace Movement: Ideals and Activism* (New York: Twayne, 1992); and Charles Chatfield and Peter van den Dungen, eds., *Peace Movements and Political Cultures* (Knoxville: Univ. of Tennessee Press, 1988).

18. Note here Lawrence Wittner, *One World or None: A History of the World Nuclear Disarmament Movement* (Stanford, Calif.: Stanford Univ. Press, 1993).

19. Gene Sharp, *The Politics of Nonviolent Action* (Boston: Porter Sargent, 1973); also, Ronald McCarthy and Gene Sharp, *Nonviolent Action: A Research Guide* (New York and London: Garland, 1997).

20. Sharp, *Politics of Nonviolent Action*, 75–76.

21. An important example of the new sophistication is found in George Lakey, *Powerful Peacemaking: A Strategy for a Living Revolution* (Philadelphia, Pa.: New Society, 1987).

22. Important early feminist peace activist writing is found in Pam McAllister, ed., *Reweaving the Web of Life* (Philadelphia, Pa.: New Society, 1987); and Barbara Deming, *Revolution and Equilibrium* (New York: Grossman, 1971).

23. A valuable example of feminist peace research perspectives is found in Birgit Brock-Utne, *Educating for Peace: A Feminist Perspective* (New York: Pergamon, 1985).

24. Among the landmark books in the early peace research movement are: Kenneth Boulding, *The Economics of Peace* (New York: Prentice-Hall, 1945), which has been translated into French, German, Japanese, and Spanish, and *Conflict and Defense: A General Theory* (New York: Harper, 1962); Anatol Rapoport, *Fights, Games and Debates* (Ann Arbor: Univ. of Michigan Press, 1960); Theodore Lenz, *Toward a Science of Peace* (New York: Bookman Associates, 1961); Johan Galtung, *Peace: Research, Education, Action*, vol. 1 of Essays in Peace Research (Copenhagen: Ejlers Christian, 1975). See also Herbert Kelman, *International Behavior* (New York: Holt, Rinehart & Winston, 1965).

25. An early documentation of this process is found in Clinton Fink and Elise Boulding, eds., "Peace Research in Transition: A Symposium," *Journal of Conflict Resolution* 16, no. 4 (1972).

26. Michael Klare, ed., *Peace and World Society Studies: A Curriculum Guide*, 6th ed. (Boulder, Colo.: Westview, 1994).

27. Alva Myrdal, *The Game of Disarmament* (New York: Pantheon, 1976).

28. Adam Roberts, ed., *The Strategy of Civilian Defense* (London: Faber & Faber, 1967).

29. Sharp, *Politics of Nonviolent Action*.

30. This Commission built heavily on the work of Louis Kriesberg and colleagues, reflected in *Intractable Conflicts and Their Transformation* (Syracuse, N.Y.: Syracuse Univ. Press, 1989). See also Elise Boulding, ed., *Building Peace in the Middle East: Challenges to States and Civil Society* (Boulder, Colo.: Lynne Rienner, 1994).

31. Scilla Elworthy McLean, ed., *How Nuclear Weapons Decisions Are Made* (London: Macmillan Press and Oxford Research Group, 1986); and Hugh Miall, *Nuclear Weapons: Who's in Charge?* (London: Macmillan, 1987).

32. International Commission for the Study of Communication Problems (MacBride Commission), *Many Voices, One World* (London: Kogan, 1980); Independent Commission on Disarmament and Security Issues (Palme Commission), *Common Security: A Blueprint for Survival* (New York: Simon & Schuster, 1982); Independent Commission on International Development Issues (Brandt Commission), *Common Crisis North-South: Cooperation for World Recovery* (Cambridge, Mass.: MIT Press, 1983); World Commission on Environment and Development (Brundtland Commission), *Our Common Future* (Oxford: Oxford Univ. Press, 1987); and South Commission (Nyerere Commission), *The Challenge to the South* (New York: Oxford Univ. Press, 1990).

33. This alliance is described in Francine Blume, "Peace Zones: Examplars and Potential," *The Acorn. Journal of Gandhi-King Society*, spring-summer 1993.

34. David Adams, ed., *The Seville Statement on Violence: Preparing the Ground for the Construction of Peace* (Paris: UNESCO, 1991).

35. John Burton, *Conflict and Communication: The Use of Controlled Communication in International Relations* (London: Macmillan, 1969).

36. Adam Curle, *Making Peace* (London: Tavistock, 1971).

37. John Paul Lederach, *Preparing for Peace: Conflict Transformation Across Cultures* (Syracuse, N.Y.: Syracuse Univ. Press, 1995), and *Building Peace: Sustainable Reconciliation in Divided Societies* (Washington, D.C.: U.S. Institute of Peace, 1997).

38. Saul Mendlovitz, ed., *On the Creation of a Just World Order: Preferred Worlds for the 1990s* (New York: Free Press, 1975).

39. This research is described in Kumar, *Nonviolence: Contemporary Issues and Challenges.*

40. This history is described in M. Annette Jaimes, ed., *The State of Native America: Genocide, Colonization and Resistance* (Boston, Mass.: South End, 1992); and John Kicza, *The Indian in Latin American History: Resistance, Resilience, and Acculturation* (New York: Scholarly Resources, 1993).

41. Institute for Defense and Disarmament Studies, *1988–89 Peace Resource Book: A Comprehensive Guide to Issues, Groups, and Literature* (Cambridge, Mass.: Ballinger, 1988).

42. The commission's findings are described in Lydia Dotto, *Planet Earth in Jeopardy: Environmental Consequences of Nuclear War* (New York: Wiley, 1986).

43. Devi Prasad and Tony Smythe, eds., *Conscription—A World Survey* (London: War Resisters International, 1968).

44. Ed Hedemann and Ruth Benn, *War Tax Resistance* (New York: War Resisters International, 1994).

45. Petra K. Kelly, *Nonviolence Speaks to Power* (Honolulu: Univ. of Hawaii Press, 1992).

46. Howard Zinn, SNCC: *The New Abolitionists* (Boston, Mass.: Beacon, 1964), and *Failure to Quit: Reflections of an Optimistic Historian* (Monroe, Maine: Common Courage, 1993).

47. Documentation of this growth is found in Sam Marullo and John Lofland, eds., *Peace Action in the Eighties: Social Science Perspectives* (New Brunswick, N.J.: Rutgers Univ. Press, 1990).

48. Institute for Defense and Disarmament Studies, *1988–89 Peace Resource Book*.

49. Examples of Buddhist peace work are found in Thich Nhat Hanh, *Love in Action* (Berkeley, Calif.: Parallax, 1993).

50. These activities are described in Glenn D. Paige and Sarah Gilliatt, eds., *Buddhism and Nonviolent Global Problem-Solving* (Honolulu: Univ. of Hawaii Press, 1991). Note especially the essay by Ariyaratne. See also "George Bond, A. T. Ariyaratne and the Sarvodaya Shramadana Movement in Sri Lanka," in *Engaged Buddhism: Buddhist Liberation Movements in Asia*, ed. Christopher Queen and Sallie King, 121–46 (Albany: SUNY Press, 1996).

51. Sulak Sivaraksa, *A Buddhist Vision for Renewing Society* (Bangkok: Thai Inter-Religious Commission for Development, 1994), and *Loyalty Demands Dissent* (Berkeley, Calif.: Parallax Press, 1998).

52. The Coalition for Peace and Reconciliation in Phnom Penh publishes a newsletter about these activities.

53. Aung San Suu Kyi, *The Political Legacy of Aung San* (Ithaca, N.Y.: Southeast Asia Program, Cornell University, 1972).

54. Daniel Metraux, "The Soka Gakkai: Buddhism in the Creation of a Harmonious and Peaceful Society," in *Engaged Buddhism*, ed. Christopher Queen and Sallie King, 365–400.

55. Jose Ignacio Cabezon, "Buddhist Principles in the Tibetan Liberation Movement," in *Engaged Buddhism*, ed. Christopher Queen and Sallie King, 295–320.

56. Christopher Chapple, "Jainism and Nonviolence," in *Subverting Hatred*, ed. Daniel Smith-Christopher, 13–24 (Cambridge: Boston Research Center for the 21st Century, 1998).

57. These protest movements are described in Vandana Shiva, *The Violence of the Green Revolution* (Dehra Dun, India: Vandana Shiva, 1989).

58. Alan Sponberg, "TBMSG: A Dhamma Revolution in Contemporary India," in *Engaged Buddhism*, ed. Christopher Queen and Sallie King, 73–120.

59. Note such articles as the following: International Fellowship of Reconciliation, "Islam and Peacemaking," *Reconciliation International* (London), February 1988; Fellowship of Reconciliation U.S., "Islam, Peacemaking and Nonviolence," *Fellowship* (Nyack, N.Y.), May-June 1994.

60. Ralph E. Crow, Philip Grant, and Saad E. Ibrahim, eds., *Arab Nonviolent Political Struggle in the Middle East* (Boulder, Colo.: Lynne Rienner, 1990).

61. Easwaren, *Man to Match His Mountains*.

62. Fouad Ajami, *The Dream Palace of the Arabs* (New York: Pantheon, 1998).

63. These activities are described in Nagasawa Madale, "Nonviolent Alternative in a Crisis Situation," *Gandhi Marg* (New Delhi) 14, no. 1 (Apr.-June 1992): 166–79; Susan Evangelista, "The Anti-Bases Campaign in the Philippines," *Gandhi Marg* 14, no. 1 (Apr.-June 1992): 215–31; and Blume, "Peace Zones."

64. M. R. Bawa Muhaiyaddeen, *Islam and World Peace: Explanations of a Sufi* (Philadelphia, Pa.: Fellowship Press, 1987).

65. This story has begun to be told by Pierre Pradervand, *Listening to Africa: Developing Africa from the Grassroots* (New York: Praeger, 1989).

66. An account of the South African nonviolence movement is found in Lyle Tatum, ed., *South Africa: Challenge and Hope* (Philadelphia: American Friends Service Committee, 1982).

67. The National Peace Accord story is found in Hendrik W. van der Merwe, *Pursuing Justice and Peace in South Africa* (New York: Routledge, 1989).

68. The rise of civil society in South Africa is described in Michael Bratton, "Beyond the State: Civil Society and Associational Life in Africa," *Transnational Associations* 3 (May-June 1991): 130–40; and Horace Campbell, "Challenging the Apartheid Regime from Below," in *Popular Struggles for Democracy in Africa*, ed. Peter Anyan'g Nyong'o (London: Zed Press, 1987), 142–69.

69. Leonardo Boff, *The Base Communities Reinvent the Church* (Maryknoll, N.Y.: Orbis, 1986).

70. Philip McManus and Gerald Schlabach, eds., *Relentless Persistence* (Philadelphia, Pa.: New Society, 1991).

## 4. Peaceful Societies and Everyday Behavior

1. Hans Hass, *The Human Animal: The Mystery of Man's Behavior* (New York: G. P. Putnam's Sons, 1970).

2. Hans Hass, *Human Animal*, 123.

3. This passage is found in Leonard Tomkinson, *Studies in the Theory and Practice of Peace and War in Chinese History and Literature* (Shanghai: Friends Center, Christian Literature Society, 1940).

4. The "10,000 societies" is a term sometimes used by anthropologists to refer to the large number of separate ethnic groups spread across the globe. Estimates of the actual number of societies range from 5,000 to 7,000, varying according to the criteria used for counting.

5. In making choices on which peoples to select and what social practices are most significant in generating societal peaceableness, I have drawn heavily on the selection of anthropological studies of peaceful societies prepared by Bruce D. Bonta and published as *Peaceful Peoples: An Annotated Bibliography* (Metuchen, N.J.: Scarecrow, 1993). I wish to express my appreciation here for his outstanding work.

6. Jean Briggs, *Never in Anger: Portrait of an Eskimo Family* (Cambridge, Mass.: Harvard Univ. Press, 1971). See also Briggs's "The Origins of Nonviolence: Inuit

Management of Aggression," in *Learning Non-Aggression: The Experience of the Non-Literate Societies*, ed. Ashley Montagu (New York: Oxford Univ. Press, 1978), 54–93.

7. Susan Isaacs, *Intellectual Growth in Young Children* (London: Routledge & Kegan Paul, 1930). Note also Elise Boulding, "The Nurturance of Adults by Children in Family Settings," in *Research in the Interweave of Social Roles*, ed. Helen Lopata (Greenwich, Conn.: JAI Press, 1980), 167–89.

8. Clyde H. Farnsworth, "Envoy Defends World of Eskimo" *New York Times*, Feb. 22, 1995.

9. Colin Turnbull, *The Forest People* (New York: Simon & Schuster, 1961).

10. In 1991 the first representative of the Central African Forest Peoples made his way to Geneva to create linkage with the UN Working Group for Indigenous Populations. Since then, the newsletter of the International Work Group for Indigenous Affairs (IWGIA) is reporting increased activities among the African rainforest peoples. A linkage with other rainforest peoples took place during the 1993 International Year of the World's Indigenous Peoples. See the IWGIA Newsletters (Copenhagen), nos. 2 and 3 (1993).

11. See especially: Ruth Benedict, *Patterns of Culture* (Boston: Houghton Mifflin, 1959). See also Irving Goldman, "The Zuni Indians of New Mexico," in *Cooperation and Competition among Primitive Peoples*, ed. Margaret Mead, (New York: McGraw-Hill, 1937), 313–53; John Whiting et al., "The Learning Values," in *People of Rimrock: A Study of Values in Five Cultures*, ed. Evon Vogt and Ethel Albert, (Cambridge, Mass.: Harvard Univ. Press, 1967), 83–125.

12. For an account of new Zuni developments, see Derek Denniston's "High Priorities: Conserving Mountain Ecosystems and Cultures," *World Watch Paper* 123 (Feb. 1995): 50–51.

13. Margaret Mead, *Sex and Temperament in Three Primitive Societies* (New York: Mentor, 1950).

14. Bonta, *Peaceful Peoples*.

15. Although Pennsylvania was a colony founded by Quakers, and Quakers originally constituted a majority in the colony's legislative assembly, the issue of voting appropriations to fulfill military obligations to the king during the French and Indian Wars led most Quakers to resign from the legislature in the later years of the colony.

16. Among studies on the Anabaptist communities, see James Juhnke, *Vision, Doctrine, War: Mennonite Identity and Organization in America*, 3 vols. (Scottdale, Pa.: Herald, 1986); Duane Friesen, *Christian Peacemaking and International Conflict* (Scottdale, Pa.: Herald, 1986); and Elbert Russell, *The History of Quakerism* (New York: Macmillan, 1992).

17. During the nineteenth-century evangelical revival in the United States, a certain number of Quaker meetings shifted to the more usual pattern of having ministers, to cope with the rapidly growing numbers of adherents.

18. The consensus process does not lead to speedy decisions. It took one hundred years from the time the first proposal was made to abolish slaveholding among Friends to the time when Friends were able to unite in accepting this as a Quaker witness.

19. The Children's Creative Response to Conflict Program is now housed with the Fellowship of Reconciliation, Box 271, Nyack, NY 10960.

20. Elise Boulding, "The Family as a Small Society," and "The Family as a Way into the Future," in *One Small Plot of Heaven: Reflections of a Quaker Sociologist on Family Life* (Wallingford, Pa.: Pendle Hill, 1989).

21. A number of organizations work to spread this sense of ecological interdependence, and they all publish newsletters. U.S. mailing addresses for a few: International Society for Ecology and Culture, P.O. Box 9475, Berkeley, CA 94709; RAIN, The Planet Drum Foundation, P.O. Box 31251, San Francisco, CA 94131; Ocean Arks International, One Locus St., Falmouth, MA 02540; World Neighbors, 4127 NW 122 St., Oklahoma City, OK 73210-8869.

22. For examples, see McKim Marriott, "The Feast of Love," in *Krishna Myths, Rites and Attitudes,* ed. Milton Singer (Chicago: Univ. of Chicago Press, 1968). See also Richard Lannoy, *The Speaking Tree: A Study of Indian Culture and Society* (London: Oxford Univ. Press, 1971).

23. Marcel Mauss, *The Gift: Forms and Functions of Exchange in Archaic Societies* (New York: Norton, 1971).

24. Marshall Sahlins, *Stone Age Economics* (New York: Aldine-Atherton, 1972).

25. Alvin Gouldner, "The Norm of Reciprocity," *American Sociological Review* 25 (1960): 161–78.

26. Johan Huizinga, *Homo Ludens: A Study of the Play Element in Culture* (Boston: Beacon, 1955).

27. Mary Reilly, ed., *Play as Exploratory Learning* (Beverly Hills, Calif.: Sage, 1974).

28. Fred Polak, *The Image of the Future,* trans. Elise Boulding (San Francisco: Jossey-Bass/Elsevier, 1972). This is a one-volume abridgement of the full two-volume translation of the original Dutch (Dobbs Ferry, N.Y.: Oceana Press, 1961).

## 5. Breaking New Ground: Feminist Peacemaking

1. Naomi Black, *Social Feminism,* Ithaca, N.Y.: Cornell Univ. Press, 1989).

2. Jane Addams, Emily G. Balch, and Alice Hamilton. *Women at The Hague* (1915; reprint, New York: Garland, 1972).

3. Elise Boulding, "Feminist Inventions in the Art of Peacemaking."

4. Margaret Mead, *Cooperation and Competition among Primitive Peoples* (New York: McGraw-Hill, 1967). See also her *Continuities in Cultural Evolution* (New Haven: Yale Univ. Press, 1964); *Culture and Commitment* (Garden City, N.Y.: Natural History Press, 1972); and *Blackberry Winter: My Earlier Years* (Gloucester, Mass.: Peter Smith, 1989).

5. Mary Catherine Bateson, *With a Daughter's Eye* (New York: Harper, 1984); Sissela Bok, *Alva Myrdal: A Daughter's Memoir* (Reading, Pa.: Addison-Wesley, 1991).

6. Alva Myrdal, *Nation and Family* (New York: Harper, 1941); Alva Myrdal, with Viola Klein, *Women's Two Roles* (London: Routledge & Kegan Paul, 1956).

7. Alva Myrdal, *The Game of Disarmament* (New York: Pantheon, 1976).

8. See, for example, Berenice Carroll, "Peace Research: The Cult of Power," *Journal of Conflict Resolution* 14, no. 4 (1972): 586–615; Birgit Brock-Utne, *Educating for Peace: A Feminist Perspective* (New York: Pergamon, 1985); and Elise Boulding, "Women's Experimental Approaches to Peace Studies," in *The Knowledge Explosion*, ed. Cherie Kramarae and Dale Spender (New York: Teacher's College Press, 1992), 54–63.

9. Birgit Brock-Utne, *Feminist Perspectives on Peace and Peace Education* (New York: Pergamon, 1989).

10. ISIS International, P.O. Box 1837, Quezon City Main, Quezon City 1100, Philippines.

11. International Women's Tribune Center, 777 UN Plaza, New York, NY 10017.

12. GROOTS International, Sherman Square #27L, New York, NY 10023.

13. The Global Fund for Women, 425 Sherman Avenue, Suite 300, Palo Alto, CA 94306-1823.

14. Women's Environment and Development Organization (WEDO), 355 Lexington Avenue., New York, NY 10017-0326.

15. Huairou Commission on Women and Habitat, Two UN Plaza c/o UNCH, 9th Floor, New York, NY 10017.

16. Chattopadhyay Kamaladevi, *Inner Recesses, Outer Spaces: Memoirs* (New Delhi: Navrang, 1986).

17. Martha Dart, *Marjorie Sykes, Quaker Gandhian* (Birmingham, U.K.: Sessions Book Trust in association with Woodbroak College, 1993).

18. Jill Wallis, *Mother of World Peace: The Life of Muriel Lester* (Enfield Lock, U.K.: Hisarlik Press, 1993).

19. Elise Boulding, "Peace Education as Peace Development," *Transnational Associations* 6 (1987): 322–26.

20. Claire Salkowsky, "Peacemaking," *Montessori Life*, winter (1994): 32–38.

21. Elise Boulding, "Peace Education as Peace Development."

22. Amy Swerdlow, *Women Strike for Peace* (Chicago: Univ. of Chicago Press, 1993).

23. Women's Action for New Directions, 691 Massachusetts Avenue, Arlington, MA 02174.

24. WILPF, Swedish Section, *The Great Peace Journey Report* (Uppsala: Samhall Upsam, 1989).

25. Barbara Harford and Sarah Hopkins, *Greenham Common: Women at the Wire* (London: Women's Press, 1984).

26. Joanna Macy, "Nuclear Guardianship Project" (pamphlet) (Berkeley, Calif.: Nuclear Guardianship Project, 1989). The address for this project is c/o Tides Foundation, 1400 Shattuck Avenue, #41, Berkeley, CA 94709.

27. Mary Evelyn Jergen, *Global Peace Service* Cincinnati, Ohio: Sisters of Notre Dame, 1993).

28. Center for Strategic Initiatives of Women, 1701 K Street NW, 11th Floor, Washington, D.C. 20006.

29. Women's Peacemakers Program, International Fellowship of Reconciliation, Spoorstraat 38, 1815 BK, Alkmaar, Netherlands. See the 1998 report on the Asian Regional Consultation on Women and Conflict Resolution.

30. Women Waging Peace is an initiative of the Women and Public Policy Program of the John F. Kennedy School of Government, Harvard University, Cambridge, Massachusetts.

## 6. New Partnerships—Women and Men

1. Elise Boulding, *The Underside of History: A View of Women Through Time*, rev. ed. (Newbury Park, Calif.: Sage, 1992).

2. Riane Eisler, *The Chalice and the Blade* (New York: Harper, 1987).

3. Terry Allen Kupers, *Revisioning Men's Lives: Gender, Intimacy, and Power* (New York: Guilford, 1993); R. William Betcher and William S. Pollack, *In a Time of Fallen Heroes: The Re-creation of Masculinity* (New York: Guilford, 1993).

4. Donald Sabo and Ross Runfola, *Jock: Sports and Male Identity* (Englewood Cliffs, N.J.: Prentice-Hall, 1980).

5. Joseph Pleck, "The Male Sex Role: Definitions, Problems and Sources of Change," *Journal of Social Issues* 32, no. 3 (1976); Joseph Pleck and Jack Sawyer, *Men and Masculinity* (Englewood Cliffs, N.J.: Prentice-Hall, 1974).

6. RAVEN, *Men, Women and Violence* (St. Louis, Mo.: Rape and Violence End Now, 1982).

7. James William Gibson, *Warrior Dreams: Violence and Manhood in Post-Vietnam America* (New York: Hill and Wang, 1994).

8. Robert Bly, *Iron John* (New York: Addison-Wesley, 1990).

9. Marac F. Fosteau, *Male Machine* (New York: McGraw-Hill, 1974); Warren Farrell, *The Liberated Man: Beyond Masculinity* (New York: Random House, 1974); Joseph Pleck and Jack Sawyer, *Men and Masculinity*; James Doyle, *The Male Experience* (New York: McGraw-Hill, 1983).

10. Maurice Berger, Brian Wallis, and Simon Watson, eds., *Constructing Masculinity* (New York and London: Routledge, 1995); David Buchbinder, *Performance Anxieties: Reproducing Masculinity* (Sydney: Allen and Unwin, 1998); Michael S. Kimmel, ed., *The Politics of Manhood* (Philadelphia: Temple Univ. Press, 1995); Michael A. Messner, *Politics of Masculinities: Men in Movements* (Newbury Park, Calif.: Sage, 1997).

11. MENSTUFF is available from the national Men's Resource Center, P.O. Box 800-W, San Anselmo, CA 94979-0800, in print as well as online.

12. Daniel J. Sonkin and Michael Durphy, *Learning to Live Without Violence: A Handbook for Men* (San Francisco: Volcano Press, 1982).

13. Pleck and Sawyer, *Men and Masculinity*, 173.

14. Lori Eickmann, "While Moms Work, Dads Stay Home to Nurture Their Kids," *Boulder Camera*, July 23, 1995, p. 1B.

15. Youth MOVE is described in *Voice Male*, Newsletter of the Men's Resource Center of Western Massachusetts, Fall 1998, 5–6.

16. MIPE can be reached at P.O. Box 36, Swarthmore, PA 19081-0036.

17. Some examples of the men's rights perspective are found in Warren Farrell, *The Manipulated Man* (Berkeley, Calif.: Berkeley Publishing Group, 1986). MENSTUFF carries information about the men's rights movement.

18. Reports mentioned can be found in *Women in Action* 1 (1995): 72–73.

19. Dorothy Dinnerstein, *The Mermaid and the Minotaur* (New York: Harper & Row, 1976).

20. Nancy Myron and Charlotte Bunch, eds., *Lesbianism and the Women's Movement* (Baltimore: Diana Press, 1975); E. M. Ettorre, *Lesbians, Women and Society* (London: Routledge & Kegan Paul, 1980).

21. *Communities Directory: A Guide to Cooperative Living* (Langley, Wash.: Fellowship for International Community, 1995).

22. Personal communication from James Cypser, Boulder, Colorado.

23. Rae Andre, *Homemakers: The Forgotten Workers* (Chicago: Univ. of Chicago Press, 1981).

24. Deanna Eversoll. "A Two-Generational View of Fathering," *Family Coordinator* 28, no. 4 (1979): 503–7.

25. Rhona and Robert Rapoport, eds., *Fathers, Mothers and Society: Towards New Alliances* (New York: Basic Books, 1977).

26. F. Grossman, W. Pollack, and E. Golding, "Fathers and Children: Predicting the Quality and Quantity of Fathering," *Developmental Psychology* 24 (1988): 82–91.

27. Betcher and Pollack, *In a Time of Fallen Heroes*.

28. Jessie Bernard, *Women, Wives, Mothers* (Chicago: Aldine, 1975).

29. Jeanne Holm, *Women in the Military: An Unfinished Revolution* (Novato, Calif.: Presidio, 1982).

30. Jay MacPherson, *Four Stages in Man: The Classical Myths* (Toronto: Macmillan, 1963), 123.

## 7. New Partnerships—Children and Adults

1. Philippe Aries, *Centuries of Childhood*, trans. Robert Baldick (New York: Knopf, 1962).

2. D. Noyes, F. Powers, and R. W. Kates, "Comparative Assessments of the Environmental and Technological Hazards of Small Children" (paper presented at the session "Children and Their Social Environments," at the annual meeting of the Association of American Geographers, 1979).

3. Elise Boulding, "The Nurturance of Adults by Children in Family Settings."

4. Roger Hart, *Children's Experience of Place* (New York: Irvington, 1979).

5. Gareth Matthews, in *The Philosophy of Childhood* (Cambridge, Mass.: Harvard Univ. Press, 1994), provides a thoughtful critique of age-related stages and points out the similarities between the thought processes of children and adults.

6. Aikido is, of course, far more than a method of defense. It is a spiritually based approach to violence that aims to rechannel the energies and attitudes of the attacker.

7. Children's Express has the motto "By Children for Everyone." Its mailing address is 1440 New York Avenue NW, Suite 510, Washington, D.C. 20005.

8. A vivid account of the Taizé Youth Assembly in Paris by Morlise Simons appeared in the *New York Times,* Jan. 2, 1995.

9. "An Interview with Satish Kumar," *Timeline* (Foundation for Global Community, Palo Alto, Calif.), Sept./Oct. 1995, 3, 4.

10. Robert Coles, *The Spiritual Life of Children* (Boston: Houghton Mifflin, 1990). For a Quaker perspective, see my essays on children and family life in *One Small Plot of Heaven: Reflections of a Quaker Sociologist on Family Life* (Wallingford, Pa.: Pendle Hill, 1989).

11. Age categories referring to children and youths can be confusing. The most common usage is as follows: 0–4, 5–9: children; 10–14: adolescents; 15–19: youth; 20–24: young adults.

12. The Peace Child theater project and the organization called Peace Child were started by David Woollcombe and headquartered at the White House, Buntingford, Herts, England SG9 9AH.

13. Carolina Garcia Travesi was so interested in the questions I put to her that she wrote me a substantial essay on her activities in flawless English!

14. Rescue Mission Planet Earth is the successor organization to Peace Child and shares its address (see n. 12). *Global Network News* is edited and published from the White House, Buntingford, Hertz, England SG9 9AH.

15. See the March 1998 issue of *Alpe/Adria* on "Solidarity and Tolerance Can be Learned: The European Youth Academy," Villach: Rathausgasse 8, Austria.

16. The office for the Coalition for Children of the Earth is at Peaceways, 324 Catalpa Avenue, Suite 318, San Mateo, CA 94401.

17. Section IV of the International Keeping the Promise Document, published by Peaceways (see n. 16) for the Coalition for Children of the Earth. The United Nations, in spite of its key role, mentioned above, in providing the framework for addressing the concerns and needs of the young, is very resistant to actual participation of children in its affairs. Sad to say, it refused to admit the several hundred children gathered at the World Summit of Children in San Francisco in the summer of 1995 to the ceremony celebrating the signing of the UN Charter, an event in which the children had counted on participating. This action was of a piece with the UN's refusal to have a child address the first UN World Summit for Children in 1990. Old patriarchal habits die hard.

18. *Hague Appeal Youth News* is sent out from the office of the International Peace Bureau, 41 rue de Zurich, 1201 Geneva, Switzerland.

19. The Northern Secretariat for Voice of Children is PO Box 8844 Youngstorget 0028, Oslo, Norway. The Southern Secretariat is FUNAM, Casilla de Correo 83, Correo Central, 5000 Cordoba, Argentina.

20. Kidspeace, at 1650 Broadway, Bethlehem, PA 18015-3998, has been in existence since 1882. Global Kids can be contacted at 561 Broadway, New York, NY 10017.

21. Outreach is an organization affiliated with the UN Environment Program (UNEP) based in Nairobi, Kenya, which publishes information packets to be used for educational purposes in low-income countries. The material on street children comes from Outreach Packets, nos. 96 and 97, on "Children in Especially Difficult Circumstances," ed. G. Dorfman, J. Connor, and S. Kahkonen. These packets are prepared at Outreach, Teaching and Learning Center, 200 East B239 Greene Street, New York University, New York, NY 10003.

22. Graca Machel's *Impact of Armed Conflict on Children* is available from the Public Information Department of the United Nations, New York, NY.

23. David and Micki Colfax, *Homeschooling for Excellence* (New York: Warner Books, 1988).

24. Grace Llewellyn, *Teenage Liberation Handbook: How to Quit School and Get a Real Life and Education* (Eugene, Oregon: Lowry House, 1991).

25. *TRANET*, a Bi-Monthly Digest for Alternative and Transformational Movements (Rangeley, Maine 04970), edited by William Ellis, unfortunately, ceased publication in 1998.

26. *Young and Powerful* is edited by Sam Firth, 271 Amhurst Road, Stoke Newington, London N167OP, England.

## Part 3: Introduction

1. For an excellent exposition of the mutuality model, see Gordon Fellman's *Rambo and the Dalai Lama, the Compulsion to Win and Its Threat to Human Survival* (Albany: SUNY Press, 1998).

## 8. Peoples and States

1. The "10,000 societies" is a term loosely used by some anthropologists (see "Peace Culture: An Overview," n. 5).

2. See *A Practical Guide to the World Decade for Cultural Development, 1988–97* (Paris: UNESCO, 1987). For accounts of the struggle to develop a UN Declaration on the rights of indigenous peoples, and to define the year and the Decade of Indigenous Peoples, see the *Indigenous World* (Copenhagen, International Work Group for Indigenous Affairs), 1993–94, 153–80; and 1994–95, 201–39.

3. See E. Boulding, "Ethnic Separatism and World Development." See also *Peace Review* 10, no. 2 (June 1998), an issue on national self-determination.

4. See, I. William Zartman, *Traditional Cures for Modern Conflict* (Boulder, Colo.: Lynne Rienner, 1999). Also see issues of the journal *International Peacekeeping*, esp. vol. 2, no. 3 (autumn 1995); and those of *New Routes*, published by the Life and Peace Institute, Uppsala, Sweden, esp. vol. 4, no. 1 (1999).

5. See the annual IWGIA yearbooks (International Work Group for Indigenous Affairs, Copenhagen) for documentation of the process.

6. World Bank, *Tribal People and Economic Development: Human Ecologic Considerations* (Washington, D.C.: World Bank, 1982).

7. Michael Barkun, *Law Without Sanctions: Order in Primitive Societies and the World Community* (New Haven, Conn.: Yale Univ. Press, 1968).

8. Ferdinand Tönnies, *Community and Society*, trans. Charles Loomis (New York: Harper & Rowe, 1976).

9. Kenneth Boulding, *Stable Peace* (Austin: Univ. of Texas Press, 1978).

10. The term "minorities at risk" comes from a 1989 study of 260 nonsovereign peoples who are both numerically significant and accorded separate and unequal treatment; see Gurr and Scarritt, "Minorities Rights at Risk, A Global Survey."

11. Lance Clark, *Early Warning of Refugee Flows* (Washington, D.C.: Refugee Policy Group, 1989); Thomas Weiss, "Whether International Efforts for Internally Displaced Peoples?" *Journal of Peace Research* vol. 36, no. 3 (1999): 363–74.

12. Michael Hechter, *International Colonialism: The Celtic Fringe in British National Development, 1536–1966* (Berkeley: Univ. of California Press, 1975).

13. Anthony Judge, "And When the Bombing Stops?" Union of International Associations Welcome Page (http://www.uia.org/uiadocs/mathbom.htm), Brussels, April 11, 1999.

14. Geoff Gilbert, "The Council of Europe and Minority Rights" in *Human Rights Quarterly* 18, no. 1 (1996). The text of the Convention is to be found in *International Legal Materials* 34, no. 1 (1995).

15. Valerii Tishkov, "Glasnost and Nationalities Within the Soviet Union," *Third World Quarterly* 11, no. 4 (Oct. 1989): 191–207.

16. Tishkov, "Glasnost and Nationalities," 194.

17. For further analyses of the consociational democracies discussed, see two issues of *Catalonia Culture* (Barcelona): no. 15 (Sept. 1989) on "Linguistic Normalization" and no. 16 (Nov. 1989) on "Territorial Planning and Public Works"; Jurg Steiner, "Power-Sharing: Another Swiss Export?" in *Conflict and Peacemaking in Multi-Ethnic Societies*, ed. Joseph Montville (Lexington, Mass.: Heath, 1989), 107–14; and Martin Heisler, "Hyphenating Belgium: Changing State and Regime to Cope with Cultural Division," in *Conflict and Peacemaking*, ed. Joseph Montville, 177–96.

18. France, which has overlapping ethnic groups with Spain, has so far been able to avoid the issue of autonomous regions and to deal with its ethnies primarily at the cultural level by recognizing four regional languages for instructional purposes in the schools: Breton, Basque, Catalan, and Occitan.

19. The report of Norway's action is found in *The Indigenous World, 1993–4* (Copenhagen: IWGIA, 1994), 24–26.

20. The report of Greenland's Home Rule developments is found in *The Indigenous World, 1993–4* (Copenhagen: IWGIA, 1994), 20–24. The report on a permanent forum for indigenous peoples is in *The Indigenous World, 1994–5* (Copenhagen: IWGIA, 1995), 213–25.

21. For helpful analyses of Sri Lanka, see two essays in *Conflict and Peacemaking*,

ed. Joseph Montville: Bryan Pfaffenberger, "Ethnic Conflict and Youth Insurgency in Sri Lanka: The Social Origins of Tamil Separation," 214–58; and Marshall Singer, "Prospects for Conflict Management in the Sri Lankan Ethnic Crisis," 259–86.

22. For helpful analyses of Malaysia, see Richard Stubbs, "Malaysia: Avoiding Ethnic Strife in a Deeply Divided Society," in *Conflict and Peacemaking*, ed. Joseph Montville, 287–300; and Jomo Sundaram, "Malaysia's New Economic Policy and National Unity," *Third World Quarterly* 11, no. 4 (Oct. 1989): 36–53.

23. Selig Harrison (1989), "Ethnic Conflict in Pakistan: The Boluch, Pashtuns, and Sundhis," in *Conflict and Peacemaking*, ed. Joseph Montville, 301–26.

24. Sam Noluk Hungu, "Fragments of a Democracy: Reflections on Class and Politics in Nigeria," *Third World Quarterly* 12, no. 1 (Jan. 1990): 86–115; and John Poden, "National System Development and Conflict Resolution in Nigeria," in *Conflict and Peacemaking*, ed. Joseph Montville, 411–32.

25. On Sudan, see two essays in *Conflict and Peacemaking*, ed. Joseph Montville: Frances Deng, "The Identity Factor in the Sudanese Conflict," 343–62; and Nelson Kasfir, "Peacemaking and Social Cleavages in Sudan," 363–88.

26. Kenneth D. McRae, "Canada: Reflections on Two Conflicts," in *Conflict and Peacemaking*, ed. Joseph Montville, 197–218; and *Cantilevers* (Center for Global Peace, American University, Washington, D.C.) 6 (spring 1999), an issue on Quebec and Northern Ireland.

27. For an activist view of this litigation, see Rick Whaley and Walter Bresette, *Walleye Warriors* (Philadelphia: New Society, 1994). A more general presentation is found in Vine Deloria, *For We Talk, You Listen: New Timbers, New Turf* (New York: Macmillan, 1970).

28. James Paul Allen and Eugene Jones Turner, *We the People: An Atlas of American Ethnic Diversity* (New York: Macmillan, 1988).

29. AISES, the American Indian Science and Engineering Society, publishes an *Annual College Guide for American Indians* as well as a remarkable and informative quarterly, *Winds of Change* (Boulder, Colo.).

30. Donald Horowitz, "Making Moderation Pay: The Comparative Politics of Ethnic Conflict Management," in *Conflict and Peacemaking*, ed. Joseph Montville, 451–76; Ted Gurr, "Peoples Against States: Ethnopolitical Conflicts and the Changing World System," *International Studies Quarterly* 38 (1994): 347–77; Raimo Vayrynen, "Towards a Theory of Ethnic Conflicts and Their Resolution," Notre Dame, Joan B. Kroc Institute for International Peace Studies, Inaugural Lecture, 1994; J. Milton Yinger, *Ethnicity: Source of Strength? Source of Conflict?* (Albany: SUNY Press, 1994); and Arend Lijphart, "The Power Sharing Approach," in *Conflict and Peacemaking*, ed. Joseph Montville, 491–511.

31. E. Boulding, "Ethnic Separatism and World Development."

32. As part of the activities of the International Year of the Indigenous People of the World, the UN Center for Human Rights (Palais des Nations, Geneva) published a *List of Indigenous Organizations* in 1994.

## 9. Gaia, the Technosphere, and Development

1. The gaia hypothesis, that the Earth's living matter, air, oceans, and land surface form a complex system that can be seen as a single organism having the capacity to keep our planet a fit place for life, was first developed by James E. Lovelock in *Gaia, A New Look at Life on Earth* (New York: Oxford Univ. Press, 1979).

2. See, for example, S. Boyden, *Biohistory: The Interplay Between Human Society and the Biosphere,* Man and the Biosphere Series, vol. 8 (Paris: UNESCO and the Parthenon Publishing Group, 1992). See also *Global Change, Geographical Approaches,* ed. John R. Mather and Galina V. Sdasyuk (Tucson: Univ. of Arizona Press, 1991).

3. For an overview of the United States as a complex of bioregions, see the Bioregional Directory and Map, in *Raise the Stakes, The Planet Drum Review,* no. 24 (winter 1994/spring 1995), published by the Planet Drum Foundation, San Francisco, Calif.

4. See Mohamed Suliman, *Ecology, Politics, Violent Conflict* (London: Zed Books, 1999).

5. From *Webster's New Universal Unabridged Dictionary,* 2d ed., s.v. "economize."

6. *Dominance of the West over the Rest* (Penang, Malaysia: Just World Trust, 1995).

7. These perspectives can be found in Claude Alvares, *Decolonizing History: Technology and Culture in India, China, and the West, 1492 to the Present Day* (New York: Apex, 1991); also in Herb Addo, *Imperialism: the Permanent Stage of Capitalism* (Tokyo: UN Univ. Press, 1986).

8. The Ifa system is described by Claude Alvares in *Dominance of the West over the Rest,* 1–21.

9. This quotation is found in Alvares, *Decolonizing History,* 139.

10. These startling words are used by C. Cobb, T. Halstead, and J. Rowe in "If the GDP Is Up, Why Is America Down?" *Atlantic Monthly,* Oct. 1995.

11. See James H. Mittelman and Robert Johnston, "The Globalization of Organized Crime, the Courtesan State, and the Corruption of Civil Society," *Global Governance* 5, no. 1 (1999): 103–26.

12. Kenneth Boulding, *The Organizational Revolution, A Study in the Ethics of Economic Organization,* published for the Federal Council of the Churches of Christ in America (New York: Harper, 1953; rpt., Chicago: Quadrangle Books, 1968).

13. Donella H. Meadows, Dennis L. Meadows, Jørgen Randers, and William L. Behrens, *Limits to Growth* (New York: Universe, 1972) was published for the Club of Rome.

14. E. F. Schumacher, *Small Is Beautiful* (New York: Harper & Rowe, 1973).

15. *Rio, Reshaping the International Order,* a report to the club of Rome, by Jan Tinbergen, was published in English by E. P. Dutton, New York, in 1976.

16. The International Commission for the Study of Communication Problems, chaired by Sean MacBride, began work in 1974; its report, *Many Voices, One World,* was published in 1980 by UNESCO.

17. Brandt Commission, *North-South: A Programme for Survival* (London: Pan Books, 1980), and *Common Crisis North-South: Cooperation for World Recovery* |

(Cambridge, Mass.: MIT Press, 1983); Palme Commission, *Common Security, A Blueprint for Survival* (New York: Simon & Schuster, 1982); World Commission on Environment and Development (Brundtland Commission), *Our Common Future* (New York: Oxford Univ. Press, 1987).

18. Ester Boserup, *Women's Role in Economic Development* (New York: St. Martin's, 1970).

19. The UNDP has prepared *Human Development Reports* annually since 1990; they are published by Oxford University Press. UNICEF's annual reports on *The State of the World's Children* are also published by Oxford University Press, as was the 1995 *Progress of Nations*. UNRISD's report *States in Disarray: The Social Effects of Globalization* was published by Banson in London, 1995. The report of the Bled Seminar, *Ethical and Spiritual Dimensions of Social Progress*, is UN Publication E95IV.2.

20. *The Challenge to the South*, Report of the South Commission (New York: Oxford Univ. Press, 1990).

21. Herman E. Daly, *Beyond Growth* (Boston: Beacon, 1996).

22. The GPI, a valuable new measure of development, is fully described by the International Forum on Globalization in "The Genuine Progress Indicator: Summary of Data and Methodology," *Redefining Progress* (San Francisco: International Forum on Globalization, 1995).

23. This passage is from chapter 5 of David C. Korten, *When Corporations Rule the World* (West Hartford, Conn.: Kumarian, 1995).

24. Severyn Bruyn, *The Self-Governing Economy, A Vision for Society in the Twenty-first Century* (Ann Arbor: Univ. of Michigan Press, in press).

25. Note Jerry Mander and Edward Goldsmith, eds., *The Case against the Global Economy* (San Francisco: Sierra Club Books, 1996), especially part 4, "Steps toward Relocalization."

26. This 16-point version of the original 18 points of the Earth Charter is taken from the Draft Summary Report of Earth Charter Initiatives, 1998, published by the Earth Charter Drafting Committee, P.O. Box 648, Middlebury, VT 05753.

27. For more on these recommendations, see *Development Dialogue* Uppsala, Sweden: Dag Hammarskjöld Foundation no. 2 (1995), a special issue on Autonomous Development Funds.

28. Note that LETS is an acronym used for various nonmonetary trading systems.

29. "Microenterprise as a Worldwide Movement," by the Small Enterprise Education and Promotion Network associated with PACT, appeared in the December 1994 issue of their newsletter, *Nexus*. See also David B. Purman, "LETS Creates Community and Community Creates Peace" in *Peace Magazine*, May/June 1994, 16–19; and two special issues of *Yes! A Journal of Positive Future*: no. 2 (1996) on "Money: Print Your Own!" and no. 9 (1999) on "Economics as if Life Matters." Information on alternative economics can be found in the following books by Hazel Henderson: *Creating Alternative Futures* (West Hartford, Conn.: Kumarian, 1996), and *Paradigms in Progress* (Indianapolis, Ind.: Knowledge Systems, 1978).

30. Anita Anand, "Saving Trees, Saving Lives," chap. 25 in *Reclaim the Earth: Women Speak Out for Life on Earth*, ed. Leonia Caldicott and Stephanie Leland (London: Women's Press, 1983), 182–88.

31. Vandana Shiva, *Staying Alive: Women, Ecology and Development* (London: Zed Books, 1989).

32. Wangari Maathai and Maggie Jones, "Greening the Desert," chap. 13 in Caldicott and Leland, *Reclaim the Earth*.

33. See n. 1.

## 10. Information, Communication, and Learning

1. *Many Voices, One World*, report by the International Commission for the Study of Communication Problems (MacBride Commission) (Paris: UNESCO, 1980).

2. See UNESCO, *A Practical Guide to the World Decade for Cultural Development, 1988–97*. Paris: UNESCO, 1987.

3. This list is based on a summary from Howard Frederick, "Communication, Peace, and International Law," in *Communication and Culture in War and Peace*, ed. Colleen Roach (Newbury Park, Calif.: Sage, 1993), 238–41.

4. Reported in *Action*, a newsletter of the World Association for Christian Communication, no. 204, Mar. 1998.

5. See *Peace Review* 11, no. 1 (Mar. 1999), a special issue devoted to the theme of media and democratic action, for a thought-provoking overview of the issues involved in media activism.

6. See *Culture of Peace*, a newsletter published by UNESCO, no. 2 (Apr. 1997).

7. Dr. Elders's statement was quoted in the fall 1994 newsletter of the North Central Regional office of the American Friends Service Committee.

8. *National Television Violence Study*, vol. 3, *Executive Summary* (Univ. of California, Santa Barbara, 1998).

9. Note the report "Violence Against Women" in *Women in Action*, no. 1, 1998, published by ISIS from the Philippines.

10. *WETV News* is a newsletter published by WETV, the Global Access Television Network, from its office in Ottawa, Canada.

11. David Shenk, *Data Smog: Surviving the Information Glut* (San Francisco: Harper, 1997), 225.

12. David Abrams, *The Spell of the Sensuous* (New York and Toronto: Random House, 1996), 273.

13. United Nations, *The World Social Situation in the 1990s* (New York: United Nations, 1994), 9.

14. Arpanet is described by Vincent Mosco in "Communication and Information: Technology for War and Peace," in *Communication and Culture in War and Peace*, ed. Colleen Roach (Newbury Park, Calif.: Sage, 1993), 52.

15. Colleen Roach, ed., *Communication and Culture in War and Peace* (Newbury Park, Calif.: Sage, 1993).

16. Seth Shulman, *Owning the Future: Staking Claims on the Knowledge Frontier* (Boston: Houghton-Mifflin, 1999).

17. The quotation is from the program description of the International Online Training Program: *More Constructive Approaches to Intractable Conflict*, written by Guy and Heidi Burgess et al. at the University of Colorado Conflict Research Consortium.

18. This work by Johan Galtung has evolved into a book, *Peace by Peaceful Means* (Oslo: Peace Research Institute Oslo [PRIO], and Thousand Oaks, Calif.: Sage, 1996).

19. The Julian of Norwich website is maintained by Sister Julia Holloway, hermit of the Holy Family, from Montebene, Fiesole, Italy.

20. Omar Antar, "Creation of an Islamic Internet Consortium," from abstracts of papers presented at the conference on "Muslims and the Information Superhighway: Tools for the Twenty-first Century," sponsored by the Islamic Society of North America. Published in *Islamic Horizons*, May/June 1419/1998.

21. For glimpses into how the minds of scientists work in dealing with the concept of chaos, including particularly how clues are picked up from the natural world, read James Gleich, *Chaos: Making a New Science* (New York: Penguin, 1987).

22. John E. Young, *Global Network: Computers in a Sustainable Society*, Worldwatch Paper no. 115, 1993.

23. Note the article by Howard Schuman, Alex Inkeles, and David Smith, "Some Psychological Effects and Non-effects of Literacy in a New Nation," *Economic Development and Cultural Change* 16 (Oct. 1967). Note also *Literacy in Traditional Societies*, ed. Jack Goody (Cambridge: Cambridge Univ. Press, 1968).

24. See *World Social Situation* in the 1990s (New York: United Nations, 1994), chap. 8, "Education and Literacy." See also the UNICEF report *The State of the World's Children 1997* (Oxford: Oxford Univ. Press, 1997).

25. Salli Rasberry and Robert Greenway, *How to Start Your Own School . . . and Make a Book* (Freestone, Calif.: Freestone Publishing Co., 1970).

26. Archibald Shaw, "The Random Falls Idea," *School Executive*, Mar. 1956.

27. A rich source of information about self-schooling is Grace Llewellyn, *Teenage Liberation Handbook: How to Quit School and Get a Real Life and Education* (Eugene, Ore.: Lowry House. 1991).

28. The development of service learning in peace studies programs is described in *Teaching for Justice: Concepts and Models for Service-Learning in Peace Studies*, ed. Kathleen Maas Weigert and Robin J. Crews, a volume in the monograph series Service Learning in the Disciplines (Washington, D.C.: American Association for Higher Education, 1999).

29. The headquarters of the United Nations University is in Tokyo, Japan. The university's Annual Report summarizes the many and varied research projects in process and provides a listing of new publications and ongoing journals.

## 11. Demilitarization: The Hardest Challenge for States and Civil Society

1. Ruth Leger Sivard, *World Military and Social Expenditures 1996*, 16th ed. (Washington, D.C.: World Priorities Inc.), 7.

2. *Prevention and Management of Violent Conflicts: An International Directory* (Utrecht: European Platform for Conflict Prevention and Transformation, 1998), 43–44.

3. The World Order Models Project (WOMP) is an international group of scholars founded in the 1960s to explore world order in terms of the values of peace, economic and social justice, human rights, and environmental quality.

4. Alan Kay, *Locating Consensus for Democracy* (St. Augustine, Fla.: Americans Talk Issues Foundation, 1998). Another important recent study documents the actual impact of citizens' movements on U.S. arms control policy: Jeffrey W. Knopf, *Domestic Society and International Cooperation* (Cambridge: Cambridge Univ. Press, 1998).

5. Thoughtful analyses of the effect of the treaty-making process on the states involved include the following: Fanny Benedette and John L. Washburn, "Drafting the International Criminal Court Treaty," *Global Governance* 5, no. 1 (1999): 1–38; Linda Camp Keith, "The United Nations International Covenant on Civil and Political Rights," *Journal of Peace Research* 36, no. 1 (1999): 95–118.

6. Beseat Kiflé Sélassié, ed., *Consensus and Peace* (Paris: UNESCO, 1960).

7. See Elise Boulding, "The Intergovernmental Order," chap. 2 in *Building a Global Civic Culture* (Syracuse: Syracuse Univ. Press, 1988).

8. The quotation is from the explanatory blurb found on the last page of each issue of *Terra Viva*.

9. The UN University has its headquarters in Tokyo, with affiliated research institutes around the world. The University for Peace, also created by the UN General Assembly, is located in San José, Costa Rica.

10. See Erskine Childers and Brian Urquhart, "Renewing the United Nations System," *Development Dialogue*, no. 1 (1994) (a journal published by the Dag Hammarskjöld Foundation in Uppsala, Sweden); see also Childers and Urquhart's *A World in Need of Leadership: Tomorrow's United Nations* (Uppsala: Dag Hammarskjöld Foundation, 1996).

11. Written by an international team of scientists at a UNESCO conference at Seville in 1986, the Seville Statement on Violence addresses the myth that violence is inherent in human nature. "Biology does not condemn humanity to war," the scientists concluded, after reviewing data from the relevant physical and social sciences. Adopted by the General Conference of UNESCO in 1989, it has since been formally confirmed by many international scientific associations and widely disseminated to the general public. See *UNESCO and a Culture of Peace*, ed. David Adams (Paris: UNESCO, 1995).

12. *Nuclear-Weapon-Free Zones in the Twenty-first Century*, ed. Pericles Gasparin and Daiana Belinda Cipollone (Geneva: United Nations Institute for Disarmament Research, 1997).

13. See *International Peacekeeping* 3, no. 4 (1996): *The UN, Peace and Force*, a special issue, edited by Michael Pugh. Also note *International Peacekeeping* 5, nos. 2 and 3 (1998), and more recent issues.

14. These possibilities are further discussed by Elise Boulding and Jan Oberg in "UN Peacekeeping and NGO Peacebuilding: Towards Partnership," in *The Future of the UN System: Potential for the Twenty-first Century,* ed. Chadwick Alger (Tokyo: United Nations Univ. Press, 1998), 127–54).

15. The year 2000 by the Jewish calendar would be the year 5761; by the Muslim calendar, the year 1420.

16. Although there is widespread debate about whether the new millennium actually begins in 2000 or 2001, most activist groups are using the year 2000 as the symbolic beginning of the third millennium.

17. The *Pugwash Newsletter,* a quarterly publication, has for thirty-five years reported on the numerous special meetings and annual conferences in which relevant research on weapons and regulatory systems is discussed. The Pugwash organization has offices in Geneva, Rome, London, and Cambridge.

18. The following references give an idea of what the field of peace research includes. (1) Arms races: Lewis Richardson, *Arms and Insecurity: A Mathematical Study of the Causes and Origins of War* (Pittsburgh: Boxwood, 1960). (2) The instability of deterrence: Raoul Naroll et al., *Military Deterrence in History* (Albany: SUNY Press, 1974). (3) Integrative systems: Kenneth Boulding, *Three Faces of Power* (Newbury Park, Calif.: Sage, 1989). (4) Positive vs. negative peace: Johan Galtung, "Violence, Peace and Peace Research," *Journal of Peace Research* 6, 3 (1969): 67–92. (5) Strategic nonviolence: Gene Sharp, *The Politics of Nonviolent Action* (Boston: Porter Sargent, 1973). (6) Nonoffensive defense: Bjorn Moller, editor, *NOD and Conversion* newsletter, University of Copenhagen. (7) Ecological security: Patricia Mische, "Security through Defending the Environment," in *New Agendas for Peace Research,* ed. Elise Boulding (Boulder, Colo.: Lynne Rienner, 1992). (8) Conflict resolution: Louis Kriesberg, *Constructive Conflicts: From Escalation to Resolution* (Boulder, Colo.: Rowman & Littlefield, 1998); Johan Galtung, *Peace by Peaceful Means* (Oslo: Peace Research Institute Oslo [PRIO], 1996); Hugh Miall, Oliver Ramsbotham, and Tom Woodhouse, *Contemporary Conflict Resolution* (Cambridge, U.K.: Polity Press, 1999).

19. An early groundbreaking publication was Scilla Elworthy McLean, ed., *How Nuclear Weapons Decisions Are Made* (London: Macmillan, 1986).

20. Peace Brigades International publishes a newsletter with reports of Brigade activities from 5 Caledonia Road, London N19DX, England.

21. See n. 2. The Center also published *People Building Peace: 35 Inspiring Stories from Around the World* (Utrecht: European Center for Conflict Prevention, 1999).

22. Johan Galtung's *Conflict Transformation by Peaceful Means* (New York: United Nations, 1998) describes the work of the Transcend network.

23. The Hague Appeal Youth Programme can be reached c/o IPB, 41 rue de Zurich, 1201 Geneva, Switzerland.

24. An account of this pilgrimage by Rusty Wright, entitled "Christians Retrace Crusaders' Steps," appeared in *Christianity Today*, Oct. 7, 1996. Another account by Rabia Harris of the Muslim Peace Fellowship appeared in *Fellowship*, September-October 1999, 24.

## 12. A Possible Future

1. Quoted in Herman E. Daly, *Beyond Growth* (Boston: Beacon, 1996), 104.

2. See the following publications: International Federation of Red Cross and Red Crescent Societies, *World Disasters Report, 1998* (New York: Oxford Univ. Press, 1998); *State of the World, 1999*, Worldwatch Institute Report (New York: Norton, 1999).

3. Such workshops were described in Joanna Macy and Molly Brown, *Coming Back to Life: Practices to Reconnect Our Lives, Our World* (Gabriola Island, B.C., Canada: New Society, 1998).

4. "Top 10 Trends for 1997 as Predicted by the Trends Research Institute in Rhinebeck, NY," *Detroit News*, Dec. 29, 1996, A-10, quoted in David Korten, *The Post-Corporate World: Life After Capitalism* (West Hartford, Conn.: Kumarian, 1999).

5. Korten, *Post-Corporate World*, 213.

6. Peace News (London), no. 2433 (Jan. 1999): 5.

7. Note Gary Gardner and Payal Sampat, *Mind Over Matter: Recasting the Role of Materials in Our Lives*, Worldwatch Paper no. 144, Dec. 1998.

8. Note Wolfgang Auckerman, *End of the Road: From World Car Crisis to Sustainable Transportation* (Post Mills, Vt.: Chelsea Green, 1991).

9. Slow Food in 1999 could be accessed on the Internet (www.slowfood.com).

10. Joe Dominguez and Vicki Robin, *Your Money or Your Life* (New York: Penguin, 1992).

11. Herman Daly, *Beyond Growth*. A somewhat different but related scenario is developed by Alan Atkisson in *Believing Cassandra* (White River Junction, Vt.: Chelsea Green, 1999).

12. This scenario is based on suggestions by Herman Daly, *Beyond Growth*, esp. chap. 5.

13. The Binding Triad was a proposal first developed by Richard Hudson, director of the Center for War/Peace Studies, New York, in the 1970s.

14. Early examples of such developments appeared in Martha Minow, *Between Vengeance and Forgiveness* (Boston: Beacon Press, 1998), and also in Rupert Ross, *Returning to the Teachings* (Toronto, Canada: Penguin Books, 1996).

15. See *Conflict Trends*, a new publication by ACCORD, the African Center for the Constructive Resolution of Disputes, in Durban, South Africa. Note also *Traditional Cures for Modern Conflicts: African Conflict Medicine*, ed. I William Zartman (Boulder, Colo.: Lynne Rienner, 1999).

16. Examples of the new thinking are found in Richard Holloway, "NGOs: Losing the High Moral Ground," *Transnational Associations*, May 1998, 233–48, and in Mary Anderson, *Do No Harm* (Boulder, Colo.: Lynne Rienner Publishers, 1999).

17. "Coulleurs Lomé: Giving a Voice to Peasant Organizations," in *Interdependent*, no. 65 (Mar. 1998): 4.

18. For an example of these networks, see "International Women's Day for Peace and Disarmament, May 24, 1999," a joint publication of the International Fellowship of Reconciliation and the International Peace Bureau. Also note Frank Wilmer, *The Indigenous Voice in World Politics* (Newbury Park, Calif.: Sage, 1993), and the steady stream of publications from the International Work Group for Indigenous Affairs, Copenhagen.

19. See *Engaged Buddhism, Buddhist Liberation Movements in Asia*, ed. Christopher Queen and Sallie King (Albany: SUNY Press, 1966).

20. See Jack Forbes, "Native Nations in the United Nations," in *News from Indian Country*, Mid-May 1998, 15A.

21. In the 1990s the newsletter of the International Movement for a Just World was published in Petaling Jaya, Malaysia.

22. In the 1990s the *Muslim World*, the weekly newsletter of the Muslim NGO the Motamar, was published in Karachi, Pakistan.

23. Examples of PAPSL are described in *Choices: The Human Development Magazine*, published by the UN Development Program, July 1998, 6–11, in an article entitled, "Local Know-How" by Kristen Helmore.

24. See Michael Shuman, *Towards a Global Village: International Community Development Initiatives* (Boulder, Colo.: Pluto Press, 1994).

25. Global Action Plan is described in Nadia McLaren, "Citizens Initiatives on Sustainable Consumption," *Transnational Associations*, Mar. 1998, 130–47.

26. For examples, see *In Context*, spring 1995, "Creating a Future We Can Live With"; also, any issue of *Plain*, published by the Center for Plain Living, Barnesville, Ohio; and *Countryside* 82, no. 4 (July-August 1998), "Preview of Homesteading in the Twenty-first Century."

27. Note UN Development Program, *Urban Agriculture* (New York: United Nations, 1996).

28. See Robert Swann and Susan Witt, *Local Currencies: Catalysts for Sustainable Regional Economies*, based on the Eighth Annual E. F. Schumacher Lecture, E. F. Schumacher Society (Great Barrington, Mass.: 1995). Also note David Pergman, "LETS Creates Community and Community Creates Peace," in the Canadian journal *Peace*, May-June 1994.

29. Note Howard Zehr, *Changing Lenses: A New Focus for Crime and Justice* (Scottdale, Pa.: Herald, 1990).

30. Note Marshall Sahlin, *Stone Age Economics* (Chicago: Aldine-Atherton, 1972); also, Paul Shepard, *The Tender Carnivore and the Sacred Game* (New York: Scribner, 1973).

# Bibliography

Abrams, David. *The Spell of the Sensuous*. New York and Toronto: Random House, 1996.

Adams, David, ed. *The Seville Statement on Violence: Preparing the Ground for the Construction of Peace*. Paris: UNESCO, 1991.

———. *UNESCO and a Culture of Peace*. Paris: UNESCO, 1995.

Addams, Jane. *Peace and Bread in Time of War*. 1922. Reprint, New York: Garland, 1972.

Addams, Jane, Emily G. Balch, and Alice Hamilton. *Women at The Hague*. 1915. Reprint, New York: Garland, 1972.

Addo, Herb. *Imperialism: The Permanent Stage of Capitalism*. Tokyo: United Nations Univ. Press, 1986.

Ajami, Fouad. *The Dream Palace of the Arabs*. New York: Pantheon, 1998.

Al-Bakhit, M. A., L. Bazin, and S. M. Cissoko, eds. *From the Seventh to the Sixteenth Century*. Vol. 4 of *History of Humanity*. Paris: UNESCO and Routledge, 1998.

Alger, Chadwick, ed. *The Future of the UN System: Potential for the Twenty-first Century*. Tokyo: United Nations Univ. Press, 1998.

Allen, James Paul, and Eugene Jones Turner. *We the People: An Atlas of American Ethnic Diversity*. New York: Macmillan, 1988.

Alvares, Claude. *Decolonizing History: Technology and Culture in India, China, and the West, 1492 to the Present Day*. New York: Apex, 1991.

Anand, Anita. "Saving Trees, Saving Lives." In *Reclaim the Earth: Women Speak Out for Life on Earth*, edited by Leonia Caldicott and Stephanie Leland, 182–88. London: Women's Press, 1983.

Anderson, Mary. *Do No Harm*. Boulder, Colo.: Lynne Rienner, 1999.

Andre, Rae. *Homemakers: The Forgotten Workers*. Chicago: Univ. of Chicago Press, 1981.

Ardrey, Robert. *African Genesis*. London: Collins, 1962.

Aries, Philippe. *Centuries of Childhood*. Translated by Robert Baldick. New York: Knopf, 1962.

Atkisson, Alan. *Believing Cassandra*. White River Junction, Vt.: Chelsea Green, 1999.

Auckerman, Wolfgang. *End of the Road: From World Car Crisis to Sustainable Transportation*. White River Junction, Vt.: Chelsea Green, 1991.

Barkun, Michael. *Law Without Sanctions: Order in Primitive Societies and the World Community.* New Haven, Conn.: Yale Univ. Press, 1968.

Bateson, Mary Catherine. *With a Daughter's Eye.* New York: Harper, 1984.

Benedette, Fanny, and John L. Washburn. "Drafting the International Criminal Court Treaty." *Global Governance* 5, no. 1 (1999): 1–38.

Benedict, Ruth. *Patterns of Culture.* Boston: Houghton-Mifflin, 1959.

Berger, Maurice, Brian Wallis, and Simon Watson, eds. *Constructing Masculinity.* New York and London: Routledge, 1995.

Bernard, Jessie. *Women, Wives, Mothers.* Chicago: Aldine, 1975.

Betcher, R. William, and William S. Pollack. *In a Time of Fallen Heroes: The Re-creation of Masculinity.* New York: Guilford, 1993.

Black, Naomi. *Social Feminism.* Ithaca, N.Y.: Cornell Univ. Press, 1989.

Block, Asher. *The Jewish Tradition of Peace.* Nyack, N.Y.: Fellowship, 1953.

Blume, Francine. "Peace Zones: Examplars and Potential," *The Acorn. Journal of Gandhi-King Society* (spring/summer 1993).

Bly, Robert. *Iron John.* New York: Addison-Wesley, 1990.

Boff, Leonardo. *The Base Communities Reinvent the Church.* Maryknoll, N.Y.: Orbis, 1986.

Boguslaw, Robert. *The New Utopians: A Study of System Design and Social Change.* Englewood Cliffs, N.J.: Prentice-Hall, 1965.

Bok, Sissela. *Alva Myrdal: A Daughter's Memoir.* Reading, Pa.: Addison-Wesley, 1991.

Bondurant, Joan V. *Conquest of Violence.* Berkeley, Calif.: Univ. of California Press, 1971.

Bonner, Edwin. *William Penn's "Holy Experiment": The Founding of Pennsylvania, 1681–1701.* Philadelphia: Temple Univ. Press, 1962.

Bonta, Bruce D. *Peaceful Peoples: An Annotated Bibliography.* Metuchen, N.J.: Scarecrow, 1993.

Borkenau, Franz. *The Spanish Cockpit.* Ann Arbor: Univ. of Michigan Press, 1963.

Borsodi, Ralph. *Flight from the City.* New York: Harper & Row, 1933.

Boserup, Ester. *Women's Role in Economic Development.* New York: St. Martin's, 1970.

Boulding, Elise. *Building a Global Civic Culture.* Syracuse, N.Y.: Syracuse Univ. Press, 1988.

———. "Ethnicity and New Constitutive Orders: An Approach to Peace in the Twenty-first Century." In *From Chaos to Order.* Vol. 1 of *Crisis and Renaissance of the World Society,* edited by Hisakazu Usui and Takeo Uchida. Tokyo: Yushindo Publishers, 1990.

——— "Ethnic Separatism and World Development." In *Research in Social Movements, Conflicts and Change,* edited by Louis Kriesberg, 259–81. Greenwich, Conn.: JAI Press, 1979.

———. "Feminist Inventions in the Art of Peacemaking." *Peace and Change* 20, no. 4 (1995): 408–38.

———. "The Nurturance of Adults by Children in Family Settings." In *Research in the Interweave of Social Roles*, edited by Helen Lopata, 167–89. Greenwich, Conn.: JAI Press, 1980.

———. *One Small Plot of Heaven: Reflections of a Quaker Sociologist on Family Life*. Wallingford, Pa.: Pendle Hill, 1989.

———. "Peace Behaviors in Various Societies." In *From a Culture of Violence to a Culture of Peace*, 31–54. Paris: UNESCO, 1996.

———. "Peace Education as Peace Development." *Transnational Associations* 6 (1987): 322–26.

———. "Two Cultures of Religion as Obstacles to Peace." *Zygon* 21, no. 4 (1986): 501–17.

———. *The Underside of History: A View of Women Through Time*. Rev. ed. 2 vols. Newbury Park, Calif.: Sage, 1992.

Boulding, Elise, ed. *Building Peace in the Middle East*. Boulder, Colo.: Lynne Rienner, 1994.

———. *New Agendas for Peace Research*. Boulder, Colo.: Lynne Rienner, 1992.

Boulding, Elise, and Kenneth Boulding. *The Future: Images and Processes*. Thousand Oaks, Calif.: Sage, 1995.

Boulding, Kenneth. *Conflict and Defense. A General Theory*. New York: Harper, 1962.

———. *Ecodynamics: A New Theory of Societal Evolution*. Beverly Hills, Calif.: Sage, 1981.

———. *Human Betterment*. Beverly Hills, Calif.: Sage, 1985.

———. *The Economics of Peace*. New York: Prentice-Hall, 1945.

———. *The Organizational Revolution, A Study in the Ethics of Economic Organization*. New York: Harper, 1953. Reprint, Chicago: Quadrangle, 1968.

———. *Stable Peace*. Austin: Univ. of Texas Press, 1978.

———. *Three Faces of Power*. Newbury Park, Calif.: Sage, 1989.

———. *The World as a Total System*. Beverly Hills, Calif.: Sage, 1985

Boyden, S. *Biohistory: The Interplay Between Human Society and the Biosphere*. Man and the Biosphere Series, vol. 8. Paris: UNESCO and the Parthenon Publishing Group, 1992.

Bramson, Leon, and George Goethals, eds. *War: Studies from Psychology, Sociology and Anthropology*. New York: Basic Books, 1968.

Bratton, Michael. "Beyond the State: Civil Society and Associational Life in Africa." *Transnational Associations* 3 (May–June 1991): 130–40.

Briggs, Jean. *Never in Anger: Portrait of an Eskimo Family*. Cambridge, Mass.: Harvard Univ. Press, 1971.

———. "The Origins of Nonviolence: Inuit Management of Aggression." In *Learning Non-Aggression: The Experience of the Non-Literate Societies*, edited by Ashley Montagu, 54–93. New York: Oxford Univ. Press, 1978.

Brock-Utne, Birgit. *Educating for Peace: A Feminist Perspective*. New York: Pergamon, 1985.

————. *Feminist Perspectives on Peace and Peace Education.* New York: Pergamon, 1989.

Bruyn, Severyn. *The Self-Governing Economy, A Vision for Society in the Twenty-first Century.* Ann Arbor: Univ. of Michigan Press, in press.

Buber, Martin. *Israel and the World.* New York: Schocken, 1948.

————. *Paths in Utopia.* Boston: Beacon, 1958.

Buchbinder, David. *Performance Anxieties: Reproducing Masculinity.* Sydney: Allen & Unwin, 1998.

Burton, John. *Conflict and Communication: The Use of Controlled Communication in International Relations.* London: Macmillan, 1969.

Bussey, Gertrude, and Margaret Tims. *Women's International League for Peace and Freedom, 1915–1965: A Record of Fifty Years' Work.* London: Allen & Unwin, 1965.

Cabezon, Jose Ignacio. "Buddhist Principles in the Tibetan Liberation Movement." In *Engaged Buddhism,* edited by Christopher Queen and Sallie King, 295–320. Albany, N.Y.: SUNY Press, 1996.

Caldicott, Leonia, and Stephanie Leland, eds. *Reclaim the Earth: Women Speak Out for Life on Earth.* London: Women's Press, 1983.

Carroll, Berenice A. "Peace Research: The Cult of Power." *Journal of Conflict Resolution* 14, no. 4 (1972): 586–615.

Carroll, Berenice A., Clinton F. Fink, and Jane E. Mohraz. *Peace and War: A Guide to Bibliographies.* Santa Barbara, Calif.: ABC-Clio, 1983.

Chatfield, Charles. *The American Peace Movement: Ideals and Activism.* New York: Twayne, 1992.

Chatfield, Charles, and Peter van der Dungen. *Peace Movements and Political Cultures.* Knoxville: Univ. of Tennessee Press, 1988.

Chattopadhyaya, Kamaladevi. *Indian Women's Battle for Freedom.* New Delhi: Abhinav, 1983.

————. *Inner Recesses, Outer Spaces: Memoirs.* New Delhi: Navrang, 1986.

Childers, Erskine, and Brian Urquhart. "Renewing the United Nations System." *Development Dialogue,* no. 1 (1994) (Dag Hammarskjöld Foundation).

————. *A World in Need of Leadership: Tomorrow's United Nations.* Uppsala: Dag Hammarskjöld Foundation, 1996.

Clark, Lance. *Early Warning of Refugee Flows.* Washington, D.C.: Refugee Policy Group, 1989.

Cohn, Norman. *The Pursuit of the Millennium.* New York: Oxford Univ. Press, 1957.

Coles, Robert. *The Spiritual Life of Children.* Boston: Houghton-Mifflin, 1990.

Colfax, David, and Micki Colfax. *Homeschooling for Excellence.* New York: Warner, 1988.

*Communities Directory: A Guide to Cooperative Living.* Langley, Wash.: Fellowship for International Community, 1995.

Cooper, Sandi E. *Patriotic Pacifism: Waging War on War in Europe, 1815–1914.* Oxford: Oxford Univ. Press, 1991.

Cotta, Sergio. *Why Violence?* Translated by Giovanni Gullace. Gainesville: Univ. of Florida Press, 1985.

Creasy, E. S. *Fifteen Decisive Battles of the World: From Marathon to Waterloo.* New York: Dorset, 1987.

Crow, Ralph E., Philip Grant, and Saad E. Ibrahim, eds. *Arab Nonviolent Political Struggle in the Middle East.* Boulder, Colo.: Lynne Rienner, 1990.

Curle, Adam. *Making Peace.* London: Tavistock, 1971.

Daly, Herman E. *Beyond Growth.* Boston: Beacon, 1996.

Dart, Martha. *Marjorie Sykes, Quaker Gandhian.* Birmingham, U.K.: Sessions Book Trust in association with Woodbrook College, 1993.

Deloria, Vine. *For We Talk, You Listen: New Timbers, New Turf.* New York: Macmillan, 1970.

Deming, Barbara. *Revolution and Equilibrium.* New York: Grossman, 1971.

Deng, Frances. "The Identity Factor in the Sudanese Conflict." In *Conflict and Peacemaking in Multi-Ethnic Societies,* edited by Joseph Montville, 343–62. Lexington, Mass.: Heath, 1989.

Denniston, Derek. "High Priorities: Conserving Mountain Ecosystems and Cultures." *Worldwatch Paper* 123 (Feb. 1995): 50–51.

de Waal, Frans. *Good Natured.* Cambridge, Mass.: Harvard Univ. Press, 1996.

Dinnerstein, Dorothy. *The Mermaid and the Minotaur.* New York: Harper & Row, 1976.

*Dominance of the West over the Rest.* Penang, Malaysia: Just World Trust, 1995.

Dominguez, Joe, and Vicki Robin. *Your Money or Your Life.* New York: Penguin, 1992.

Dotto, Lydia. *Planet Earth in Jeopardy: Environmental Consequences of Nuclear War.* New York: Wiley, 1986.

Doyle, James. *The Male Experience.* New York: McGraw-Hill, 1983.

Dumas, Lloyd. *Overburdened Economy.* Berkeley: Univ. of California Press, 1986.

Easwaran, Eknath. *A Man to Match His Mountains.* Petaluma, Calif.: Nilgiri, 1984.

Eibl-Eibesfeldt, Irennaus. *Love and Hate.* New York: Holt, Rinehart and Winston, 1972.

Eisler, Riane. *The Chalice and the Blade.* New York: Harper, 1987.

Ember, Carol R., and Melvin Ember. "War, Socialization and Interpersonal Violence: A Cross-Cultural Study," *Journal of Conflict Resolution* 38, no. 4 (1994): 620–46.

Ettorre, E. M. *Lesbians, Women and Society.* London: Routledge and Kegan Paul, 1980.

European Center for Conflict Prevention. *People Building Peace: Thirty-five Inspiring Stories from Around the World.* Utrecht: European Center for Conflict Prevention, 1999.

European Platform for Conflict Prevention and Transformation. *Prevention and Management of Violent Conflicts: An International Directory.* Utrecht: European Platform for Conflict Prevention and Transformation, 1998.

Eversoll, Deanna. "A Two-Generational View of Fathering," *Family Coordinator* 28, no. 4 (1979): 503–7.

Falk, Richard, Robert Johansen, and Samuel Kim, eds. *The Constitutional Foundations of World Peace.* Albany, N.Y.: SUNY Press, 1993.

Fanon, Franz. *The Wretched of the Earth.* New York: Grove, 1963.

Farrell, Warren. *The Liberated Man: Beyond Masculinity.* New York: Random House, 1974.

———. *The Manipulated Man.* Berkeley, Calif.: Berkeley Publishing Group, 1986.

Fellman, Gordon. *Rambo and the Dalai Lama: The Compulsion to Win and Its Threat to Human Survival.* Albany, N.Y.: SUNY Press, 1998.

Fink, Clinton, and Elise Boulding, eds. "Peace Research in Transition: A Symposium," a special issue of *Journal of Conflict Resolution* 16, no. 4 (1972).

Forbes, Jack. "Native Nations in the United Nations." *News from Indian Country,* Mid-May 1998, 15A.

Fosteau, Marac F. *Male Machine.* New York: McGraw-Hill, 1974.

Fourier, Charles. *Theory of Social Organization.* New York: C. P. Somerby, 1876.

Frederick, Howard. "Communication, Peace, and International Law." In *Communication and Culture in War and Peace,* edited by Colleen Roach, 238–41. Newbury Park, Calif.: Sage, 1993.

Friesen, Duane. Christian Peacemaking and International Conflict. Scottdale, Pa.: Herald, 1986.

Galtung, Johan. *Peace by Peaceful Means.* Oslo: Peace Research Institute Oslo [PRIO], 1996; and Thousand Oaks, Calif.: Sage, 1996.

———. *Peace: Research, Education, Action.* Vol. 1 of *Essays in Peace Research.* Copenhagen: Ejlers Christian, 1975.

———. "Violence, Peace and Peace Research." *Journal of Peace Research* 6, no. 3 (1969): 67–92.

Gandhi, Mohandas. *Nonviolence in Peace and War.* 1942. Reprint, New York: Garland, 1971.

Gardner, Gary, and Payal Sampat. *Mind Over Matter: Recasting the Role of Materials in Our Lives.* Worldwatch Paper no. 144, Dec. 1998.

Garthoff, R. L. *The Great Transition: American-Soviet Relations and the End of the Cold War.* Washington, D.C.: Brookings Institution, 1994.

Gaskin, Stephen. *Rendered Infamous.* Summertown, Tenn.: Book Publishing Co., 1982.

Gasparin, Pericles and Daiana Belinda Cipollone, ed. *Nuclear-Weapon-Free Zones in the 21st Century.* Geneva: United Nations Institute for Disarmament Research, 1997.

Gerth, Hans, and C. Wright Mills. *From Max Weber: Essays in Sociology.* New York: Oxford Univ. Press, 1946.

Gibson, James William. *Warrior Dreams: Violence and Manhood in Post-Vietnam America.* New York: Hill & Wang, 1994.

Gilbert, Geoff. "The Council of Europe and Minority Rights." *Human Rights Quarterly* 18, no. 1 (1996).

Gilman, Charlotte Perkins. *Herland.* New York: Pantheon, 1979.

Gleick, James. *Chaos: Making a New Science.* New York: Penguin, 1987.

Goldman, Irving. "The Zuni Indians of New Mexico." In *Cooperation and Competition among Primitive Peoples,* edited by Margaret Mead, 313–53. New York: McGraw-Hill, 1937.

Goody, Jack, ed. *Literacy in Traditional Societies.* Cambridge: Cambridge Univ. Press, 1968.

Goonatilake, Susantha. "Future of Asian Cultures: Between Localization and Globalization." In *The Futures of Asian Cultures,* edited by Eleonora Masini, 131–59. Bangkok: UNESCO Office for Asia and the Pacific, 1993.

Gouldner, Alvin. "The Norm of Reciprocity." *American Sociological Review* 25 (1960): 161–78.

Greback, Kerstin, Ragnhild Greek, and Ann-Cathrin Jarl, eds. *The Great Peace Journey.* Uppsala: Samhall Upsam, 1989.

Grossman, F. W. Pollack, and E. Golding. "Fathers and Children: Predicting the Quality and Quantity of Fathering." *Developmental Psychology* 24 (1988): 82–91.

Grun, Bernard. *The Timetables of History: A Horizontal Linkage of People and Events.* New York: Simon & Schuster, 1975. (Based on Werner Stein, *Kulturfahrplan,* 1946.)

Gurr, Ted. "Peoples Against States: Ethnopolitical Conflicts and the Changing World System," *International Studies Quarterly* 38 (1994): 347–77.

Gurr, Ted, and James Scarritt. "Minorities' Rights at Risk: A Global Survey," *Human Rights Quarterly* 11 (1989): 375.

Hanh, Thich Nhat. *Love in Action.* Berkeley, Calif.: Parallax, 1993.

Harford, Barbara, and Sarah Hopkins, eds. *Greenham Common: Women at the Wire.* London: Women's Press, 1984.

Harrison, Selig. "Ethnic Conflict in Pakistan: The Boluch, Pashtuns, and Sundhis." In *Conflict and Peacemaking in Multi-Ethnic Societies,* edited by Joseph Montville, 301–26. Lexington, Mass.: Heath, 1989.

Hart, Roger. *Children's Experience of Place.* New York: Irvington, 1979.

Hass, Hans. *The Human Animal: The Mystery of Man's Behavior.* New York: G. P. Putnam's Sons, 1970.

Hawkley, Louise, and James C. Juhnke, eds. *Nonviolent America: History Through the Eyes of Peace.* North Newton, Kans.: Bethel College, 1993.

Hechter, Michael. *Internal Colonialism: The Celtic Fringe in British National Development, 1536–1966.* Berkeley: Univ. of California Press, 1975.

Hedemann, Ed, and Ruth Benn. *War Tax Resistance.* New York: War Resisters International, 1994.

Heisler, Martin. "Hyphenating Belgium: Changing State and Regime to Cope with Cultural Division." In *Conflict and Peacemaking in Multi-Ethnic Societies*, edited by Joseph Montville, 177–96. Lexington, Mass.: Heath, 1989.

Helmore, Kristen. "Local Know-How." *Choices: The Human Development Magazine* (UN Development Program), July 1998.

Henderson, Hazel. *Creating Alternative Futures*. West Hartford, Conn.: Kumarian, 1996.

———. *Paradigms in Progress*. Indianapolis, Ind.: Knowledge Systems, 1978.

Hobsbawn, Eric J. *The Age of Extremes: A History of the World 1941–1991*. New York: Pantheon, 1994.

Holloway, Richard. "NGOs: Losing the High Moral Ground." *Transnational Associations*, May 1998: 233–48.

Holm, Jeanne. *Women in the Military: An Unfinished Revolution*. Novato, Calif.: Presidio, 1982.

Horowitz, Donald. "Making Moderation Pay: The Comparative Politics of Ethnic Conflict Management." In *Conflict and Peacemaking in Multi-Ethnic Societies*, edited by Joseph Montville, 451–76. Lexington, Mass.: Heath, 1989.

Huizinga, Johan. *Homo Ludens: A Study of the Play Element in Culture*. Boston: Beacon, 1955.

Hungu, Sam Noluk. "Fragments of a Democracy: Reflections on Class and Politics in Nigeria." *Third World Quarterly* 12, no. 1 (1990): 86–115.

Independent Commission on Disarmament and Security Issues (Palme Commission). *Common Security: A Blueprint for Survival*. New York: Simon & Schuster, 1982.

Independent Commission on International Development Issues (Brandt Commission). *Common Crisis North-South: Cooperation for World Recovery*. Cambridge, Mass.: MIT Press, 1983.

———. *North-South: A Programme for Survival*. London: Pan Books, 1980.

Infield, Henrik F. *Cooperative Communities at Work*. London: Kegan Paul, 1947.

Institute for Defense and Disarmament Studies. *1988–89 Peace Resource Book: A Comprehensive Guide to Issues, Groups, and Literature*. Cambridge, Mass.: Ballinger, 1988.

International Commission for the Study of Communication Problems (MacBride Commission). *Many Voices, One World*. London: Kogan, 1980.

International Federation of Red Cross and Red Crescent Societies. *World Disasters Report, 1998*. New York: Oxford Univ. Press, 1998.

International Forum on Globalization. "The Genuine Progress Indicator: Summary of Data and Methodology." In *Redefining Progress*. San Francisco: International Forum on Globalization, 1995.

Isaacs, Susan. *Intellectual Growth in Young Children.* London: Routledge & Kegan Paul, 1930.

Jaimes, M. Annette, ed. *The State of Native America: Genocide, Colonization and Resistance.* Boston, Mass.: South End, 1992.

James, William. "The Moral Equivalent of War." In *War: Studies from Psychology, Sociology and Anthropology,* edited by Leon Bramsos and George Goethals, 21–31. New York: Basic Books, 1968.

Jergen, Mary Evelyn. *Global Peace Service.* Cincinnati, Ohio: Sisters of Notre Dame, 1993.

Juhnke, James. *Vision, Doctrine, War: Mennonite Identity and Organization in America,* 3 vols. Scottdale, Pa.: Herald, 1986.

Kasfir, Nelson. "Peacemaking and Social Cleavages in Sudan." In *Conflict and Peacemaking in Multi-Ethnic Societies,* edited by Joseph Montville, 363–88. Lexington, Mass.: Heath, 1989.

Kay, Alan. *Locating Consensus for Democracy.* St. Augustine, Fla.: Americans Talk Issues Foundation, 1998.

Keeley, Lawrence. *War Before Civilization.* New York: Oxford Univ. Press, 1996.

Keith, Linda Camp. "The United Nations International Covenant on Civil and Political Rights." *Journal of Peace Research* 36, no. 1 (1999): 95–118.

Keller, Evelyn F. *A Feeling for the Organism: Life and Work of Barbara McClintock.* New York and San Francisco: W. H. Freeman, 1983.

Kellert, Stephen, and Edward Wilson. *The Biophilia Hypothesis.* Washington, D.C.: Island Press, 1993.

Kelly, Petra K. *Nonviolence Speaks to Power.* Honolulu: Univ. of Hawaii Press, 1992.

Kelman, Herbert. *International Behavior.* New York: Holt, Rinehart & Winston, 1965.

Kicza, John. *The Indian in Latin American History: Resistance, Resilience, and Acculturation.* New York: Scholarly Resources, 1993.

Kimmel, Michael S., ed. *The Politics of Manhood.* Philadelphia: Temple Univ. Press, 1995.

Kinkade, Kathleen. *A Walden Two Experiment: The First Five Years of Twin Oaks Community.* New York: Morrow, 1973.

Klare, Michael, ed. *Peace and World Society Studies: A Curriculum Guide,* 6th ed. Boulder, Colo.: Westview, 1994.

Knopf, Jeffrey W. *Domestic Society and International Cooperation.* Cambridge: Cambridge Univ. Press, 1998.

Kodama, Katsuya, and Unto Vesa, eds. *Towards a Comparative Analysis of Peace Movements.* Aldershot, Hants, U.K.: Dartmouth Publishing Group, 1990.

Korten, David C. *The Post-Corporate World: Life After Capitalism.* West Hartford, Conn.: Kumarian, 1999.

————. *When Corporations Rule the World.* West Hartford, Conn.: Kumarian, 1995.

Kramer, Samuel N. *History Begins at Sumer.* New York: Doubleday Anchor, 1959.

Kriesberg, Louis. *Constructive Conflicts: From Escalation to Resolution.* Boulder, Colo.: Rowman & Littlefield, 1998.

Kriesberg, Louis, ed. *Research in Social Movements, Conflicts and Change.* Greenwich, Conn.: JAI Press, 1979.

Kriesberg, Louis, Terrell Northrup, and Stuart Thorson, eds. *Intractable Conflicts and Their Transformation.* Syracuse, N.Y.: Syracuse Univ. Press, 1989.

Kropotkin, Peter. *The Conquest of Bread.* New York: New York Univ. Press, 1972.

Kumar, Mahendra. *Nonviolence: Contemporary Issues and Challenges.* New Delhi: Gandhi Peace Foundation, 1994.

Kupers, Terry Allen. *Revisioning Men's Lives: Gender, Intimacy, and Power.* New York: Guilford, 1993.

Kyi, Aung San Suu. *The Political Legacy of Aung San.* Ithaca, N.Y.: Southeast Asia Program, Cornell University, 1972.

Lakey, George. *Powerful Peacemaking: A Strategy for a Living Revolution.* Philadelphia: New Society, 1987.

Lannoy, Richard. *The Speaking Tree: A Study of Indian Culture and Society.* London: Oxford Univ. Press, 1971.

Lasky, Melvin J. *Utopia and Revolution.* Chicago: Univ. of Chicago Press, 1976.

Lebow, R. N., and J. G. Stein. *We All Lost the Cold War.* Princeton, N.J.: Princeton Univ. Press, 1994.

Lederach, John Paul. *Building Peace: Sustainable Reconciliation in Divided Societies.* Washington, D.C.: U.S. Institute of Peace, 1997.

————. *Preparing for Peace: Conflict Transformation Across Cultures.* Syracuse, N.Y.: Syracuse Univ. Press, 1995.

Lenz, Theodore. *Toward a Science of Peace.* New York: Bookman Associates, 1961.

Lewin, Moshe. *Lenin's Last Struggle.* New York: Pantheon, 1968.

Lijphart, Arend. "The Power Sharing Approach." In *Conflict and Peacemaking in Multi-Ethnic Societies,* edited by Joseph Montville, 491–511. Lexington, Mass.: Heath, 1989.

Llewellyn, Grace. *Teenage Liberation Handbook: How to Quit School and Get a Real Life and Education.* Eugene, Ore.: Lowry House, 1991.

Lopata, Helen, ed. *Research in the Interweave of Social Roles.* Greenwich, Conn.: JAI Press, 1980.

Lovelock, James E. *Gaia, A New Look at Life on Earth.* New York: Oxford Univ. Press, 1979.

Lynd, Staughton, ed. *Nonviolence in America: A Documentary History.* New York: Bobbs-Merrill, 1966.

Machel, Graca. *Impact of Armed Conflict on Children.* New York: United Nations, 1998.

MacPherson, Jay. *Four Stages in Man: The Classical Myths.* Toronto: Macmillan, 1963.

Macy, Joanna. *Dharma and Development.* Hartford, Conn.: Kumarian, 1983.

Macy, Joanna, and Molly Brown. *Coming Back to Life: Practices to Reconnect Our Lives, Our World.* Gabriola Island, B.C., Canada: New Society, 1998.

Madale, Nagasawa. "Nonviolent Alternative in a Crisis Situation." *Gandhi Marg* (New Delhi) 14, no. 1 (1992): 166–79.

Mander, Jerry, and Edward Goldsmith, eds. *The Case Against the Global Economy.* San Francisco: Sierra Club Books, 1996.

Mannheim, Karl. *Ideology and Utopia.* Translated by Louis Wirth and Edward Shils. London and New York: Harcourt Brace and World, 1952.

Manuel, Frank, and Fritzie Manuel. *Utopian Thought in the Western World.* Cambridge, Mass.: Belknap Press of Harvard Univ. Press, 1979.

Margulis, Lynn. *Symbiosis in Cell Evolution.* New York and San Francisco: W. H. Freeman, 1981.

———. *The Symbiotic Planet: A New Look at Evolution.* New York: Basic Books, 1998.

Margulis, Lynn, and Dorion Sagan. *What Is Life.* New York: Simon and Schuster, 1995.

Markusen, Ann, and J. Yudken. *Dismantling the Cold War Economy.* New York: Basic Books, Harper Collins, 1992.

Marriott, McKim. "The Feast of Love." In *Krishna Myths, Rites and Attitudes*, edited by Milton Singer. Chicago: University of Chicago Press, 1968.

Marshall, C. B. *The Communist Manifesto.* Washington, D.C.: School of Advanced International Studies, Johns Hopkins University, 1960.

Marullo, Sam, and John Lofland, eds. *Peace Action in the Eighties: Social Science Perspectives.* New Brunswick, N.J.: Rutgers Univ. Press, 1990.

Maruyamah, Magorah. *Mindscapes in Management: Use of Individual Differences in Multicultural Management.* Aldershot, Hants, U.K.: Dartmouth Publishing Co., 1994.

Marx, Leo. *The Machine in the Garden.* New York: Oxford Univ. Press, 1964.

Masini, Eleanora, ed. *The Future of Asian Cultures.* Bangkok: UNESCO Regional Office, 1993.

Mather, John R., and Galina V. Sdasyuk, eds. *Global Change, Geographical Approaches.* Tucson: Univ. of Arizona Press, 1991.

Matthews, Gareth. *The Philosophy of Childhood.* Cambridge, Mass.: Harvard Univ. Press, 1994.

Mauss, Marcel. *The Gift: Forms and Functions of Exchange in Archaic Societies.* New York: Norton, 1971.

McCarthy, Ronald, and Gene Sharp. *Nonviolent Action: A Research Guide.* New York and London: Garland, 1997.

McLaren, Nadia. "Citizens Initiatives on Sustainable Consumption," *Transnational Associations*, Mar. 1998, 130–47.

McLean, Scilla Elworthy, ed. *How Nuclear Weapons Decisions Are Made*. London: Macmillan Press and Oxford Research Group, 1986.

McManus, Philip, and Gerald Schlabach. *Relentless Persistence*. Philadelphia: New Society, 1991.

McNeill, William. *The Rise of the West: A History of the Human Community*. Chicago: Univ. of Chicago Press, 1963.

McRae, Kenneth D. "Canada: Reflections on Two Conflicts." In *Conflict and Peacemaking in Multi-Ethnic Societies*, edited by Joseph Montville, 197–218. Lexington, Mass.: Heath, 1989.

Mead, Margaret. *Blackberry Winter: My Earlier Years*. Gloucester, Mass.: Peter Smith, 1989.

———. *Continuities in Cultural Evolution*. New Haven, Conn.: Yale Univ. Press, 1964.

———. *Cooperation and Competition among Primitive Peoples*. New York: McGraw-Hill, 1967.

———. *Culture and Commitment*. Garden City, N.Y.: Natural History Press, 1972.

———. *Sex and Temperament in Three Primitive Societies*. New York: Mentor, 1950.

———. "Warfare Is Only an Invention—Not a Biological Necessity." In *War: Studies from Psychology, Sociology and Anthropology*, edited by Leon Bramson and George Goethals, 269–74. New York: Basic Books, 1968.

Meadows, Donella H., Dennis L. Meadows, Jørgen Randers, and William L. Behrens. *Limits to Growth*. New York: Universe, 1972.

Melman, Seymour. *The Demilitarized Society: Disarmament and Conversion*. Montreal: Harvest House, 1988.

Menashe, Louis, and Ronald Rodosh, eds. *Teach-ins: U.S.A. Reports, Opinions, Documents*. New York: Praeger, 1967.

Mendelsohn, Everett, and Helga Nowotny. *Nineteen Eighty-Four: Science Between Utopia and Dystopia*. Boston: D. Reidel, 1984.

Mendlovitz, Saul, ed. *On the Creation of a Just World Order: Preferred Worlds for the 1990s*. New York: Free Press, 1975.

Messner, Michael A. *Politics of Masculinities: Men in Movements*. Newbury Park, Calif.: Sage, 1997.

Metraux, Daniel. "The Soka Gakkai: Buddhism in the Creation of a Harmonious and Peaceful Society." In *Engaged Buddhism*, edited by Christopher Queen and Sallie King. Albany: SUNY Press, 1996.

Miall, Hugh. *Nuclear Weapons: Who's in Charge?* London: Macmillan, 1987.

Miall, Hugh, Oliver Ramsbotham, and Tom Woodhouse. *Contemporary Conflict Resolution*. Cambridge, U.K.: Polity, 1999.

Minow, Martha. *Between Vengeance and Forgiveness*. Boston, Mass.: Beacon, 1998.

Mittelman, James H., and Robert Johnston. "The Globalization of Organized Crime, the Courtesan State, and the Corruption of Civil Society." *Global Governance* 5, no. 1 (1999): 103–26.

Montagu, Ashley, ed. *Learning Non-Aggression: The Experience of the Non-Literate Societies*. New York: Oxford Univ. Press, 1978.

Montville, Joseph, ed. *Conflict and Peacemaking in Multi-Ethnic Societies*. Lexington, Mass.: Heath, 1989.

More, Thomas. *Complete Works of St. Thomas More*. Edited by Edward Surtz and J. H. Hexter. New Haven, Conn.: Yale Univ. Press, 1965.

Mosco, Vincent. "Communication and Information: Technology for War and Peace." In *Communication and Culture in War and Peace*, edited by Colleen Roach, 52. Newbury Park, Calif.: Sage, 1993.

Mouritzen, H. "The Nordic Model of a Foreign Policy Instrument: Its Rise and Fall." *Journal of Peace Research* 32, no. 1 (1995): 9–21.

Muhaiyaddeen, M. R. Bawa. *Islam and World Peace: Explanations of a Sufi*. Philadelphia: Fellowship Press, 1987.

Mumford, Lewis. *The Story of Utopias*. New York: Viking, 1962.

Musto, Ronald G. *The Catholic Peace Tradition*. Maryknoll, N.Y.: Orbis, 1986.

Myrdal, Alva. *The Game of Disarmament*. New York: Pantheon, 1976.

———. *Nation and Family*. New York: Harper, 1941.

Myrdal, Alva, with Viola Klein. *Women's Two Roles*. London: Routledge & Kegan Paul, 1956.

Myron, Nancy, and Charlotte Bunch, eds. *Lesbianism and the Women's Movement*. Baltimore: Diana Press, 1975.

Naroll, Raoul, Vern Bullough, and Frada Naroll. *Military Deterrence in History*. Albany: SUNY Press, 1974.

National Television Violence Study. Vol. 3, *Executive Summary*. University of California, Santa Barbara, 1998.

Nhat Hanh, Thich. *Love in Action*. Berkeley, Calif.: Parallax, 1993.

Nordhoff, Charles. *Communistic Societies of the United States*. 1875. Reprint, New York: Dover, 1966.

Noyes, John Humphrey. *History of American Socialism*. Philadelphia, Pa.: J. B. Lippincott, 1870.

Nyong'o, Peter Anyan'o, ed. *Popular Struggles for Democracy in Africa*. London: Zed, 1987.

Ornauer, Helmut, with Hakan Wiberg, Andrzcj Sicinsky, and Johan Galtung. *Images of the World in the Year 2000*. The Hague: Mouton, 1976.

Paige, Glenn D., and Sarah Gilliatt, eds. *Buddhism and Nonviolent Global Problem-Solving*. Honolulu: Univ. of Hawaii Press, 1991.

Paige, Glenn D., Chaiwat Satha-Anand, and Sarah Gilliatt, eds. *Islam and Nonviolence*. Honolulu: Univ. of Hawaii Press, 1993.

Park, Grenville, and Louis Sohn. *World Peace Through World Law.* 3d ed. Cambridge, Mass.: Harvard Univ. Press, 1966.

Pergman, David. "LETS Creates Community and Community Creates Peace." *Peace* (Toronto, Canada), May-June 1994.

Pfaffenberger, Bryan. "Ethnic Conflict and Youth Insurgency in Sri Lanka: The Social Origins of Tamil Separation." In *Conflict and Peacemaking in Multi-Ethnic Societies,* edited by Joseph Montville, 214–58. Lexington, Mass.: Heath, 1989.

Pleck, Joseph. "The Male Sex Role: Definitions, Problems and Sources of Change." *Journal of Social Issues* 32, no. 3 (1976).

Pleck, Joseph, and Jack Sawyer. *Men and Masculinity.* Englewood Cliffs, N.J.: Prentice-Hall, 1974.

Poden, John. "National System Development and Conflict Resolution in Nigeria." In *Conflict and Peacemaking in Multi-Ethnic Societies,* edited by Joseph Montville, 411–32. Lexington, Mass.: Heath, 1989.

Polak, Fred. *The Image of the Future.* Translated and abbreviated by Elise Boulding. San Francisco: Jossey-Bass/Elsevier, 1972.

Pradervand, Pierre. *Listening to Africa: Developing Africa from the Grassroots.* New York: Praeger, 1989.

Prasad, Devi, and Tony Smythe, eds. *Conscription—A World Survey.* London: War Resisters International, 1968.

Queen, Christopher, and Sallie King, eds. *Engaged Buddhism: Buddhist Liberation Movements in Asia.* Albany: SUNY Press, 1996.

Rapoport, Anatol. *Fights, Games and Debates.* Ann Arbor: Univ. of Michigan Press, 1960.

Rapoport, Rhona, and Robert Rapoport, eds. *Fathers, Mothers and Society: Towards New Alliances.* New York: Basic Books, 1977.

Rasberry, Salli, and Robert Greenway. *How to Start Your Own School . . . and Make A Book.* Freestone, Calif.: Freestone Publishing, 1970.

RAVEN. *Men, Women and Violence.* St. Louis, Mo.: Rape and Violence End Now, 1982.

Raviv, Amiram, Louis Oppenheimer, and Daniel Bar-Tal, eds. *How Children Understand War and Peace.* San Francisco: Jossey-Bass, 1999.

Reilly, Mary, ed. *Play as Exploratory Learning.* Beverly Hills, Calif.: Sage, 1974.

Richardson, Lewis F. *Arms and Insecurity: A Mathematical Study of the Causes and Origins of War.* Pittsburgh: Boxwood, 1960.

———. *Statistics of Deadly Quarrels.* Pittsburgh and Chicago: Boxwood, 1960.

Roach, Colleen, ed. *Communication and Culture in War and Peace.* Newbury Park, Calif.: Sage, 1993.

Roberts, Adam, ed. *The Strategy of Civilian Defense.* London: Faber & Faber, 1967.

Ross, Rupert. *Returning to the Teachings.* Toronto, Canada: Penguin, 1996.

Russell, Elbert. *The History of Quakerism.* New York: Macmillan, 1992.

Sabo, Donald, and Ross Runfola. *Jock: Sports and Male Identity.* Englewood Cliffs, N.J.: Prentice-Hall, 1980.

Sahlins, Marshall. *Stone Age Economics.* New York: Aldine-Atherton, 1972.

Sahtouris, Elisabet. *Earthdance: Living Systems in Evolution.* Santa Barbara, Calif.: Metalog Books, 1995.

Salkowsky, Claire. "Peacemaking." *Montessori Life,* winter 1994, 32–38.

Schumacher, E. F. *Small Is Beautiful.* New York: Harper & Row, 1973.

Schuman, Howard, Alex Inkeles, and David Smith. "Some Psychological Effects and Non-effects of Literacy in a New Nation." *Economic Development and Cultural Change* 16 (1967).

Schwarzschild, Steven. *Roots of Jewish Nonviolence.* New York: Jewish Peace Fellowship, 1985.

Sélassié, Beseat Kiflé, ed. *Consensus and Peace.* Paris: UNESCO, 1960.

Sharp, Gene. *The Politics of Nonviolent Action.* Boston: Porter Sargent, 1973.

Shaw, Archibald. "The Random Falls Idea." *School Executive,* Mar. 1956.

Shenk, David. *Data Smog: Surviving the Information Glut.* San Francisco: Harper, 1997.

Shiva, Vandana. *Staying Alive: Women, Ecology and Development.* London: Zed, 1989.

———. *The Violence of the Green Revolution.* Dehra Dun, India: Vandana Shiva, 1989.

Shulman, Seth. *Owning the Future: Staking Claims on the Knowledge Frontier.* Boston: Houghton-Mifflin, 1999.

Shuman, Michael. *Towards a Global Village: International Community Development Initiatives.* Boulder, Colo.: Pluto Press, 1994.

Singer, Marshall. "Prospects for Conflict Management in the Sri Lankan Ethnic Crisis." In *Conflict and Peacemaking in Multi-Ethnic Societies,* edited by Joseph Montville, 259–86. Lexington, Mass.; Heath, 1989.

Singer, Milton, ed. *Krishna Myths, Rites and Attitudes.* Chicago: Univ. of Chicago Press, 1968.

Sivaraksa, Sulak. *A Buddhist Vision for Renewing Society.* Bangkok: Thai Inter-Religious Commission for Development, 1994.

———. *Loyalty Demands Dissent.* Berkeley: Parallax, 1998.

Sivard, Ruth Leger. *World Military and Social Expenditures 1996,* 16th ed. Washington, D.C.: World Priorities Inc., 1996.

Sonkin, Daniel J., and Michael Durphy. *Learning to Live Without Violence: A Handbook for Men.* San Francisco: Volcano Press, 1982.

Sorokin, Pitirim. *Social and Cultural Dynamics.* Boston: Porter Sargent, 1957.

South Commission (Nyerere Commission). *The Challenge to the South.* New York: Oxford Univ. Press, 1990.

Spencer, Herbert. *The Man Versus the State with Four Essays on Politics and Society.*
1884. Reprint, edited by Donald Marcal, London: Penguin, 1969.
——. *Principles of Sociology.* New York: Appleton, 1896.
Sponberg, Alan. "TBMSG: A Dhamma Revolution in Contemporary India." In
*Engaged Buddhism,* edited by Christopher Queen and Sallie King, 73–120.
Albany: SUNY Press, 1996.
Spretnak, Charlene. *The Politics of Women's Spirituality.* Garden City: Anchor, 1982.
*State of the World, 1999.* Worldwatch Institute Report. New York: Norton, 1999.
Steiner, Jurg. "Power-Sharing: Another Swiss Export?" In *Conflict and Peacemaking
in Multi-Ethnic Societies,* edited by Joseph Montville, 107–14. Lexington, Mass.:
Heath, 1989.
Steinsland, G., and P. M. Sørenson. *Menneske Og Makter i Vikingenes Verden.* Oslo:
Universitetsforlaget, 1994.
Stubbs, Richard. "Malaysia: Avoiding Ethnic Strife in a Deeply Divided Society." In
*Conflict and Peacemaking in Multi-Ethnic Societies,* edited by Joseph
Montville, 287–300. Lexington, Mass.: Heath, 1989.
Suliman, Mohamed. *Ecology, Politics, Violent Conflict.* London: Zed, 1999.
Summy, Ralph, and M. Saunders. "Why Peace History?" *Peace and Change* 20, no. 1
(1995): 2–38.
Sundaram, Jomo. "Malaysia's New Economic Policy and National Unity." *Third
World Quarterly* 11, no. 4 (1989): 36–53.
Swann, Robert, and Susan Witt. *Local Currencies: Catalysts for Sustainable Regional
Economies.* Great Barrington, Mass.: E. F. Schumacher Society, 1995.
Swerdlow, Amy. *Women Strike for Peace.* Chicago: Univ. of Chicago Press, 1993.
Tatum, Lyle, ed. *South Africa: Challenge and Hope.* Philadelphia: American Friends
Service Committee, 1982.
Teixeira, Bryan. *A Gandhian Futurology.* Madurai, India: Valliammal Institution,
Gandhi Museum, 1992.
Thomas, John L. *Alternative America.* Cambridge, Mass.: Belknap Press of Harvard
Univ. Press, 1983.
Tinbergen, Jan. *Rio, Reshaping the International Order.* A report to the club of
Rome. New York: E. P. Dutton, 1976.
Tishkov, Valerii. "Glasnost and Nationalities within the Soviet Union." *Third World
Quarterly* 11, no. 4 (Oct. 1989): 191–207.
Tomkinson, Leonard. *Studies in the Theory and Practice of Peace and War in Chinese
History and Literature.* Shanghai: Friends Center, Christian Literature Society,
1940.
Tönnies, Ferdinand. *Community and Society.* Translated by Charles Loomis. New
York: Harper & Row, 1976.
Toynbee, Arnold. *Reconsiderations.* Vol. 12 of *A Study of History.* New York: Oxford
Univ. Press, 1964.

Turnbull, Colin. *The Forest People*. New York: Simon & Schuster, 1961.

UN Development Program. *Urban Agriculture*. New York: United Nations, 1996.

UNESCO. *From a Culture of Violence to a Culture of Peace*. Paris: UNESCO, 1996.

———. *Peace on Earth: A Peace Anthology*. Paris: UNESCO, 1980.

———. *A Practical Guide to the World Decade for Cultural Development, 1988–97*. Paris: UNESCO, 1987.

UNICEF. *The State of the World's Children 1997*. Oxford: Oxford Univ. Press, 1997.

United Nations. *The World Social Situation in the 1990s*. New York: United Nations, 1994.

Usui, Hisakazu, and Takeo Uchida, eds. *From Chaos to Order*. Vol. 1, *Crisis and Renaissance of the World Society*. Tokyo: Yushindo Publishers, 1990.

van der Merwe, Hendrik W. *Pursuing Justice and Peace in South Africa*. New York: Routledge, 1989.

Vogt, Evon, and Ethel Albert, eds. *People of Rimrock: A Study of Values in Five Cultures*. Cambridge, Mass.: Harvard Univ. Press, 1967.

Wallis, James. *The Soul of Politics*. Maryknoll, N.Y.: Orbis, 1994.

Wallis, Jill. *Mother of World Peace: The Life of Muriel Lester*. Enfield Lock, U.K.: Hisarlik, 1993.

Watson, Burton, trans. *Basic Writings of Mo Tzu, Hsun Tzu and Han Fei Tzu*. New York: Columbia Univ. Press, 1964.

Watson, Lyall. *Dark Nature*. New York: Harper Collins, 1965.

Wax, Caroline, K. M. Panikkar, and J. M. Romain. *The Twentieth Century*. Vol. 6 of *History of Mankind*. New York: Harper & Row, 1966.

Weigert, Kathleen Maas, and Robin J. Crews. *Teaching for Justice: Concepts and Models for Service Learning in Peace Studies*. Monograph Series, Service Learning in the Disciplines. Washington, D.C.: American Association for Higher Education, 1999.

Weil, Simone. *The Iliad: A Poem of Force*. Wallingford, Pa.: Pendle Hill, 1956.

Weiss, Thomas. "Whither International Efforts for Internally Displaced Peoples?" *Journal of Peace Research* 36, no. 3 (1999): 363–74.

Whaley, Rick, and Walter Bresette. *Walleye Warriors*. Philadelphia: New Society, 1994.

Whiting, John, et al. "The Learning Values." In *People of Rimrock: A Study of Values in Five Cultures*, edited by Evon Vogt and Ethel Albert, 83–125. Cambridge, Mass.: Harvard Univ. Press, 1967.

Wilmer, Frank. *The Indigenous Voice in World Politics*. Newbury Park, Calif.: Sage, 1993.

Wittner, Lawrence. *One World or None: A History of the World Nuclear Disarmament Movement*. Stanford, Calif.: Stanford Univ. Press, 1993.

World Bank. *Tribal People and Economic Development: Human Ecologic Considerations*. Washington, D.C.: World Bank, 1982.

World Commission on Environment and Development (Brundtland Commission). *Our Common Future.* Oxford: Oxford Univ. Press, 1987.

Wrangham, Richard, and Dale Peterson. *Demonic Males.* Boston: Houghton-Mifflin, 1996.

Wright, Quincy. *A Study of War.* 2nd. ed. Chicago: Univ. of Chicago Press, 1965.

Yinger, J. Milton. *Ethnicity: Source of Strength? Source of Conflict?* Albany: SUNY Press, 1994.

Zartman, I. William. *Traditional Cures for Modern Conflicts: African Conflict Medicine.* Boulder, Colo.: Lynne Rienner, 1999.

Zehr, Howard. *Changing Lenses: A New Focus for Crime and Justice.* Scottdale, Pa.: Herald, 1990.

Zinn, Howard. *Failure to Quit: Reflections of an Optimistic Historian.* Monroe, Maine: Common Courage, 1993.

———. *SNCC: The New Abolitionists.* Boston, Mass.: Beacon, 1964.

# Index

abolitionism, 60

Abolition 2000, 251

Abrams, David, 218

Abusive Men Exploring New Directions (AMEND), 128

ACCORD (African Centre for the Constructive Resolution of Disputes), 73

Accra Assembly for Disarmament, 66, 75, 82–83

ACP (African-Caribbean-Pacific) group, 245

*Action Update* (Rescue Mission Planet Earth), 150

Adams, Henry, 35

Addams, Jane, 64

adults: children as gentling, 91, 102; children nurturing, 147; literacy among, 200, 225; partnering between children and, 139–58; play, 105; sensory deprivation from television and computers, 223; teen insensitivity to, 147. *See also* men; women

Africa: Accra Assembly for Disarmament, 66, 75, 82–83; African-Caribbean-Pacific (ACP) group, 245; autonomous development approach in, 205; Center for the Strategic Initiatives of Women, 121; community-based development initiative for, 271; Ghana, 196; Grameen Banking in, 207; Great Lakes Region, 95, 184, 216, 261; illiteracy as rising in, 225; indigenous peoples of, 184; Kenya, 153, 208–9; Mbuti people, 94–95; minorities at risk in, 173; multiethnic states in, 182–84; Nairobi street children, 153; Nigeria, 182–84, 196; orature of, 194; Organization of African Unity, 232, 245, 267–68; peace movements in, 82–83; peace research in,

73; Pelindaba Treaty, 243; regional intergovernmental organization for, 267; Somalia, 261; South Africa, 73, 83, 241, 266; Sudan, 183–84, 261; Tanzania, 44–45, 239; television in, 216; village schools in, 227; world conflicts, 1995–97, 235

African-Caribbean-Pacific (ACP) group, 245

African Centre for the Constructive Resolution of Disputes (ACCORD), 73

*African Journal of Peace Research*, 73

African National Congress, 83

African Peace Research Association (AFPRA), 73

African Peace Research Institute, 73

African University of Peace and Development project, 232

*Agenda 21*, 150

aggression: ethnies containing, 170–71; in human nature, 2; Inuit on, 93; in men's socialization, 125; play in learning to control, 105; and television violence, 217; war in socialization for, 16. *See also* conflict; violence

agribusiness, 192, 205

agriculture: agribusiness, 192, 205; back-to-the-land movement, 35, 50, 263, 271; biosphere affected by, 189, 191; cooperative farms, 49–50; crop yields, 204; education integrated with, 226; food supply increased by new technologies, 195; Green Revolution's effects in India, 81; and human population growth, 191; indigenous peoples in developing new type of, 270; seed industry, 202; soil degradation, 191, 205, 209; urban agriculture, 271; women in, 199

ahimsa, 62, 81